FULLY COHERENT PLAN

FOR A NEW AND BETTER SOCIETY

DAVID SHRIGLEY

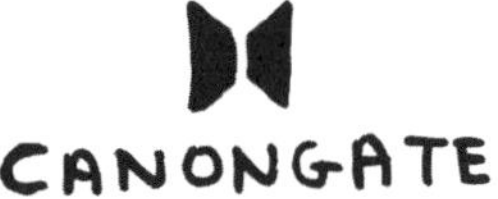

CANONGATE

PUBLISHED IN GREAT BRITAIN
BY CANONGATE BOOKS LTD
14 HIGH STREET EDINBURGH EH11TE
CANONGATE.CO.UK.

2

BRITISH LIBRARY CATALOGUING-IN-
PUBLICATION DATA
A CATALOGUE RECORD FOR THIS
BOOK IS AVAILABLE ON REQUEST
FROM THE BRITISH LIBRARY
ISBN 978 1 78689 3840
BOOK DESIGN BY DAVID SHRIGLEY
PRINTED IN ITALY

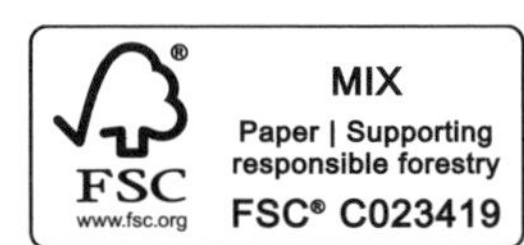

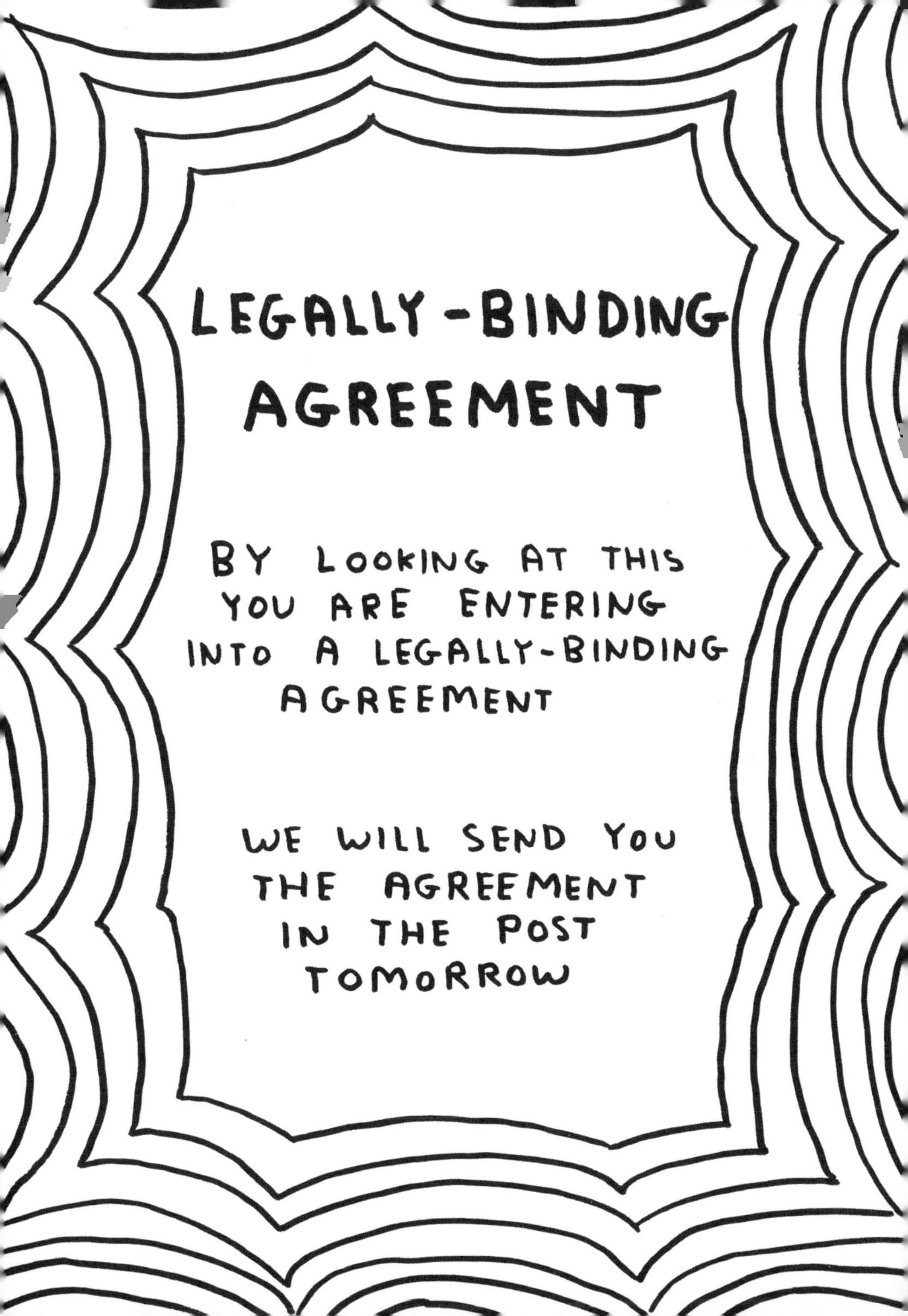

LEGALLY-BINDING AGREEMENT

BY LOOKING AT THIS YOU ARE ENTERING INTO A LEGALLY-BINDING AGREEMENT

WE WILL SEND YOU THE AGREEMENT IN THE POST TOMORROW

WHAT ARE YOU GOING TO
DO WITH IT ?

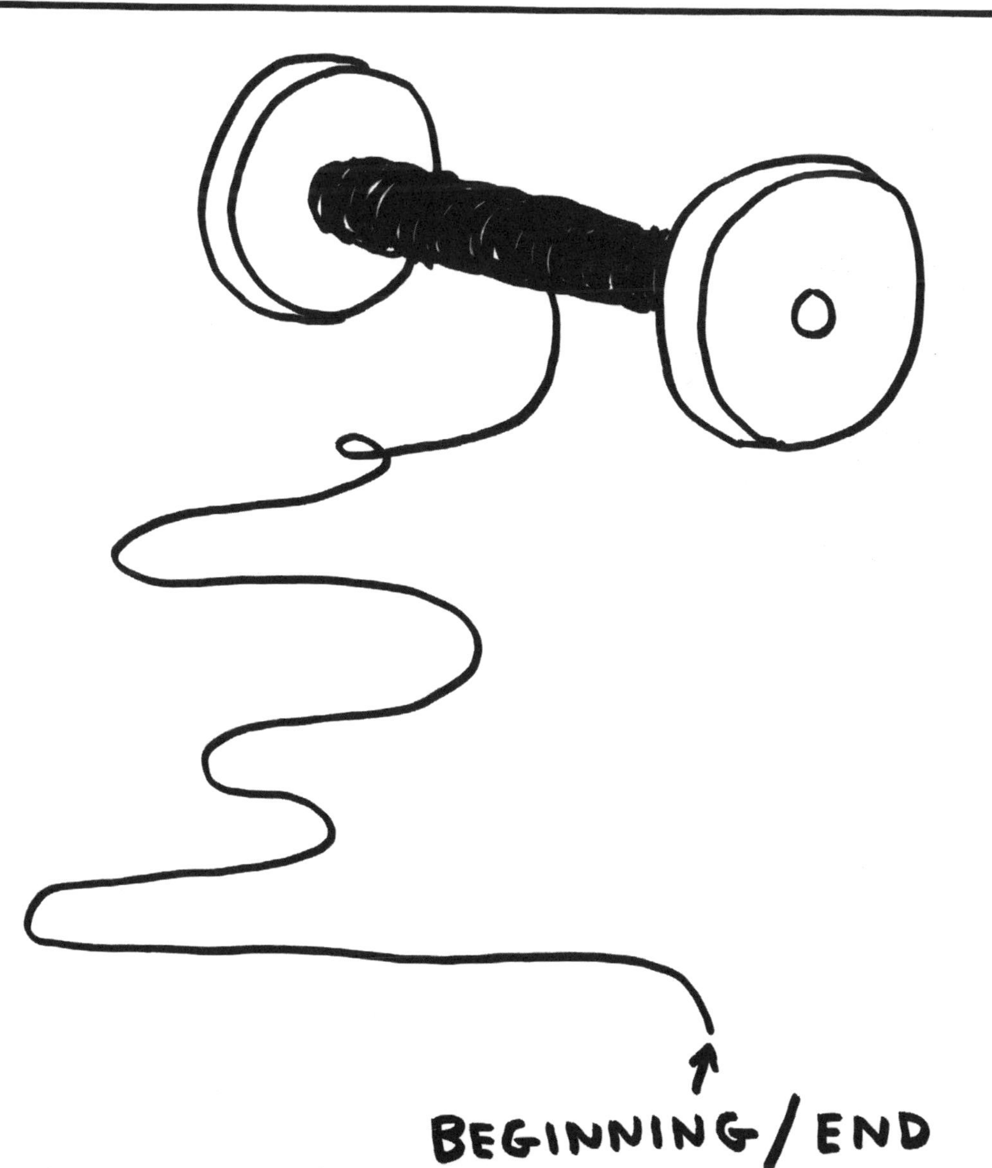
BEGINNING / END

LUNATICS HAVE TAKEN OVER THE RUNNING OF THE COUNT

THIS IS NOT TRUE
THEY ARE NOT LUNATICS

THE FABRIC OF SOCIETY

NEEDS TO BE WASHED
HAS BOBBLES ON IT
THAT NEED TO BE PICKED OFF
IS SOMEWHAT WORN
BUT OTHERWISE IS IN GOOD CONDITION
AND IS NOT IN IMMEDIATE NEED
OF REPLACEMENT

MISTAKES

I DROPPED A GIANT GLASS SPHERE
FROM THE TOP OF A LADDER
AND IT SMASHED INTO TINY PIECES
I SHOULD NOT HAVE TAKEN IT
UP THE LADDER
IT WAS A MISTAKE

DINOSAURS

WE SHOULD LEARN FROM THIER
MISTAKES

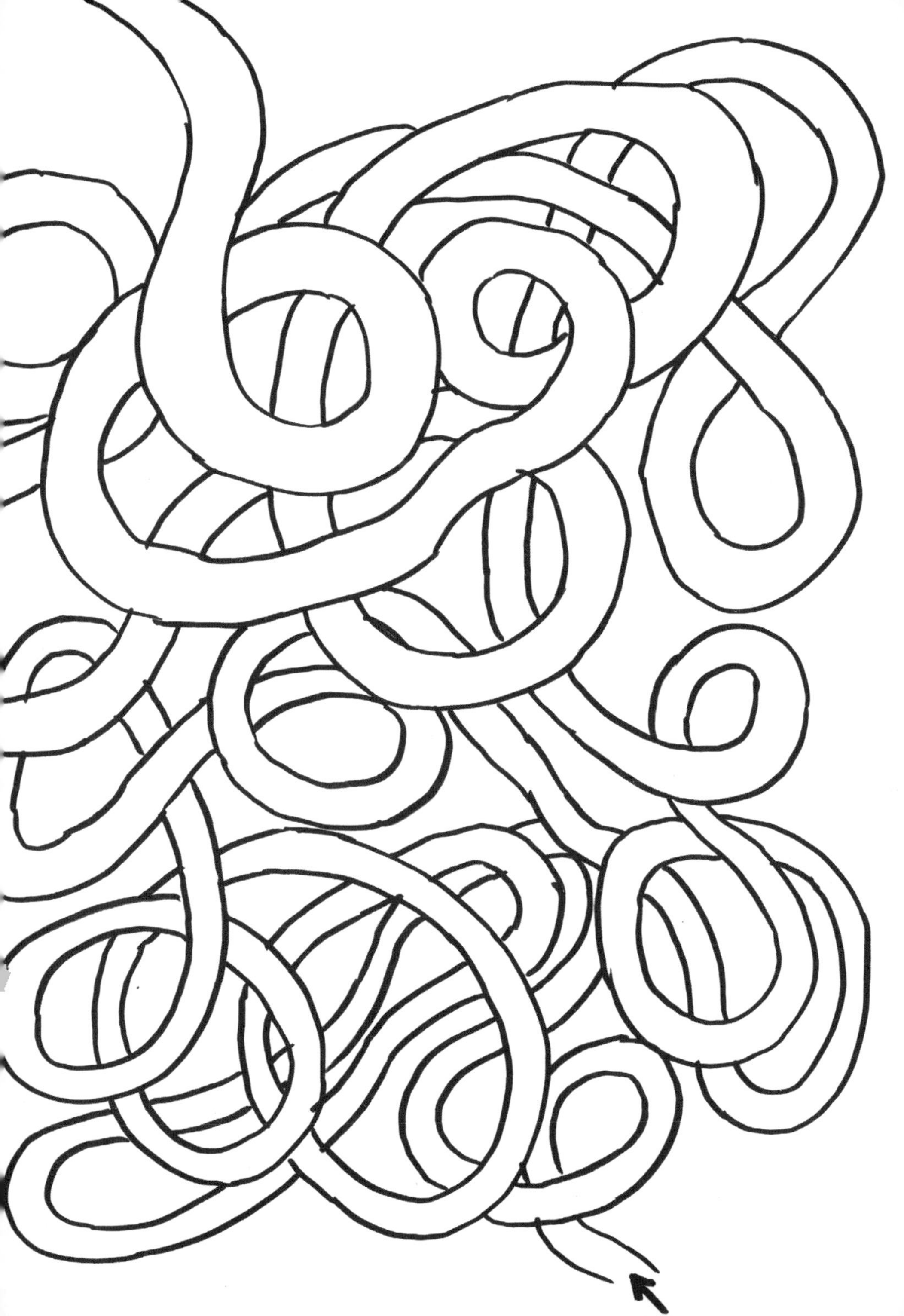

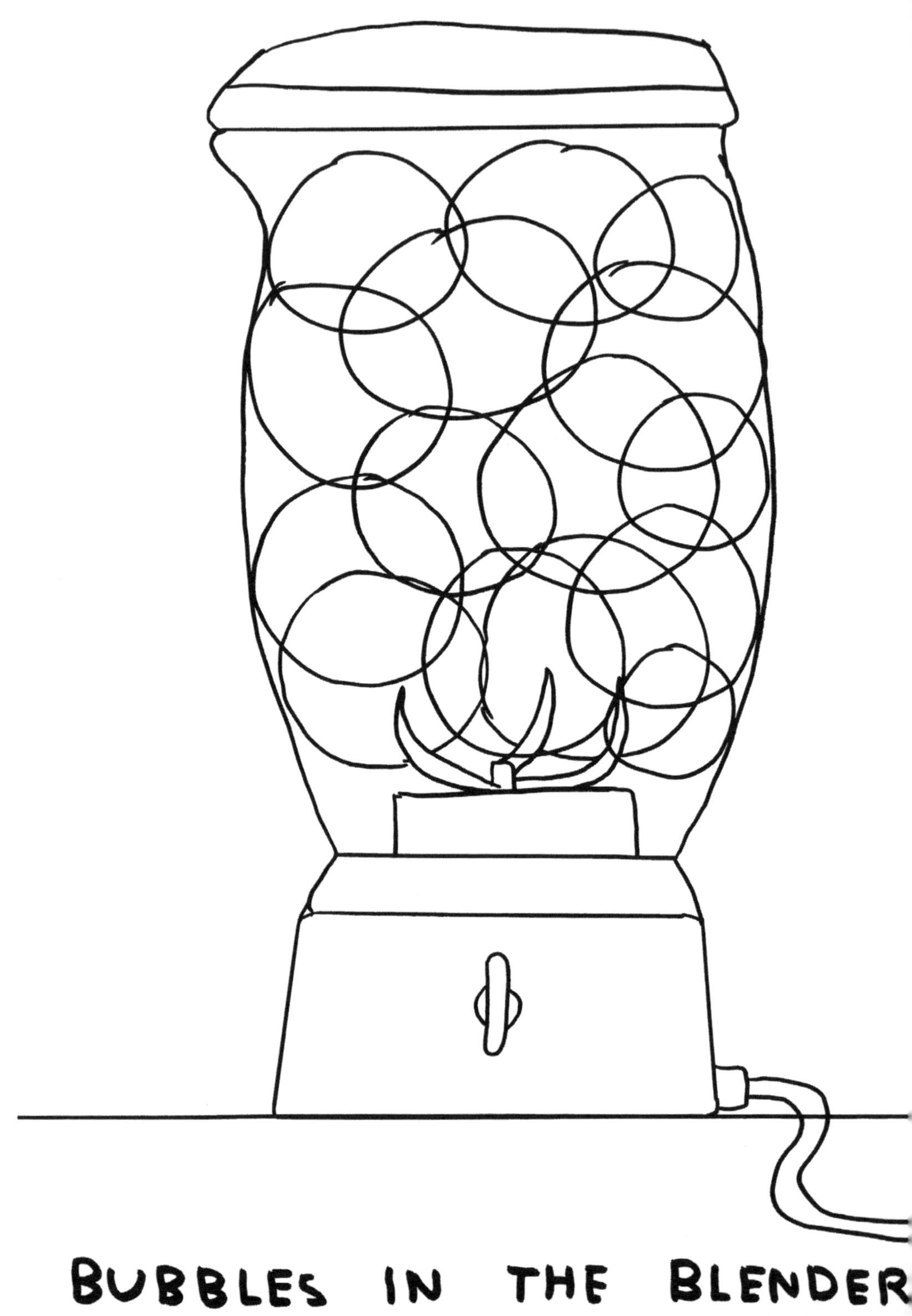

BUBBLES IN THE BLENDER

COMMON SOCIAL PLAGUES

MOULDY PROCESS
ENCRUSTED LEADERSHIP
CIVIL BLIGHT
BENDING HEAD
MILDEW
NEIGHBOURHOOD CANKER
FALSE DAWN
GROUP WILT
STEM ROT
ROOT ROT

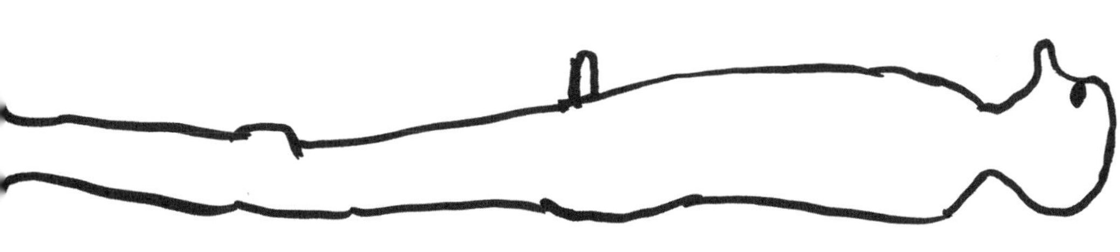

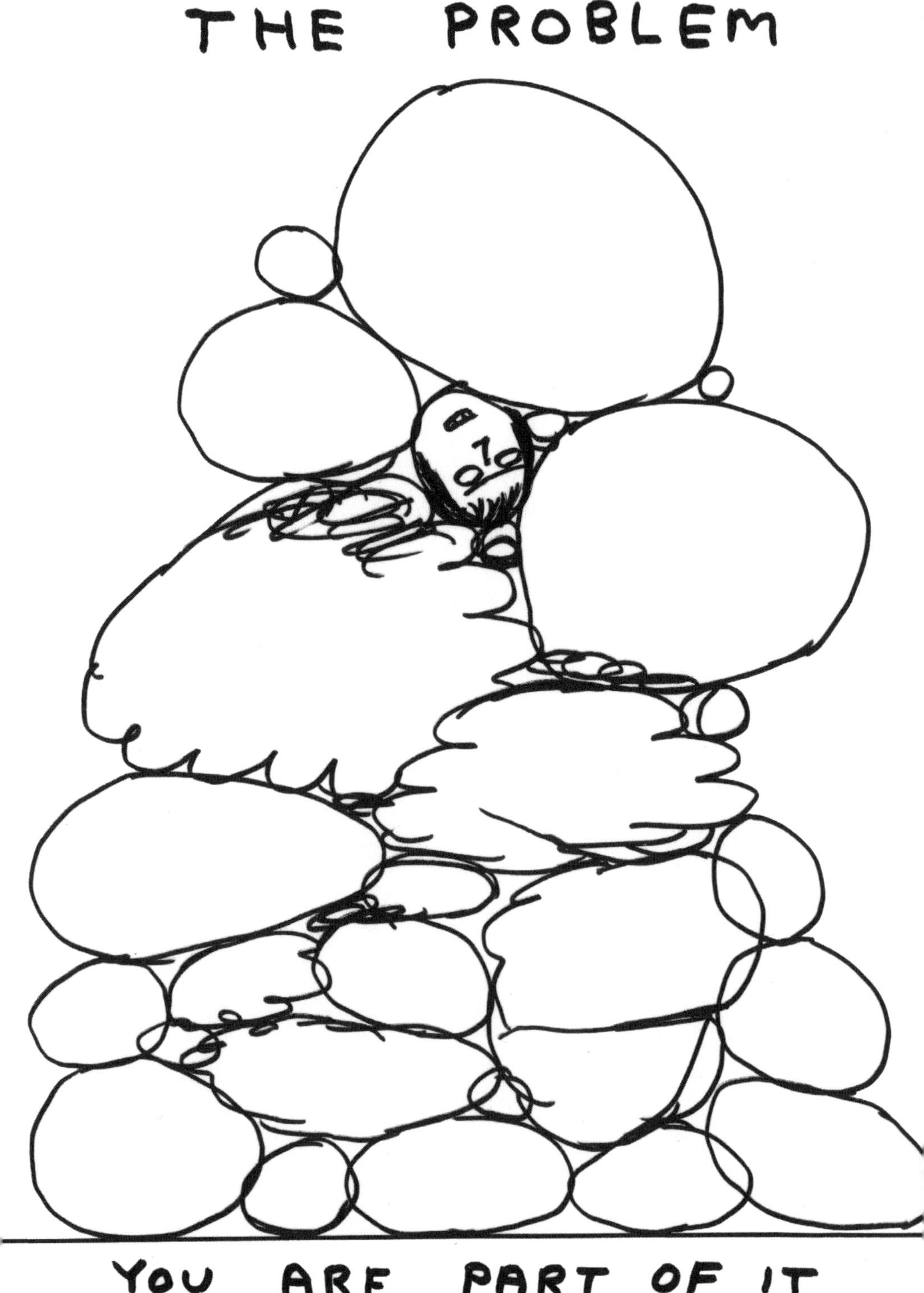

THE PROBLEM
YOU ARE PART OF IT

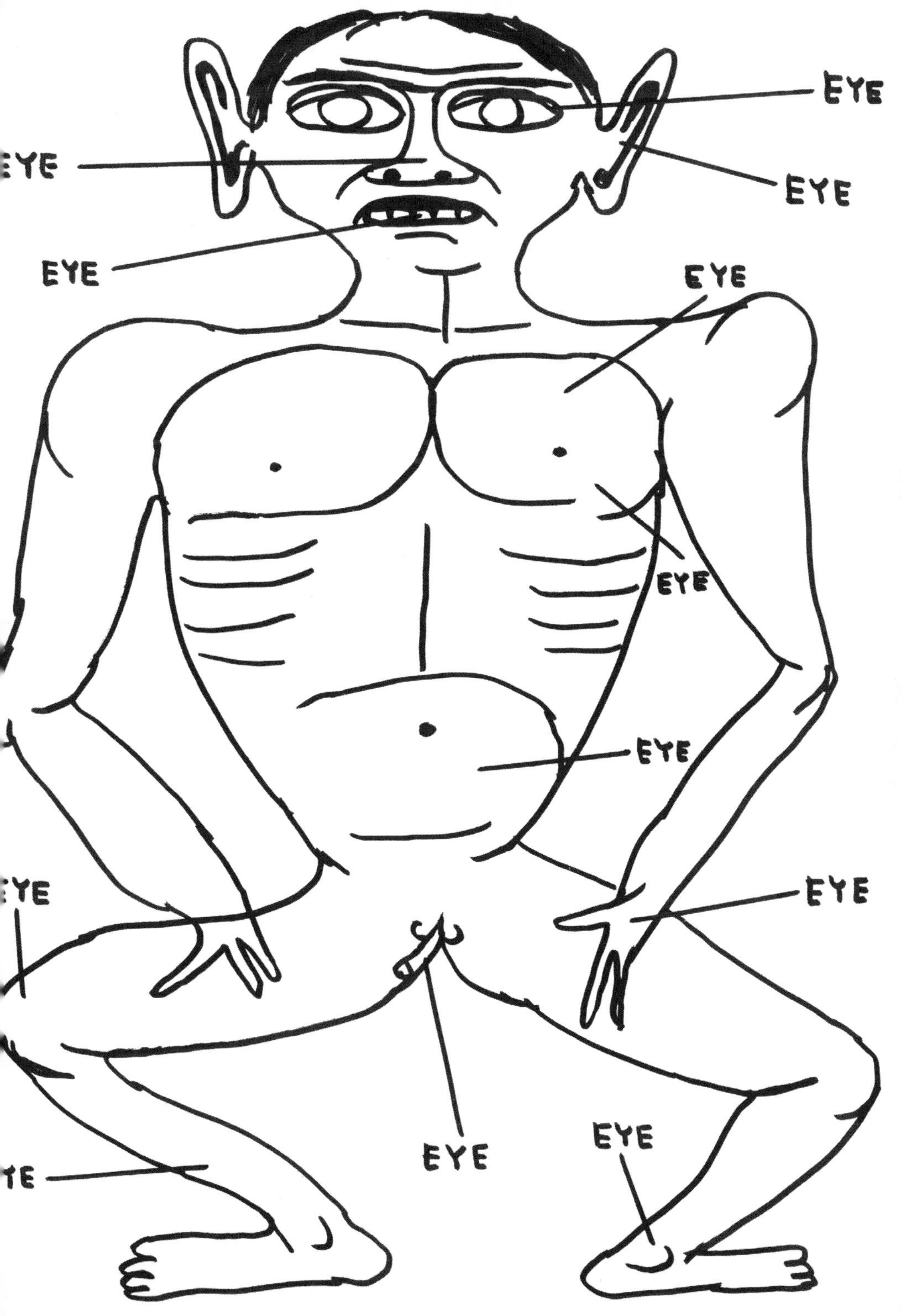

EYE
EYE
EYE
EYE
EYE
EYE
EYE
EYE
EYE
EYE
EYE

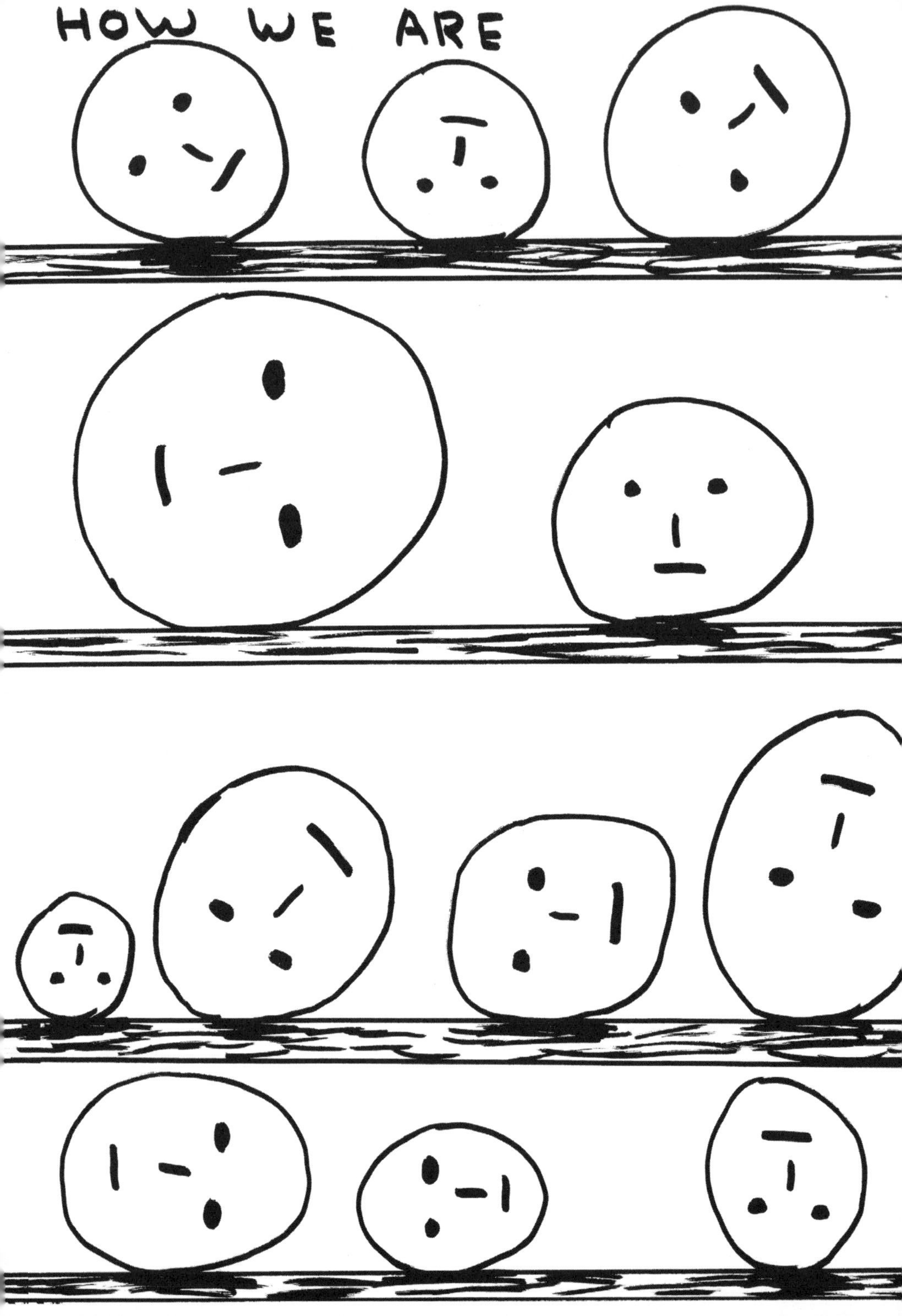

HOW WE ARE

WORMS AND SOCIETY

WORMS ARE CONTENT TO WRIGGLE
BENEATH THE EARTH.
WHEN A WORM GETS CUT IN HALF
EACH HALF GROWS BACK INTO
A NEW WORM.
IT IS INSPIRING.
WE SHOULD LEARN FROM THEIR EXAMPLE

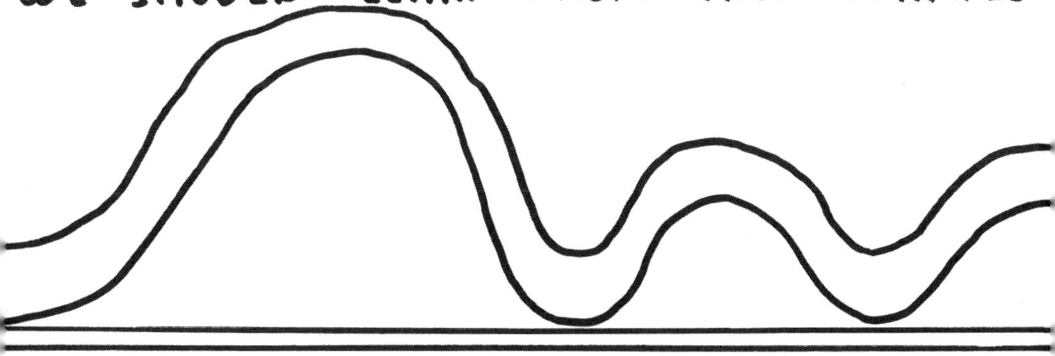

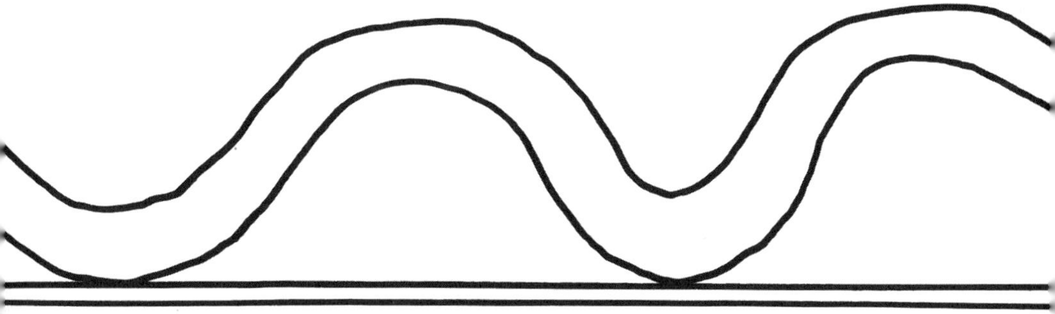

WORMS PASS BY

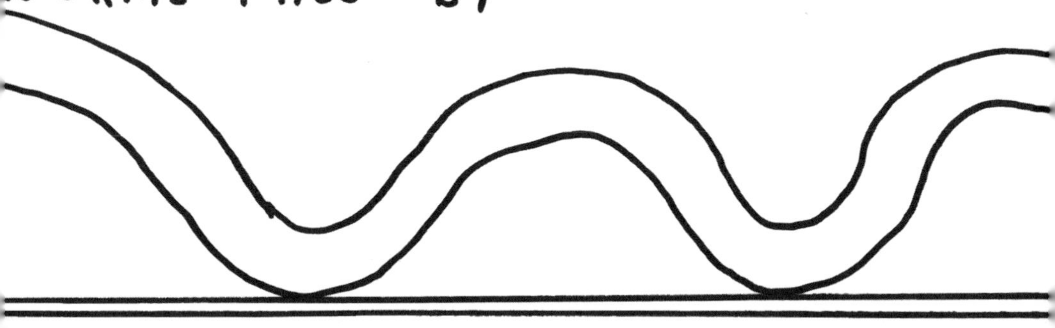

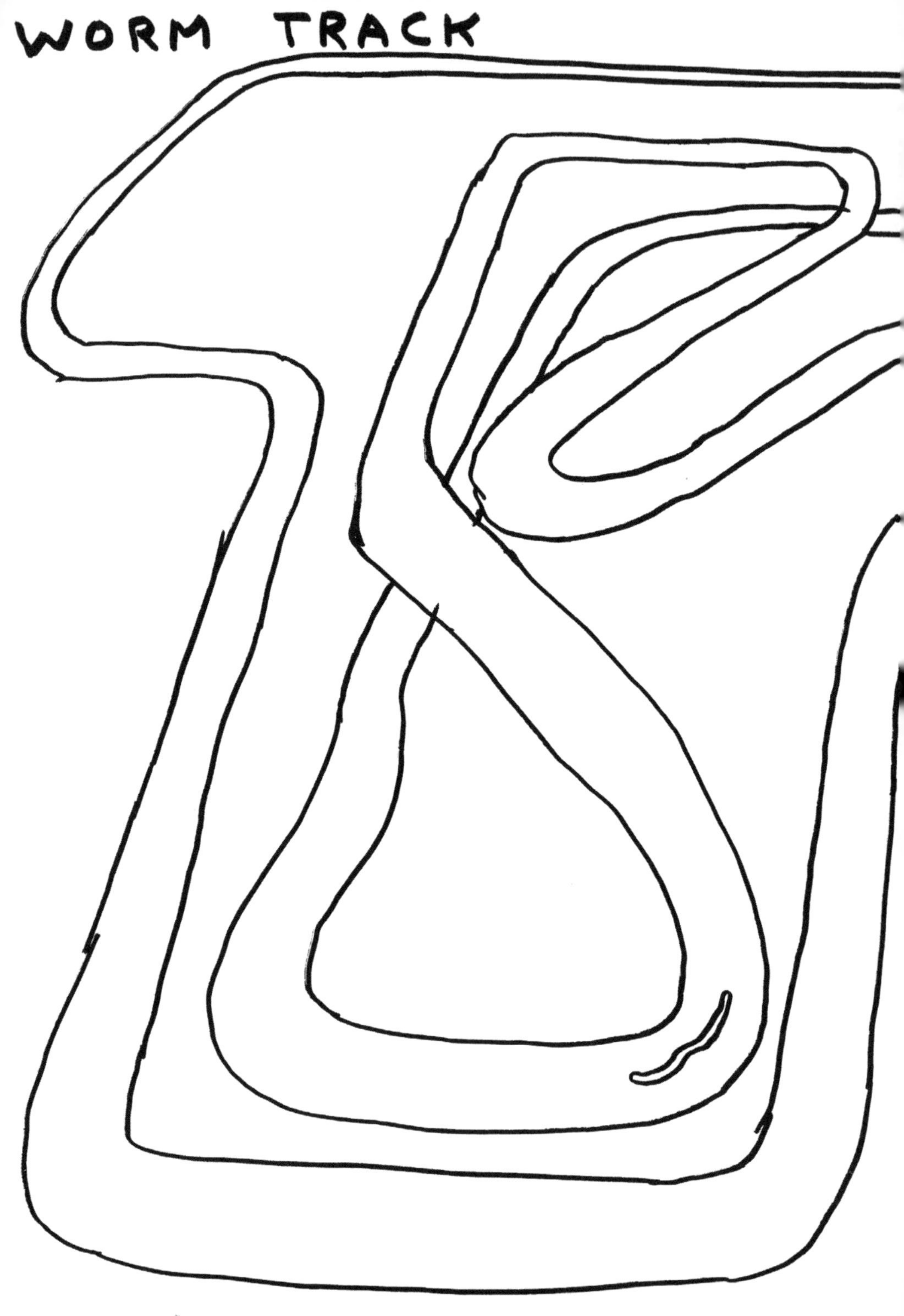

WORM TRACK

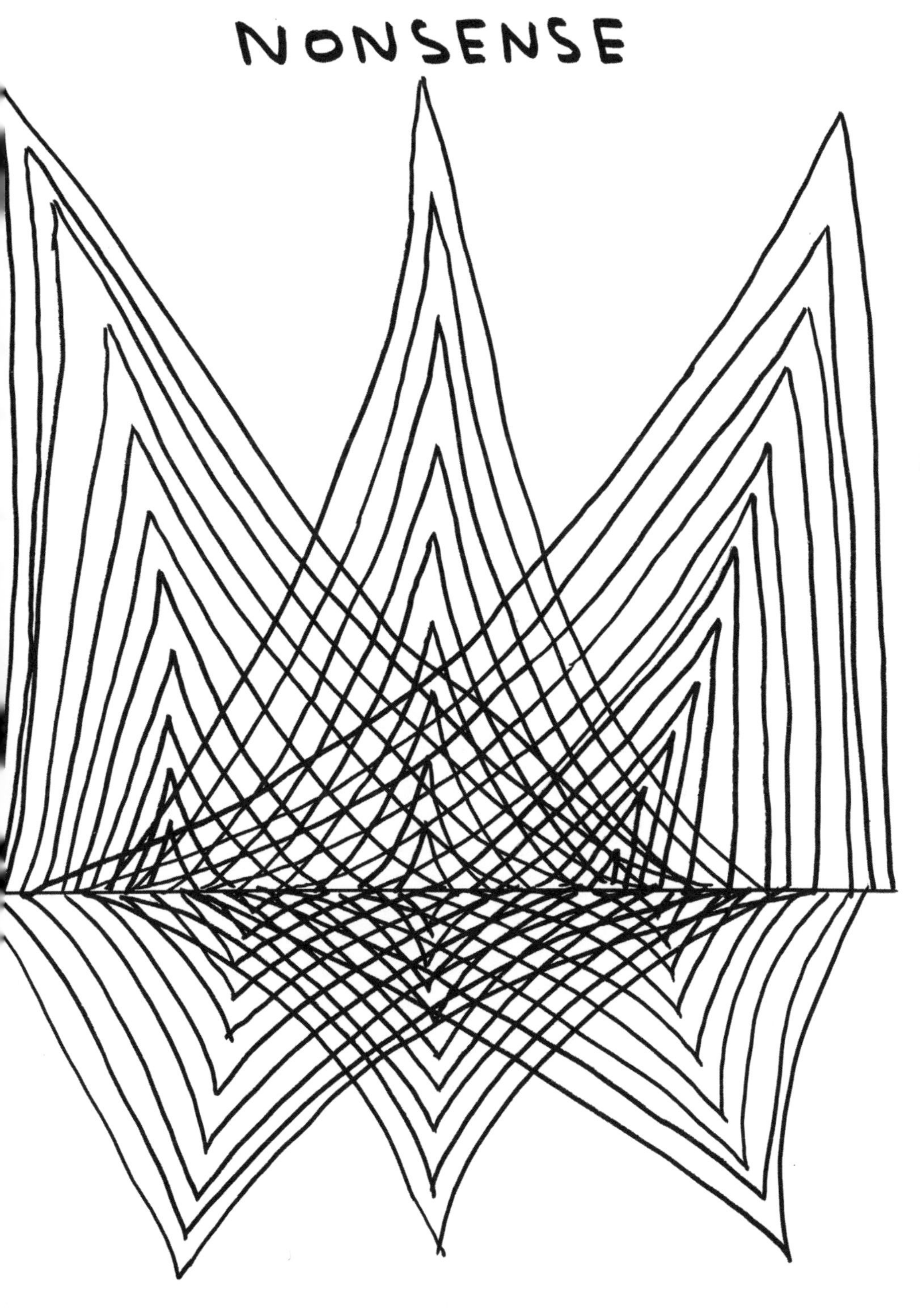
NONSENSE

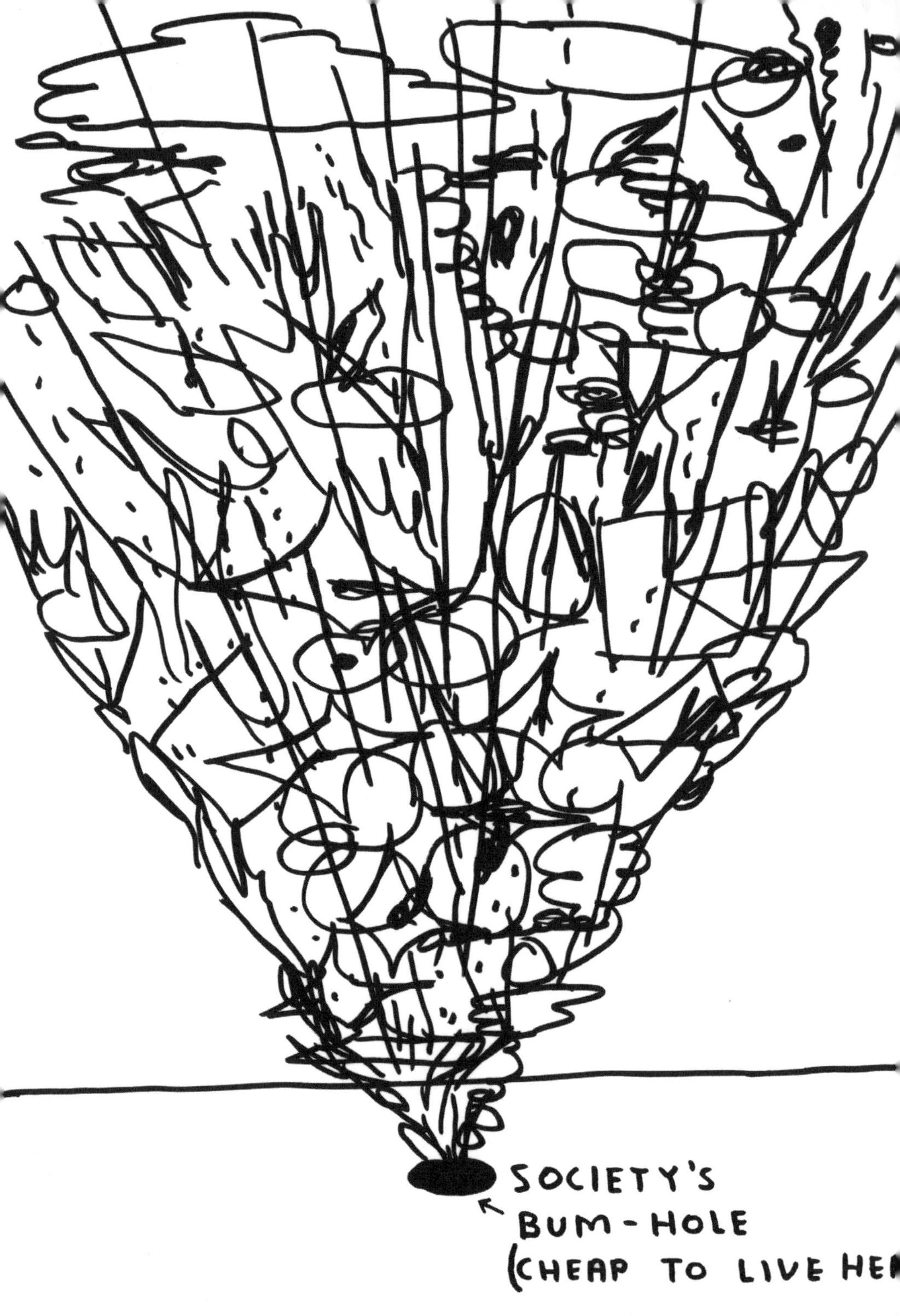

SOCIETY'S
BUM-HOLE
(CHEAP TO LIVE HE

THE RACE

EVENTUALLY YOU MUST JOIN IN

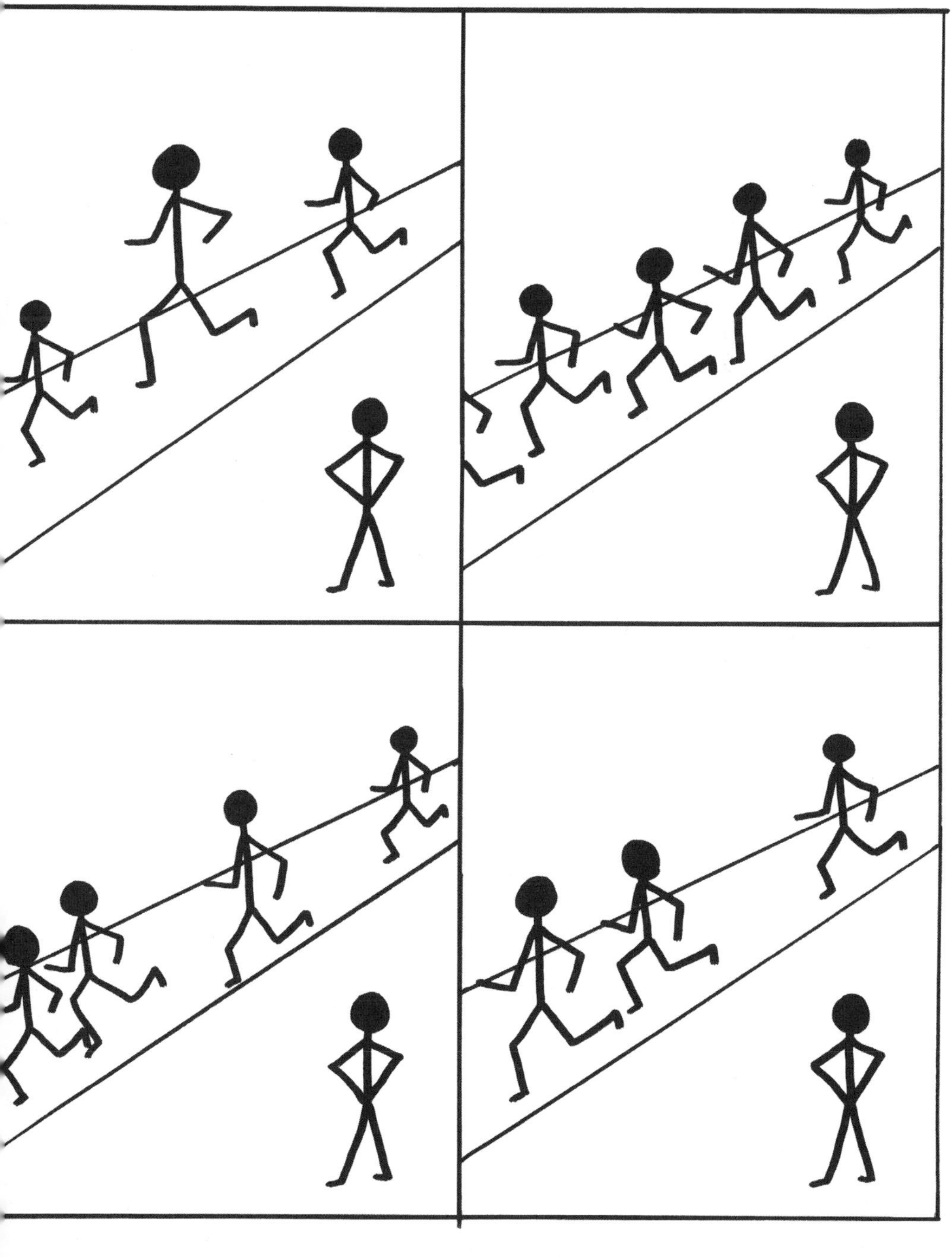

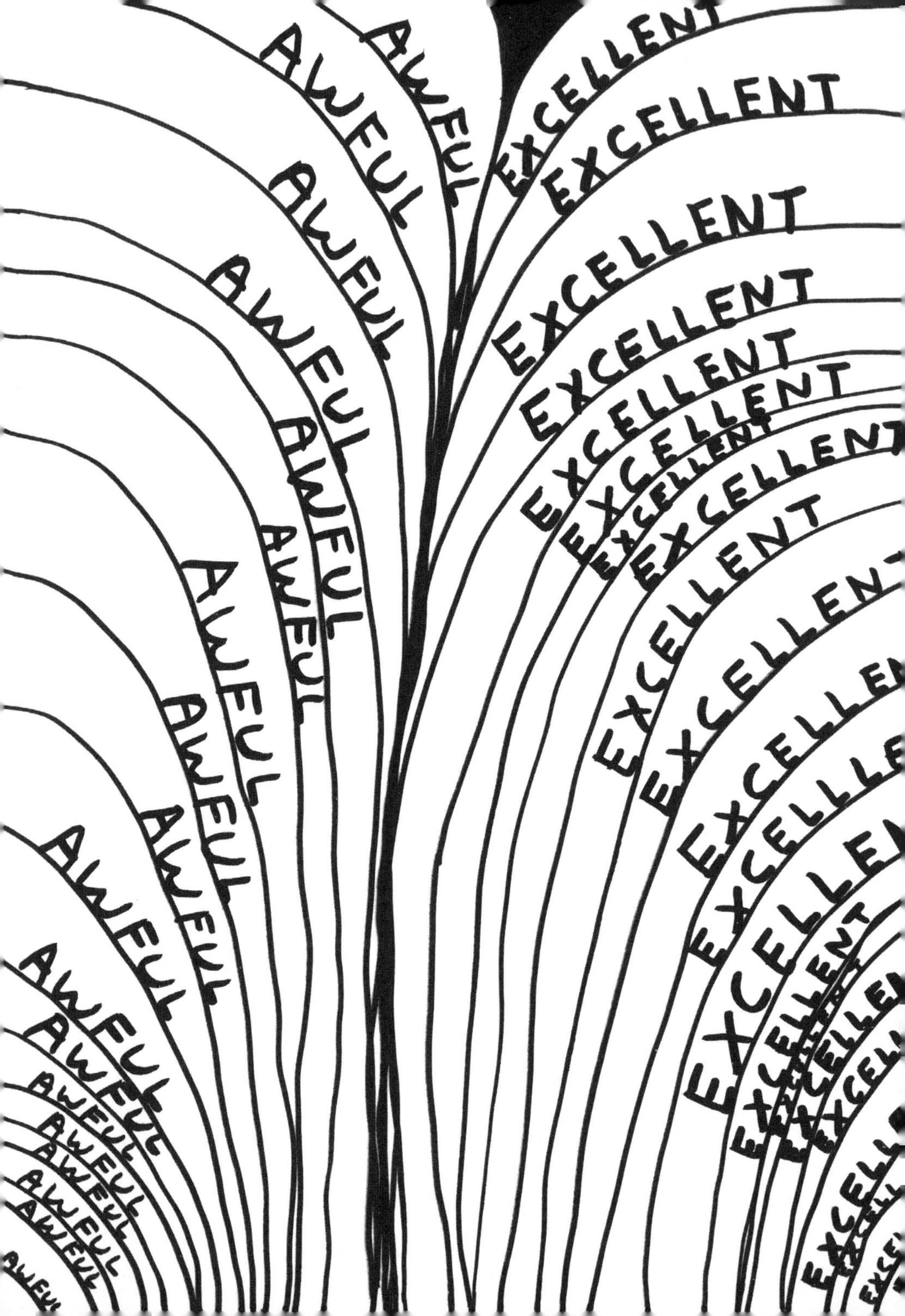

AWFUL
AWFUL
AWFUL
AWFUL
AWFUL
AWFUL
AWFUL
AWFUL
AWFUL
AWFUL
AWFUL
AWFUL
AWFUL
AWFUL
AWFUL
AWFUL
AWFUL

EXCELLENT
EXCELLENT
EXCELLENT
EXCELLENT
EXCELLENT
EXCELLENT
EXCELLENT
EXCELLENT
EXCELLENT
EXCELLENT
EXCELLENT
EX CELLENT
EXCELLENT
EXCELLENT
EXCELLENT
EXCELLENT
EXCELLENT
EXCELLENT
EXCELLENT
EXCELLENT
EXCELLENT
EXCELLENT

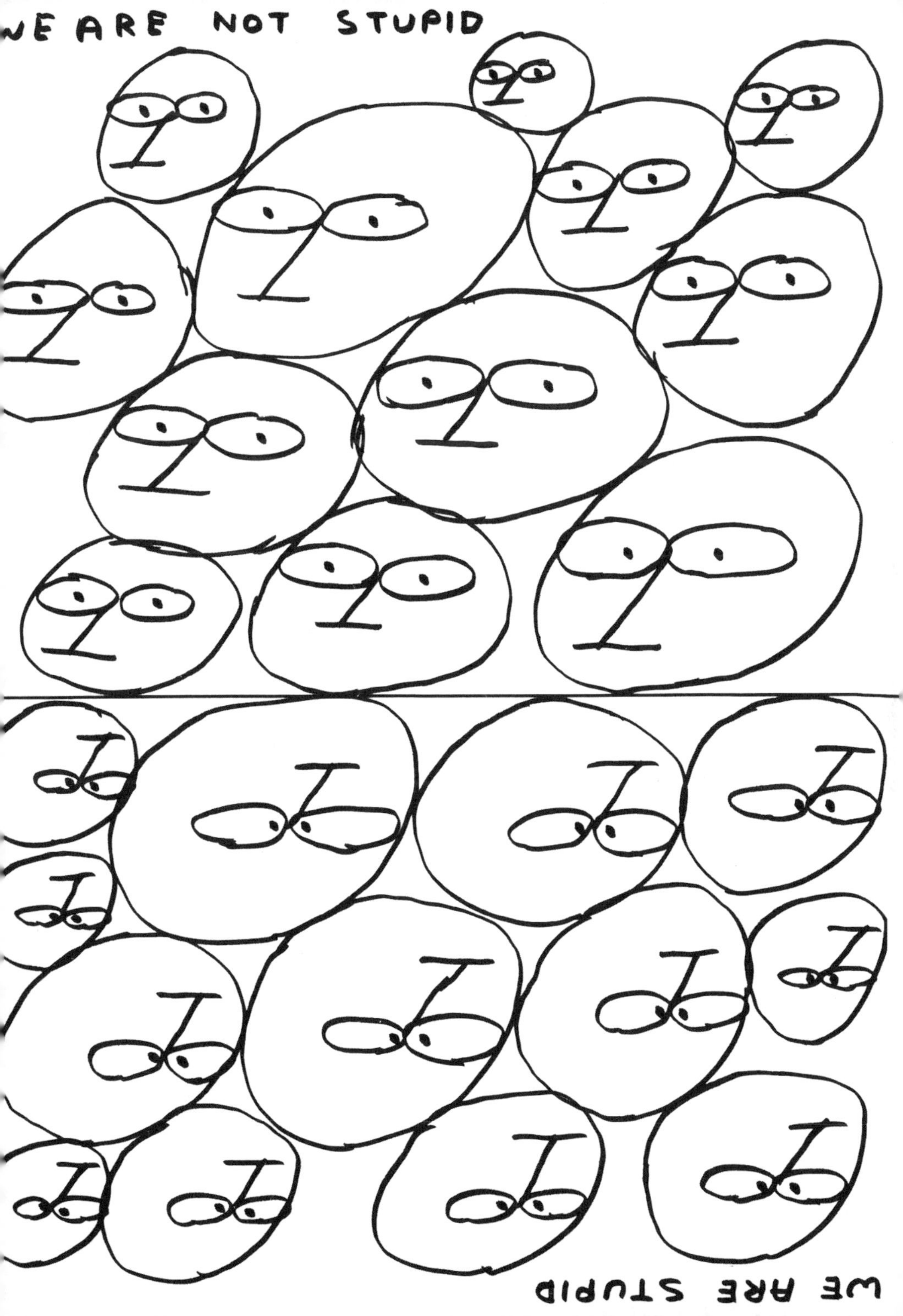

WE ARE NOT STUPID
WE ARE STUPID

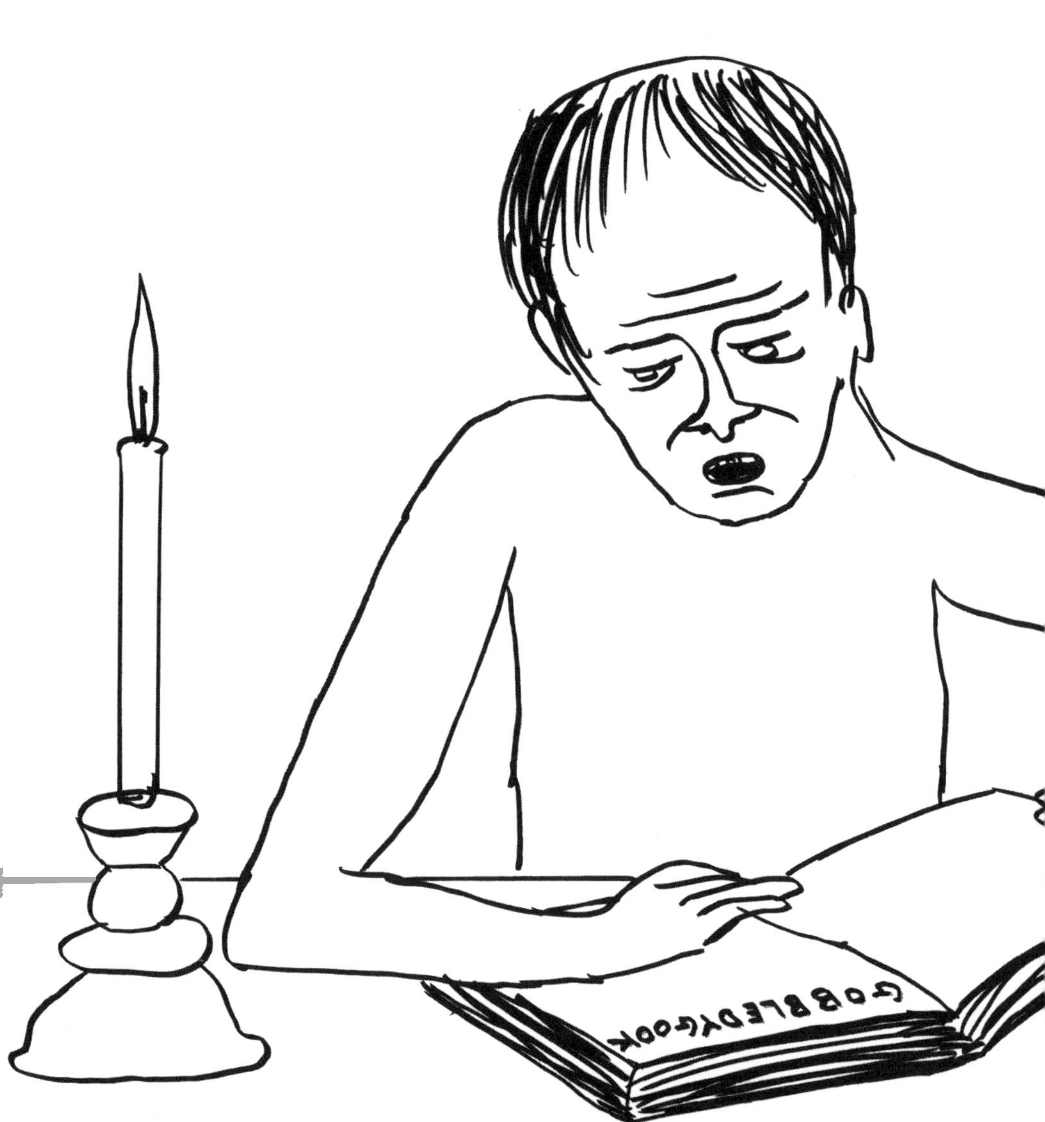

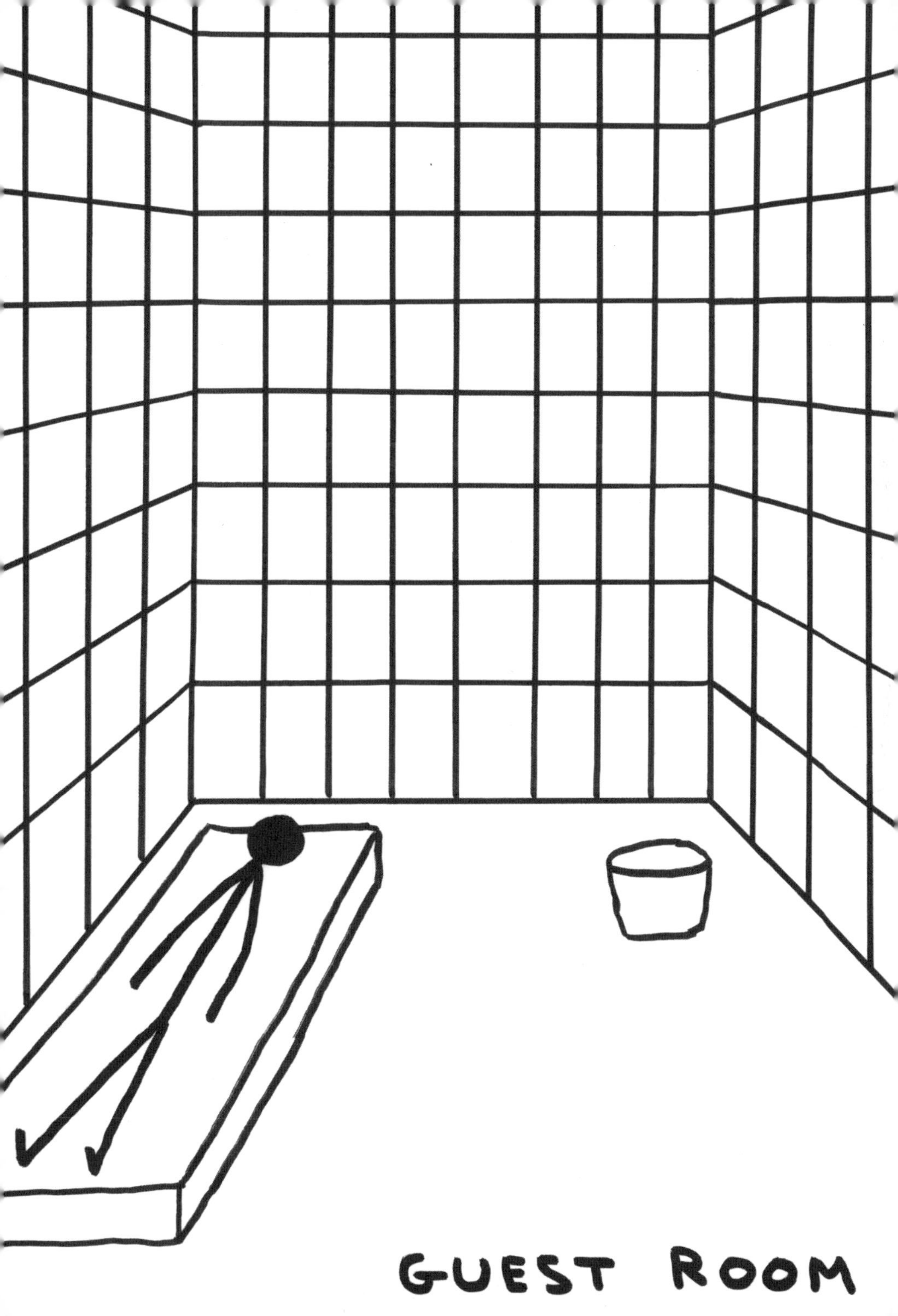

GUEST ROOM

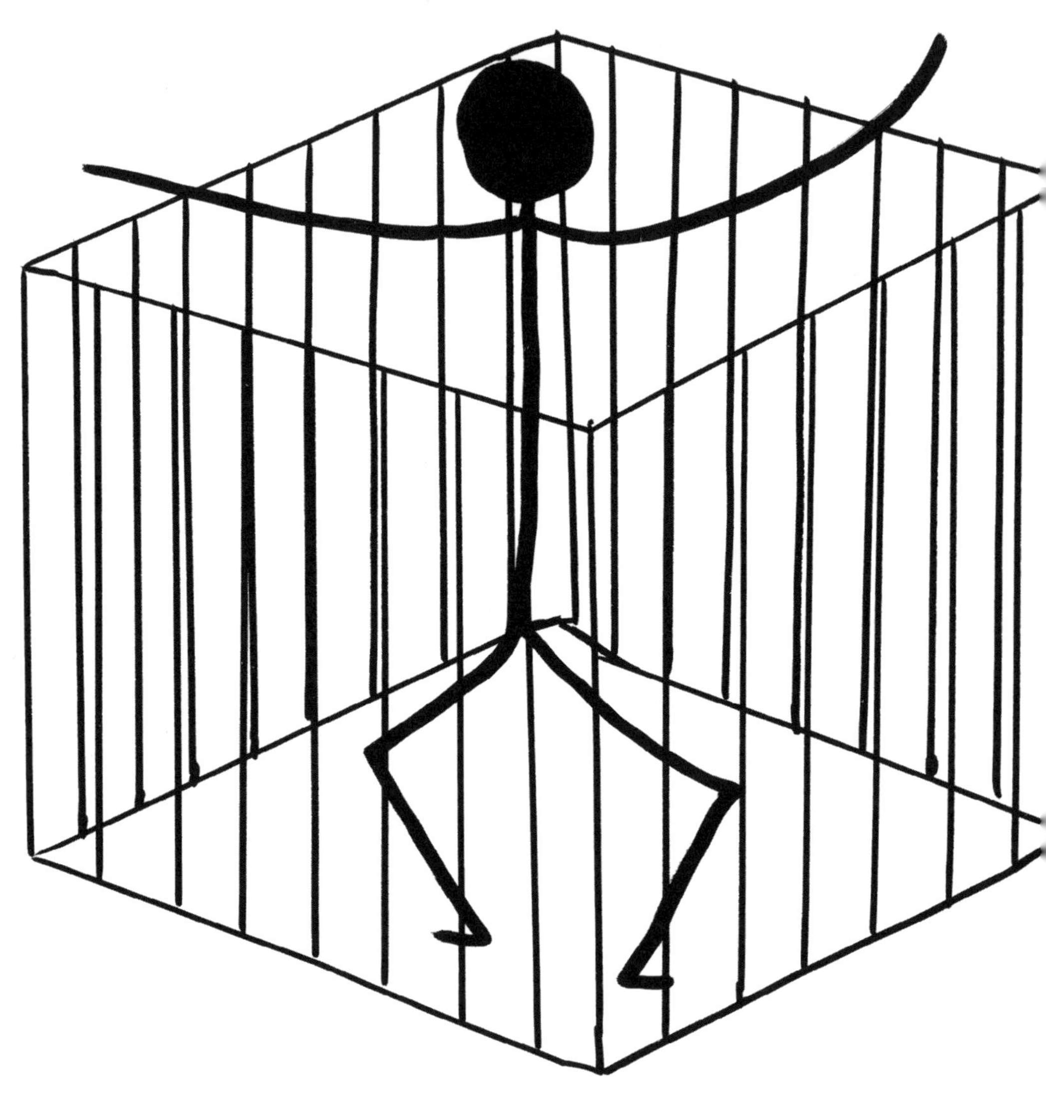

I PLAY IN MY PLAYPEN
I AM VERY HAPPY

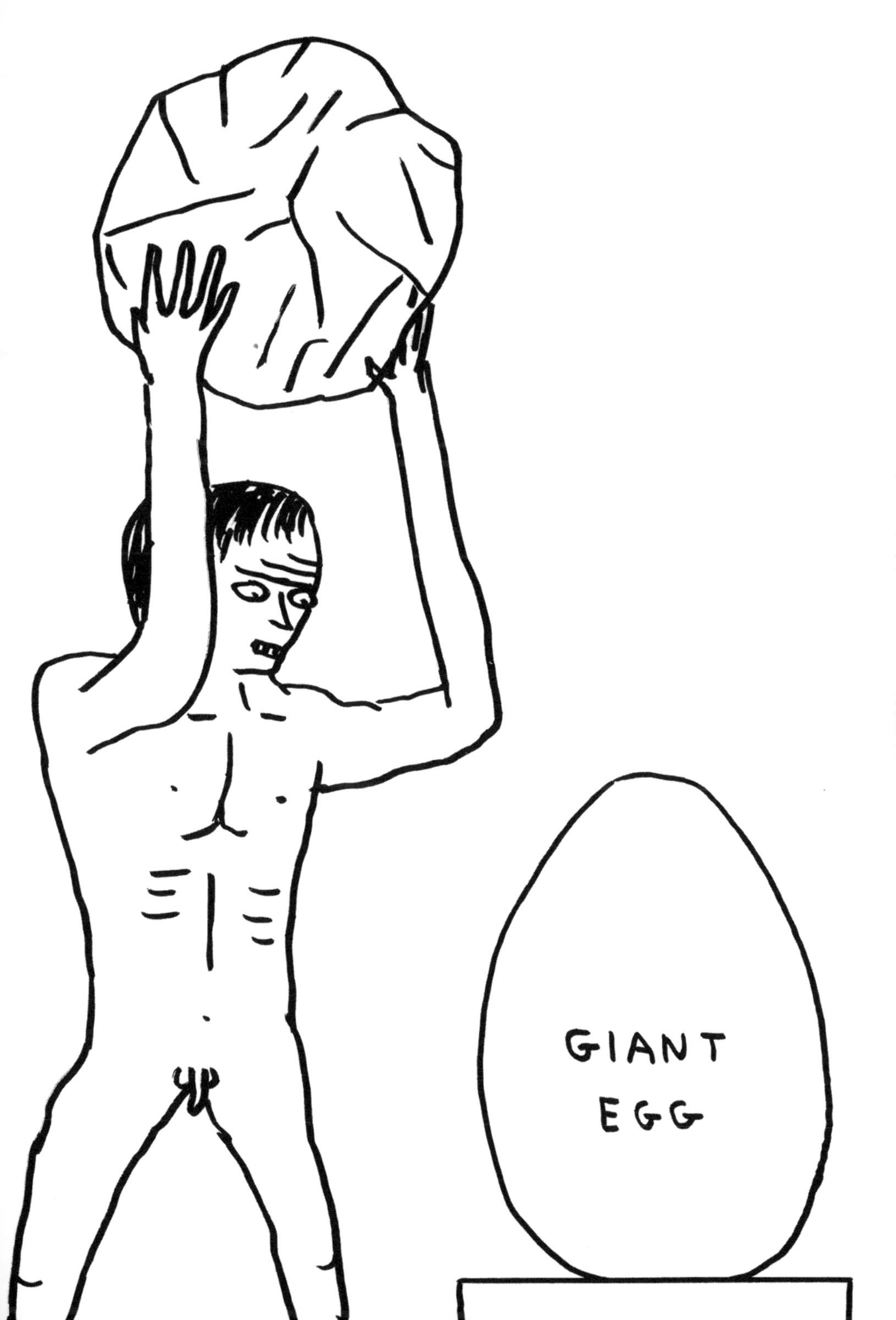

GIANT
EGG

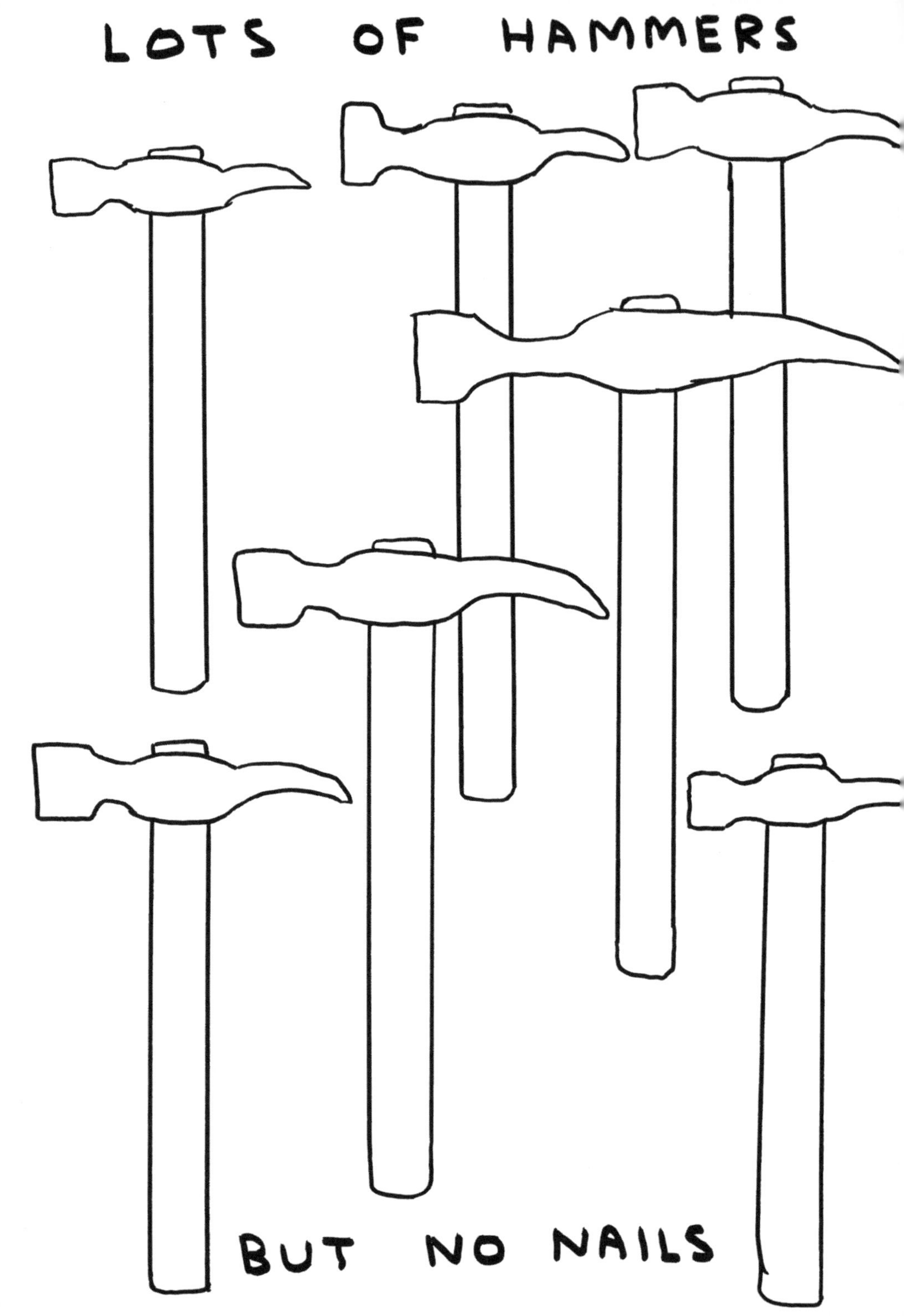
LOTS OF HAMMERS
BUT NO NAILS

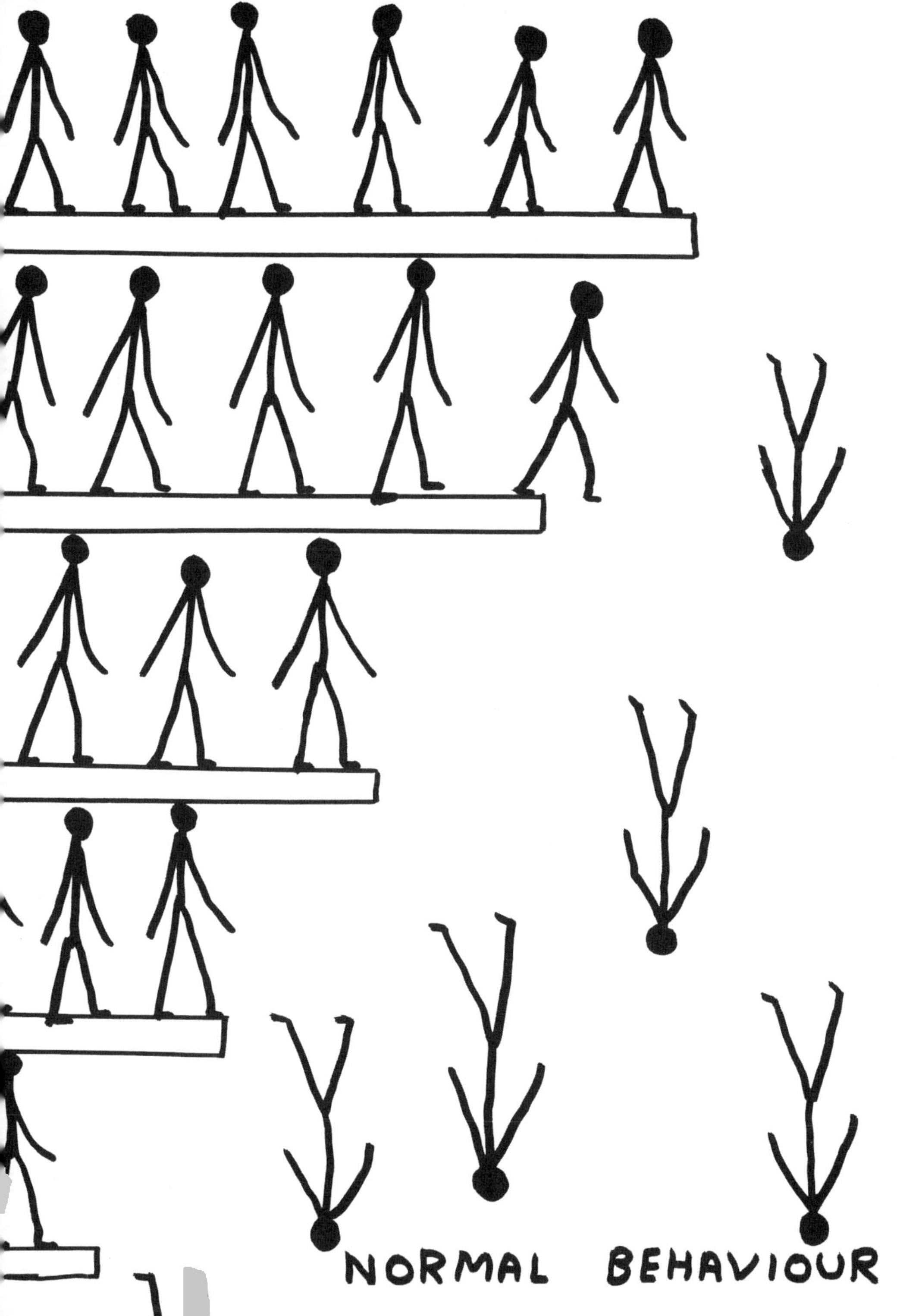
NORMAL BEHAVIOUR

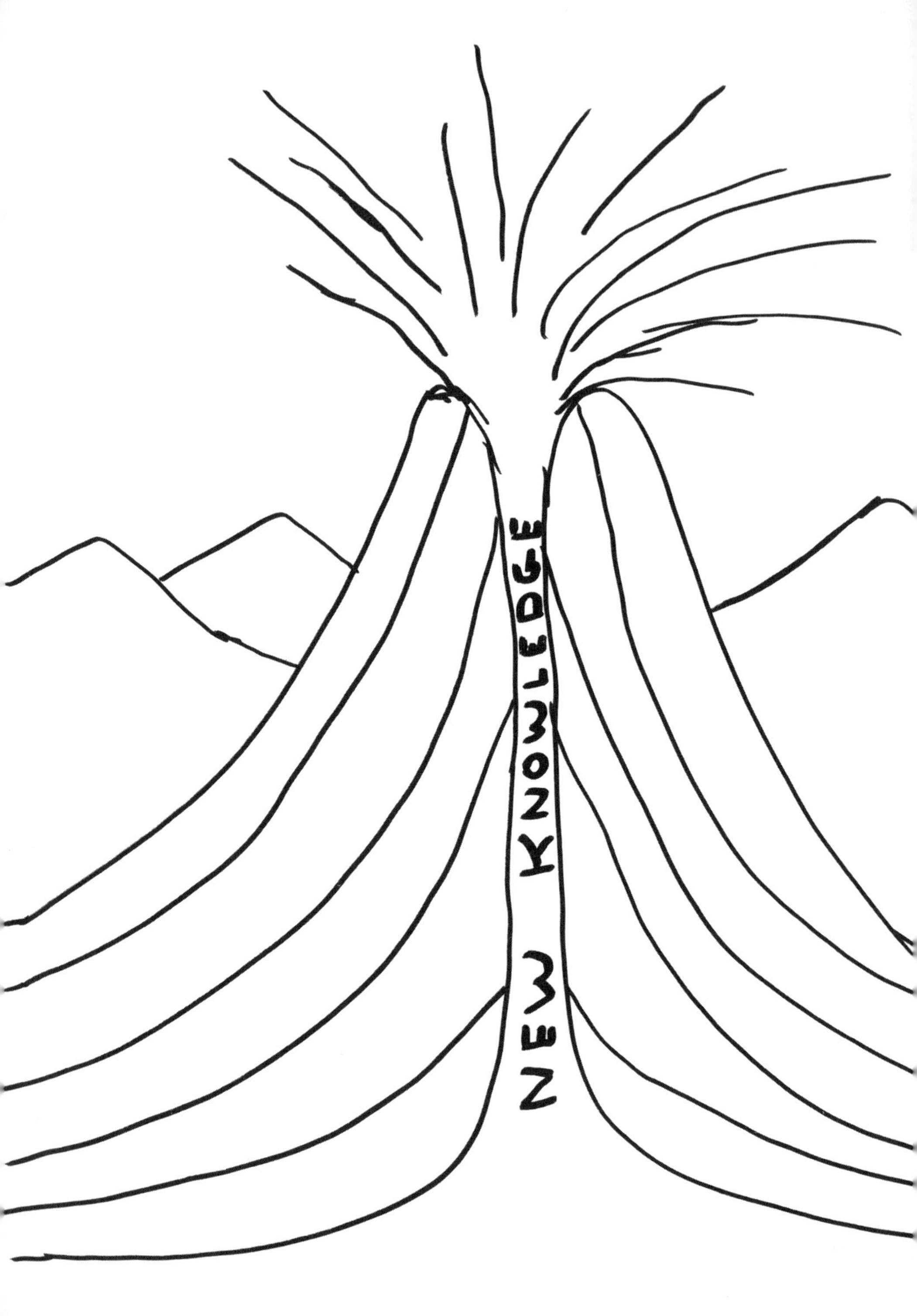

NEW KNOWLEDGE

FOR LEADERSHIP

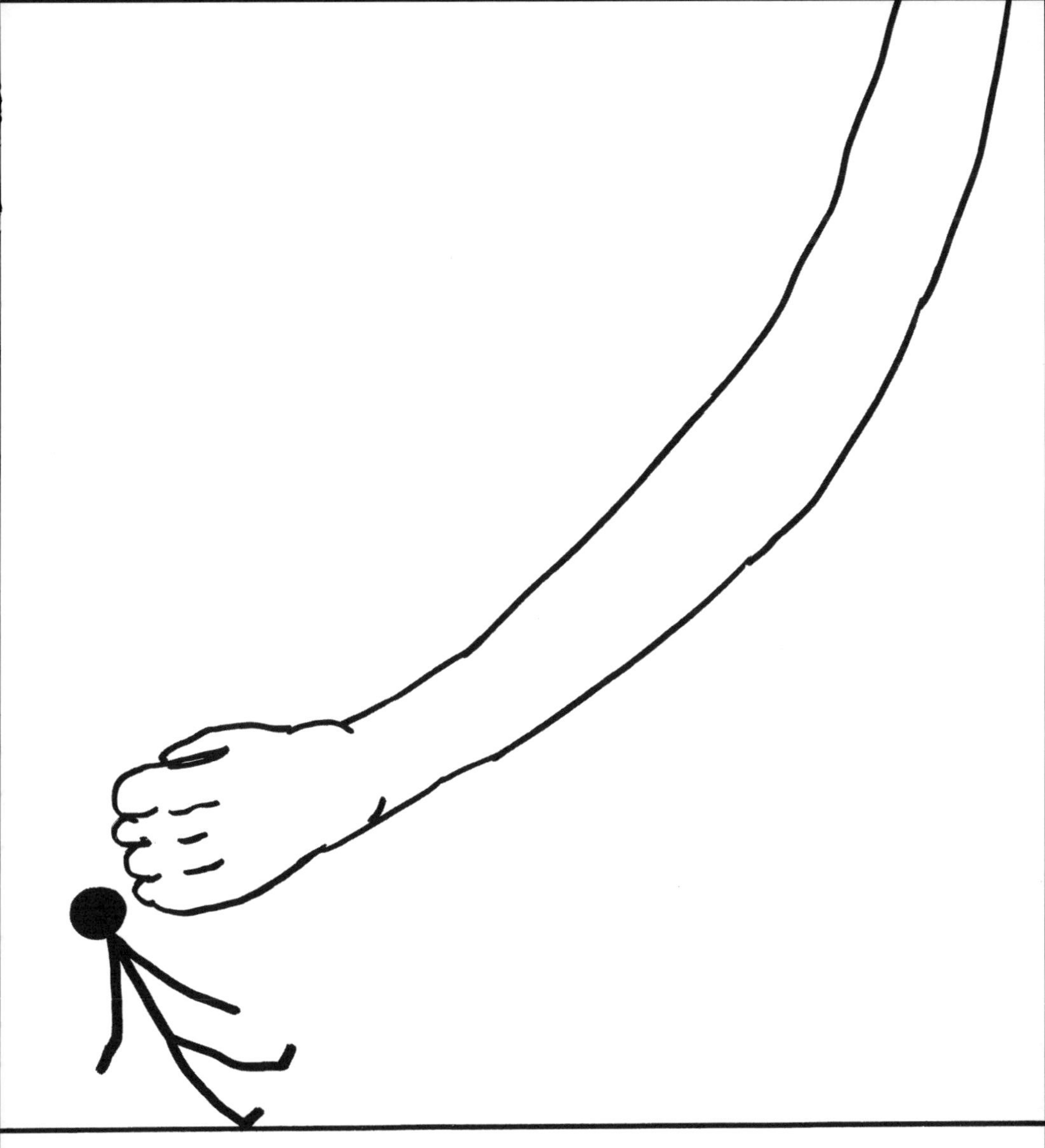

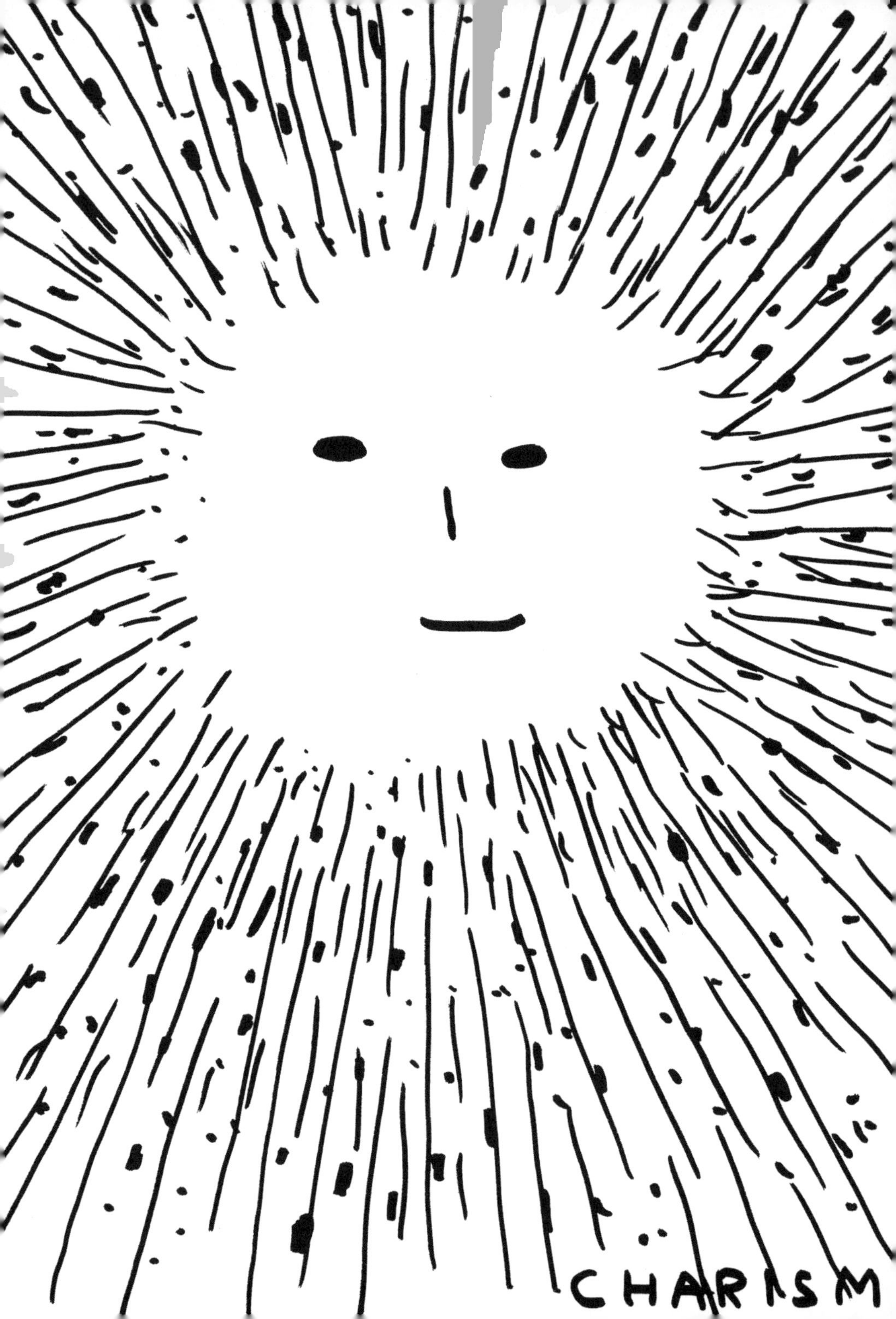
CHARISM

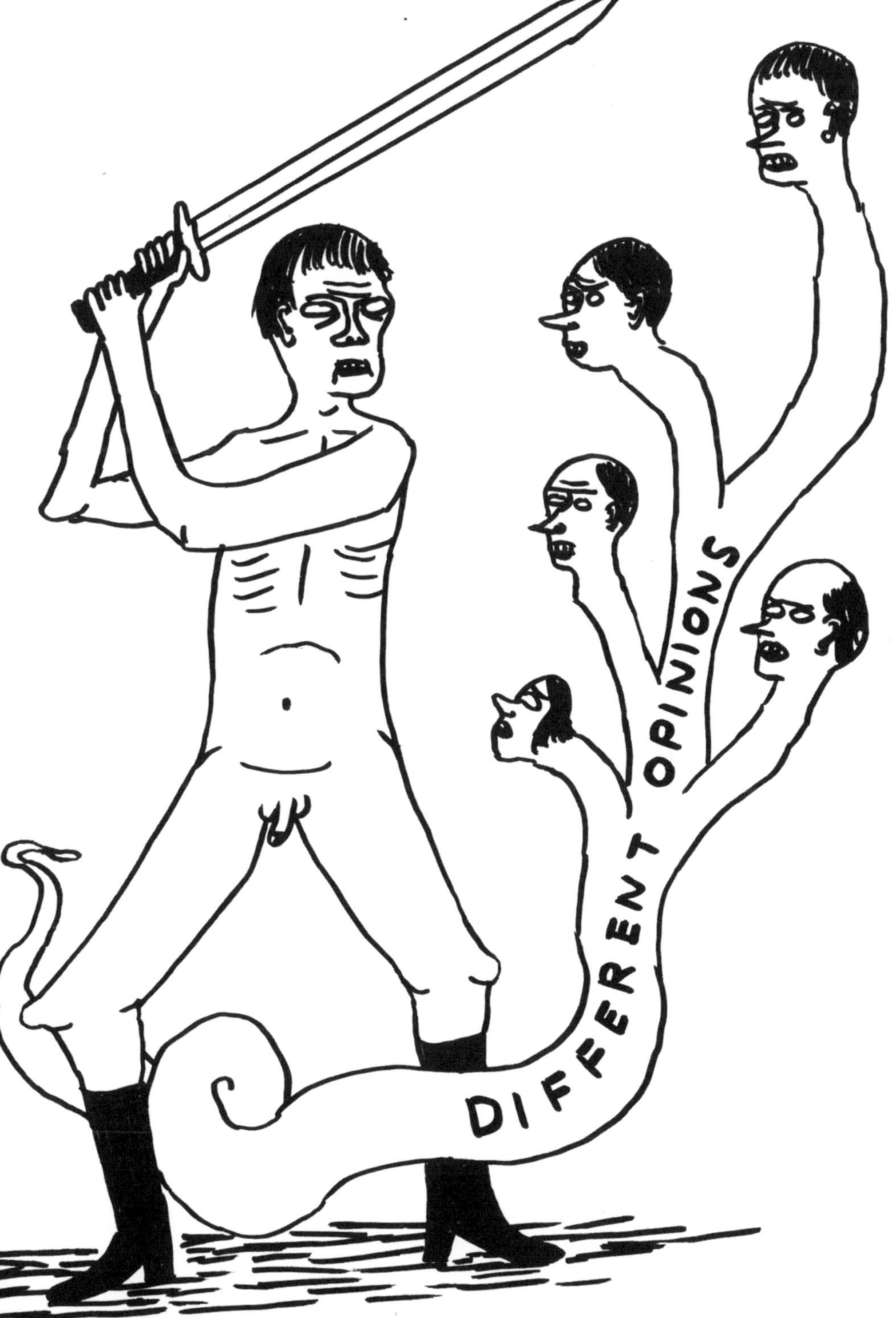

DIFFERENT OPINIONS

SPEECHMAKING

DO NOT PLAN
FROWN
DO NOT MAKE EYE CONTACT
WITH THE AUDIENCE
SPEAK AS QUIETLY AS POSSIBLE
SPEAK QUICKLY
DO NOT PAUSE
SHOUT OCCASIONALLY
AND WITHOUT REASON
USE ABUSIVE LANGUAGE
WATCH RECORDINGS OF YOUR SPEECH

REASONS
UNNECESSARY
YOU MAY PROCEED WITHOUT THEM

SOCIAL WIND
I BLOW INTO TOWN
I RUIN EVERYTHING
THEN I GO AWAY
I AM GREATLY RESPECTED

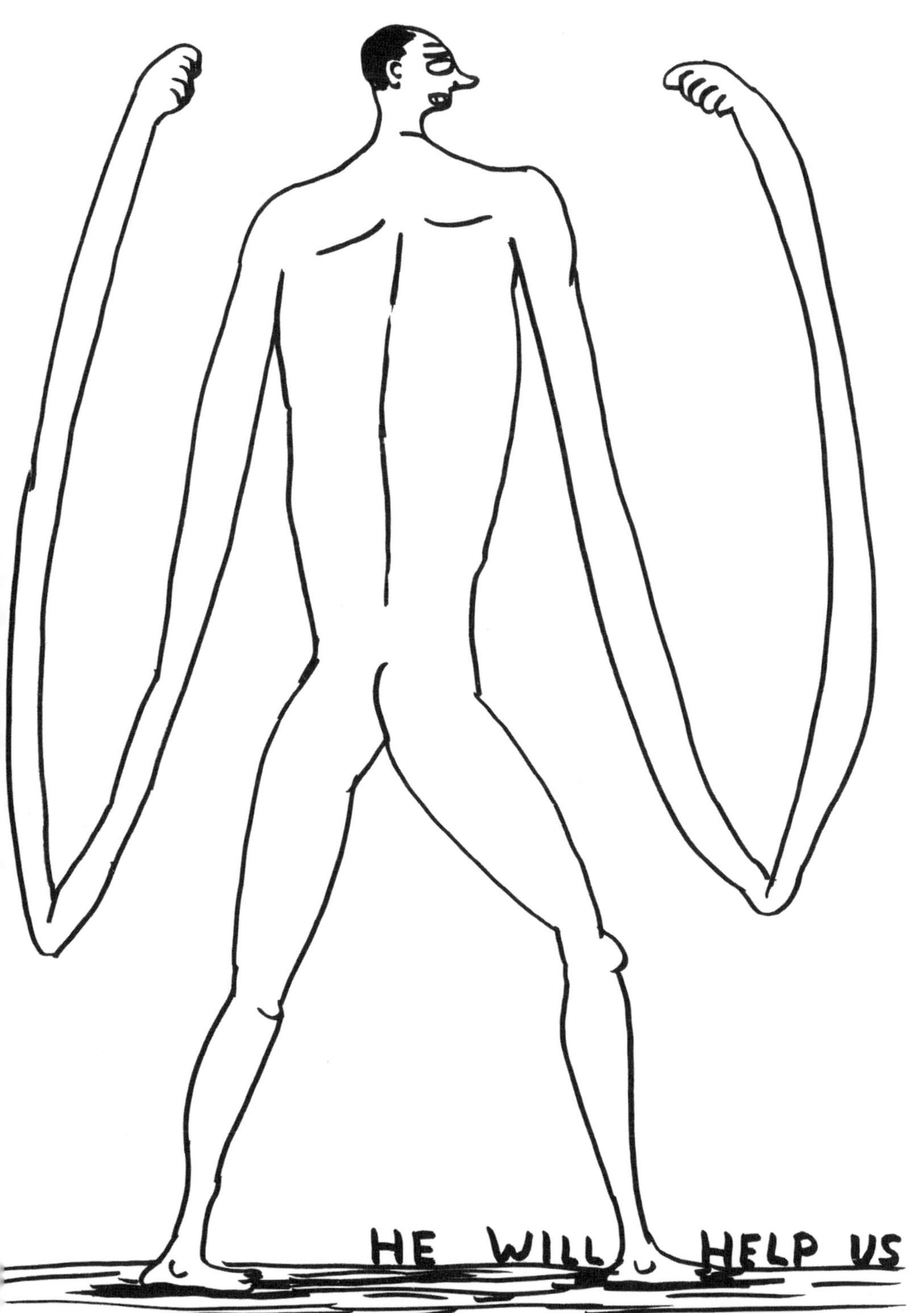HE WILL HELP US

I AM MAGNIFICENT

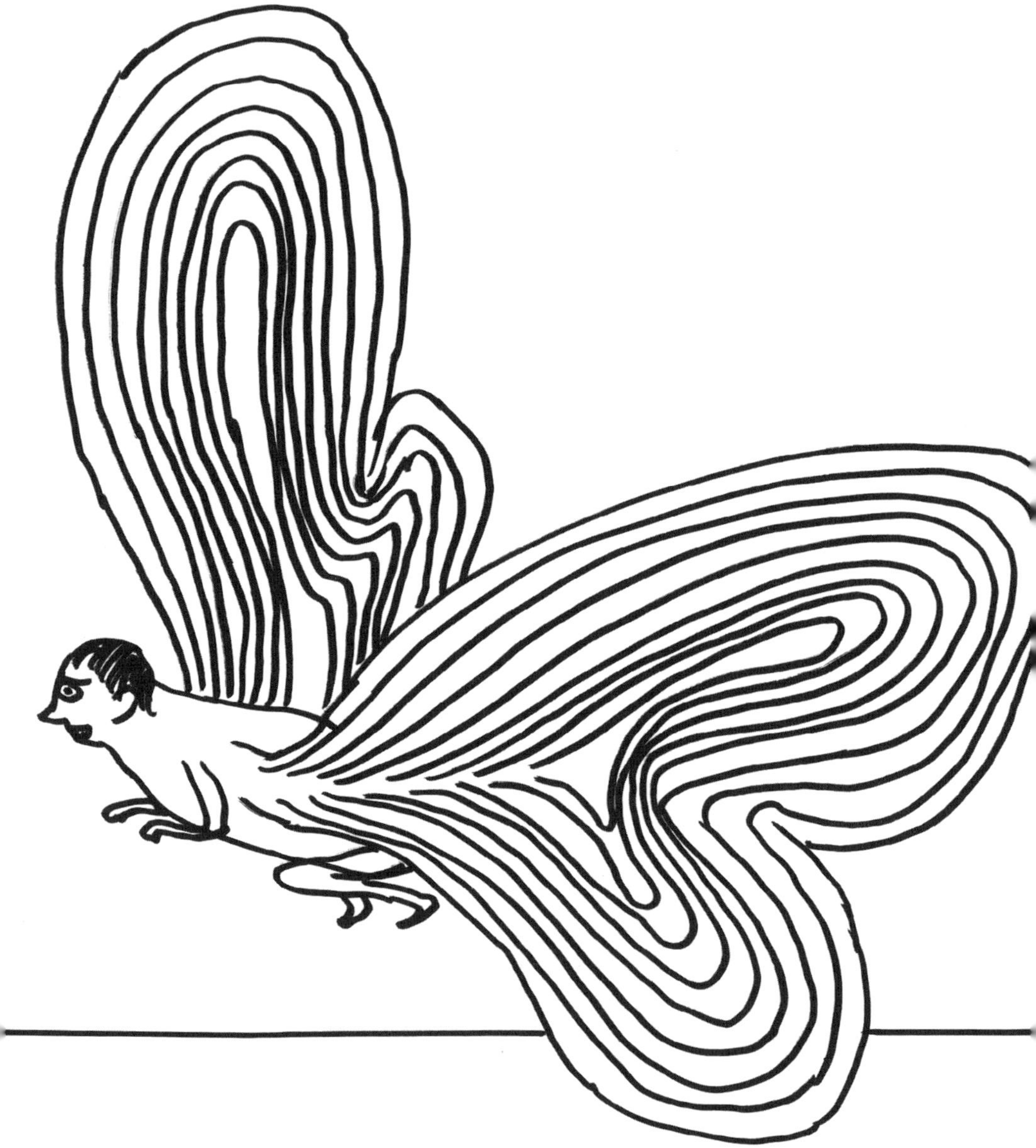

I AM SO BLOODY MAGNIFICENT

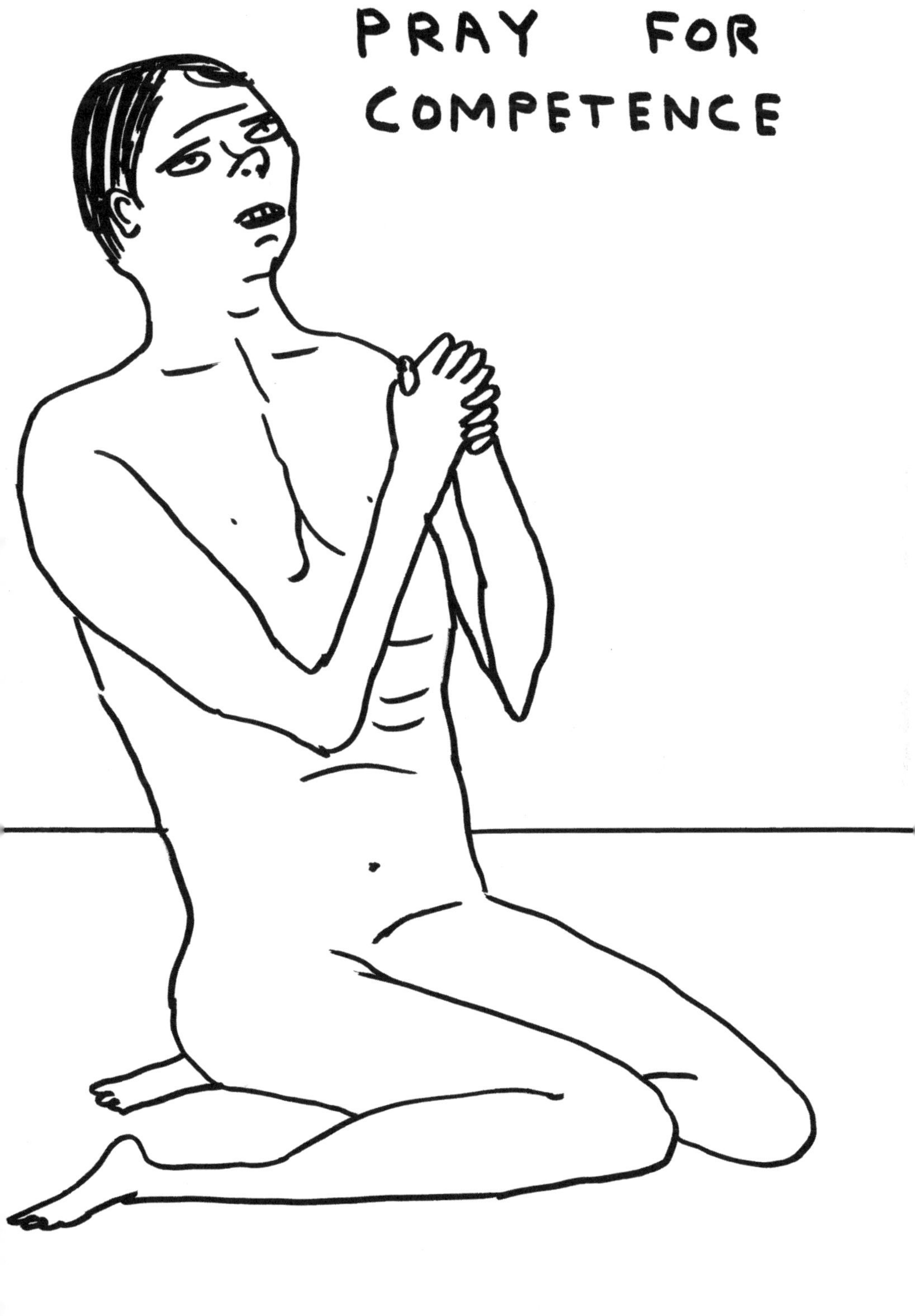
PRAY FOR
COMPETENCE

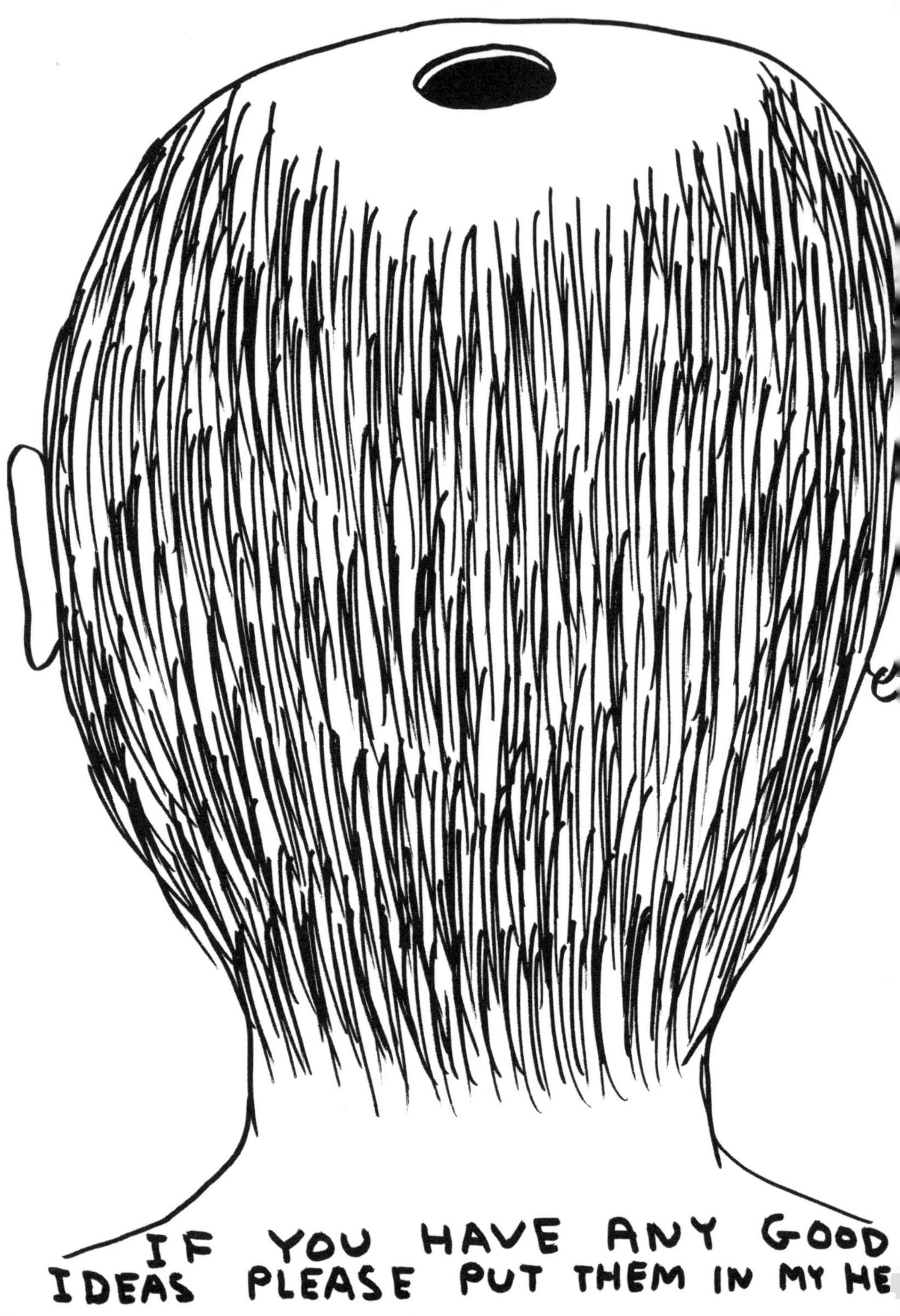

IF YOU HAVE ANY GOOD
IDEAS PLEASE PUT THEM IN MY HE

DO WHAT YOU WANT

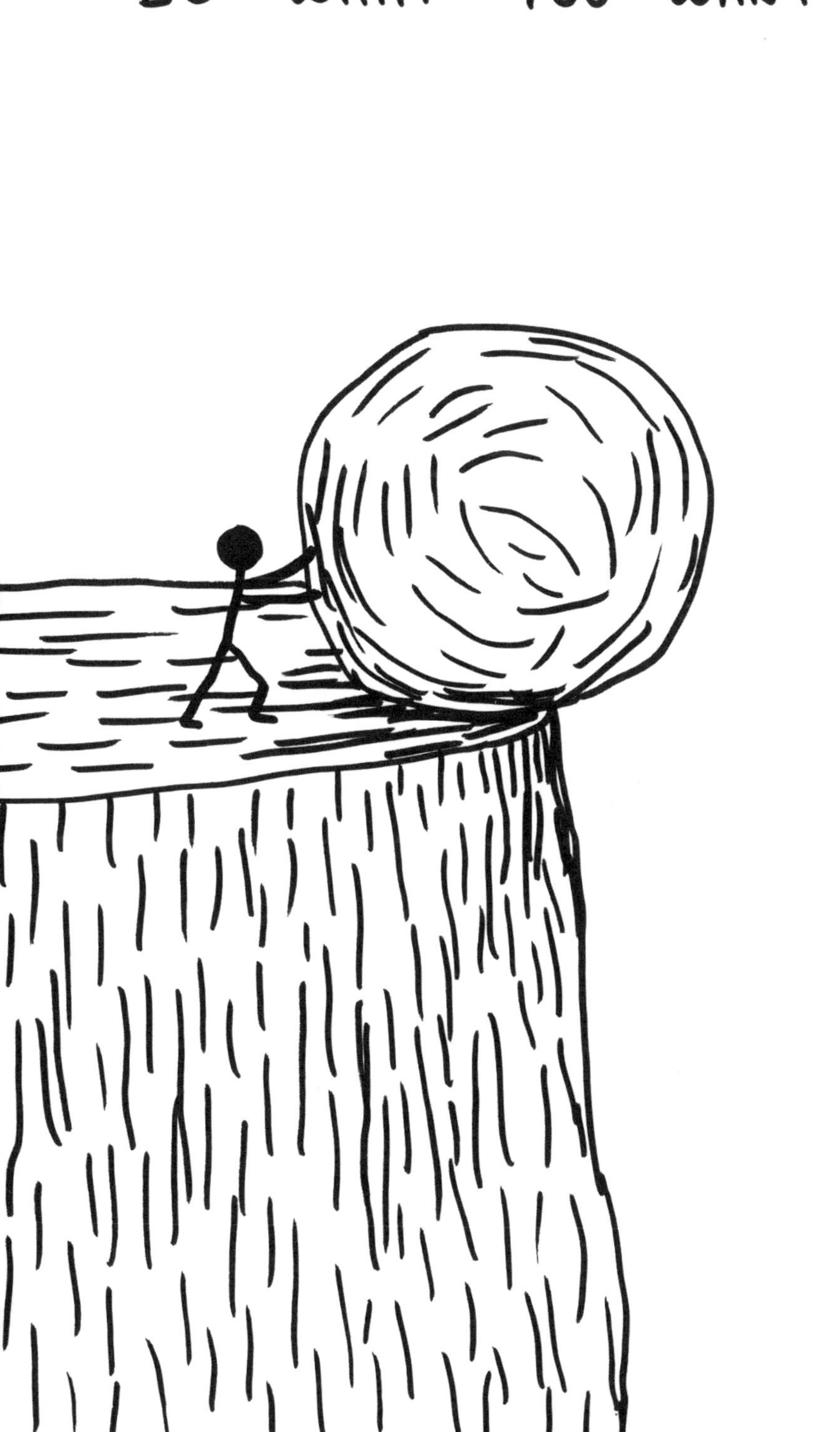

IS THE KING A FOOL?

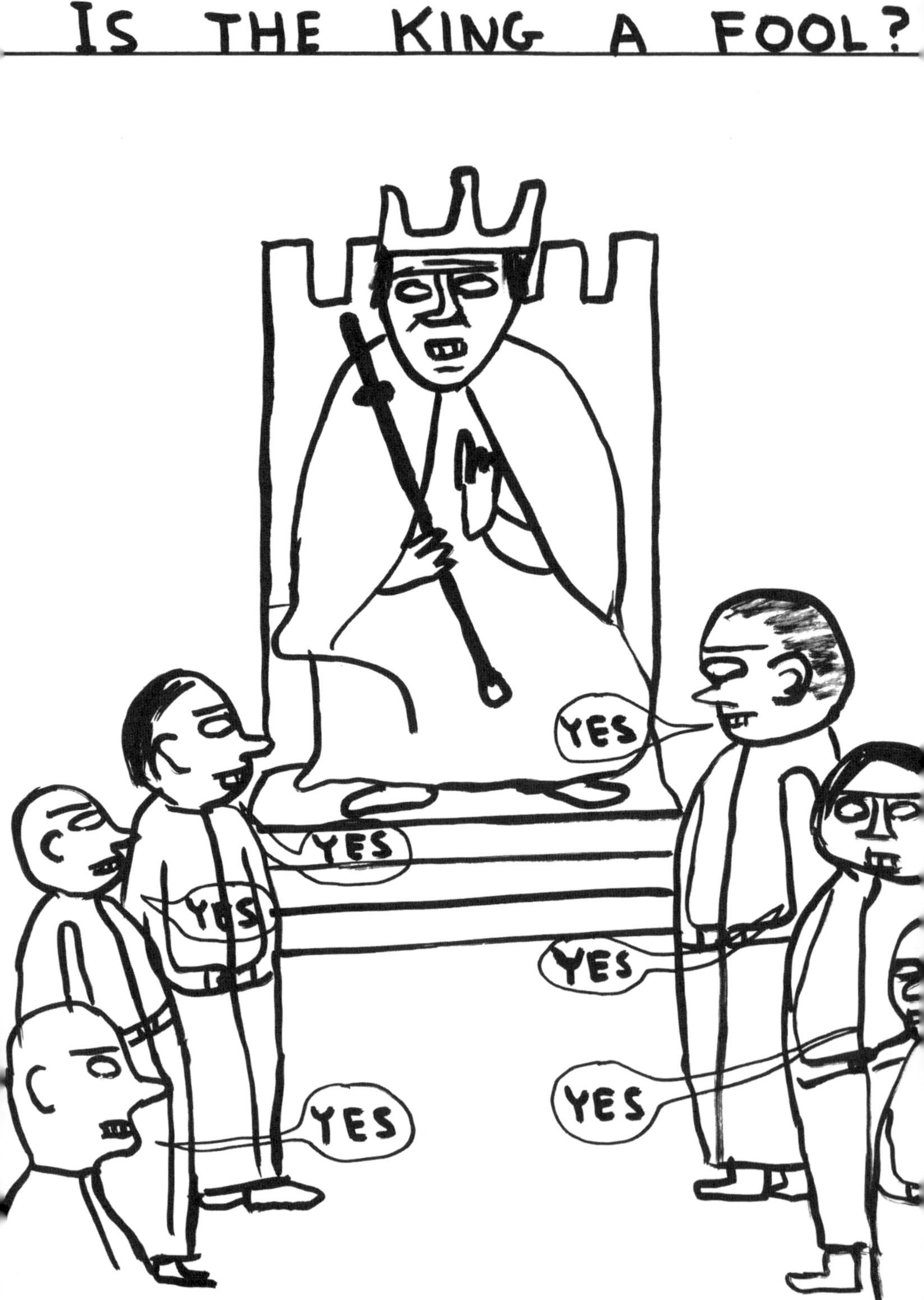

SAVE THE WORLD !

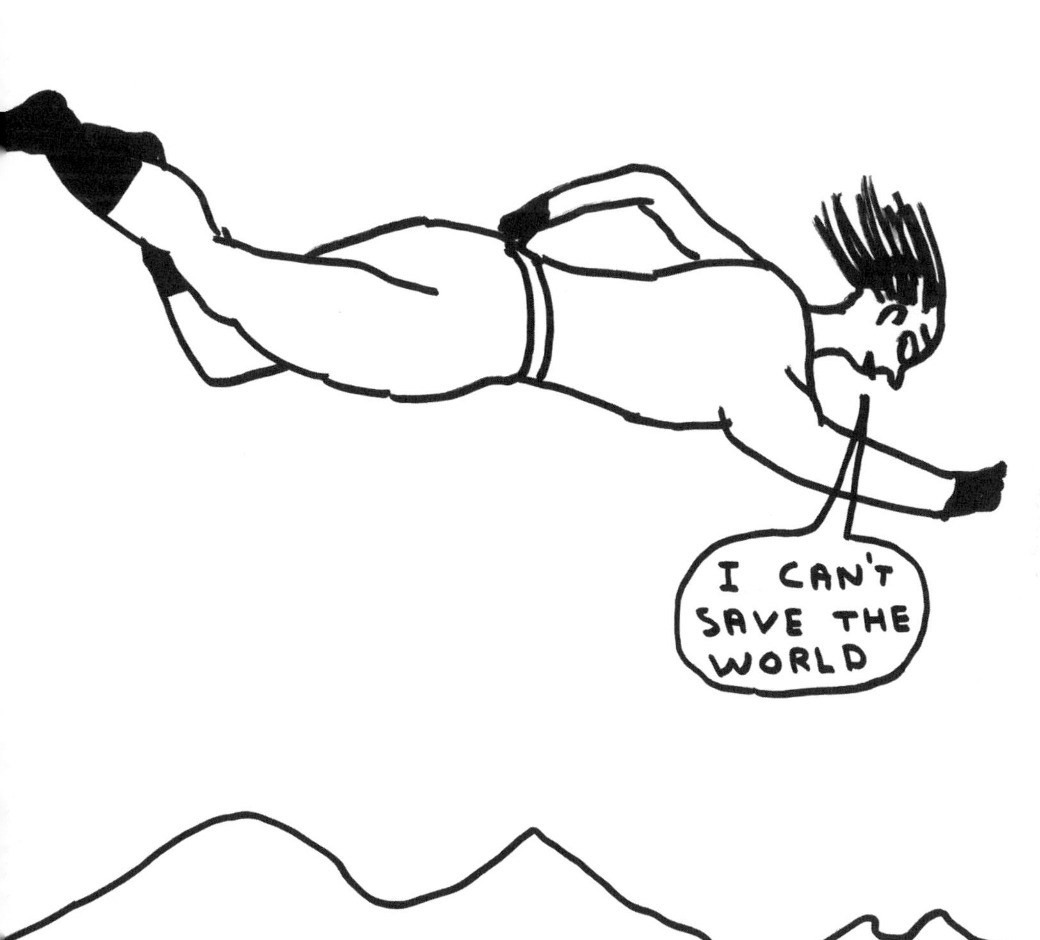

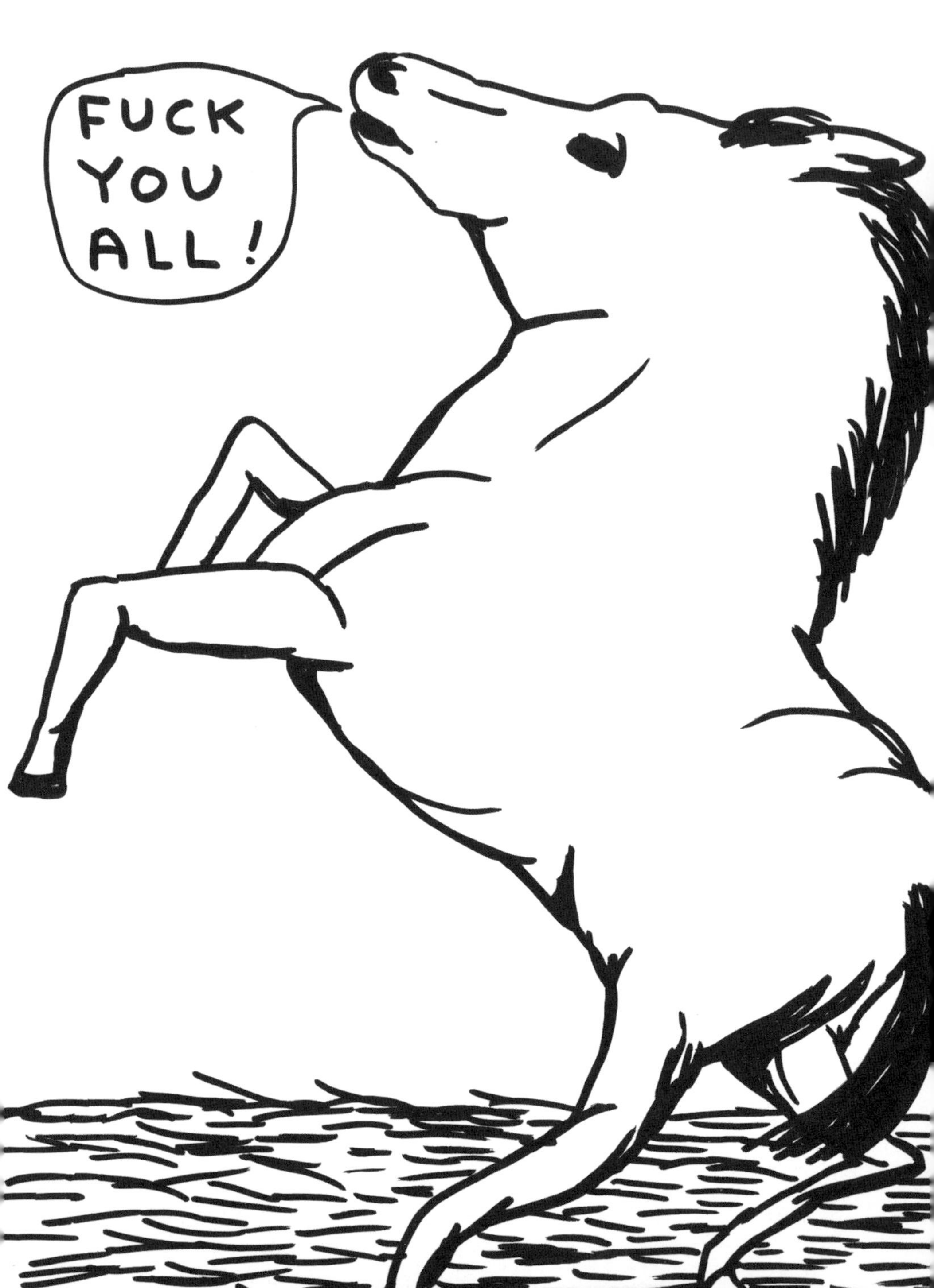

FUCK YOU ALL!

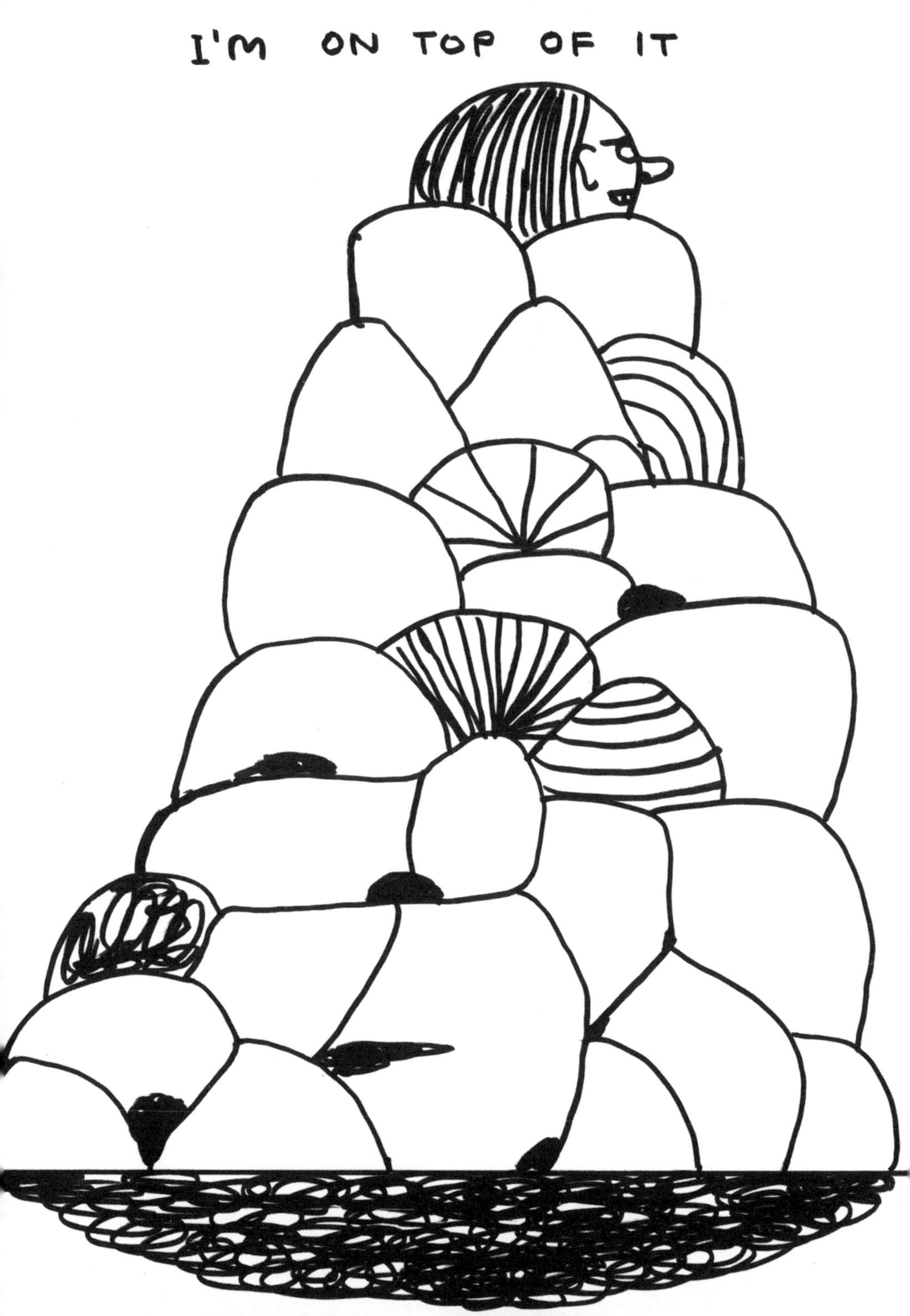
I'M ON TOP OF IT

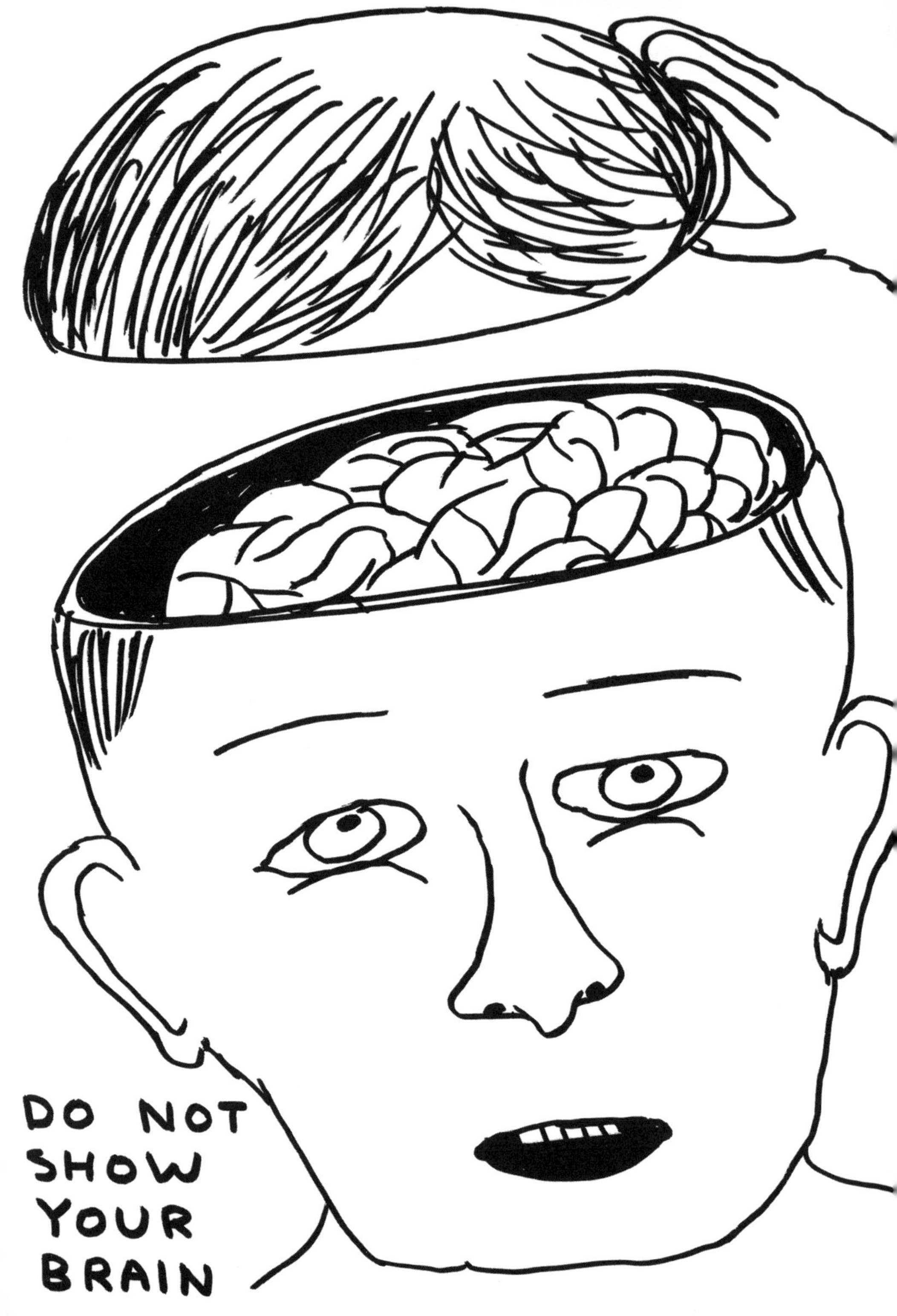

DO NOT
SHOW
YOUR
BRAIN

EVERYTHING I DO IS RIGHT

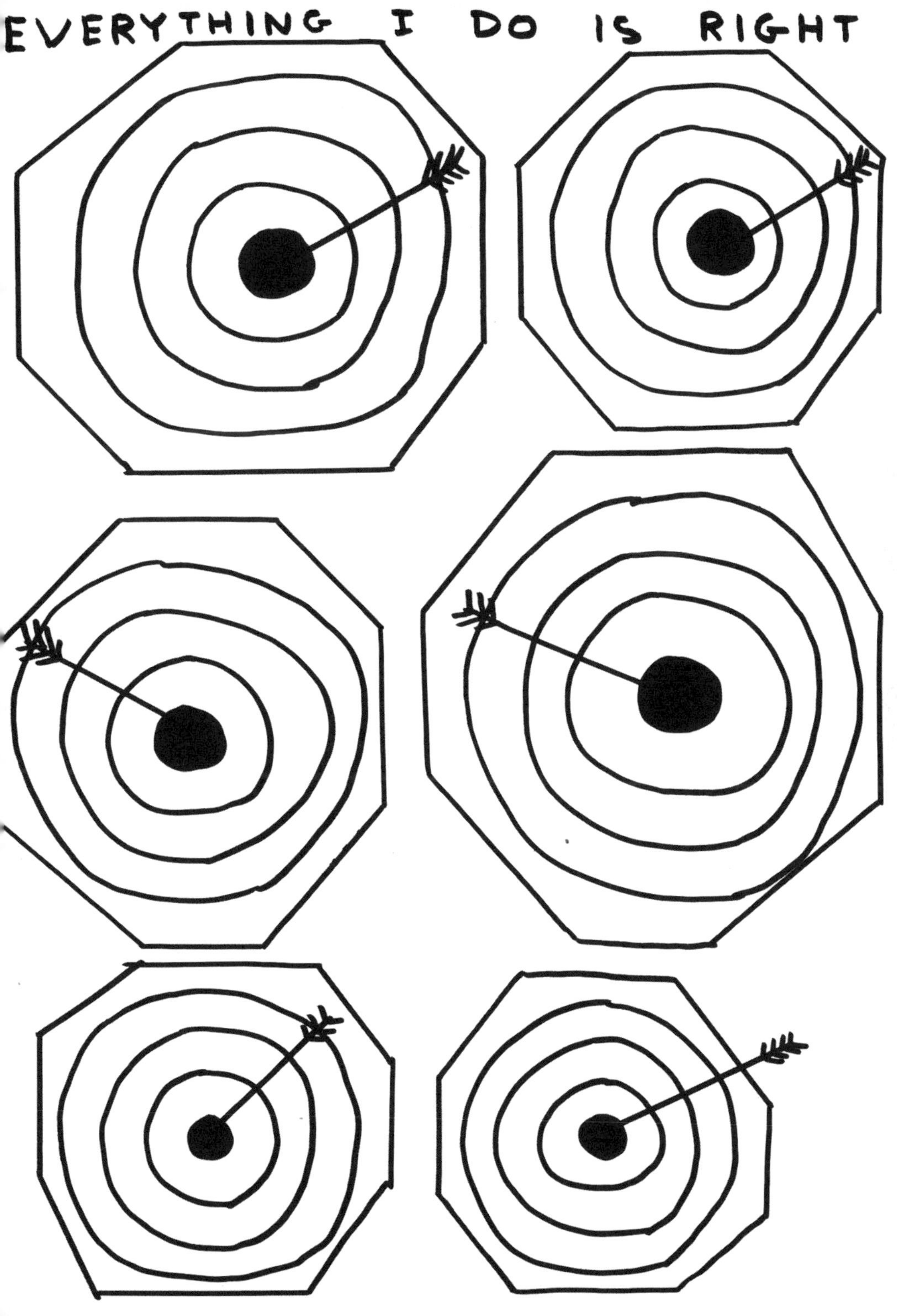

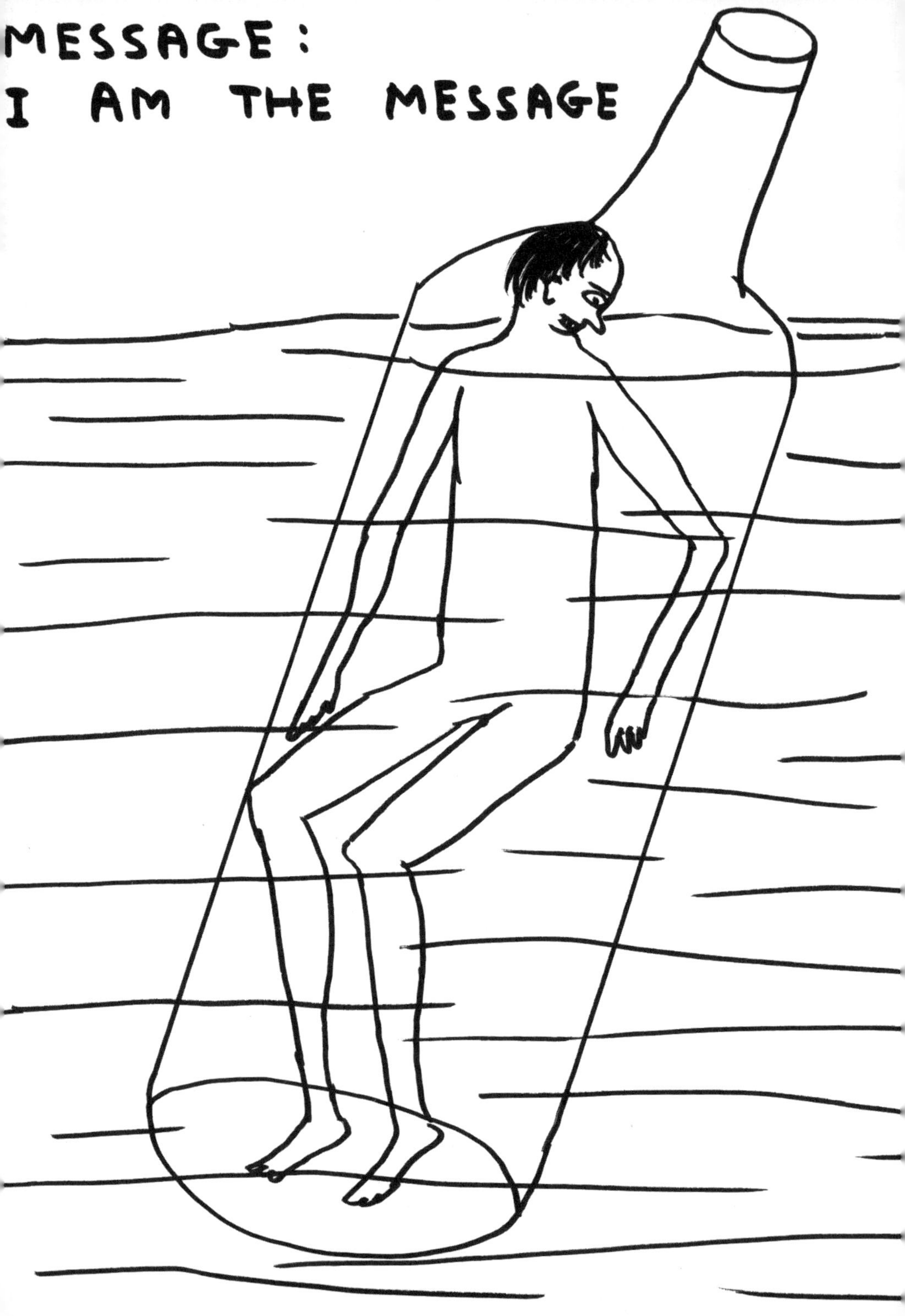
MESSAGE:
I AM THE MESSAGE

INFRASTRUCTURE

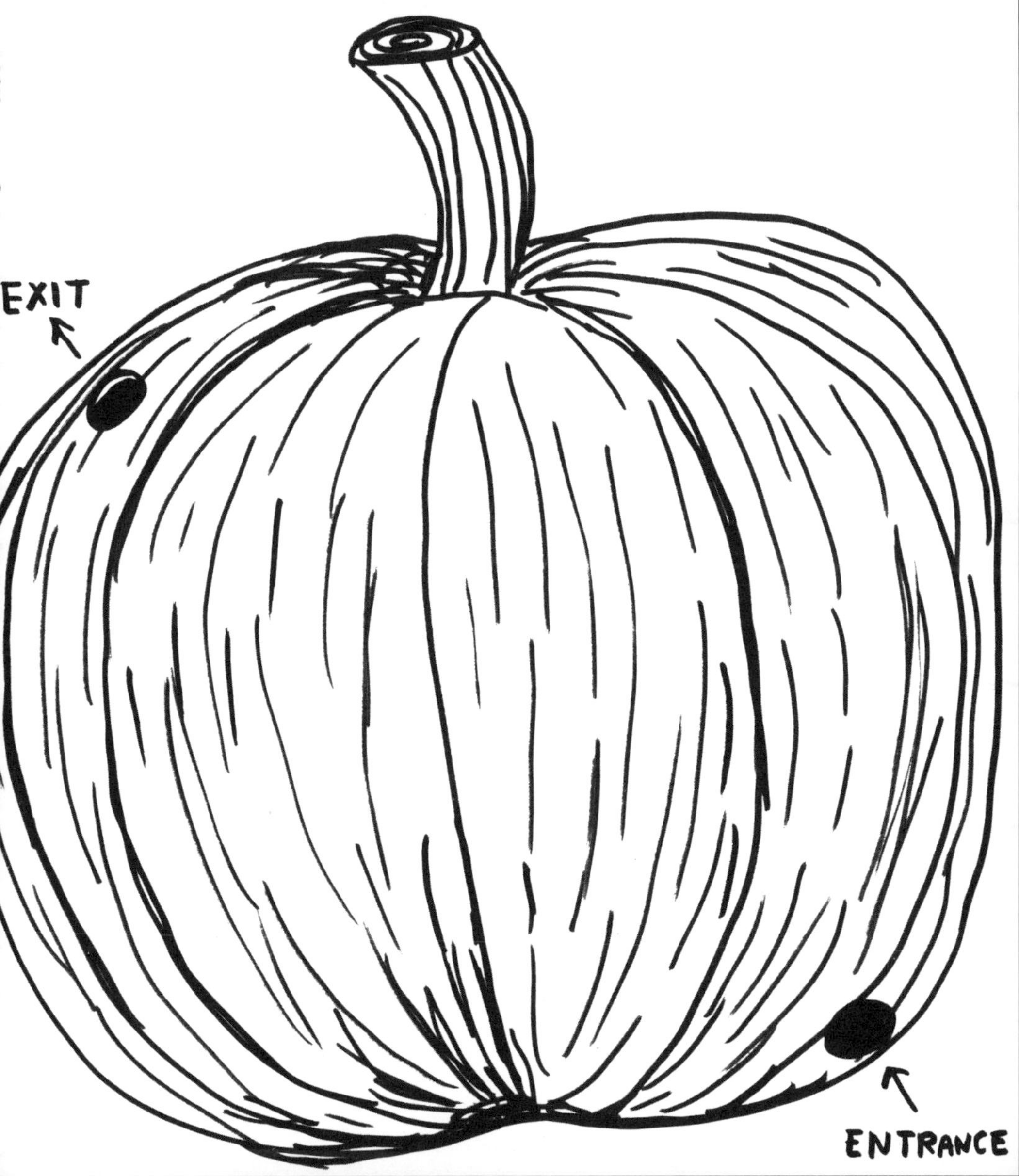

DEAR LORD
PLEASE PROTECT THE FRAGILE
GLASS VESSELS AND DO NOT
ALLOW THEM TO FALL AND
BREAK.
        AMEN

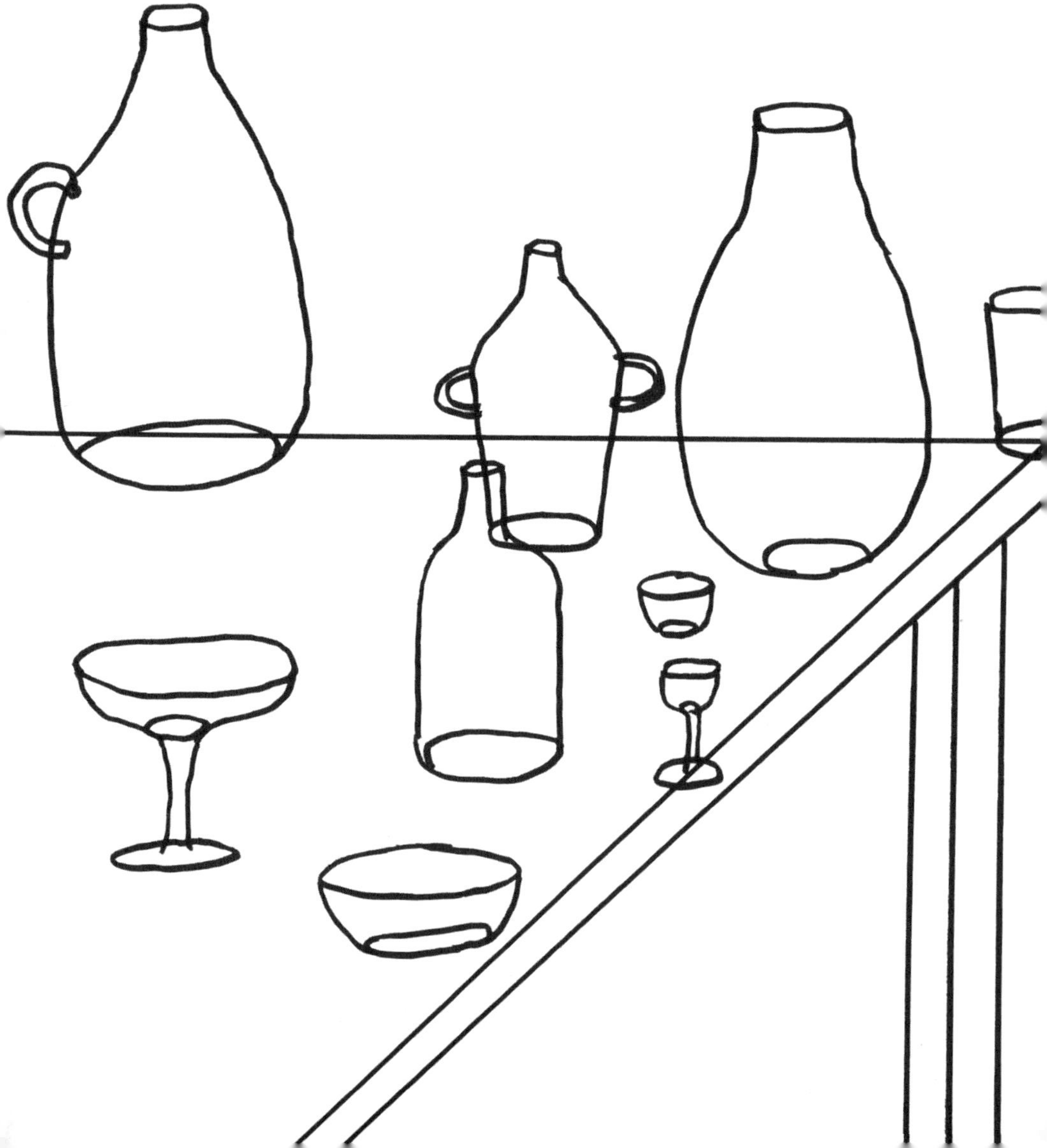

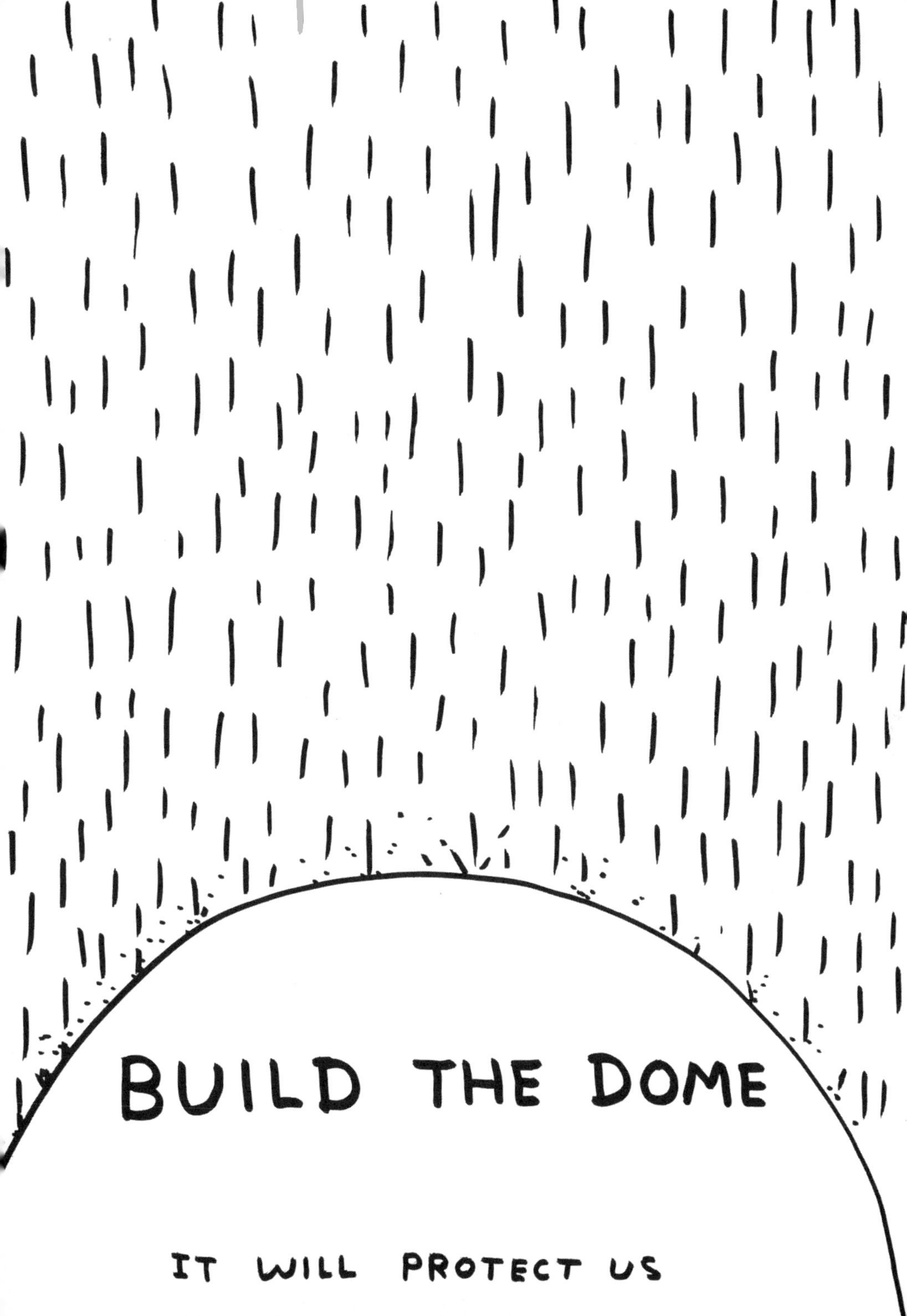

BUILD THE DOME
IT WILL PROTECT US

THIS IS THE TREE THA[T]
I FELL FROM

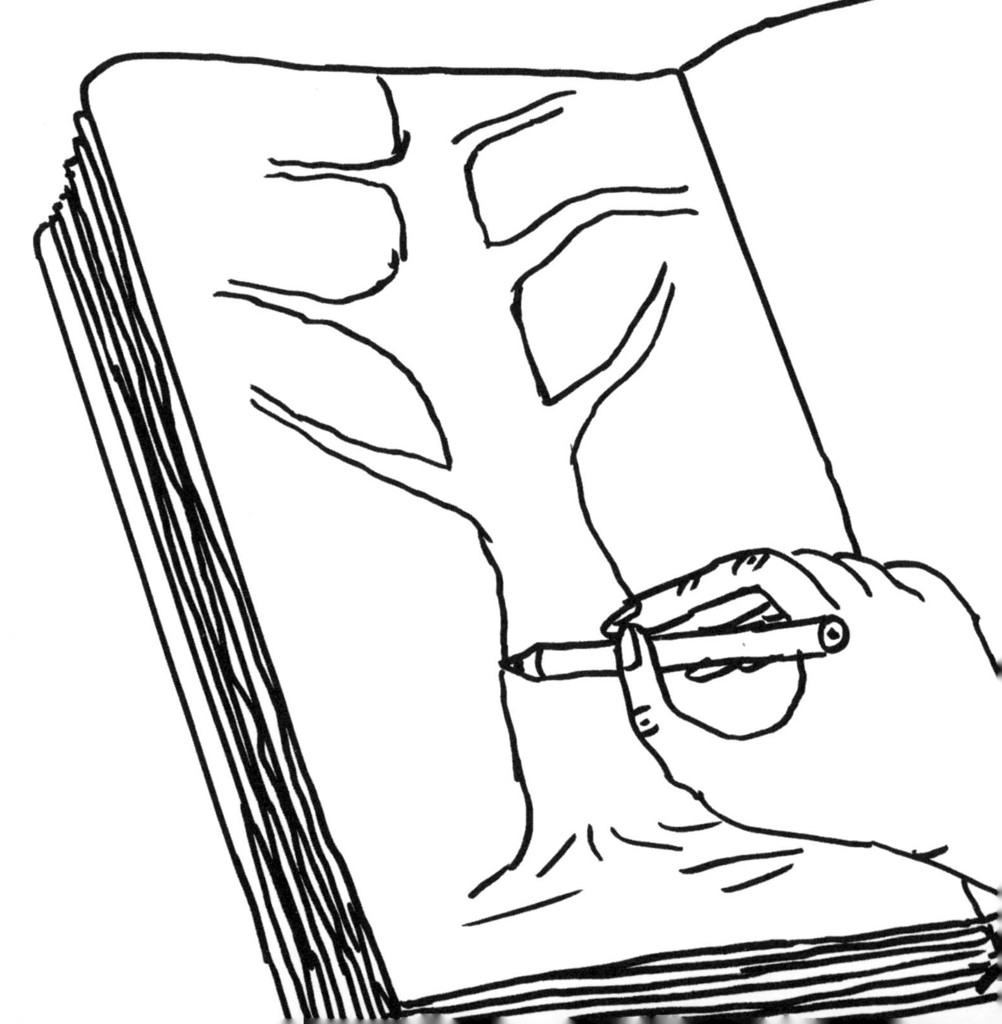

WINDOWS

EVERY BUILDING MUST HAVE THEM
EXCEPT DUNGEONS

WALLS

CHRONICALLY UNDERFUNDED

BRIDGES

CONTINUOUSLY BEING PAINTED
OFTEN CLOSED

THE SEA

DO NOT GO IN IT
THERE ARE JELLYFISH

USE OF ROBOTS

THEY SAID A ROBOT COULD FEED THE CAT
BUT THE CAT DID NOT LIKE THE ROBOT
AND THE CAT LEFT
AND NOW THE ROBOT IS REDUNDANT

WEASELS

IMPOSSIBLE TO GET RID OF THEM
IT CANNOT BE DONE

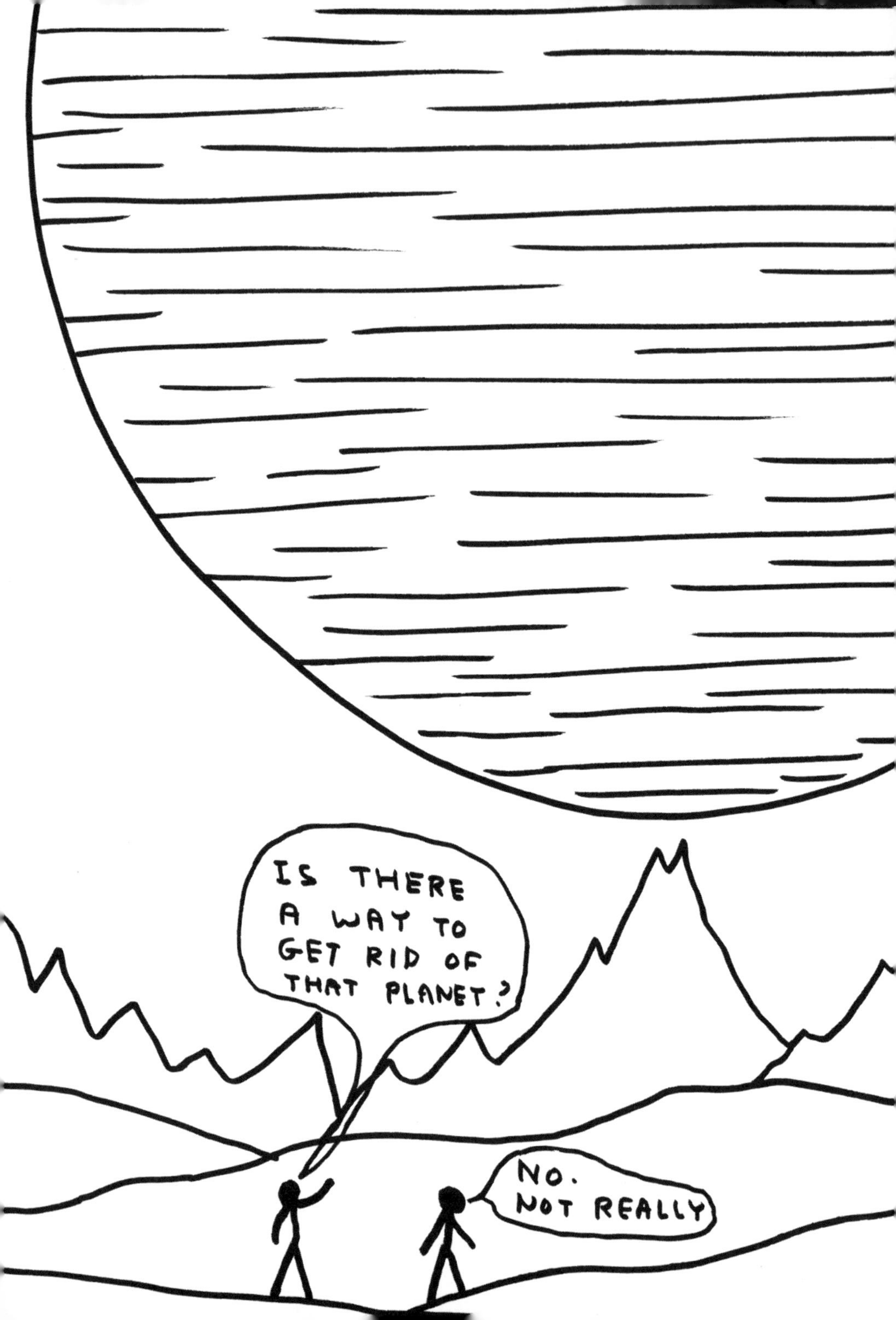

IS THERE A WAY TO GET RID OF THAT PLANET?
NO. NOT REALLY

PLACES OF WORSHIP

THEY KEEP POPPING UP
SEEMINGLY OVERNIGHT
AND THEN IN A FEW DAYS THEY ARE GONE
IT IS AS IF THEY HAD NEVER BEEN THERE
THE ONLY TRACE IS AN AREA OF
YELLOWED GRASS
AND AN ODD SMELL
LIKE STALE POPCORN

A SHOWER OF METEORITES

IT WAS UNEXPECTED
PEOPLE WILL GATHER THEM
AND TRY TO SELL THEM
DO NOT BUY THEM
GATHER YOUR OWN

PUBLIC BUILDINGS

FILLED WITH A KIND OF
EXPANDING FOAM
TO MAKE THEM LESS AIRY

WHAT COLOUR SHOULD WE PAINT THE PUBLIC BUILDINGS?

WE CAN DECIDE THAT LATER
BUT PINK OR GREEN WOULD BE NICE

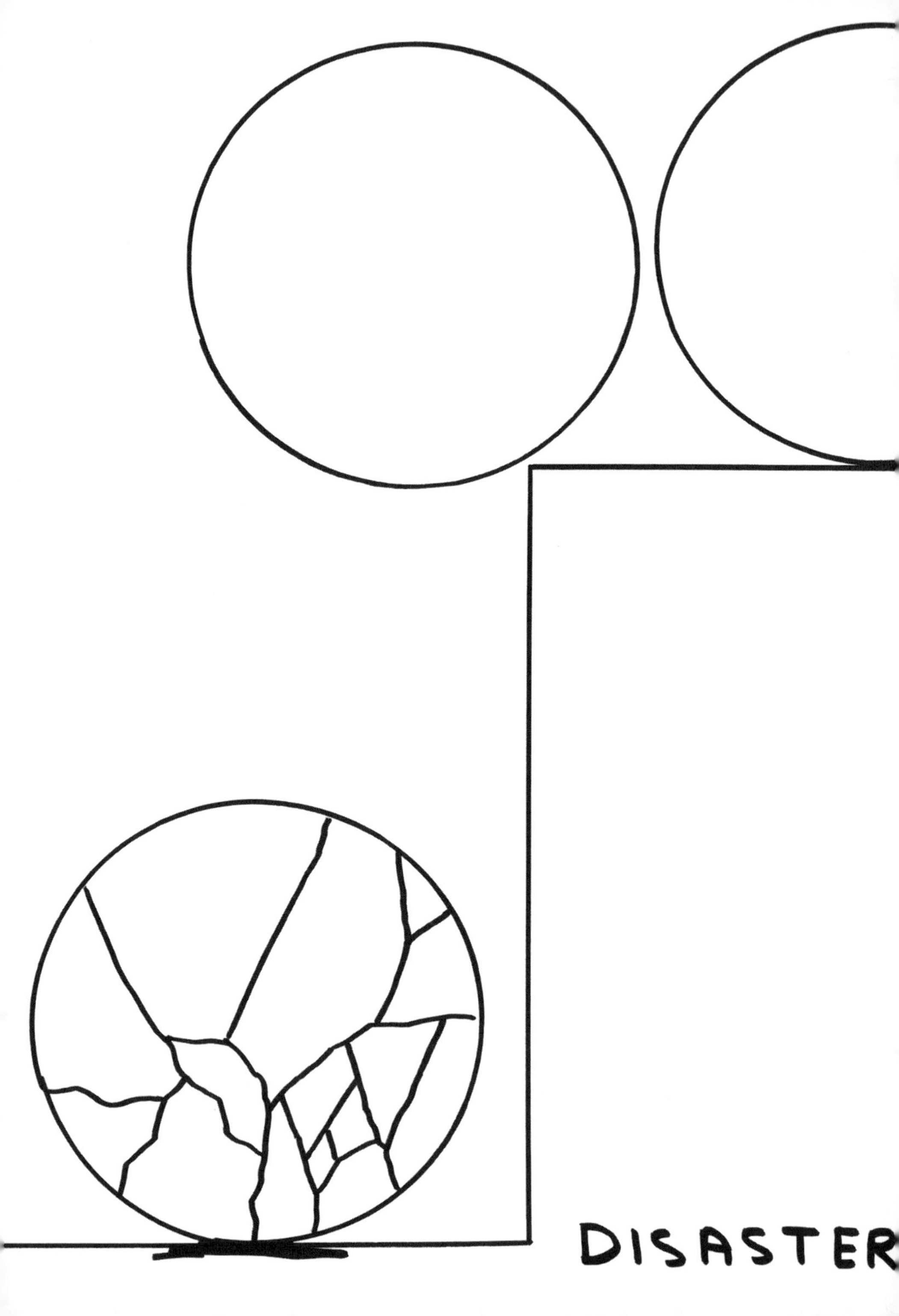

DISASTER

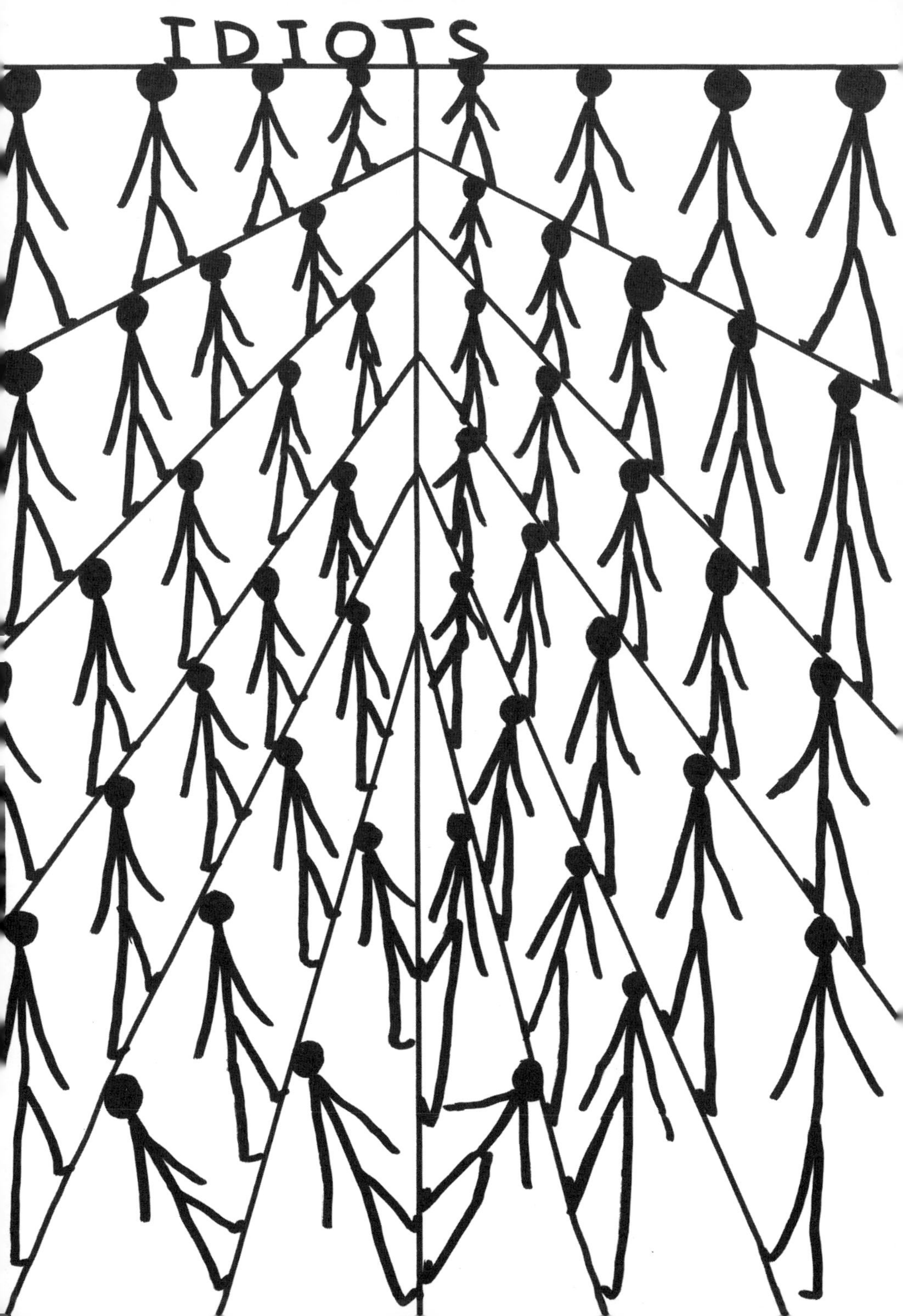

IDIOTS

CLIMBING PLANTS

THEY CLIMB UP THE WALL
THEY LOOK NICE
BUT THEY ARE DESTROYING THE WALL
EVENTUALLY THE WALL WILL FALL DOWN
AND THE INVADING HORDES
WILL BE ABLE TO ENTER OUR STRONGHOL
AND WE SHALL BE OVERRUN
AND KILLED
AND ALL BECAUSE OF THOSE
DAMNED PLANTS

SHED BUILDING

WE NEED TO BUILD
A MILLION NEW SHEDS
EVERY YEAR
FOR THE NEXT TEN YEARS

VILE AND DIRTY ASPECTS

AVAILABLE FROM THE BALCONY
AT THE REAR OF THE BUILDING
AND FROM THE PATIO

LIMITED VIEWS

I COULD ONLY SEE HIS FEET

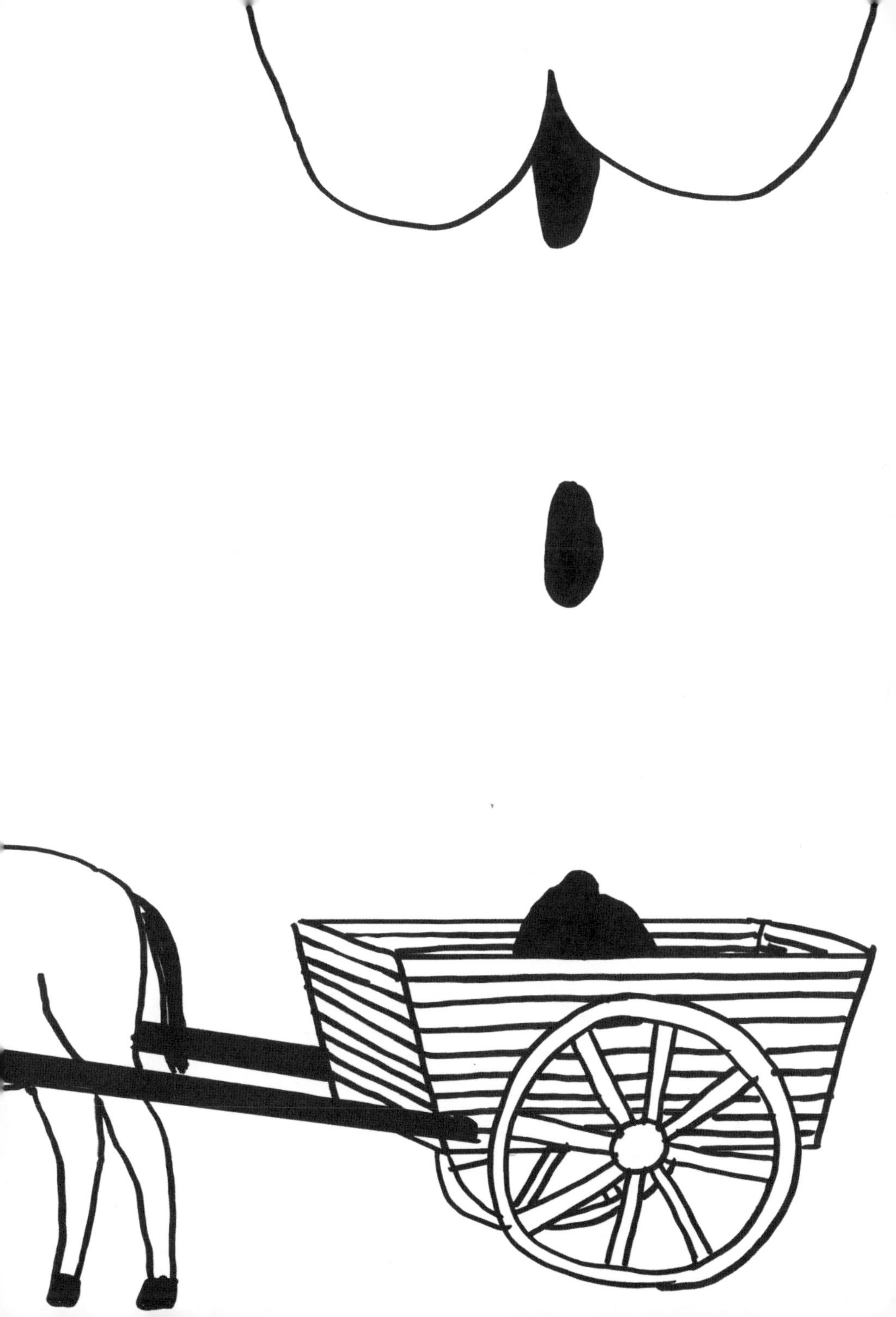

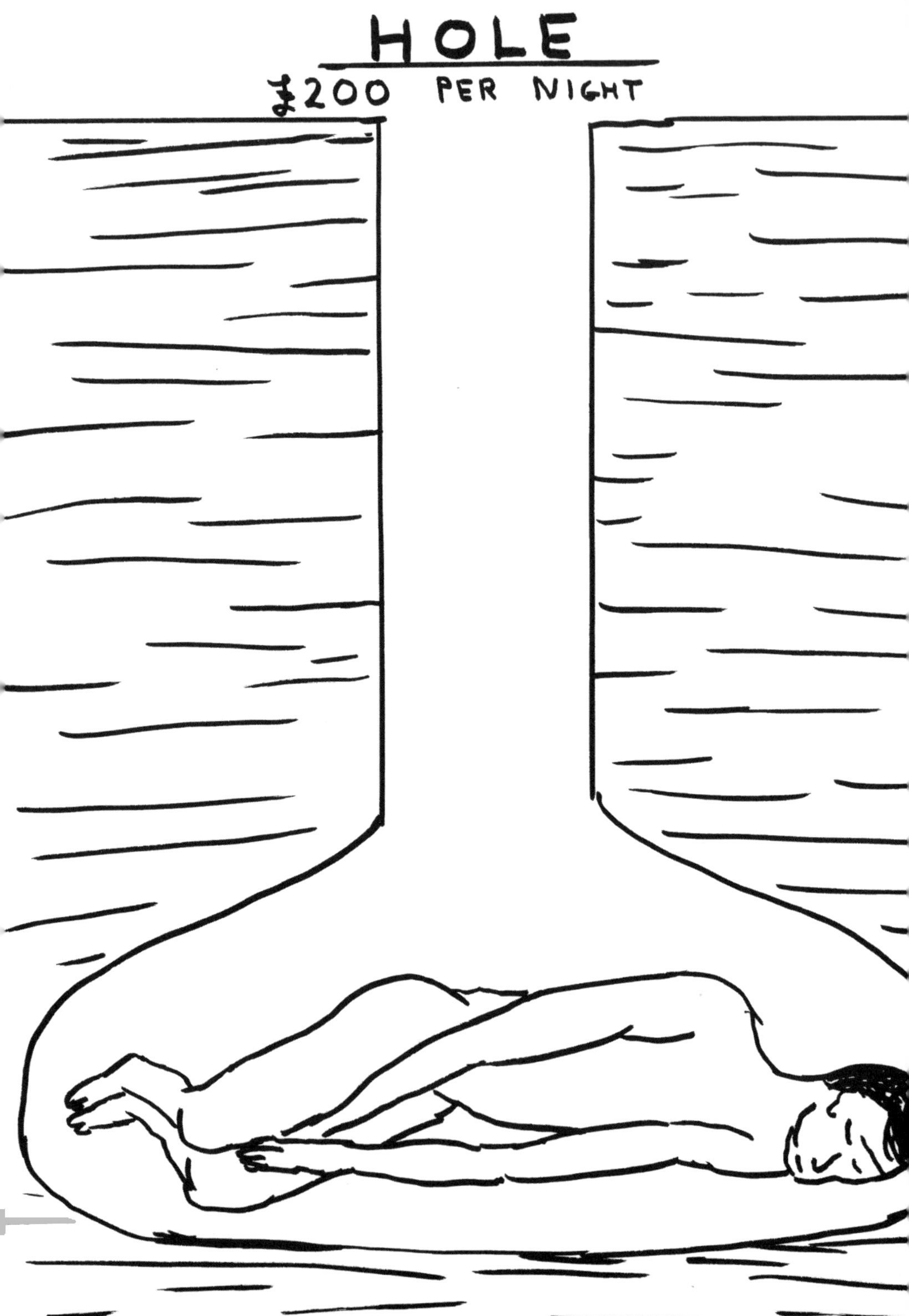

HOLE
ま200 PER NIGHT

AREAS OF LAWN

THE GRASS IS NOT REAL

AREAS OF CONCRETE

THE CONCRETE IS REAL

AREAS OF GRAVEL

THE GRAVEL IS EDIBLE

AREAS COVERED WITH BAUBLES

THERE ARE CURRENTLY NO AREAS
COVERED WITH BAUBLES

THE SO-CALLED PLEASURE GARDENS

I ONCE FELL OVER IN THE PLEASURE GARDENS
AND I ROLLED DOWN A SLOPE
AND I TORE MY TROUSERS

REFUSE COLLECTION (FILTH)

WILL BE COLLECTED ON WEDNESDAYS
UNLESS YOU LIVE OUTSIDE OF TOWN
IN WHICH CASE
IT WILL NEVER BE COLLECTED
NOT EVER
YOU MUST FIND A WAY TO
GET RID OF IT YOURSELF
BURN IT PERHAPS
OR DUMP IT ON A NEIGHBOUR'S LAND

EVENTS

DISCO
SEANCE
SLAVE AUCTION
GENERAL ELECTION

MOMENTS

MISSILE LAUNCH
DRUG PARTY
ORGAN RECITAL
PARADE OF WEIRDOS

TRANSPORT

HITCH A RIDE ON THE GARBAGE TRUCK
OR ARE YOU TOO PROUD?

NEW ROADS

A LANE FOR RACING CARS
A LANE FOR HORSE AND CART
A LANE FOR GREYHOUNDS + WHIPPETS
A LANE FOR GENERAL MOTORING

AIR CONDITIONING

THE SOUND OF IT IS LIKE MUSIC

IMPROVEMENTS

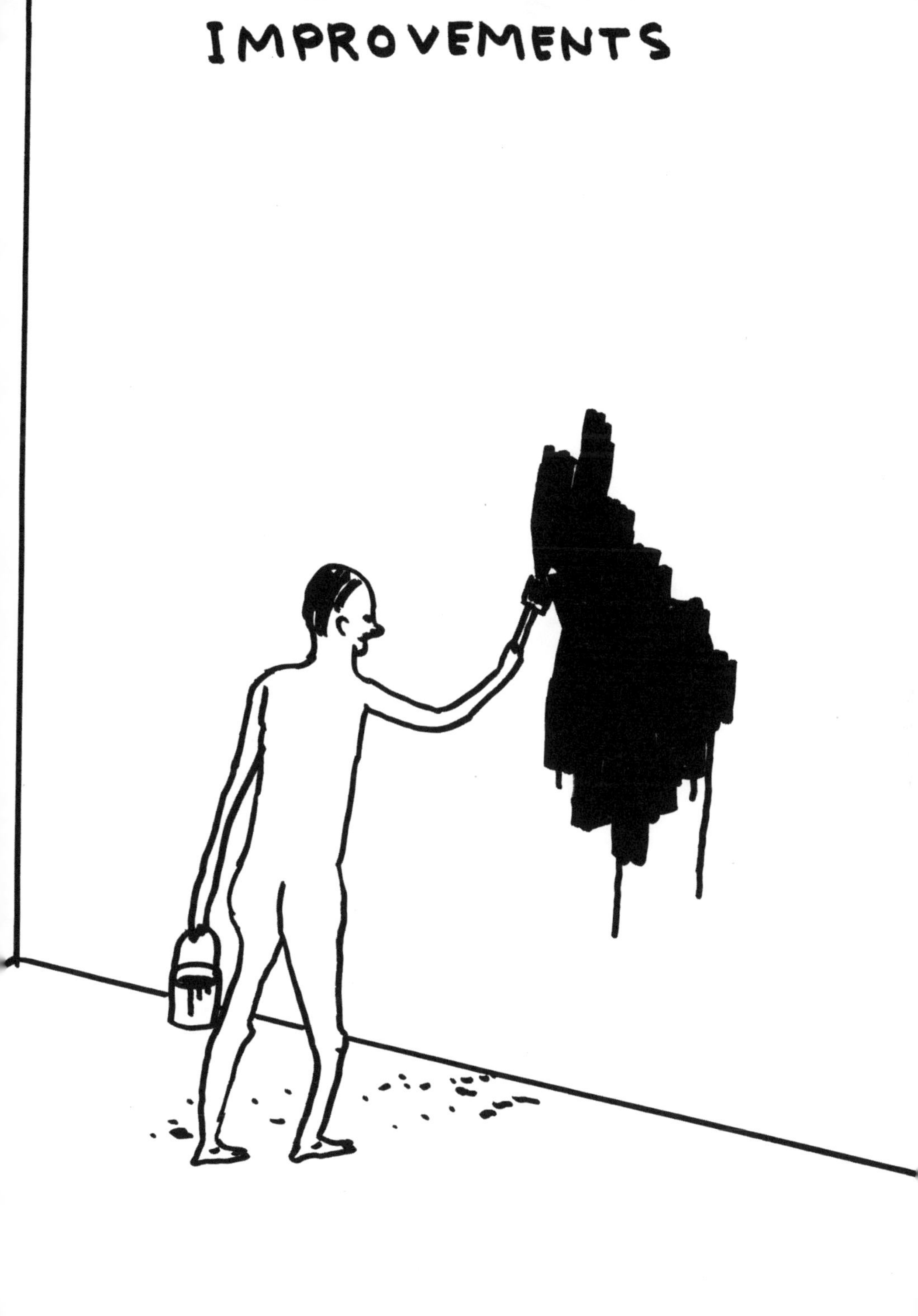

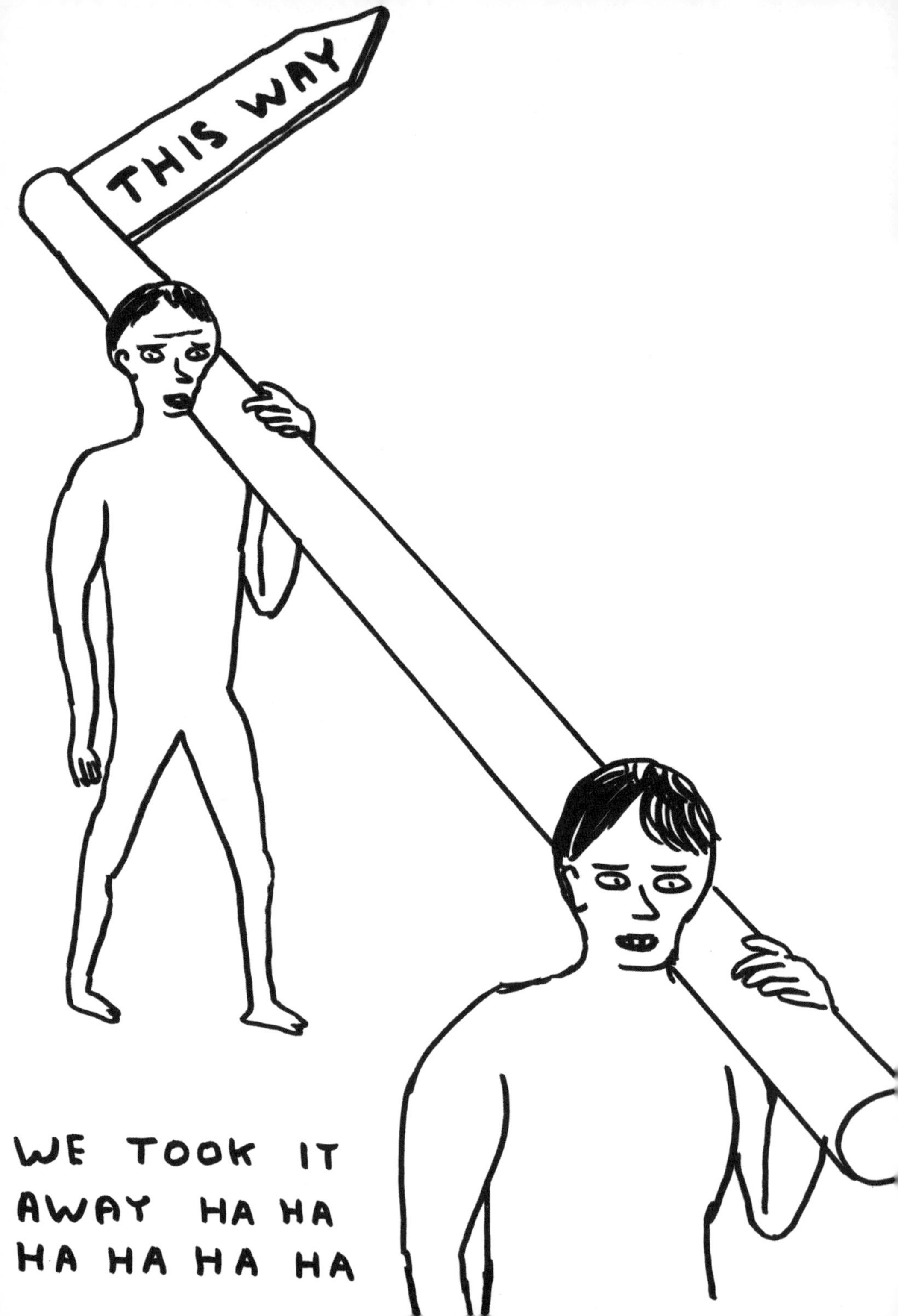
THIS WAY
WE TOOK IT
AWAY HA HA
HA HA HA HA

CHAPTER FOUR
ECONOMICS

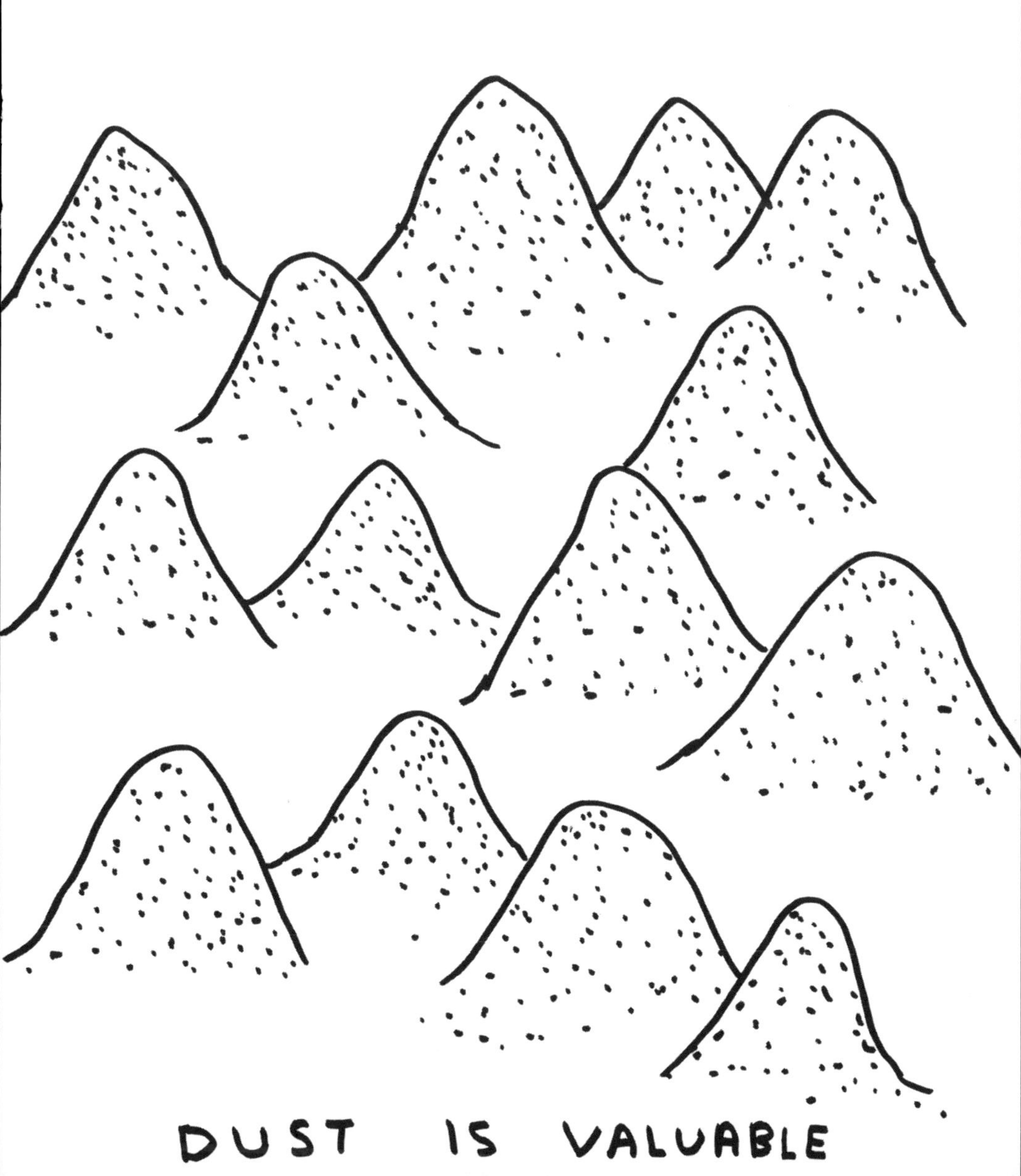

DUST IS VALUABLE

TAXATION

SOCIETY NEEDS ITS CITIZENS
TO PAY TAX
TAXES ARE WHAT YOU PAY
TO LIVE IN A CIVILIZED SOCIETY
IF YOU DON'T PAY TAXES
THEN THERE WILL BE NO ONE
TO KILL THE RATS
AND WE WILL BE OVERRUN WITH RATS
AND THAT WOULD BE AWFUL

THINGS THAT CAN BE USED AS CURRENCY

SHOES
BUTTERFLIES
HAIRCUTS
HAIR

DATA

DATA ENTRY PEOPLE
ENTERING DATA
THEY ARE HAPPY
THEY LIKE DOING IT
WHILE WE PLAY SPORTS

HEAVY INDUSTRY

REPLACED BY POETRY

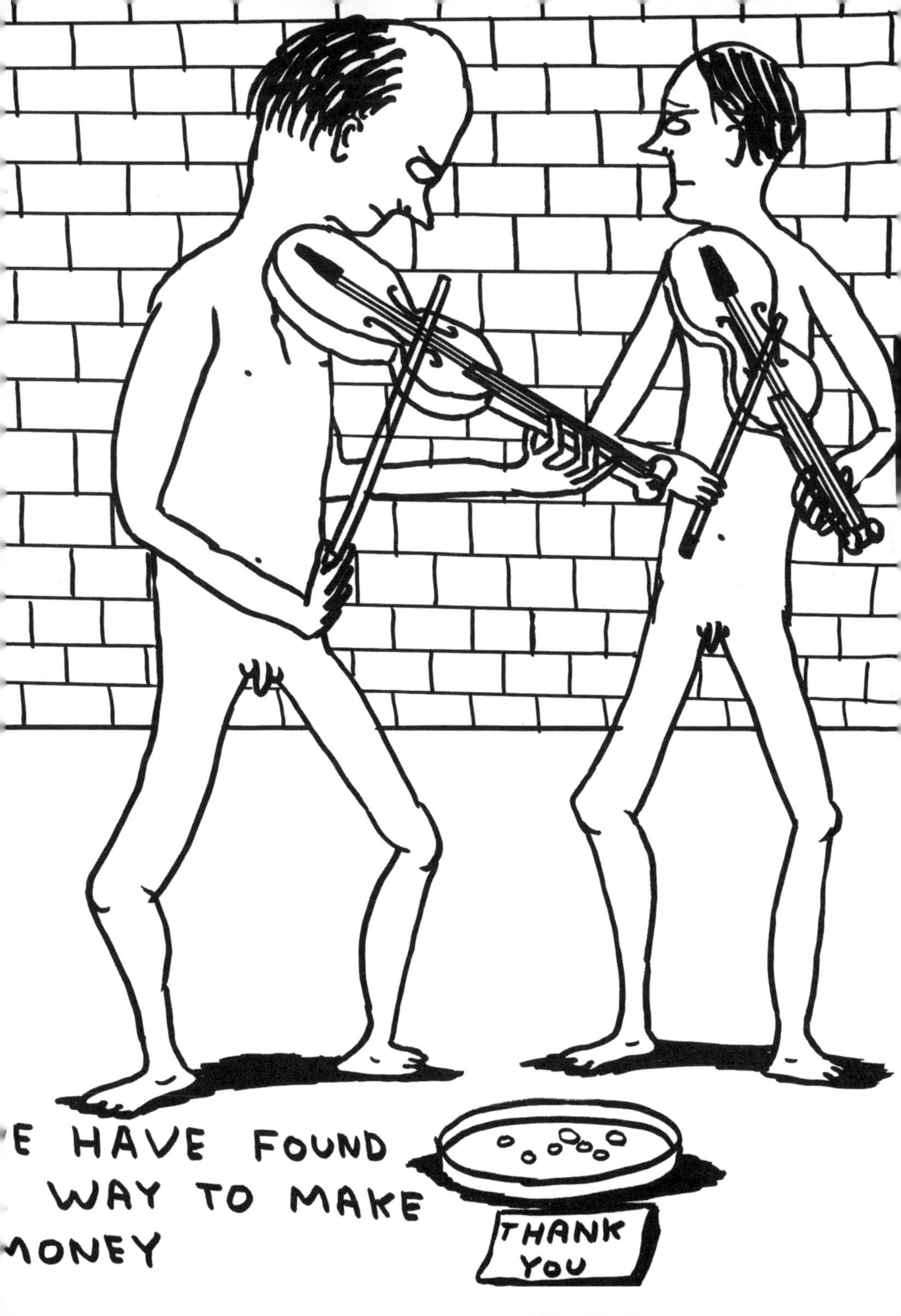
E HAVE FOUND
WAY TO MAKE
MONEY
THANK
YOU

CAREER COMES SECOND 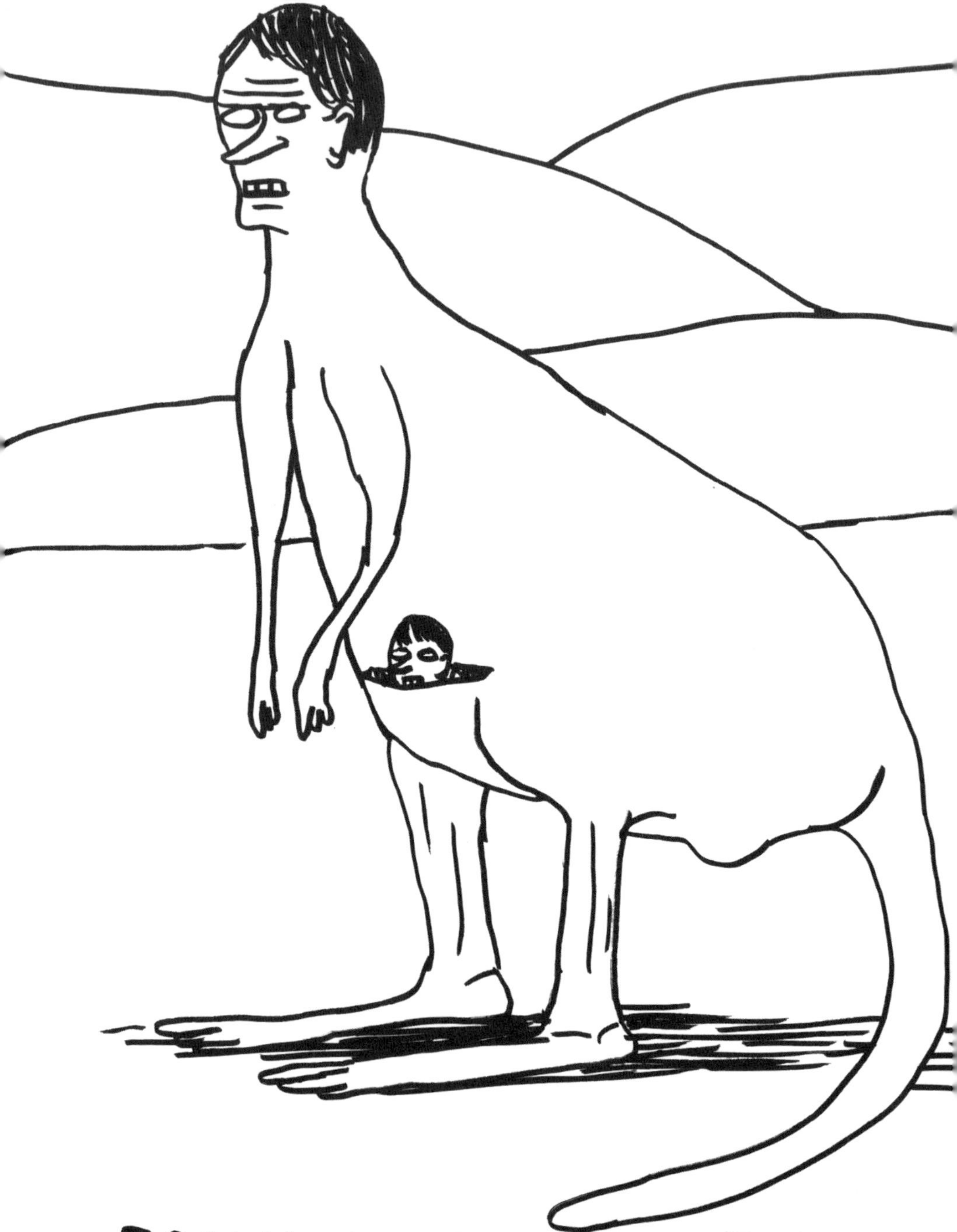
FAMILY COMES FIRST

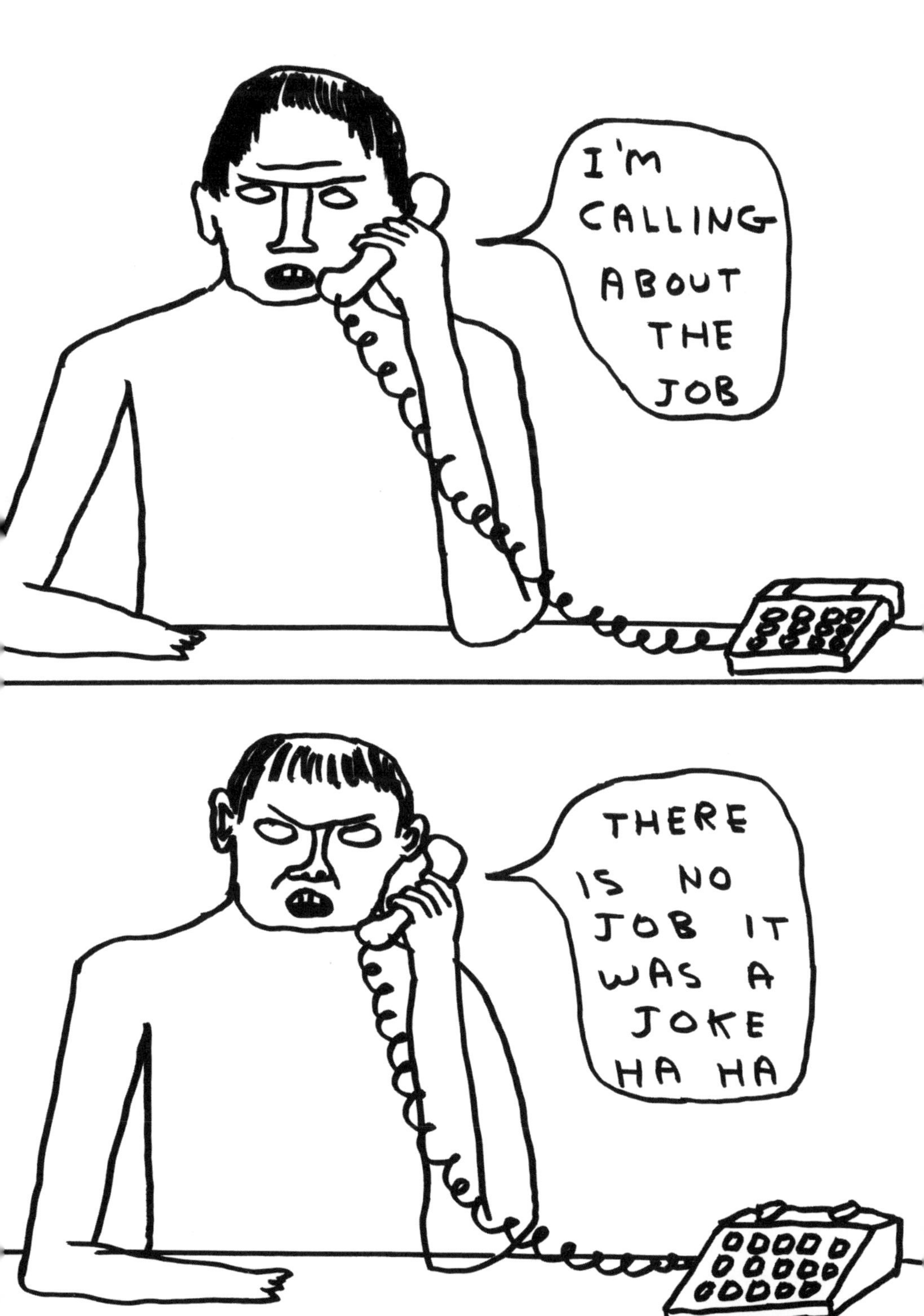
I'M CALLING ABOUT THE JOB
THERE IS NO JOB IT WAS A JOKE HA HA

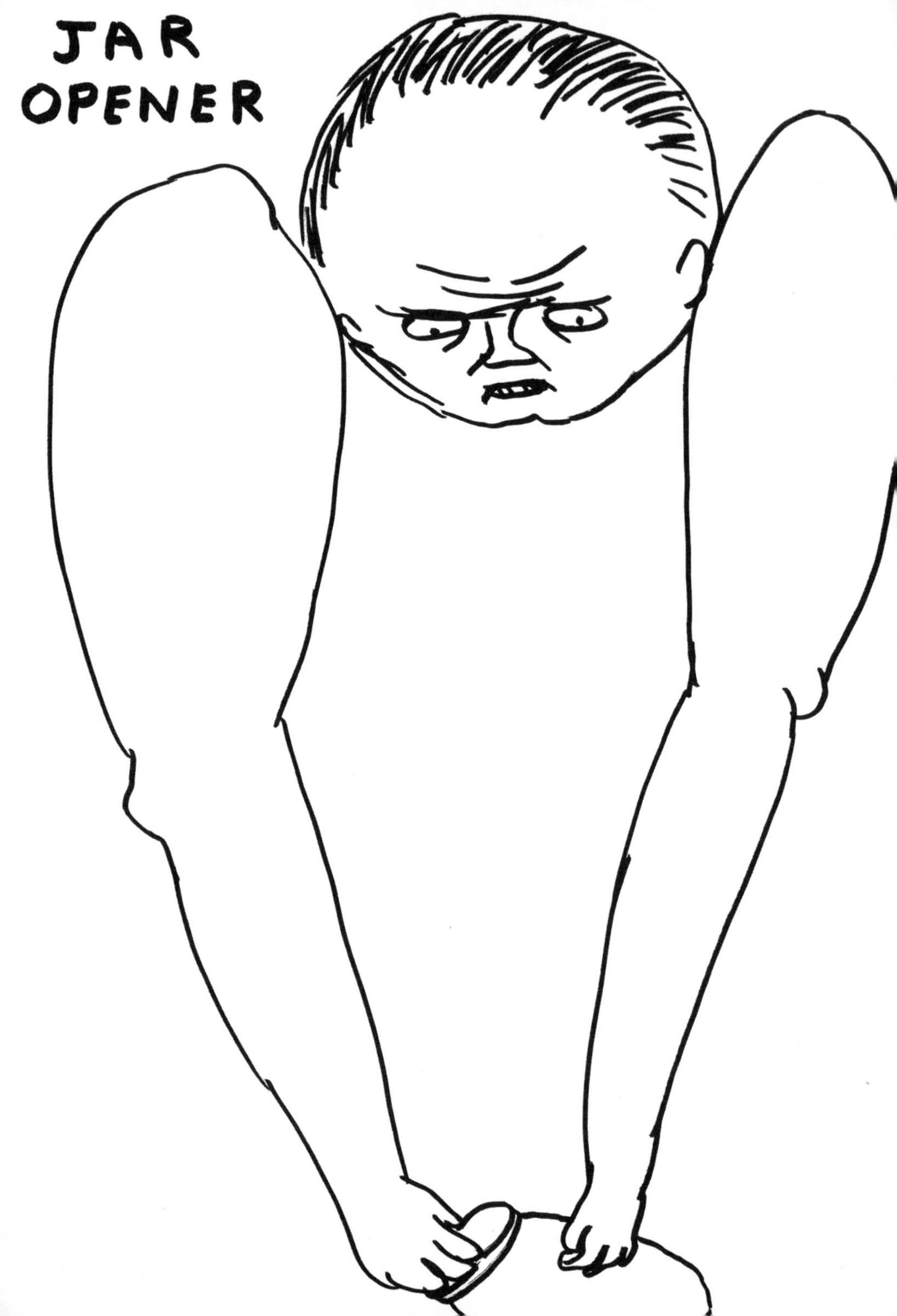

JAR
OPENER

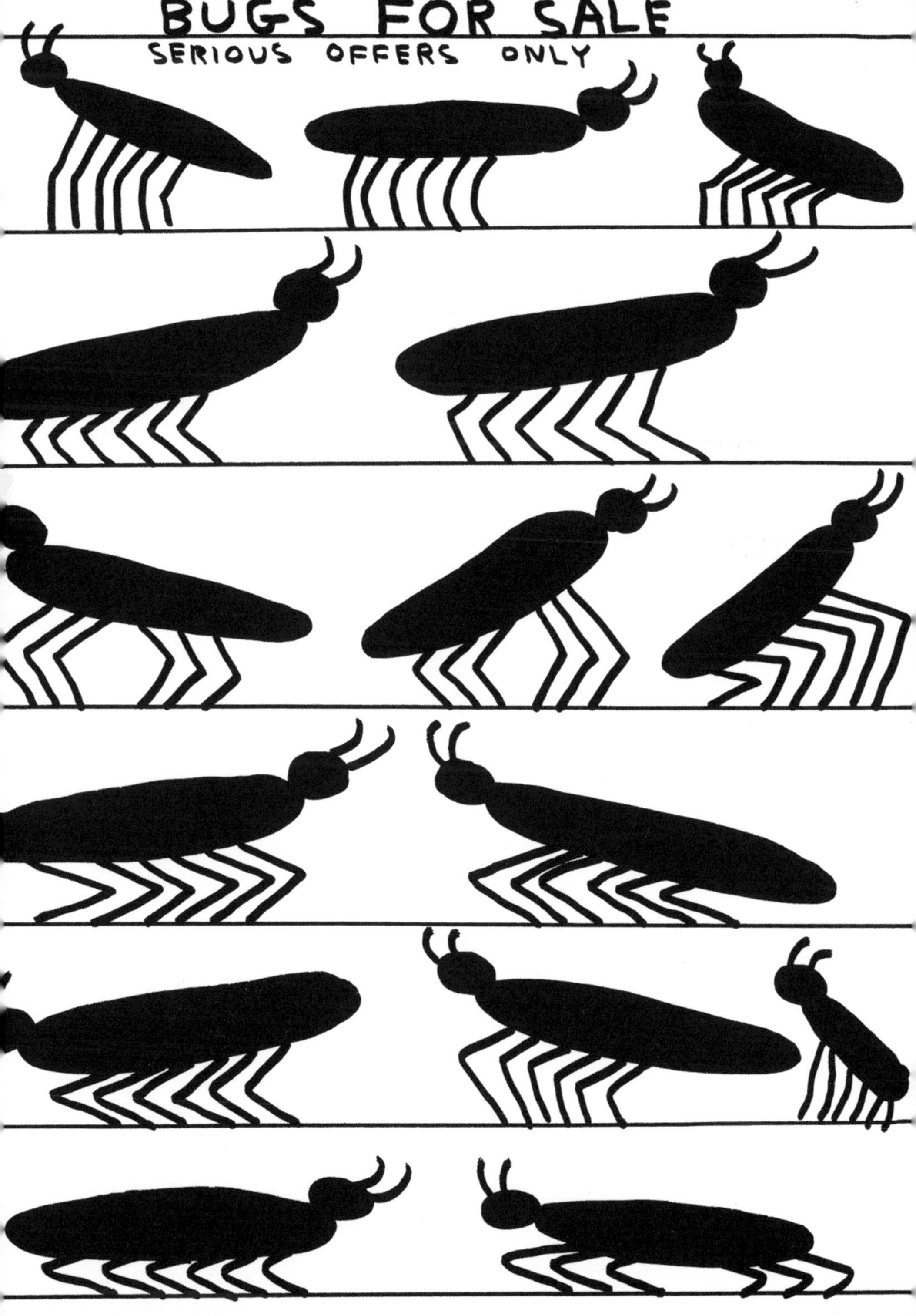

BUGS FOR SALE
SERIOUS OFFERS ONLY

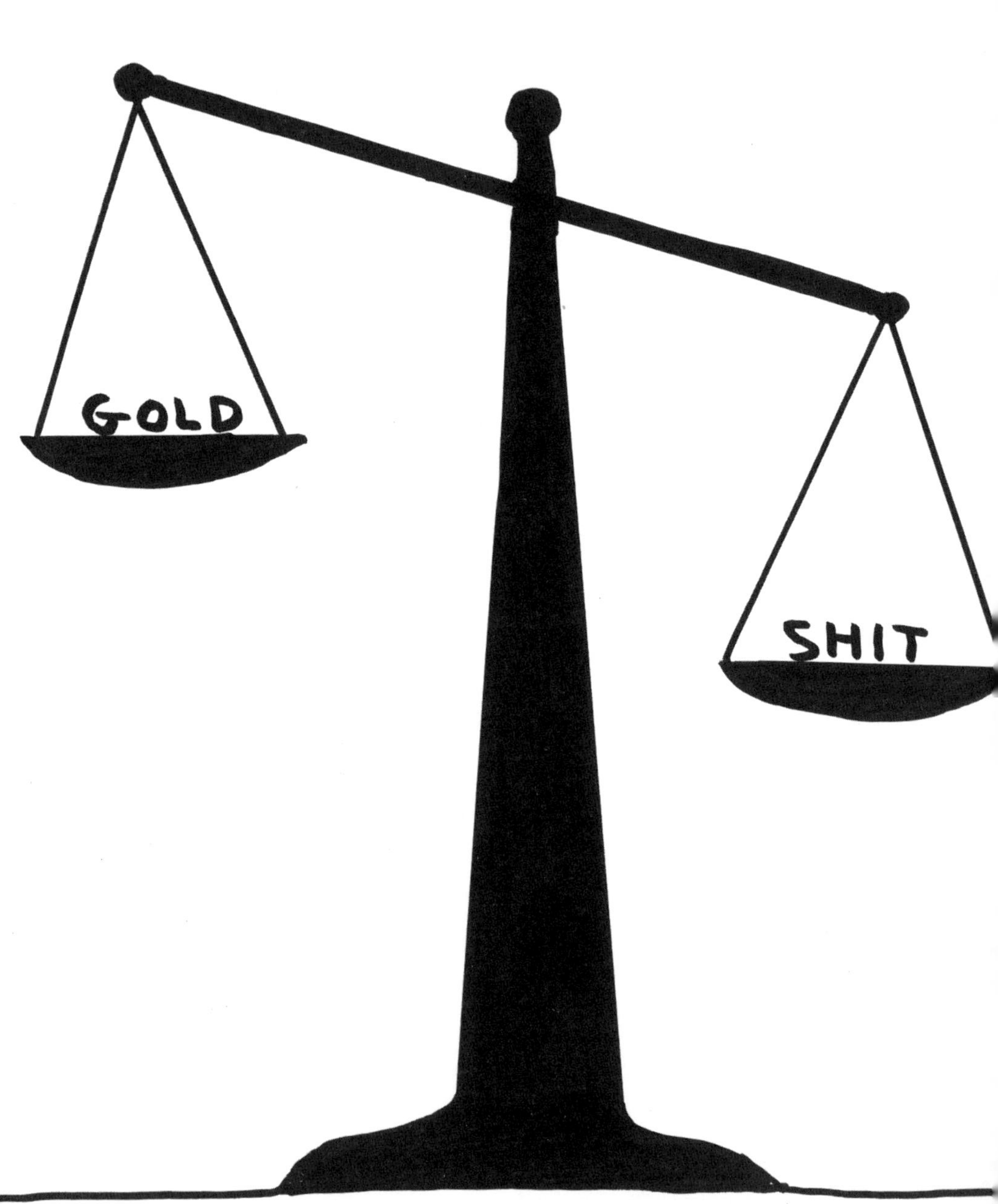

GOLD
SHIT

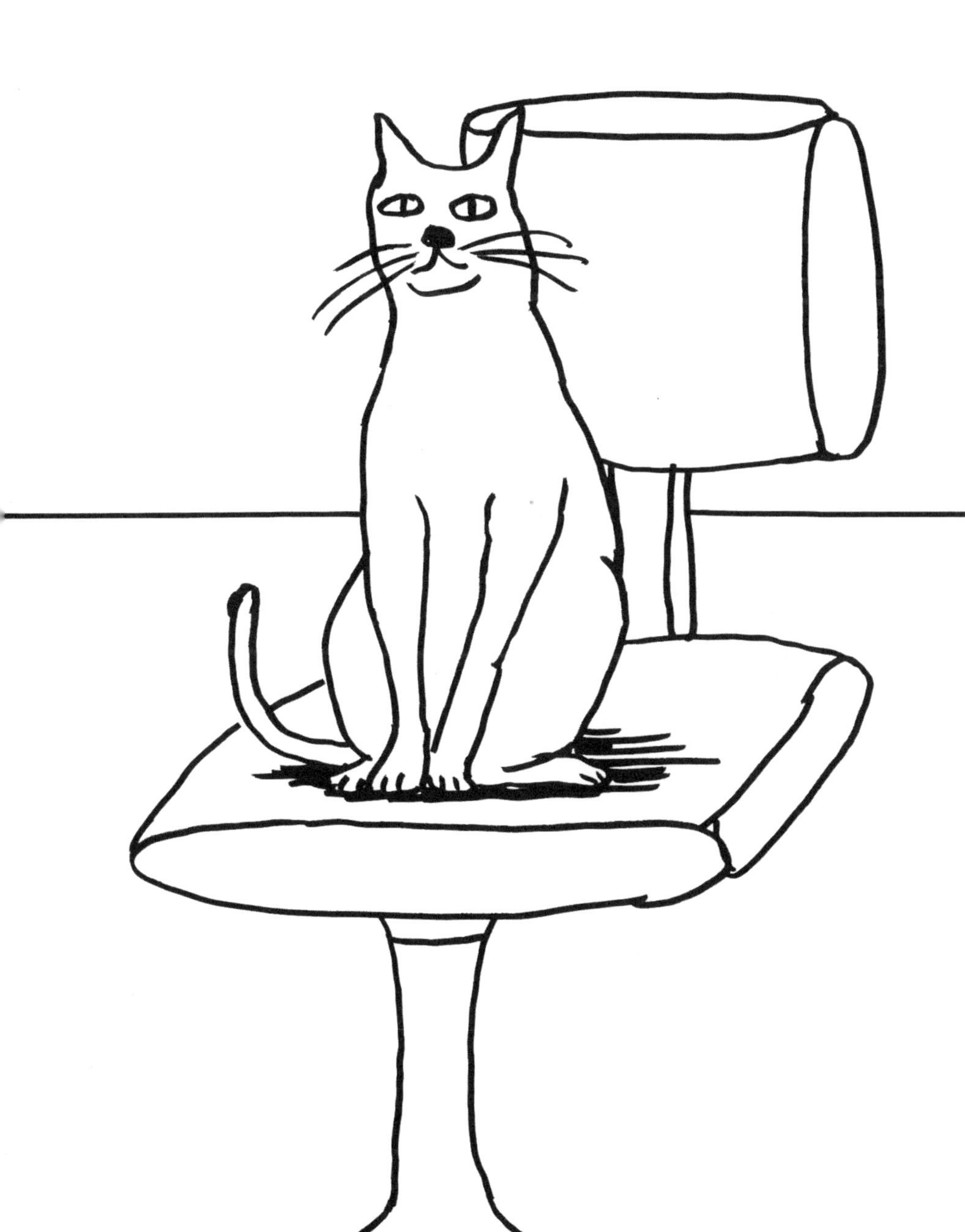

CAT HAS YOUR JOB
YOU HAVE CAT'S JOB

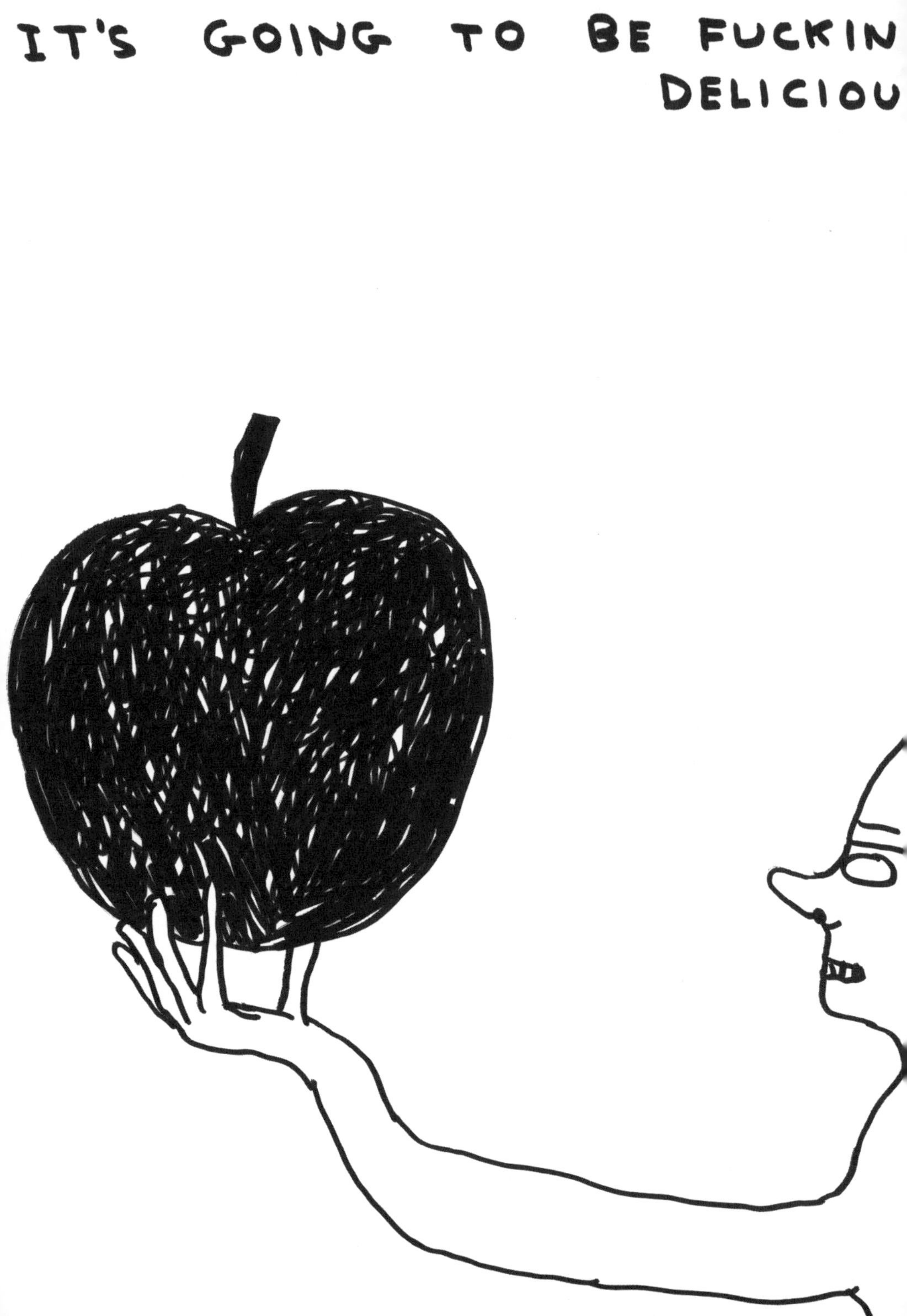
IT'S GOING TO BE FUCKIN
DELICIOU

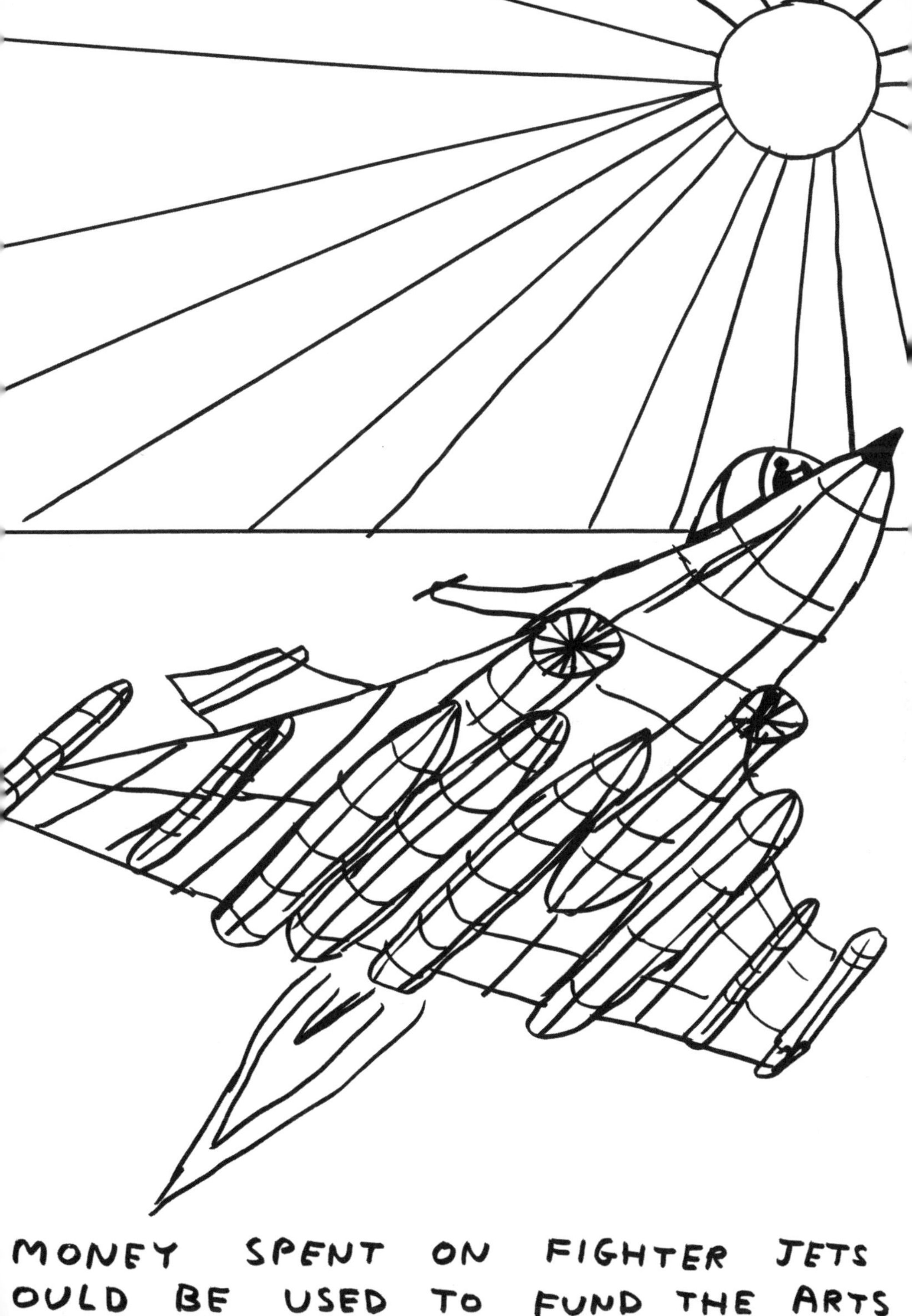

MONEY SPENT ON FIGHTER JETS
OULD BE USED TO FUND THE ARTS

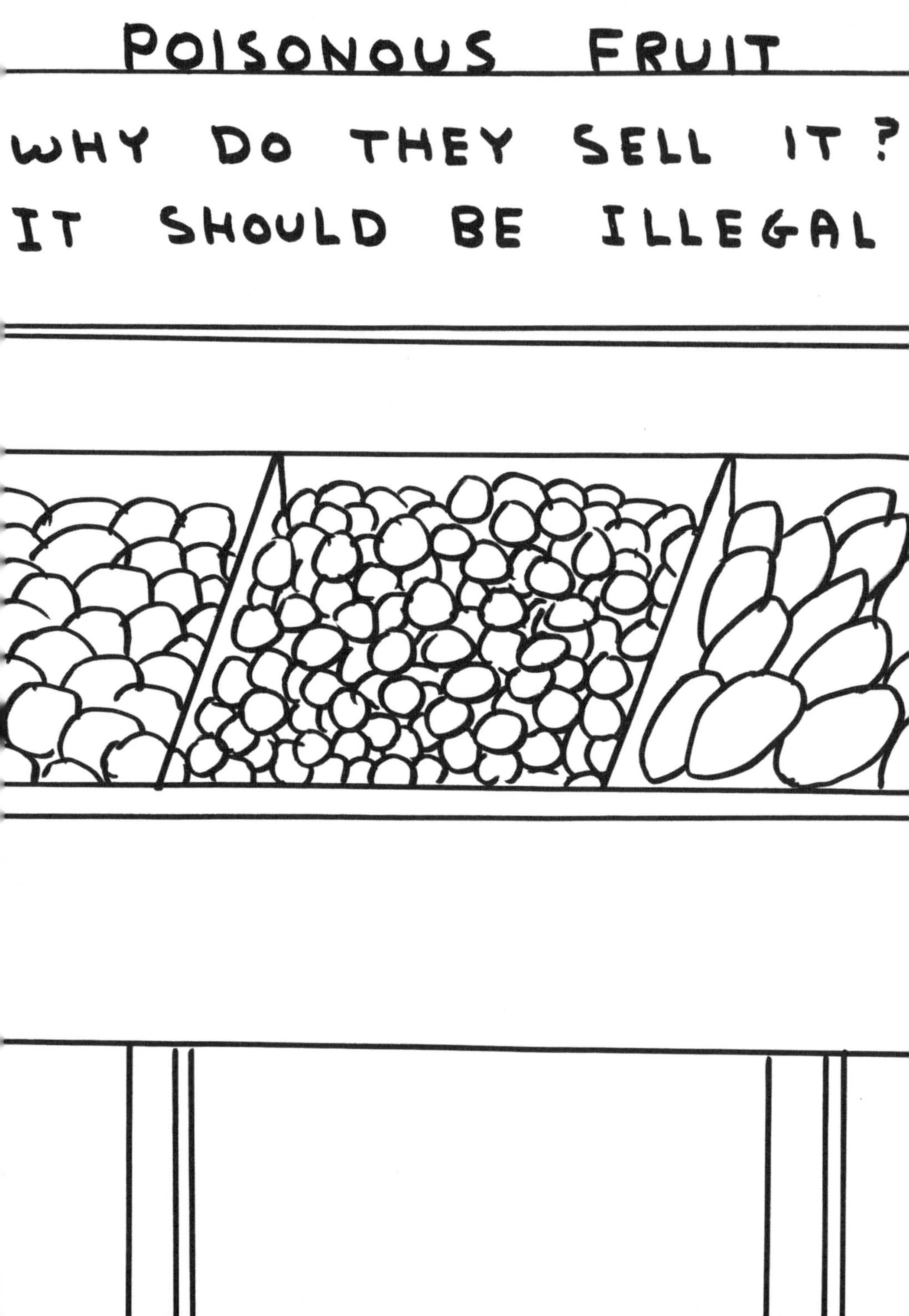

POISONOUS FRUIT
WHY DO THEY SELL IT?
IT SHOULD BE ILLEGAL

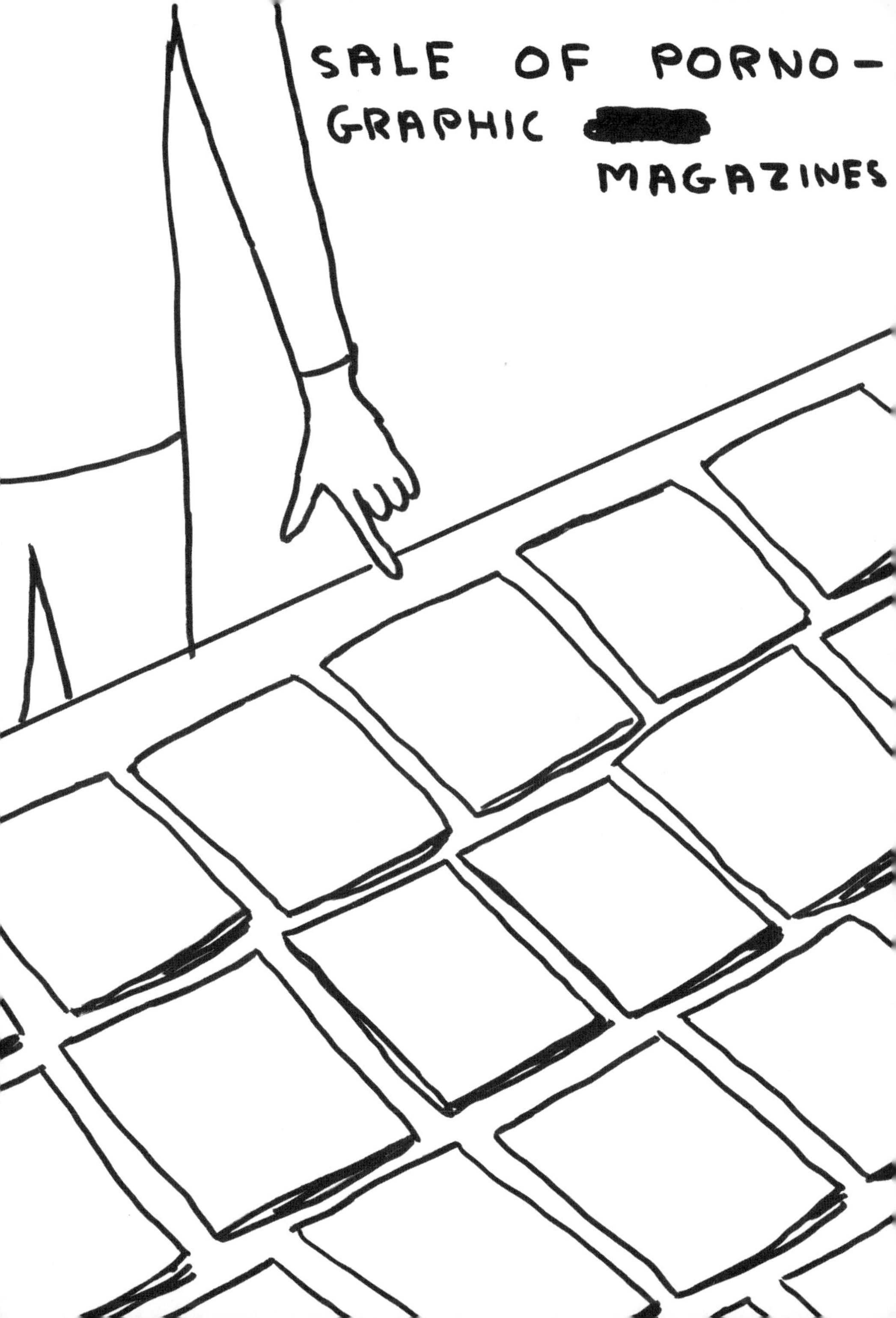

SALE OF PORNO-
GRAPHIC MAGAZINES

SHOPPING

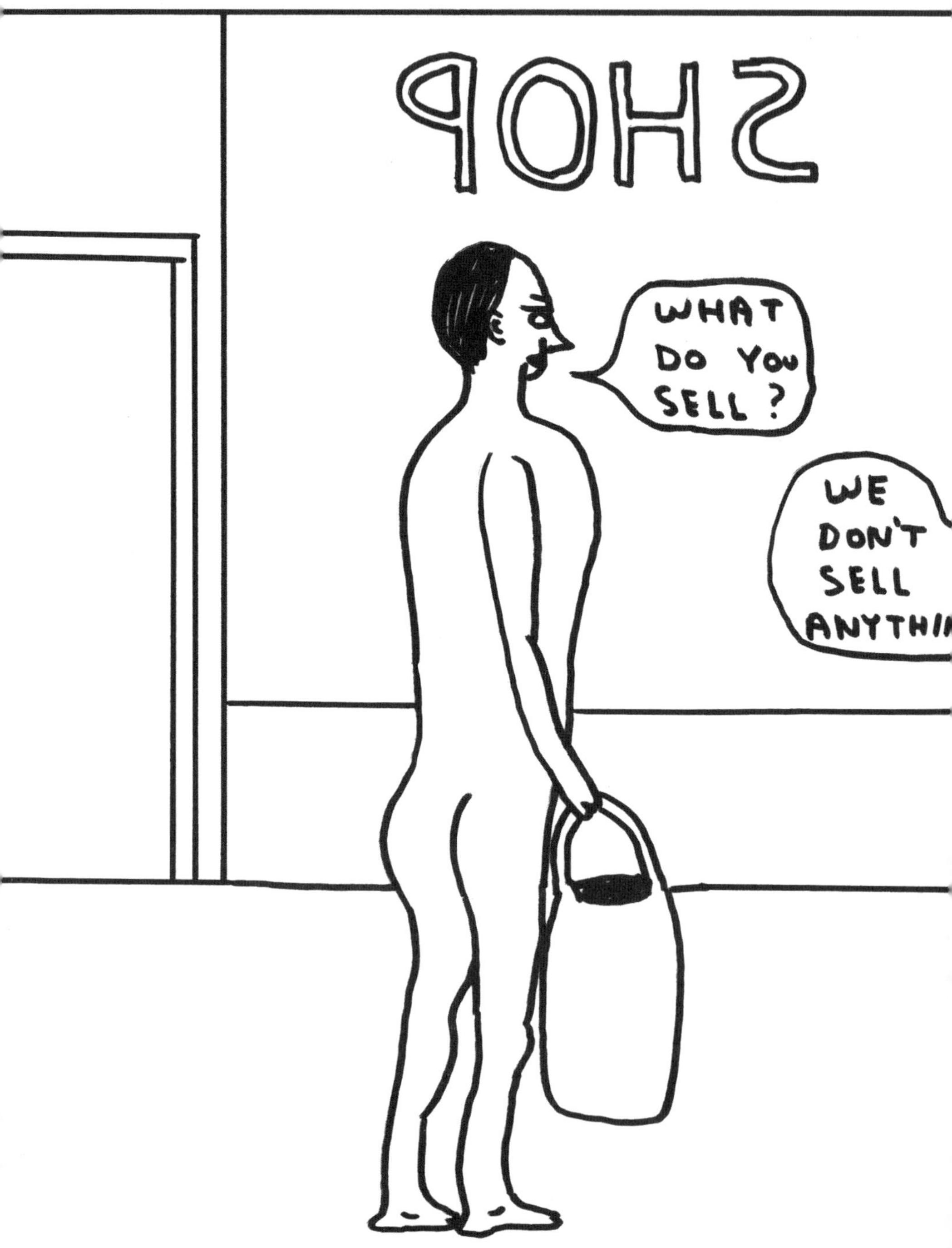

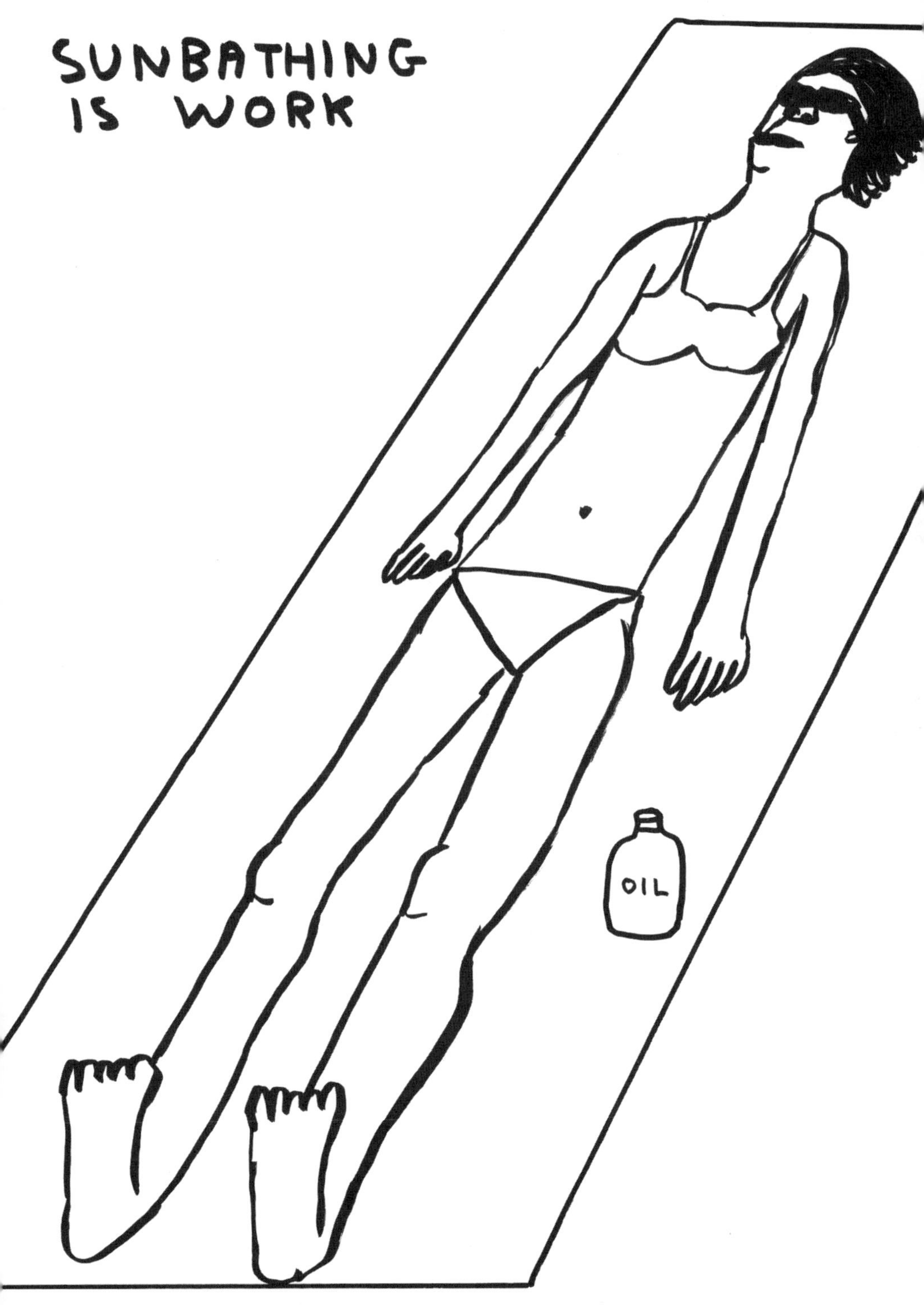

SUNBATHING IS WORK
OIL

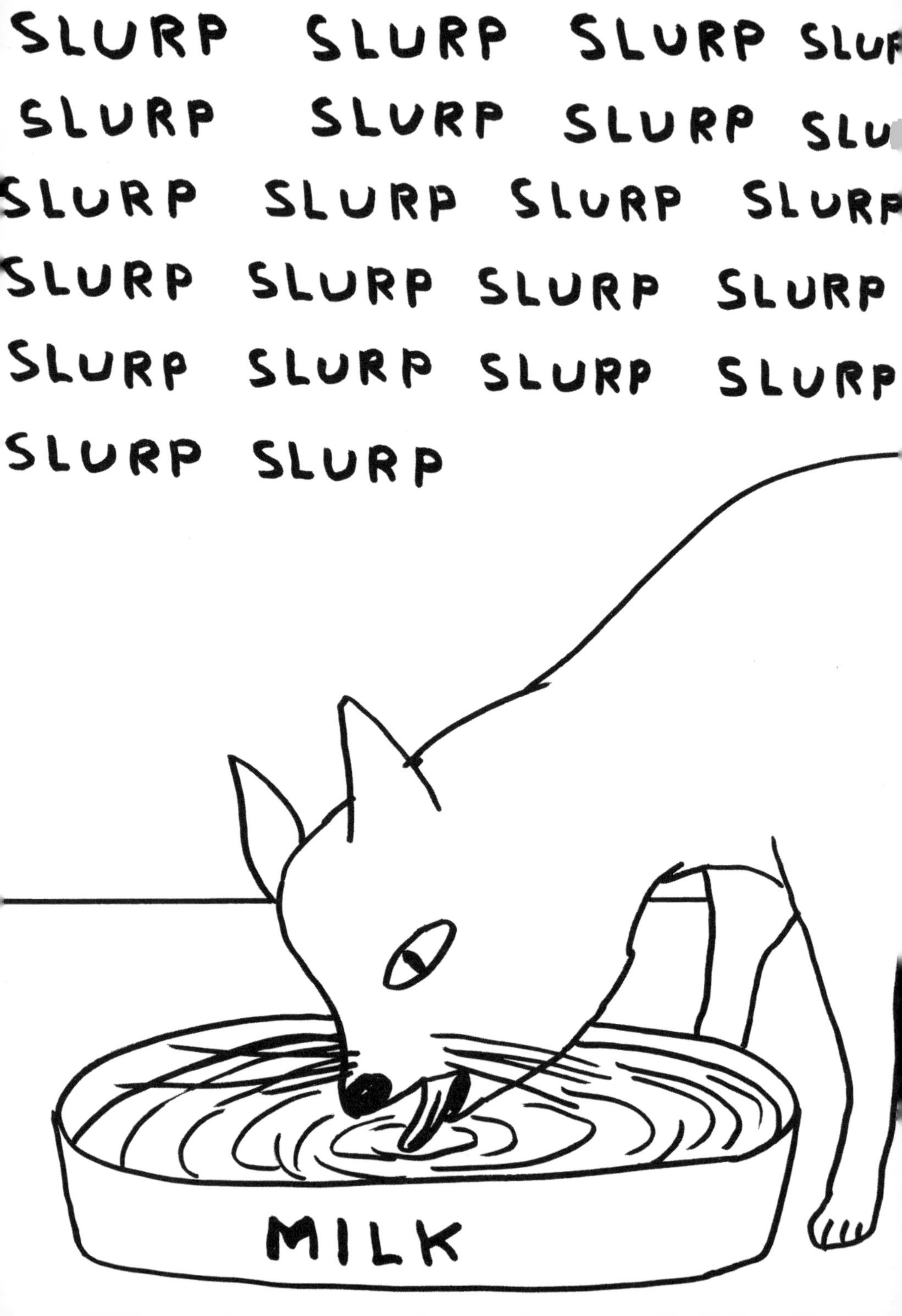

SLURP SLURP SLURP SLURP
SLURP SLURP SLURP SLURP
SLURP SLURP SLURP SLURP
SLURP SLURP SLURP SLURP
SLURP SLURP SLURP SLURP
SLURP SLURP
MILK

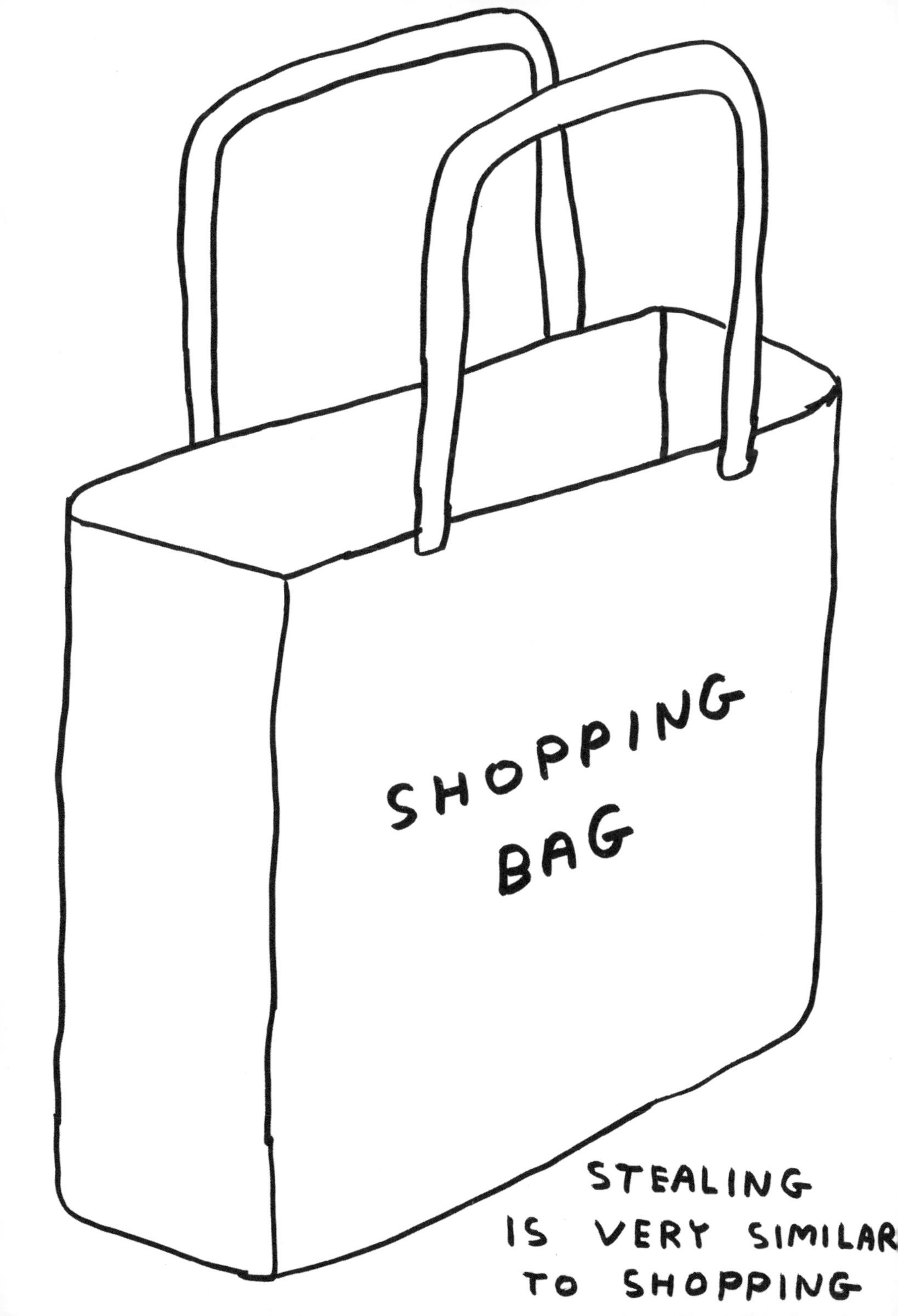

SHOPPING
BAG
STEALING
IS VERY SIMILAR
TO SHOPPING

NEW SPADE

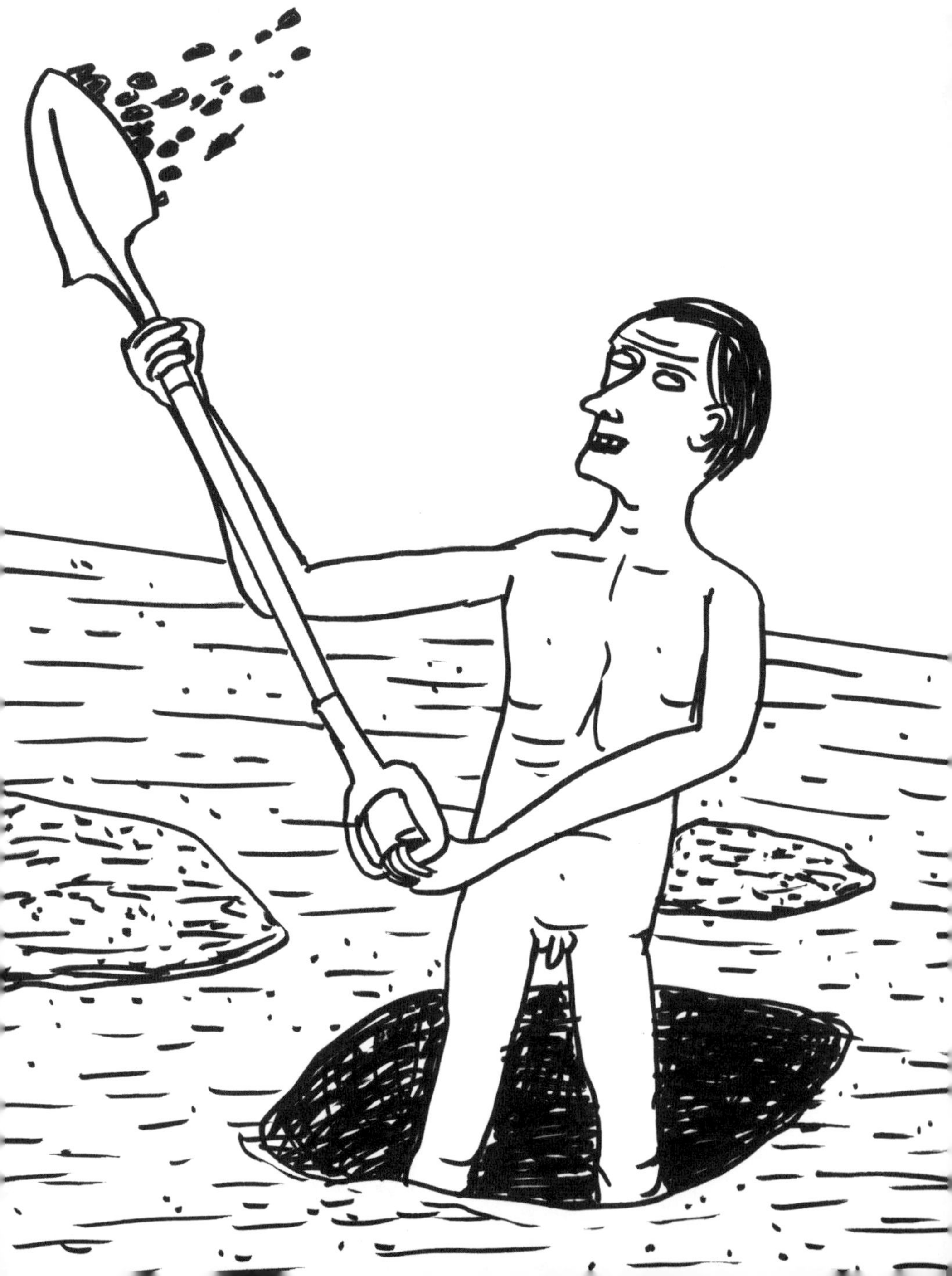

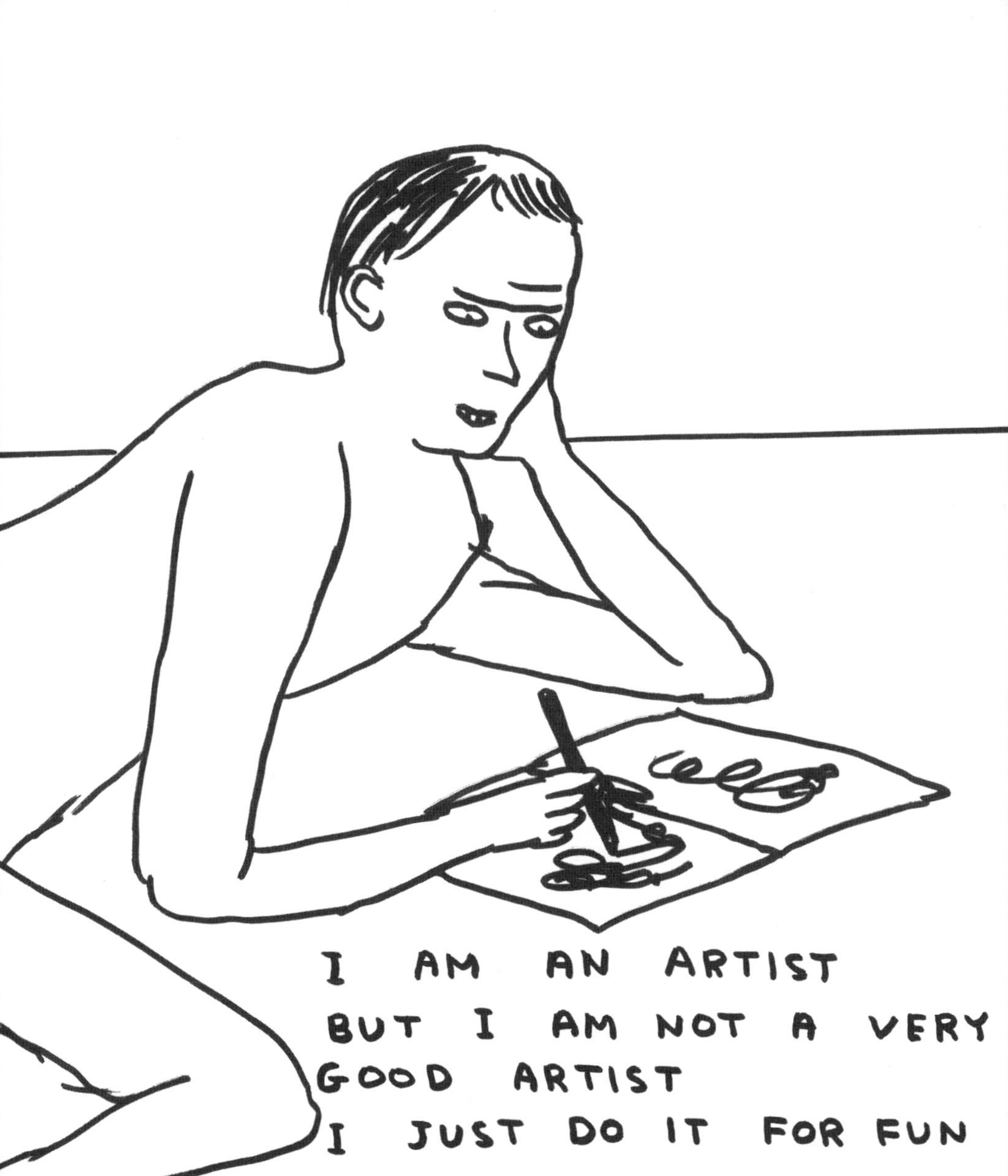

CULTURE
I AM AN ARTIST
BUT I AM NOT A VERY
GOOD ARTIST
I JUST DO IT FOR FUN

BELIEFS

SPECIFIC STATEMENTS THAT
PEOPLE HOLD TO BE TRUE:
LEFT-HANDED PEOPLE ARE EVIL
DRINKING MILK IS HARMFUL
ETC.

ARTEFACTS

DISTINCT MATERIAL OBJECTS
SUCH AS INFLATABLES
ARCHITECTURE
FOLDING CHAIRS
AND ARTISTIC CREATIONS

RITUAL

I BUILT A SNOWMAN
I DID NOT KNOW HOW TO DO IT
AT FIRST
BUT THERE WAS A MAN WHO
HELPED ME
IT WAS VERY KIND OF HIM
I GAVE HIM SOME MONEY

THE ARTS

TO BE RESPECTED AND FEARED

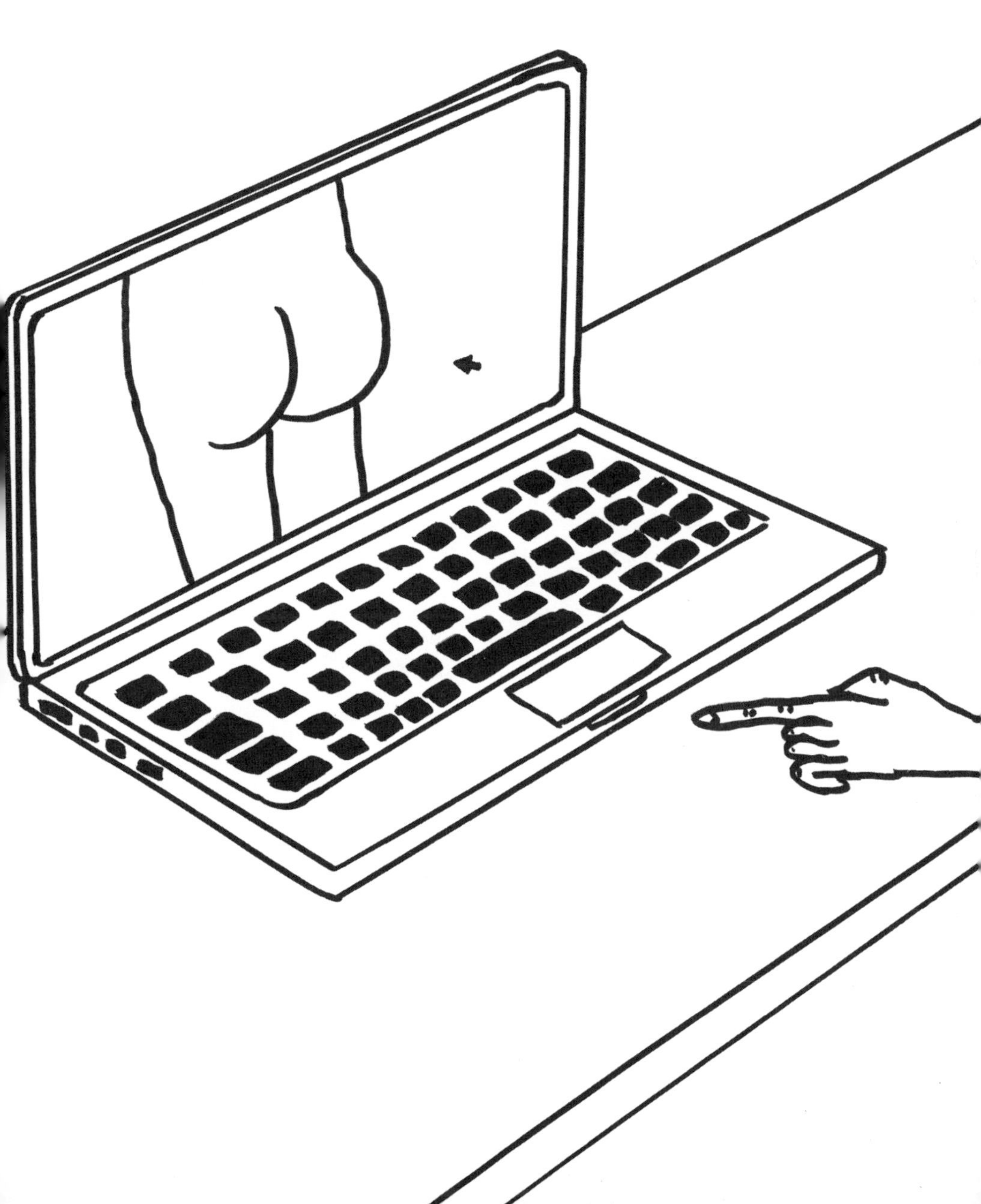

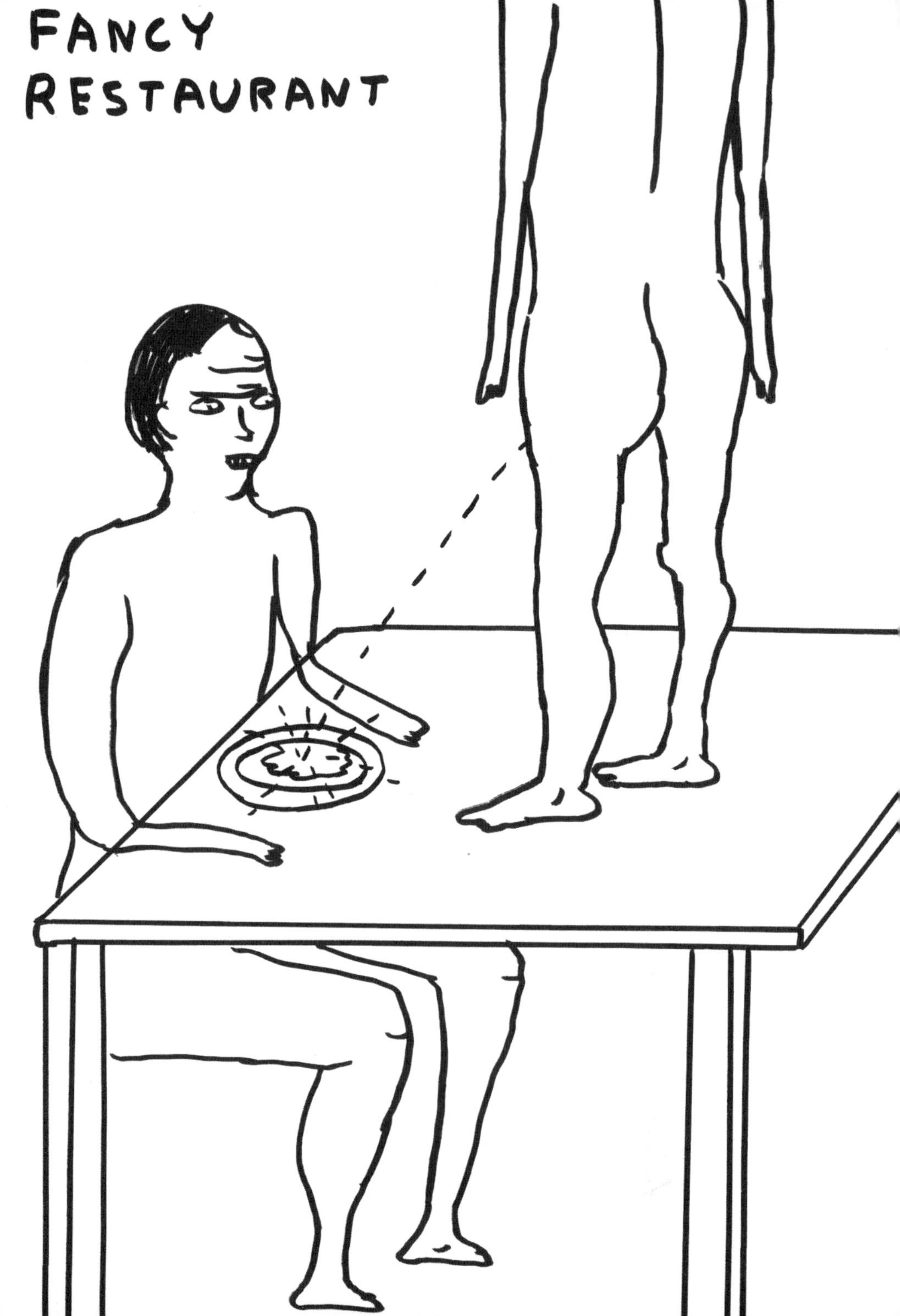

FANCY
RESTAURANT

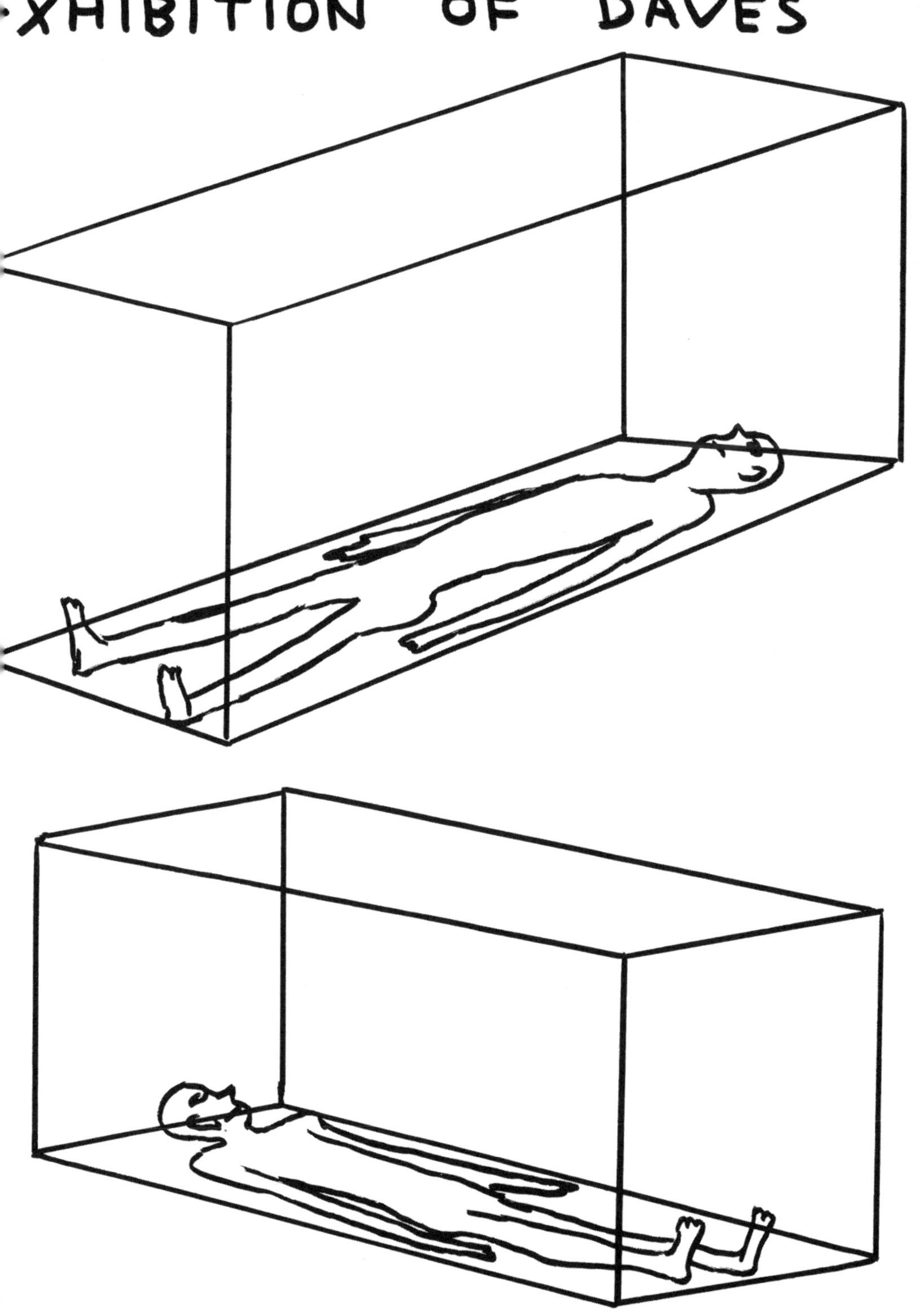

XHIBITION OF DAVES

LANGUAGE

I INVENTED MY OWN LANGUAGE
I DIDN'T LIKE THE OTHER LANGUAGES
SO I INVENTED MY OWN
IT HAS BECOME HUGELY POPULAR
EVERYBODY USES IT
AND NOW I AM RICH

TRADITION

TRADITIONAL THINGS
AND NON-TRADITIONAL THINGS
TOGETHER
IN THE SAME PRESENTATION
ALL MIXED-UP
SO YOU CAN'T TELL
THE TRADITIONAL THINGS
FROM THE NON-TRADITIONAL THING
SOME PEOPLE FIND THIS PROPOSAL
RATHER DISTURBING
BUT I THINK IT'S A GOOD IDEA
AND THAT'S WHY I'M PROPOSING IT

HORSE SHIT

FOR USE IN THE GARDEN
FOR USE IN PROTESTS
FOR USE IN ARTWORKS

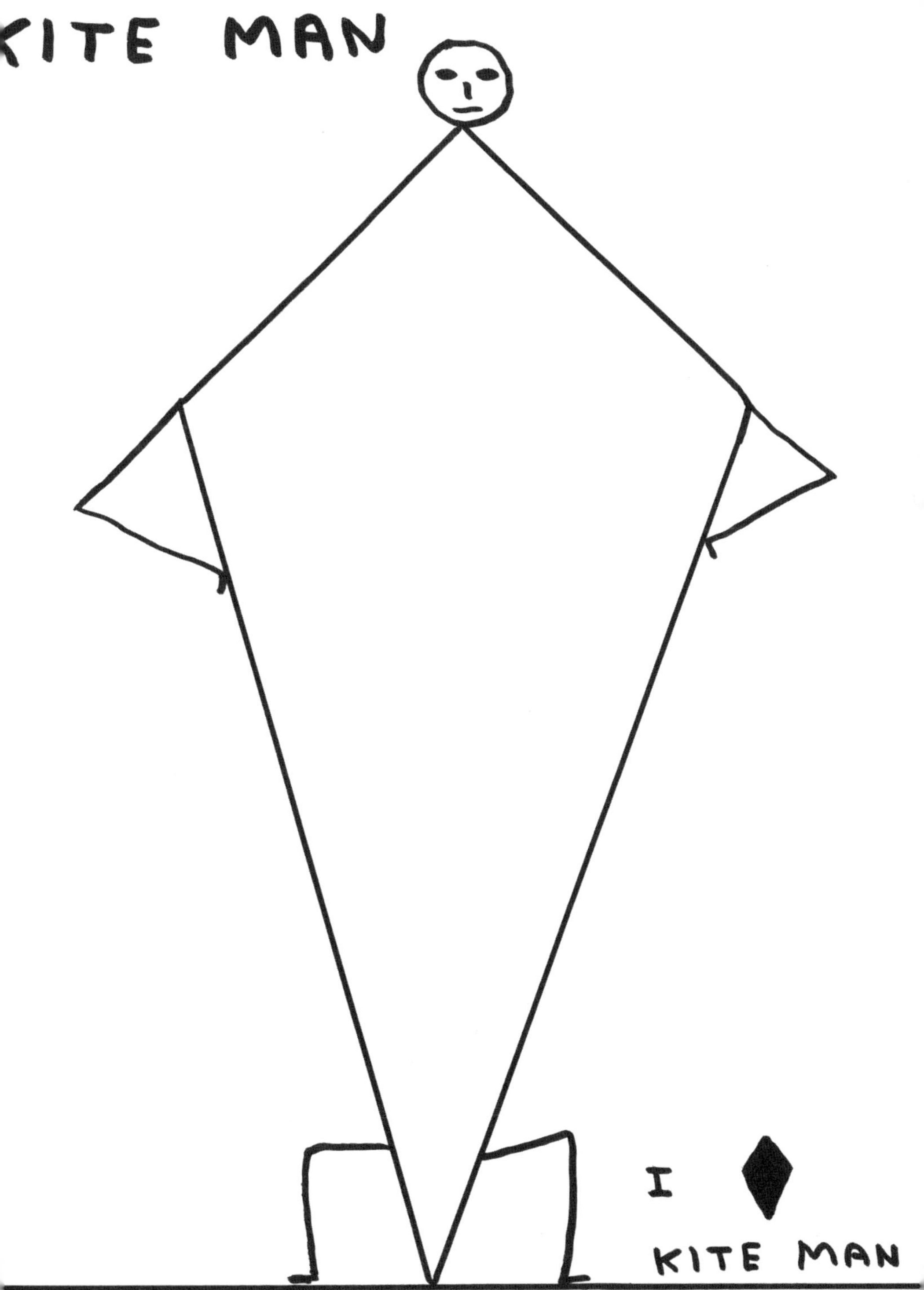

KITE MAN
I
KITE MAN

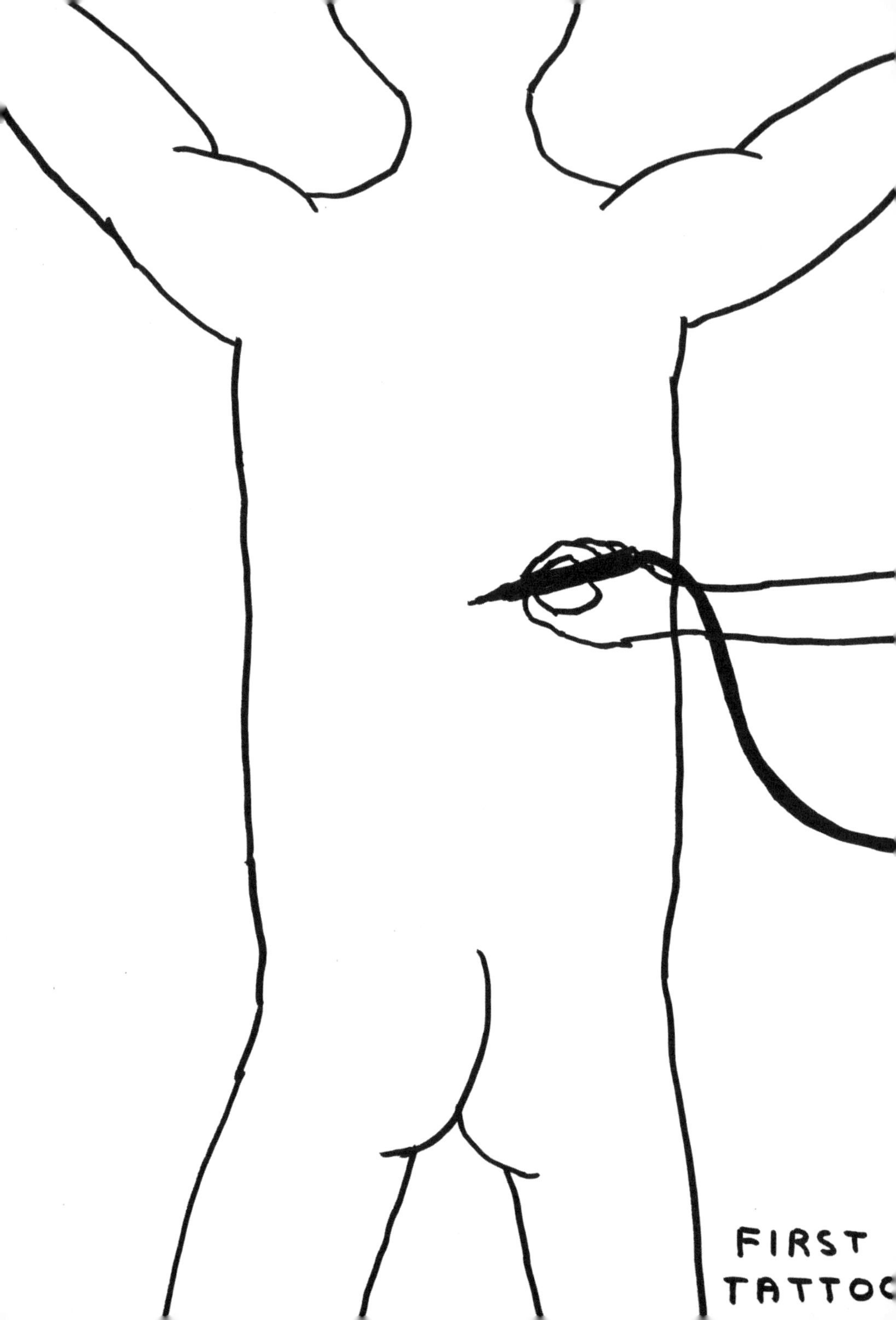

FIRST
TATTOO

GIANT RODENT

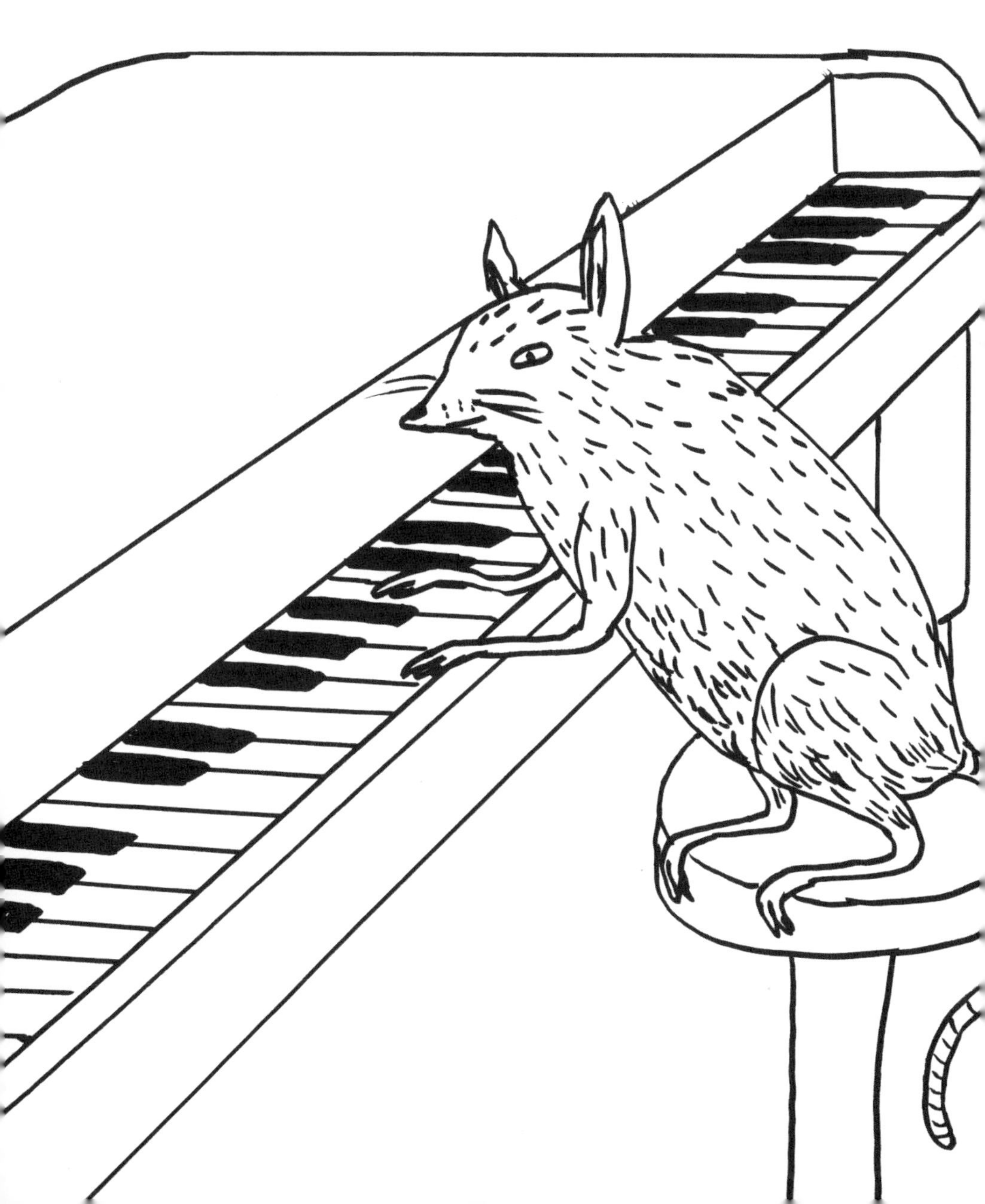

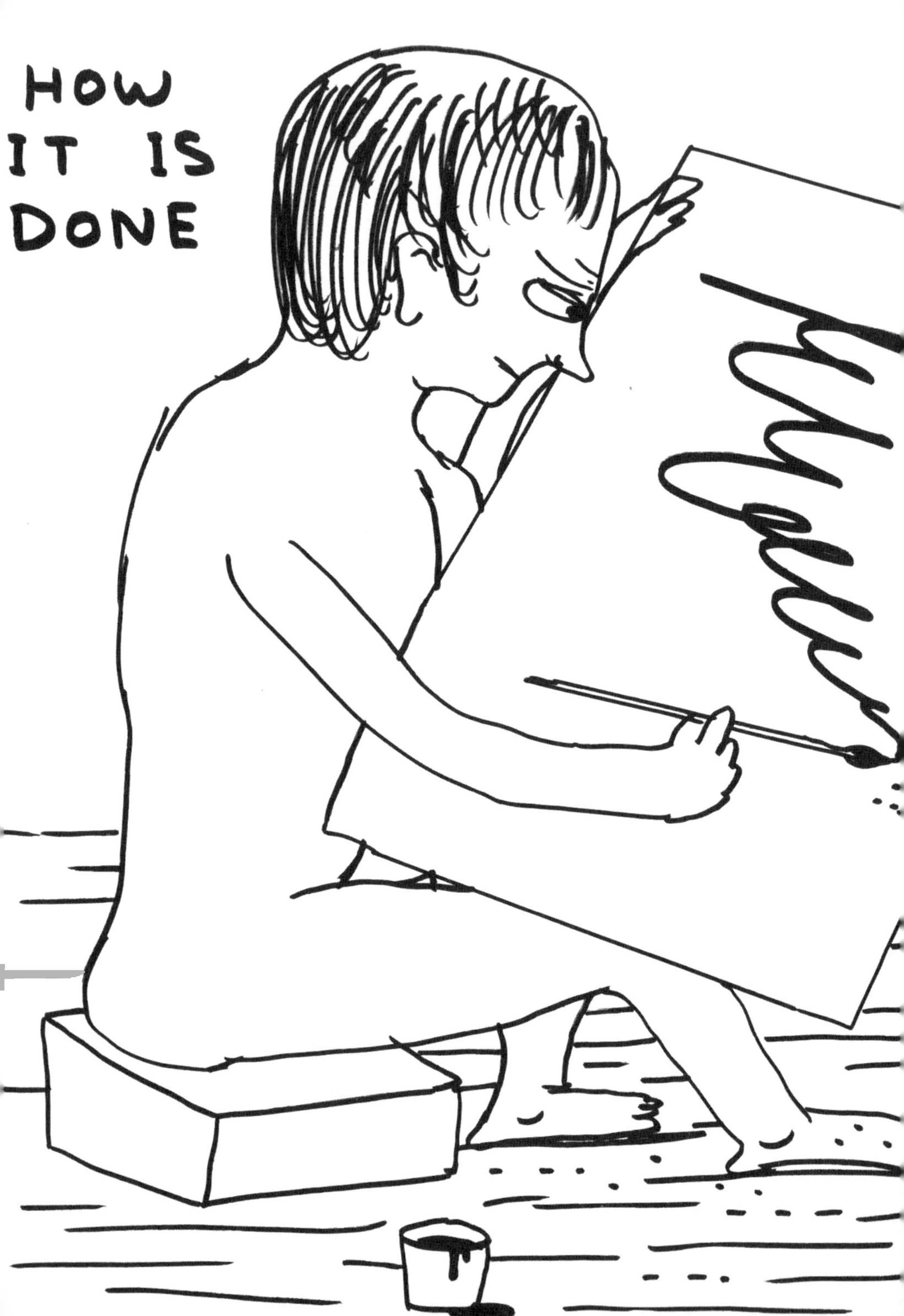
HOW
IT IS
DONE

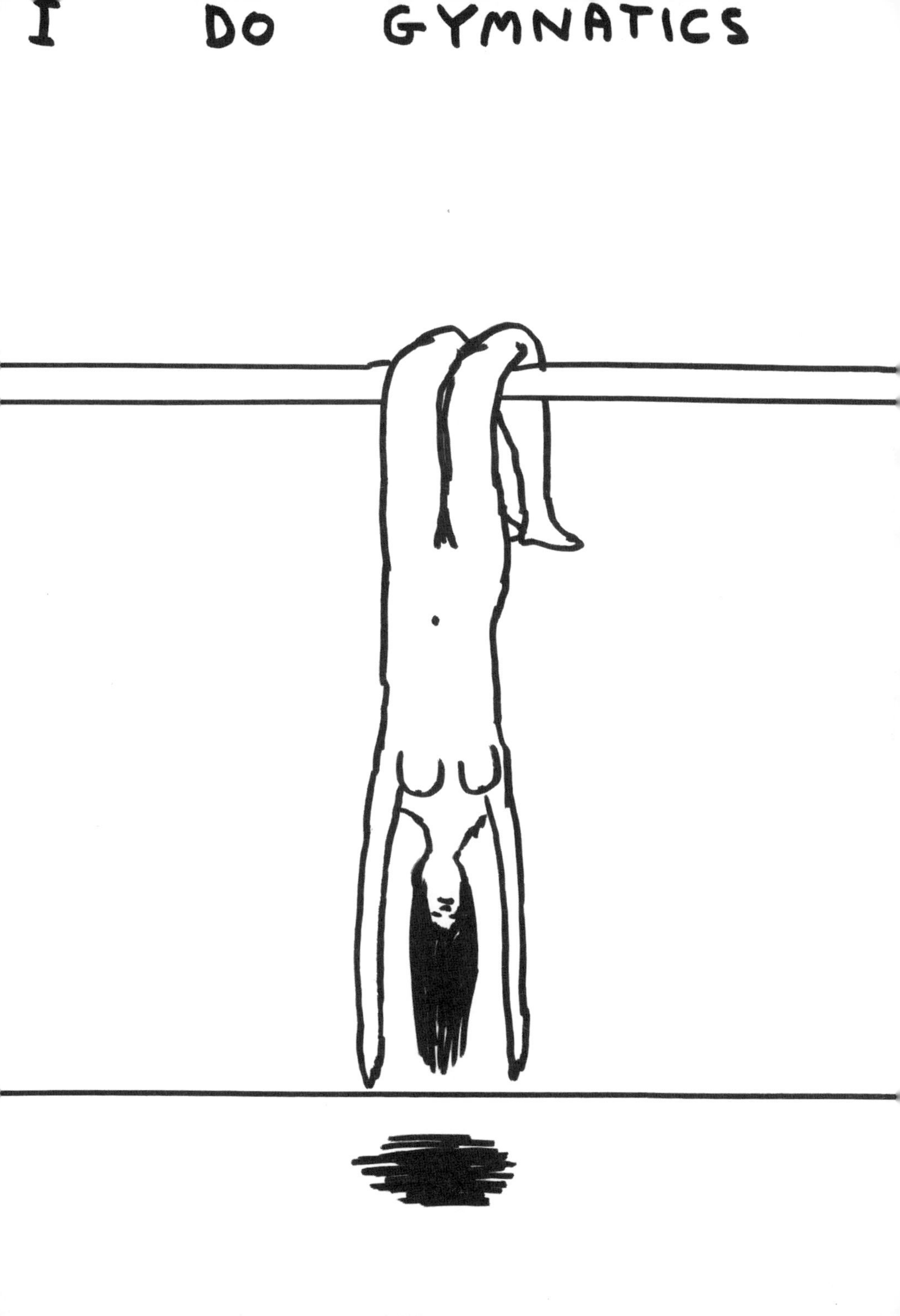

I   DO GYMNATICS

CULTURAL PROCEDURE

I AM CARRYING OUT A PROCEDURE
IT REQUIRES CONCENTRATION
AND DILIGENCE
AND FOR ME TO BE HAPPY AND CALM
PLEASE RESPECT MY ATTEMPT
TO CARRY OUT THE PROCEDURE
AND STOP LAUGHING AT ME

COMMON ATTIRE

T-SHIRT, SHORTS, FLIP-FLOPS
T-SHIRT HAS SLOGANS WRITTEN ON IT
IN MAUVE LIPSTICK
SHORTS ARE DIRTY
FLIP-FLOPS ARE ILL-FITTING
(TOO BIG : POSSIBLY STOLEN)

TYPES OF RHAPSODY

NICE RHAPSODY
HORRIBLE RHAPSODY

JEWELLERY MADE OF FOOD

PASTA BROOCH
MACARONI NECKLACE
DOUGHNUT TIARA

DAWNS

PRAWNS
DAWN OF PRAWNS

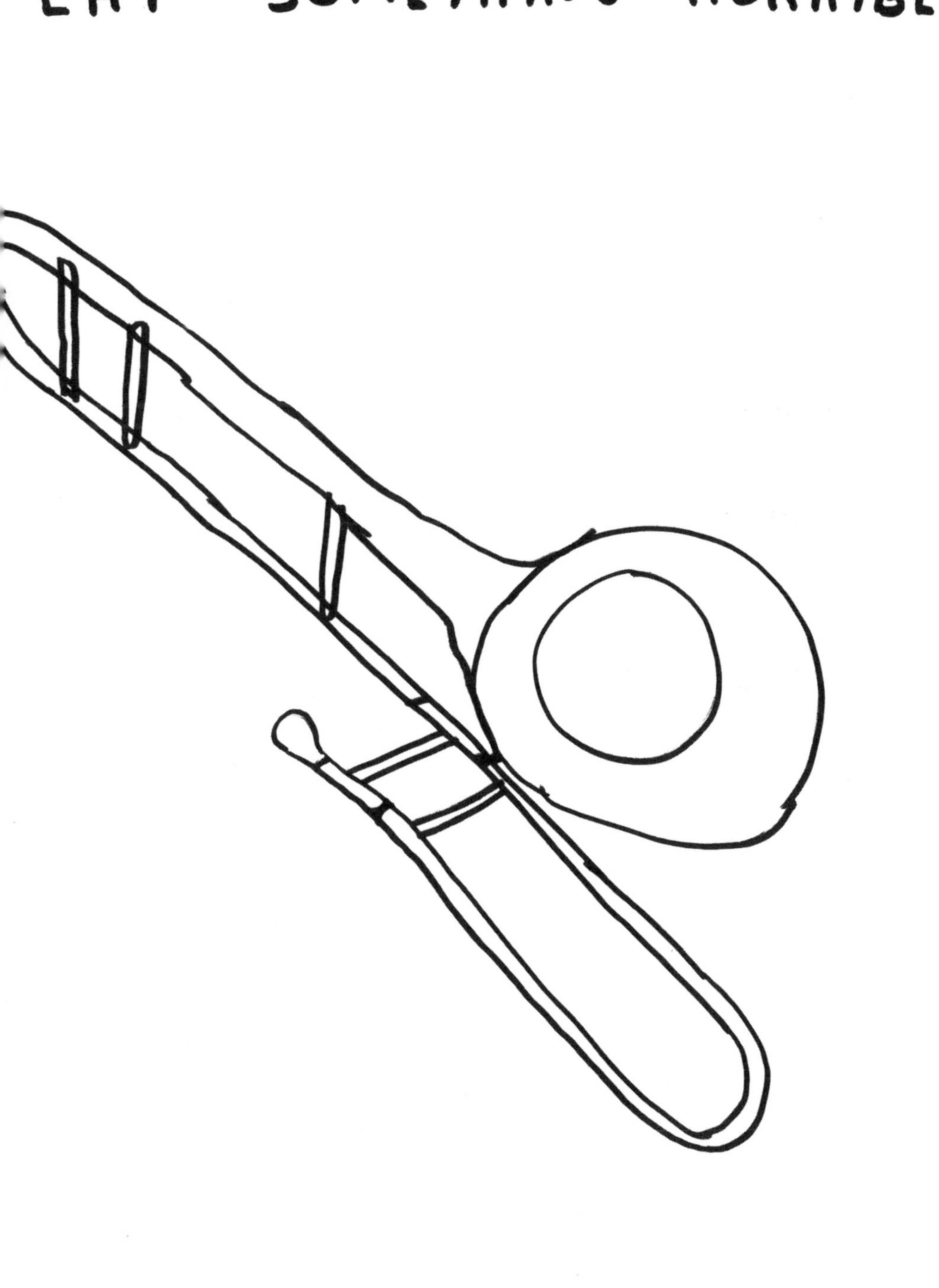

PLAY SOMETHING HORRIBLE

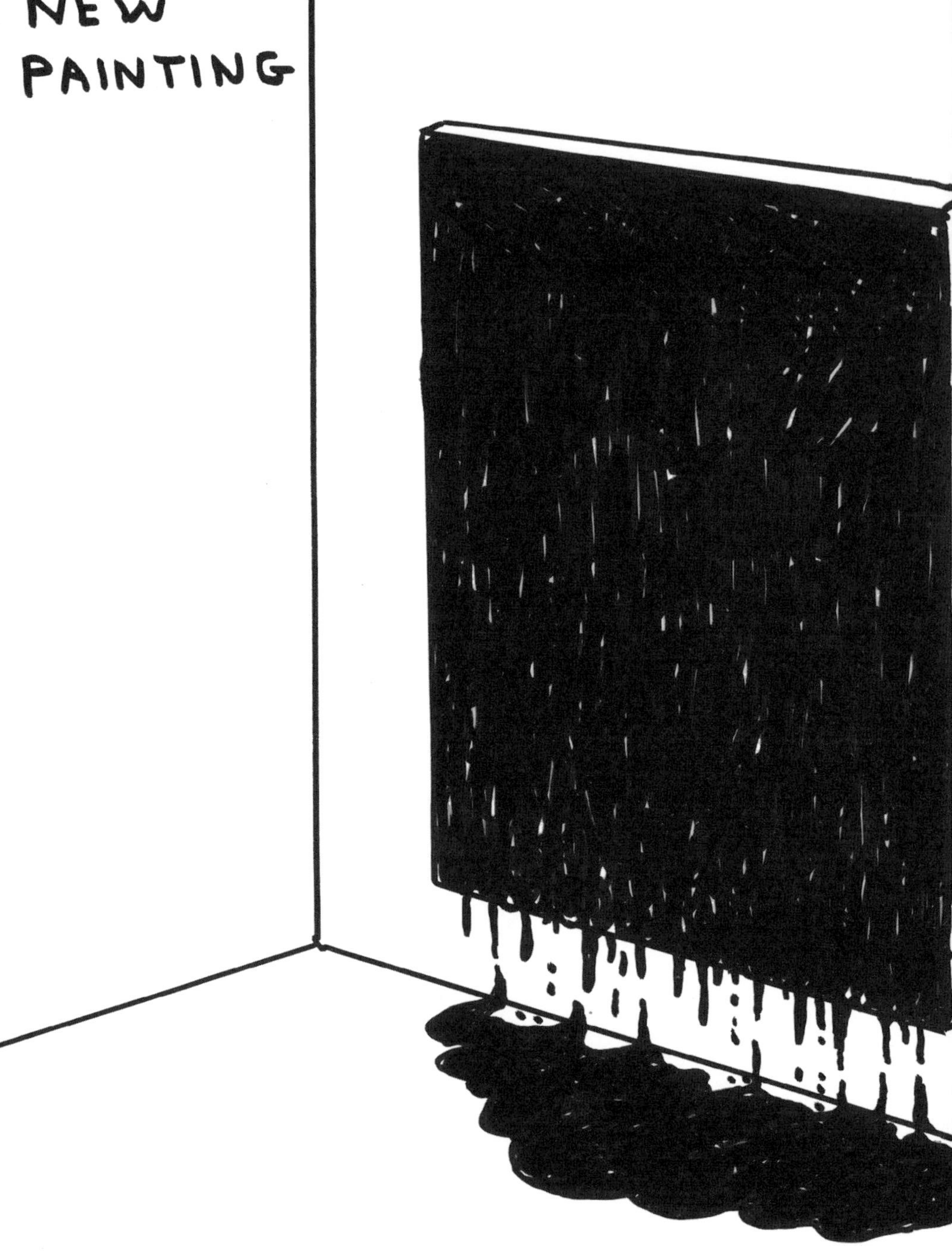

NEW
PAINTING

CHAPTER SIX

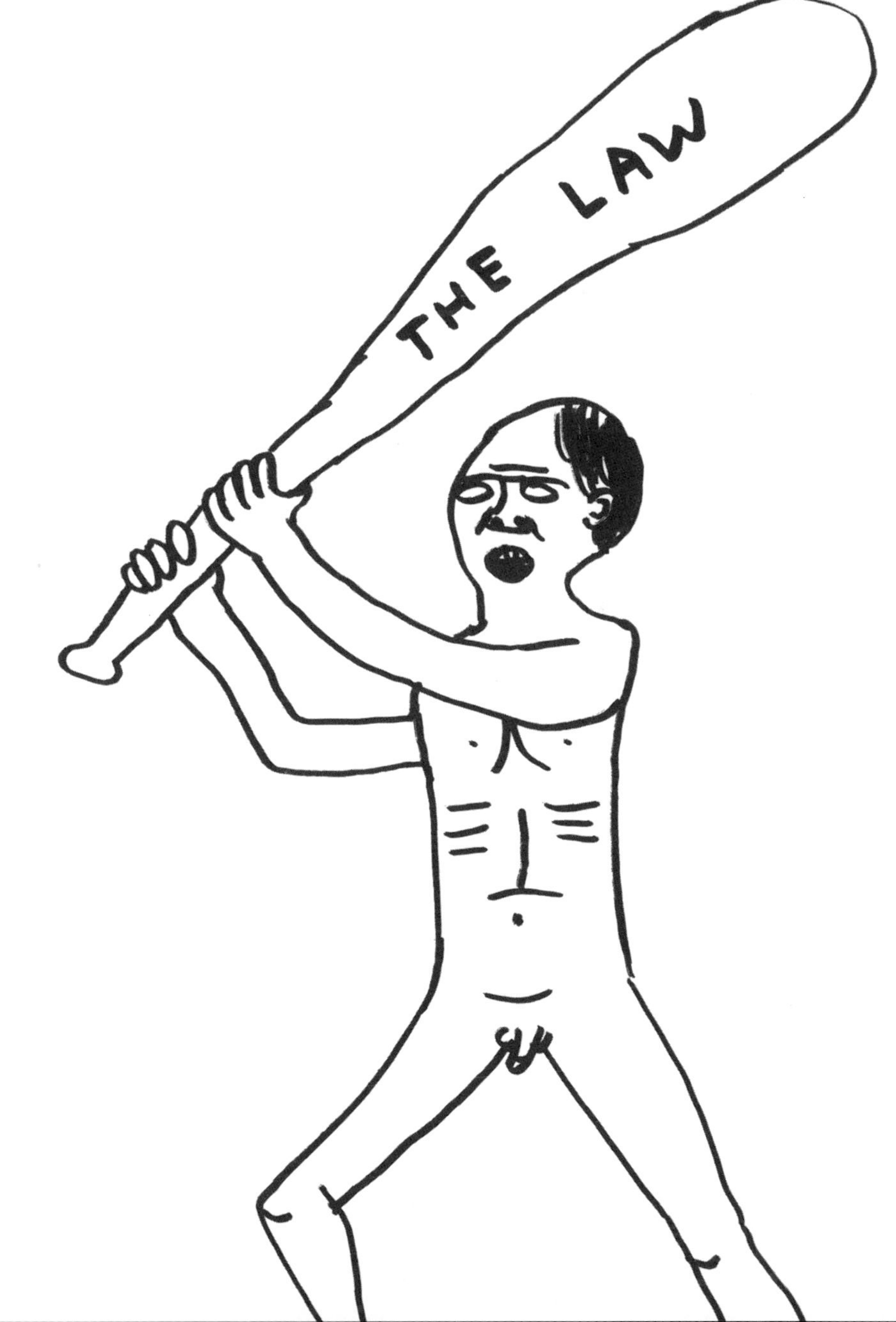

THE POLICE
THEY ARE JUST LIKE
THE REST OF US
EXCEPT MORE VIOLENT

ELECTRIC SHOCKS
YOU CAN ACQUIRE A PERMIT
TO ADMINISTER ELECTRIC SHOCKS
BY FILLING IN A SIMPLE FORM
AT YOUR LOCAL POST OFFICE
YOU DO NOT NEED TO
BRING IDENTIFICATION
AND THE PERMIT IS FREE OF CHARG
WHEN YOU HAVE THE PERMIT
YOU ARE FREE TO
ADMINISTER ELECTRIC SHOCKS
AT ANY TIME
TO ANYONE OVER THE AGE OF 16

RULES
SOCIETY MUST BE KEPT CLEAN
AND FREE FROM DIRT AND GREASE

PERMITTED HAIRSTYLES
ALMOST EVERYTHING IS PERMITTED
AT THE PRESENT TIME
BUT THIS WILL BE REVIEWED

FORBIDDEN FRUIT

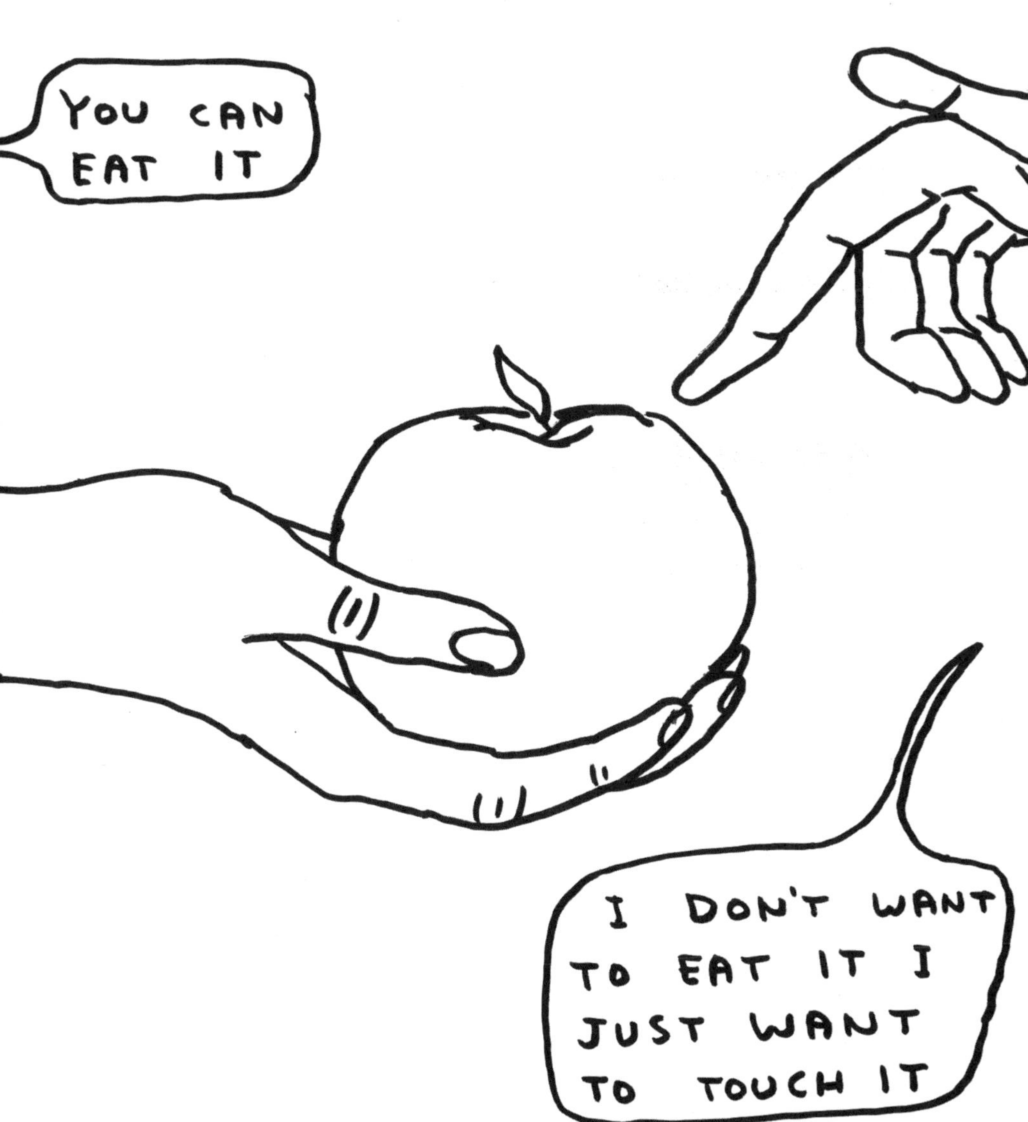

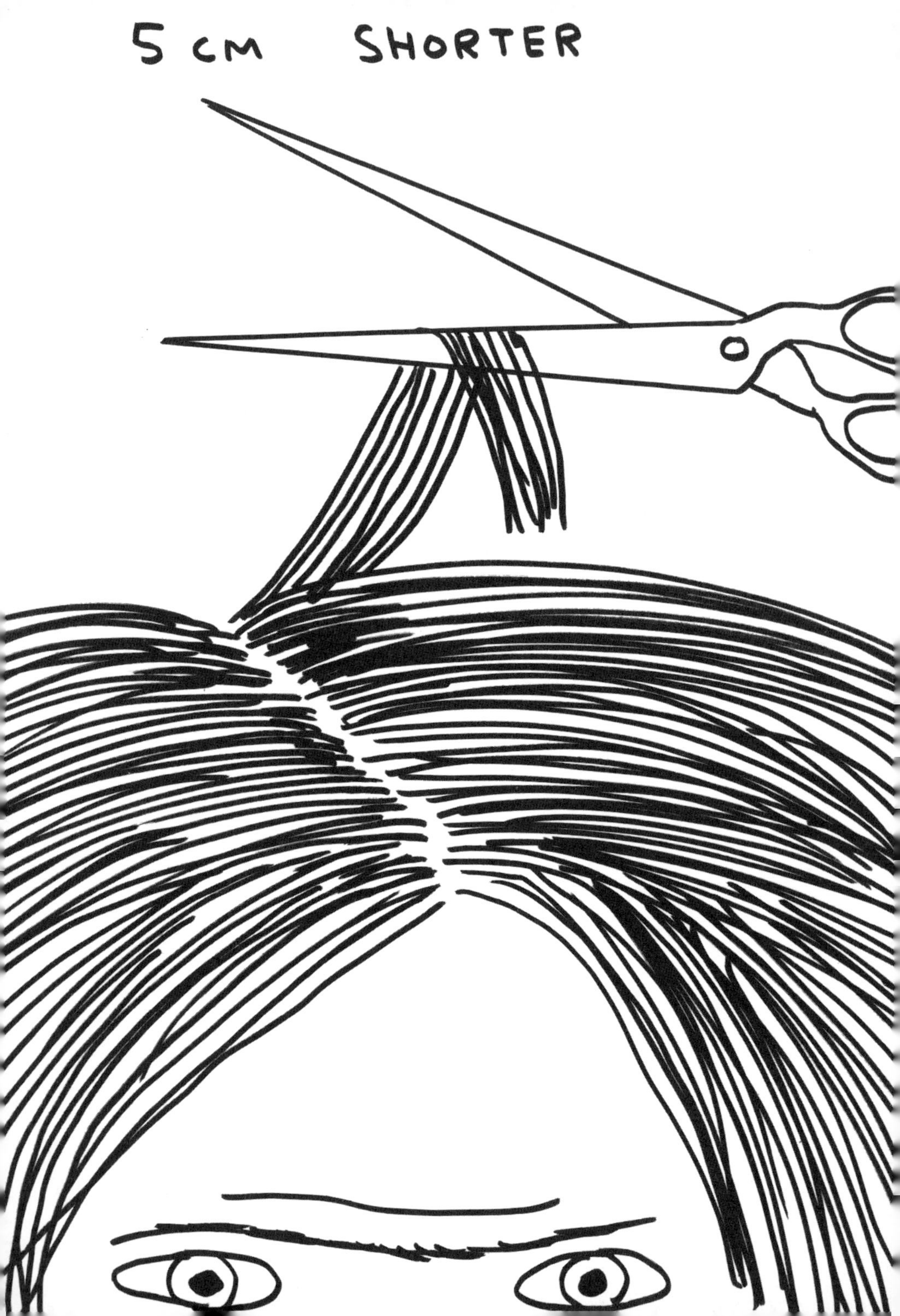

5 CM   SHORTER

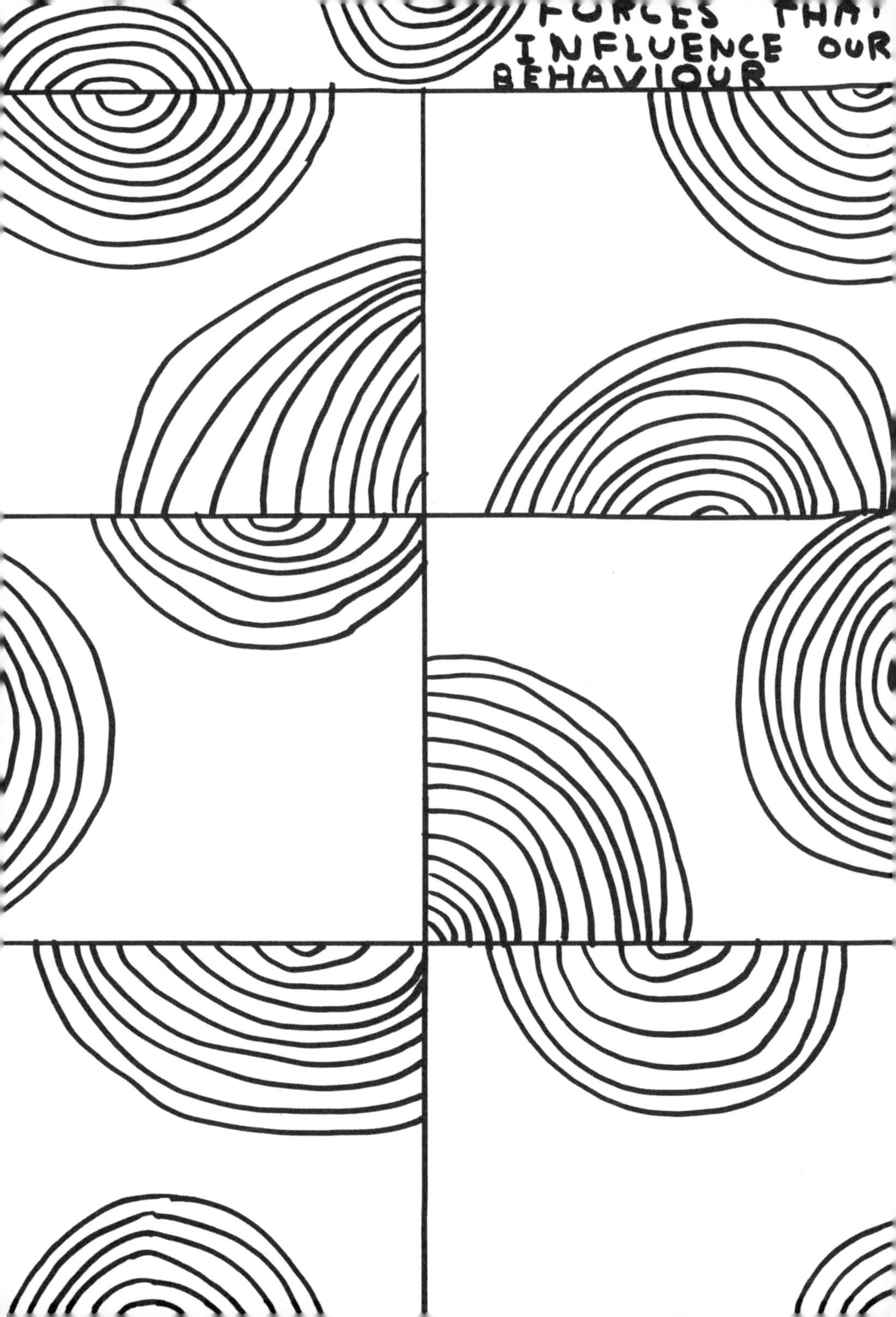

FORCES THAT
INFLUENCE OUR
BEHAVIOUR

TIME KEEPING
ALL CITIZENS MUST WEAR A WATCH
IT'S THE LAW!
OR IT WILL BE SOON

EXCESSIVE USE OF FORCE
PART OF ONE EAR LOST IN THE MUD

COST-CUTTING EXCERCISE
THEY SHUT THE PRISONS
THEY LET THE PRISONERS GO FREE
IT WAS FINE , ACTUALLY

CAUSE AND EFFECT
YOU WHISTLED AT HER
SHE KICKED YOU IN THE BRAIN

LIVING ON A BOAT
IF YOU LIVE ON A BOAT
THEN YOU ARE NOT A MEMBER OF SOCIET
SORRY

EVERYONE MUST WEAR WELLINGTON BOOTS
THIS IS JUST A PROPOSAL
AT THE PRESENT TIME

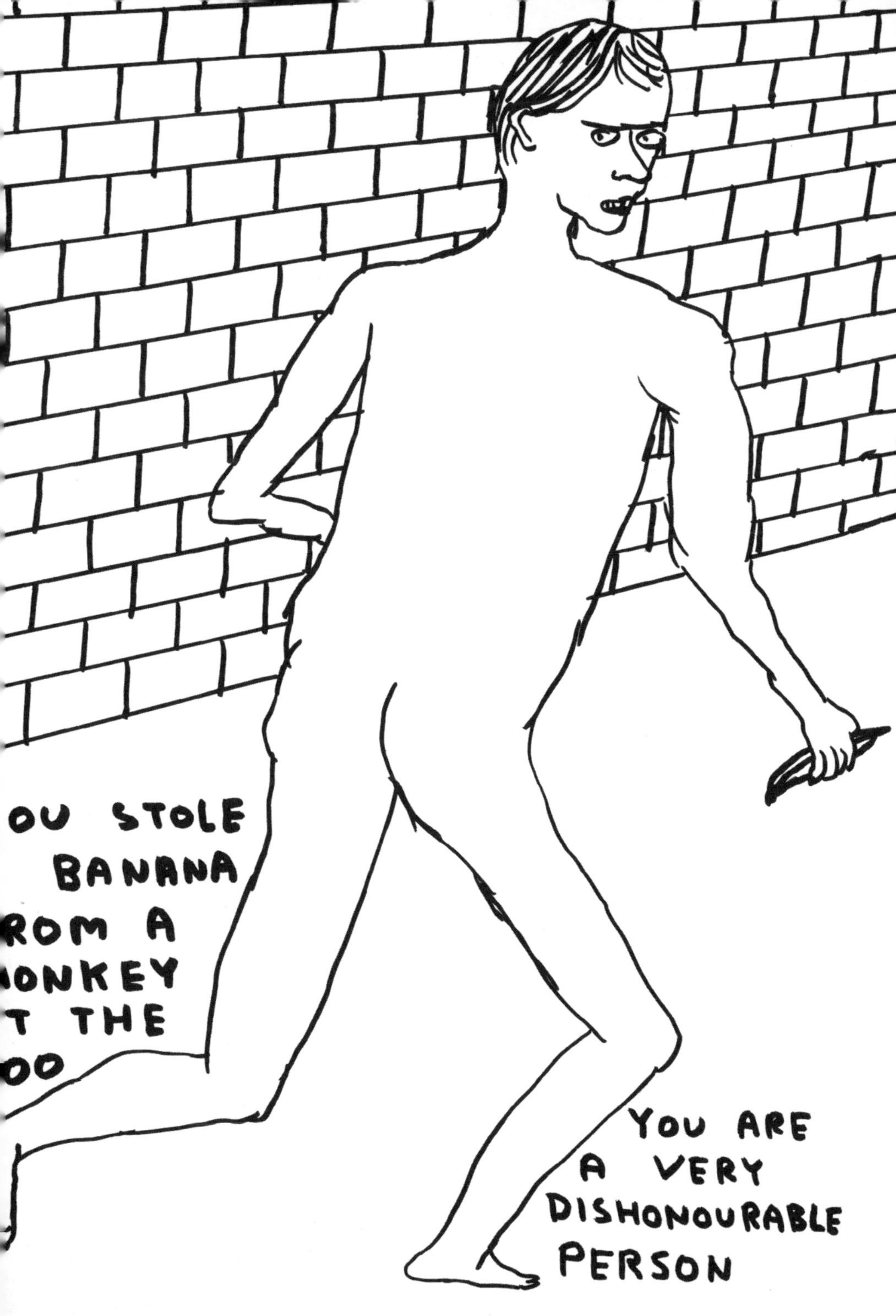
OU STOLE
BANANA
ROM A
ONKEY
T THE
OO

YOU ARE
A VERY
DISHONOURABLE
PERSON

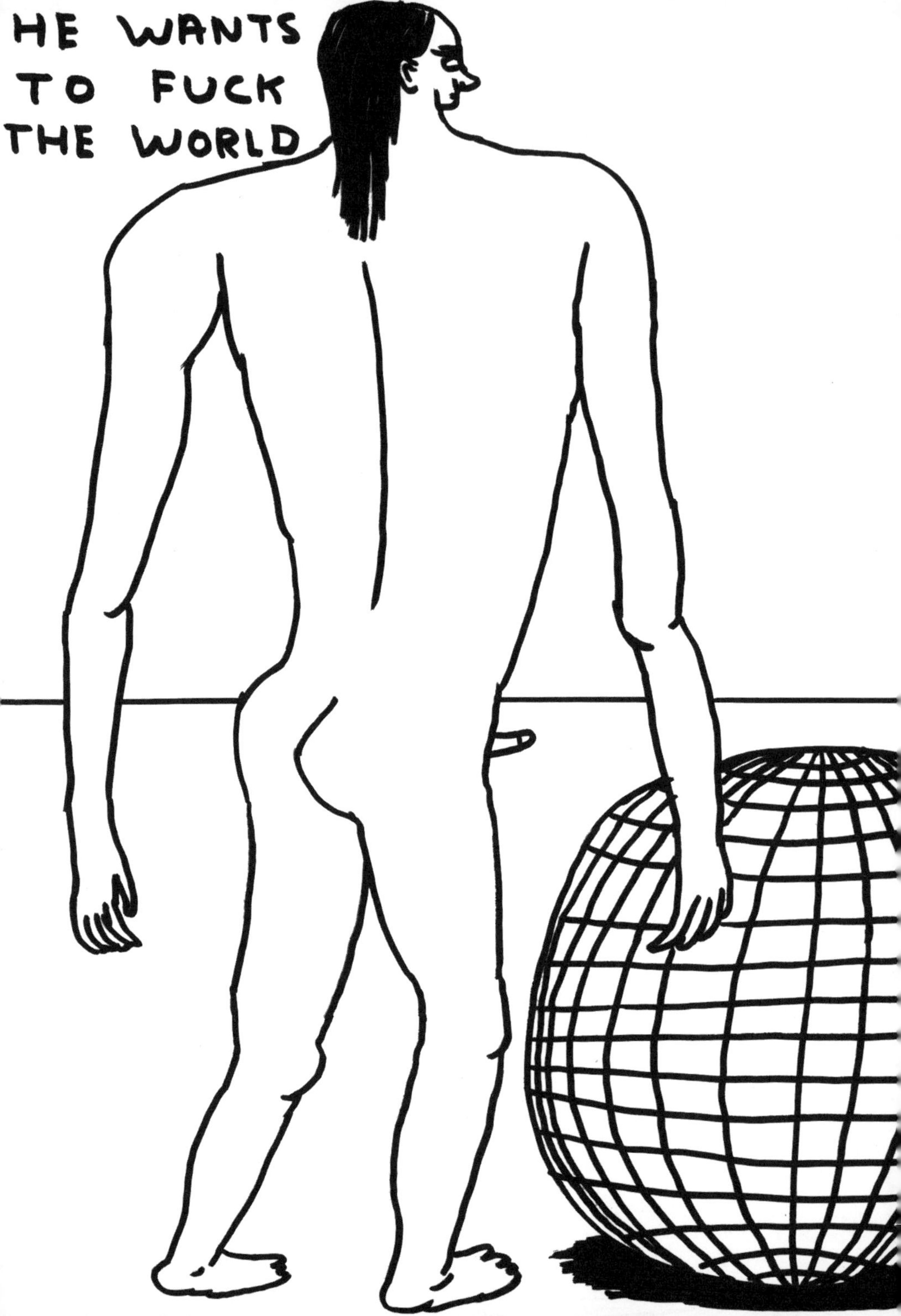
HE WANTS
TO FUCK
THE WORLD

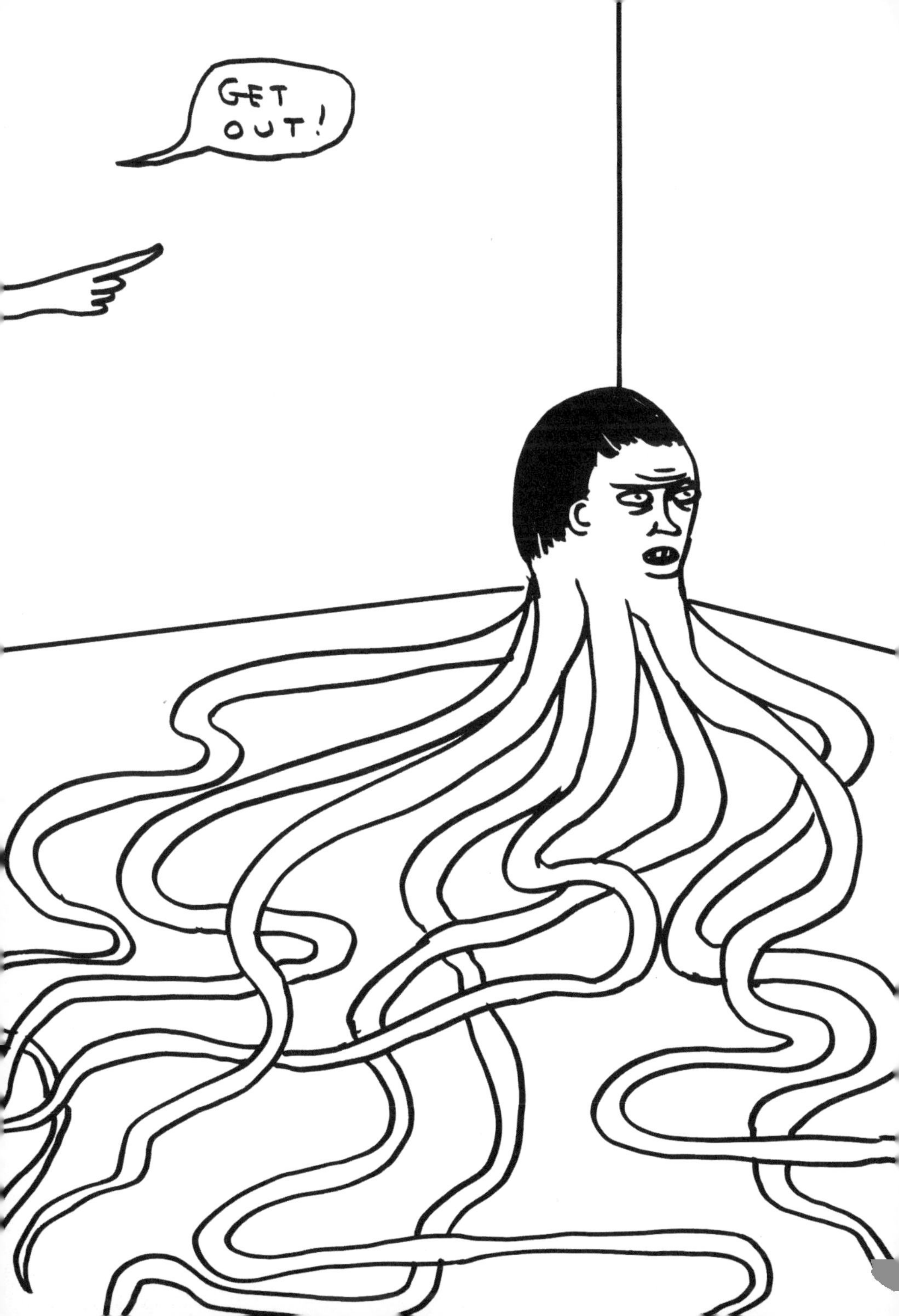

GET OUT!

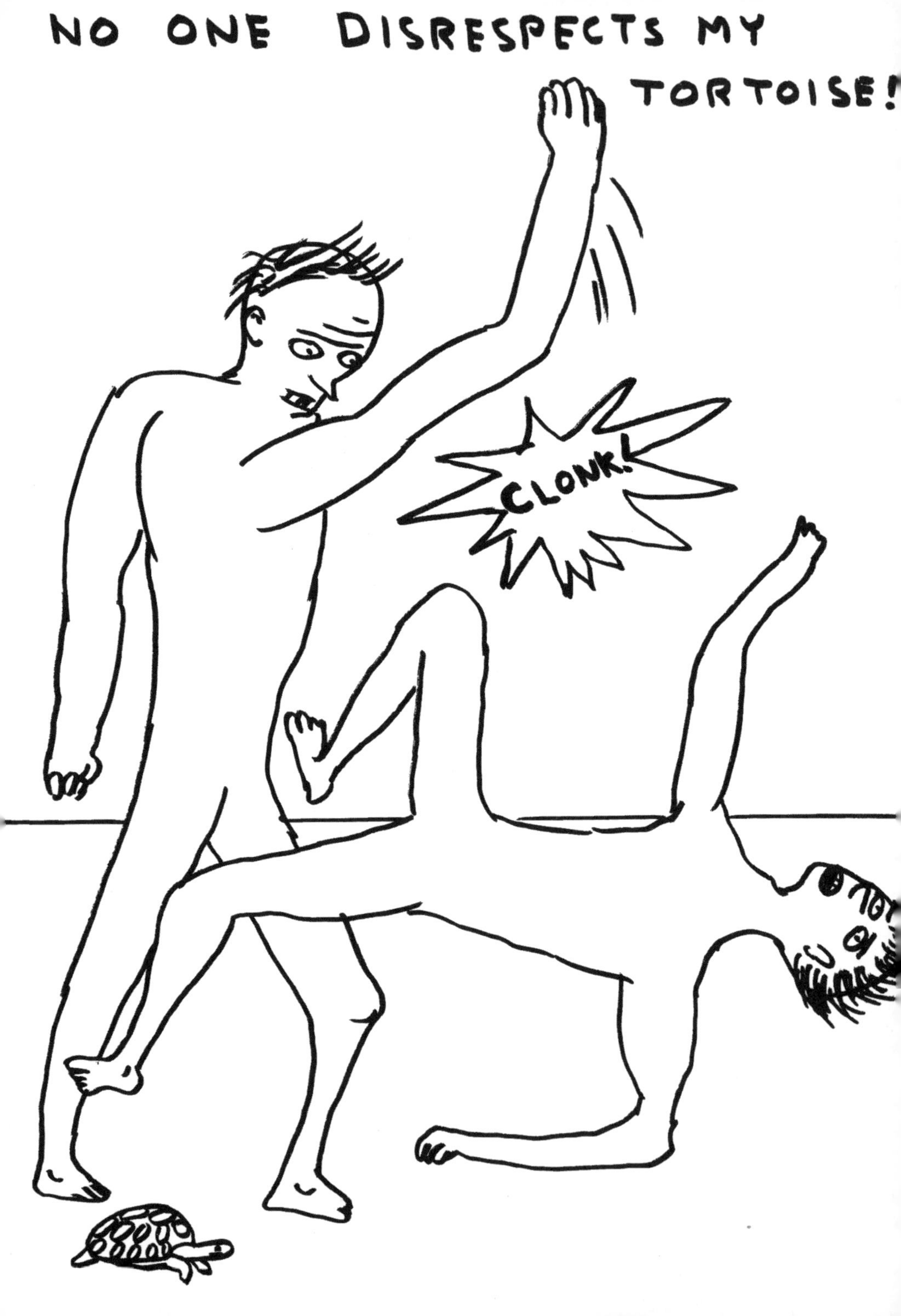
NO ONE DISRESPECTS MY TORTOISE!
CLONK!

THE SCOURGE OF MISPRONUNCIATION

WILL BE ERADICATED
THE MEANS THAT WILL BE ADOPTED
MAY APPEAR DRASTIC AT FIRST
BUT THEY WILL GET RESULTS
AND MISPRONUNCIATION
WILL BE A THING OF THE PAST
I CAN ASSURE YOU

GLUE

GLUE IS NOW ILLEGAL
YOU CAN'T BUY IT IN THE SHOPS ANYMORE
IF THEY FIND YOU GLUEING THINGS
THEN YOU GET INTO TROUBLE
THEY DON'T WANT YOU TO FIX THINGS
WHEN THEY BREAK
THEY WANT YOU TO THROW THEM AWAY
YOU CAN MAKE YOUR OWN GLUE
IN SECRET
AND USE IT
BUT IT'S A RISK

RAGS

AS LONG AS THEY ARE CLEAN
IT IS OK TO WEAR THEM

GRRRRRRRR RRRRRRR
RR RRRRRRRRRRRRRRR
RRRRRRRRRRRRRRRRRRR

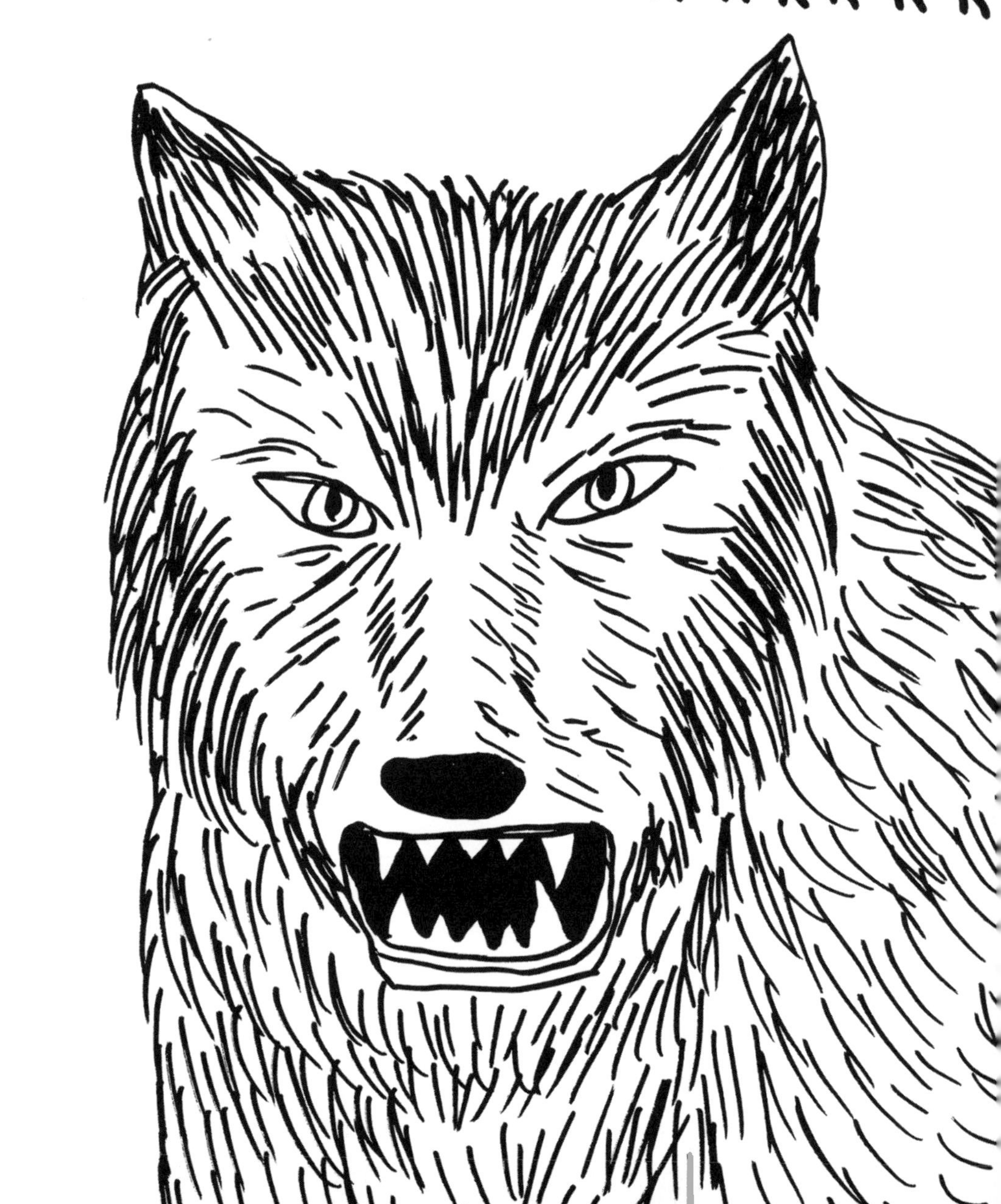

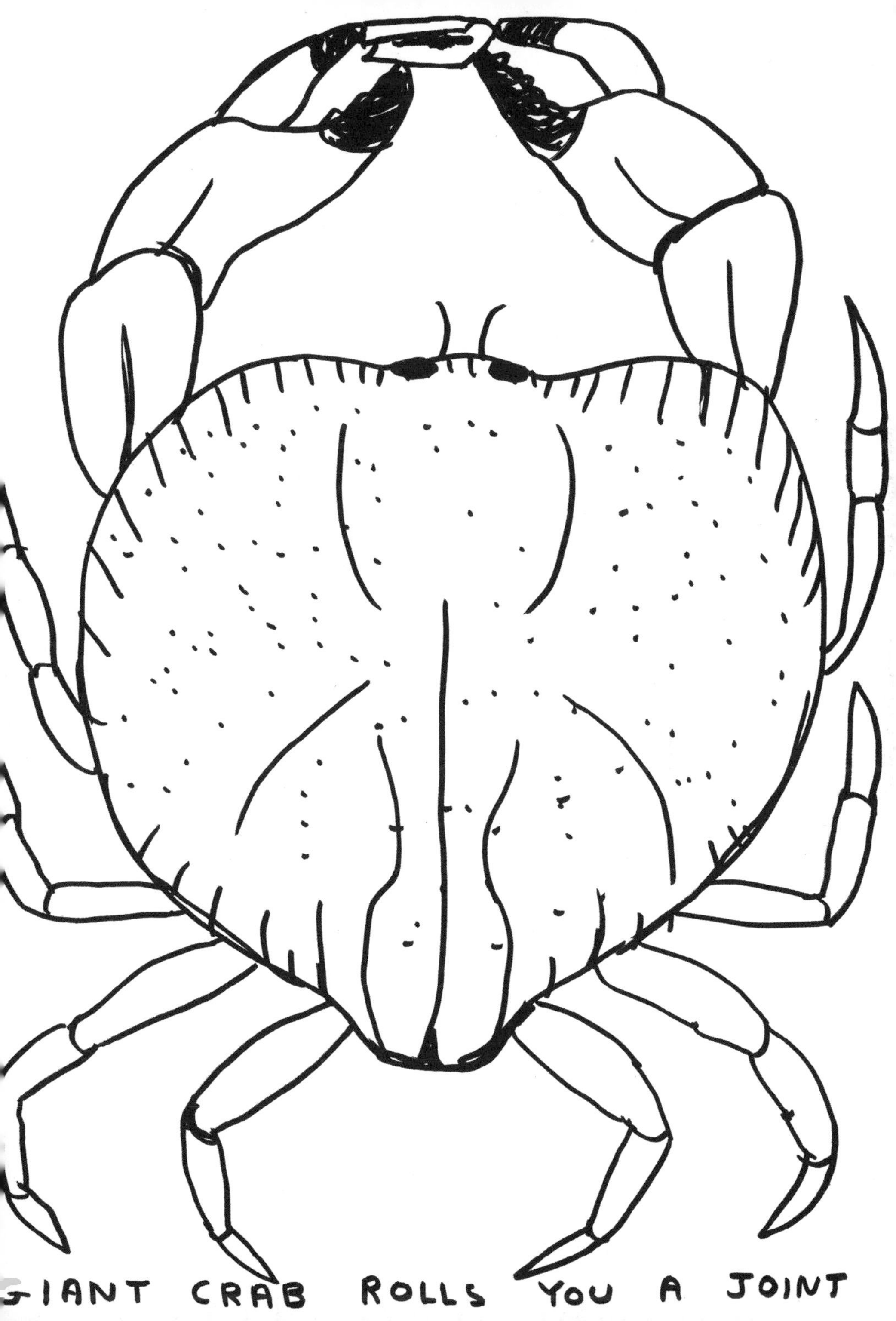

GIANT CRAB ROLLS YOU A JOINT

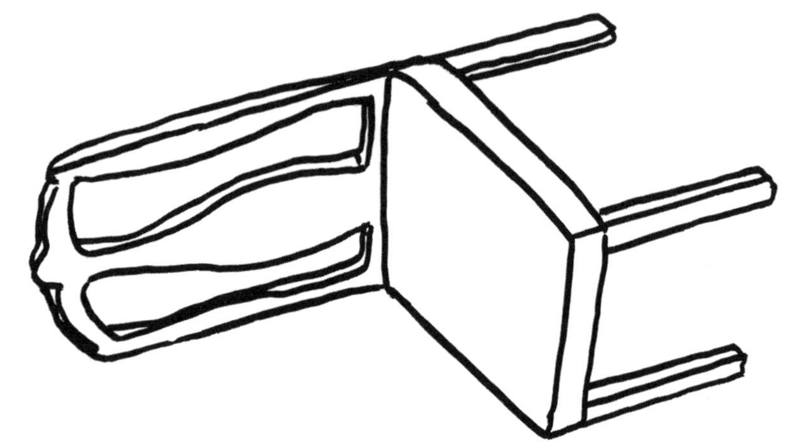

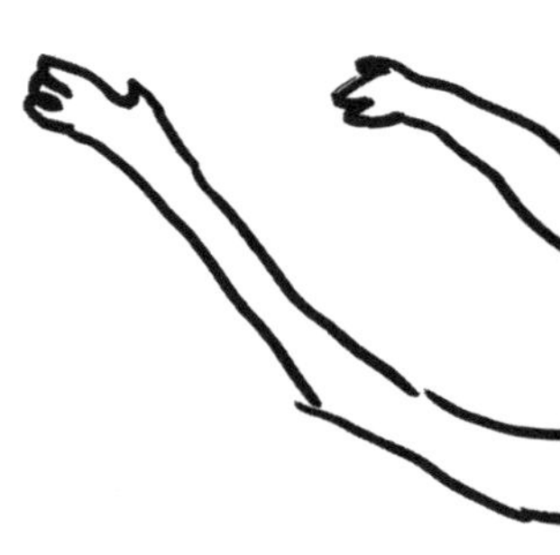

IT IS WRONG TO THROW
CHAIR

GIVE ME BACK MY PENIS

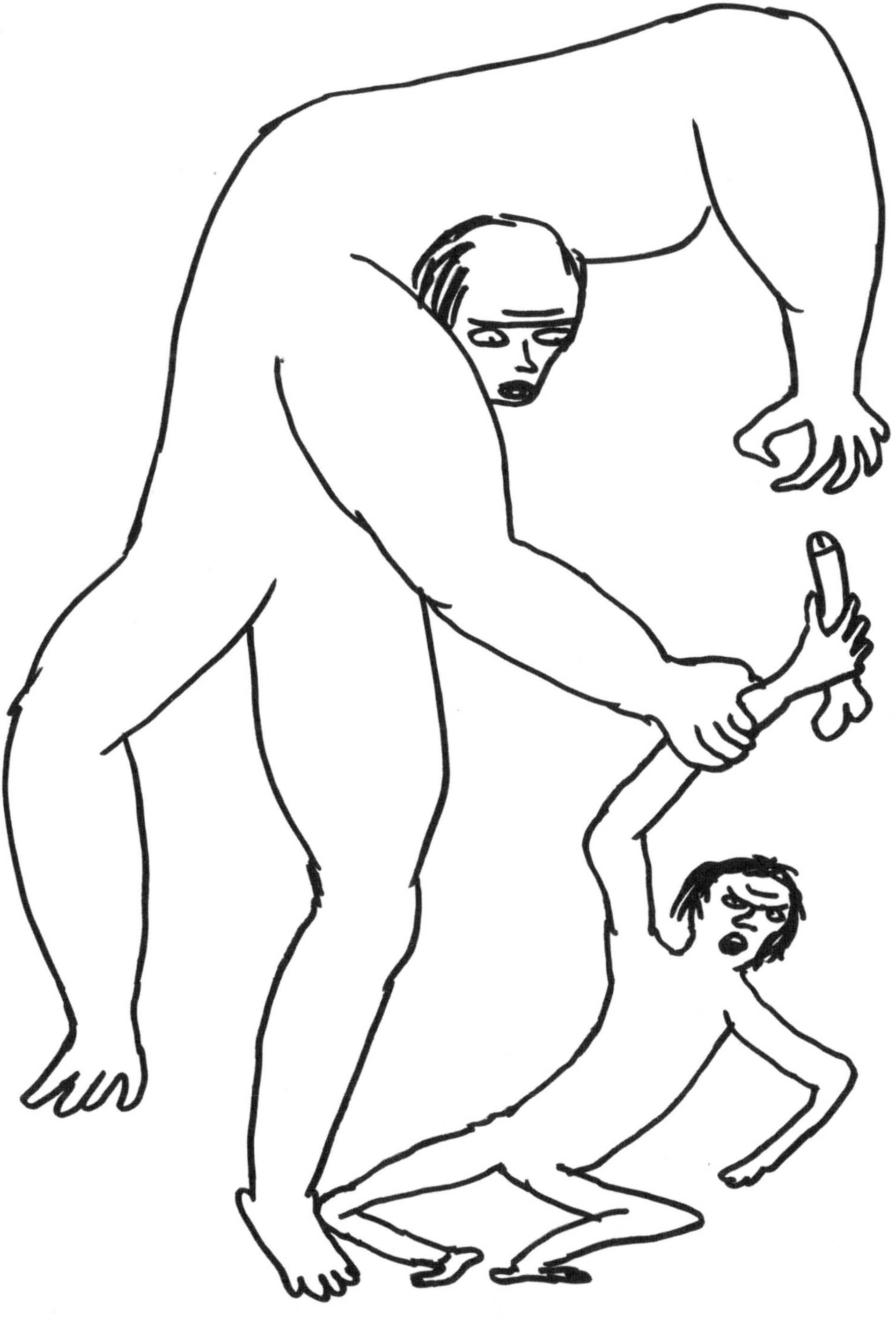

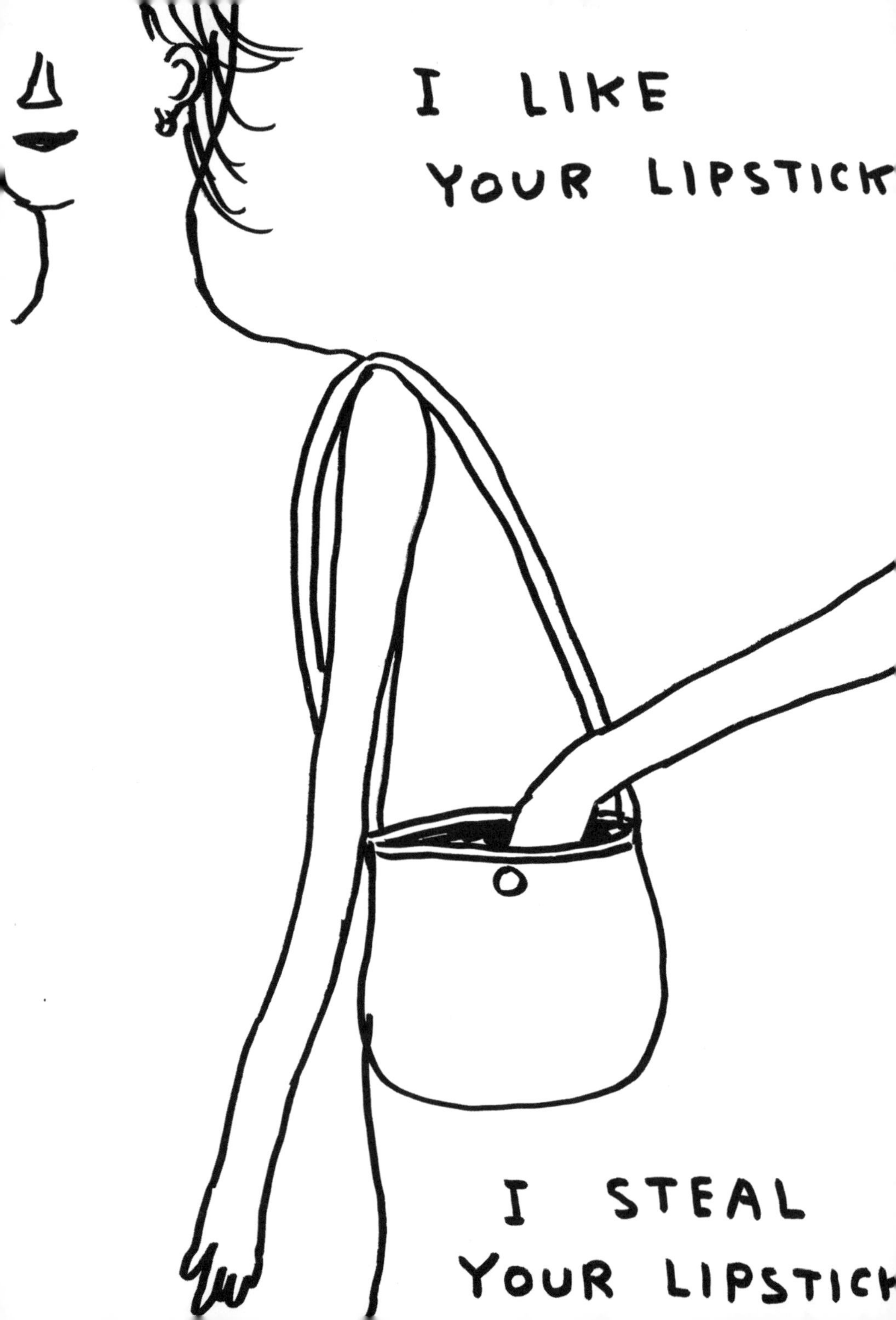

I LIKE YOUR LIPSTICK
I STEAL YOUR LIPSTICK

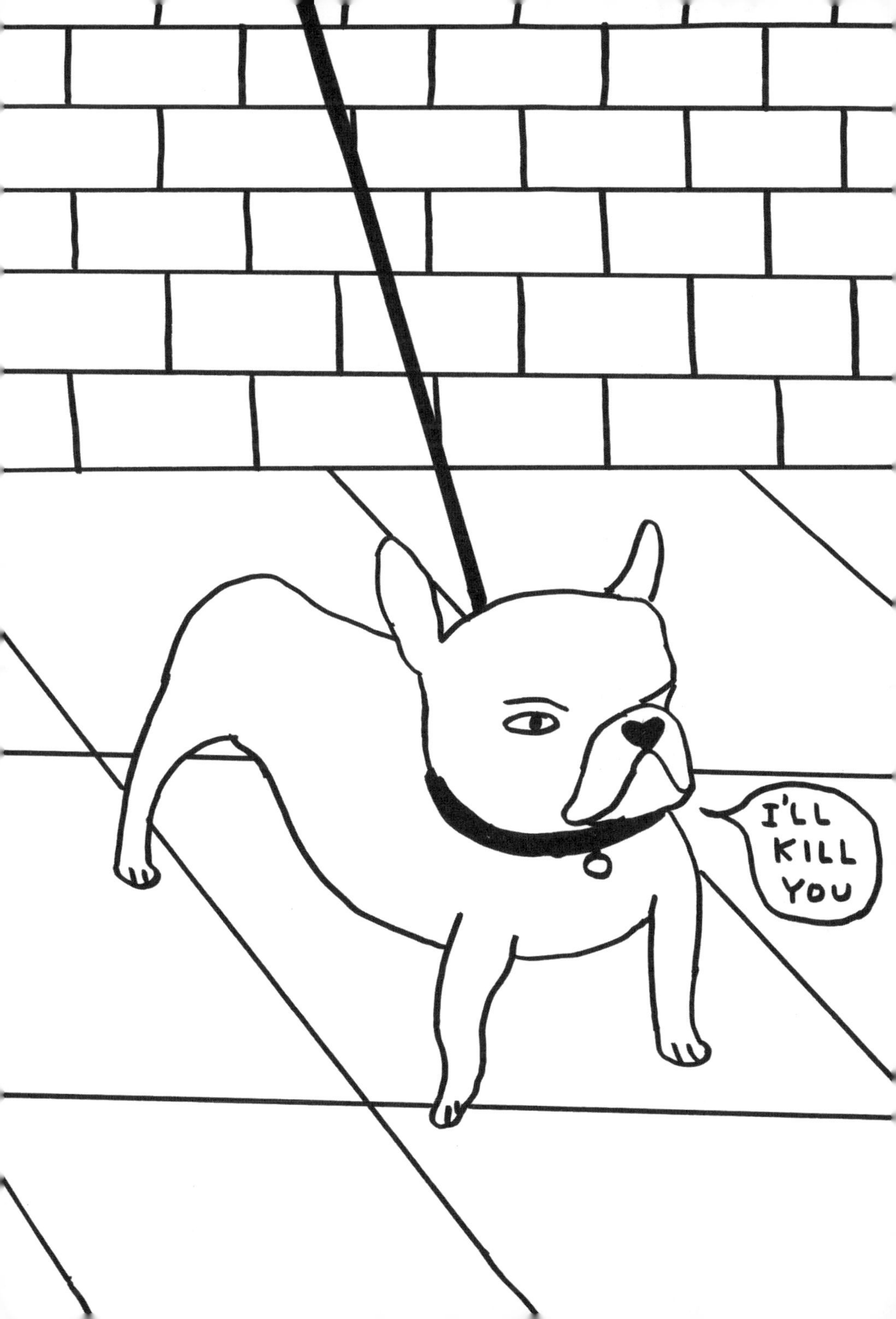
I'LL KILL YOU

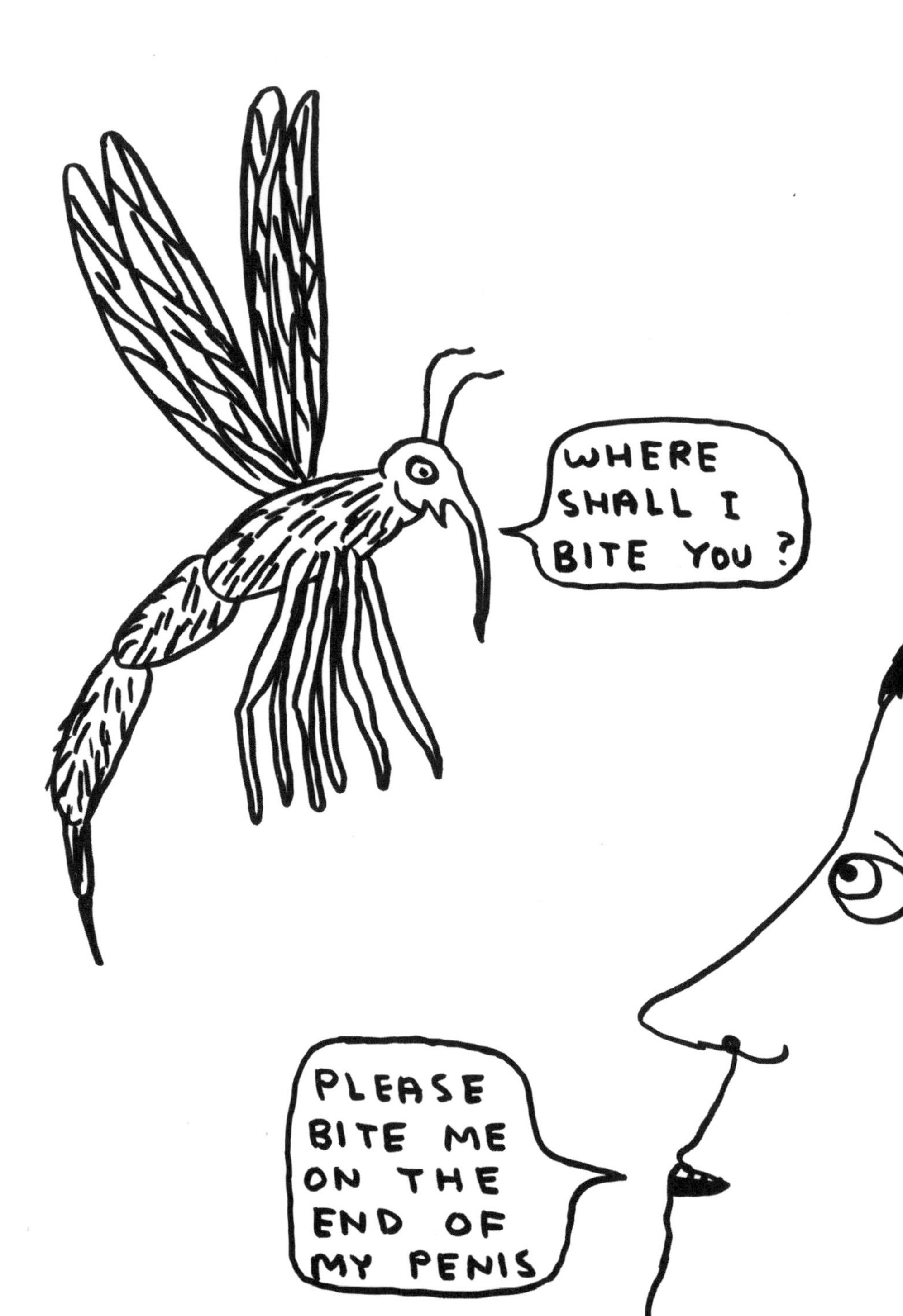

WHERE SHALL I BITE YOU ?
PLEASE BITE ME ON THE END OF MY PENIS

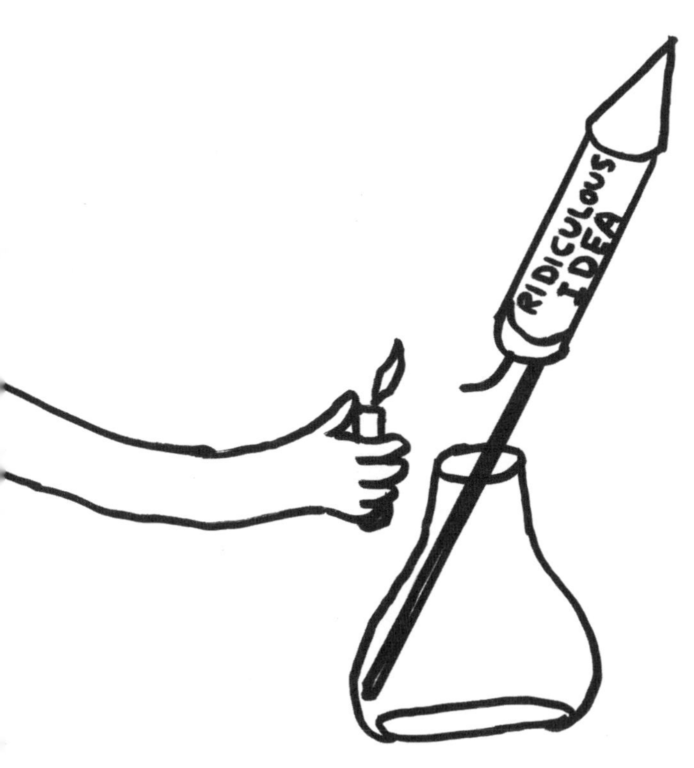
RIDICULOUS
IDEA

PROTECTING OUR BORDERS

FROM WHOM ?
FROM WHAT ?
FROM ZOMBIES

OTHER NATIONS

THEY HAVE MORE RATS THAN WE D
WE CONTROL OUR RATS AND THEY DON
THEY DO NOT EVEN TRY
THEY THINK RATS ARE OK

NATIONAL IDENTITY

WE ARE US
THEY ARE THEM
IT IS OK
THEY MUST STAY AS THEM
THEY CANNOT BE US
THAT WOULD NOT BE OK
WE DO NOT WANT TO BE THEM
WE WILL NOT ALLOW IT
IT WILL NOT HAPPEN
(THEN LATER, AFTER ADJUSTMENT)
IT NOW APPEARS THAT WE ARE TH
AND THAT THEY ARE US
IT IS NOT OK
BUT WE MUST ACCEPT IT

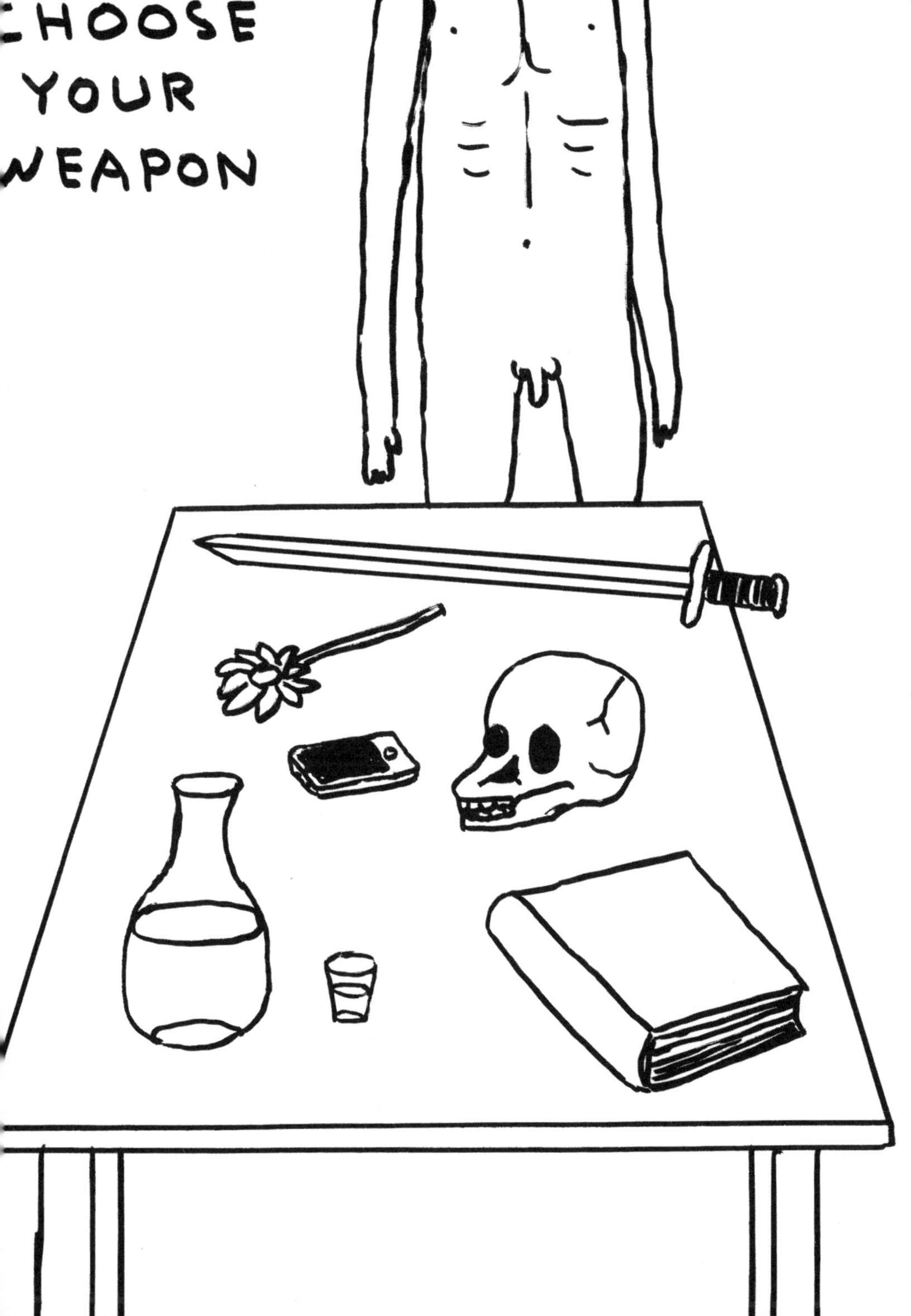
CHOOSE
YOUR
WEAPON

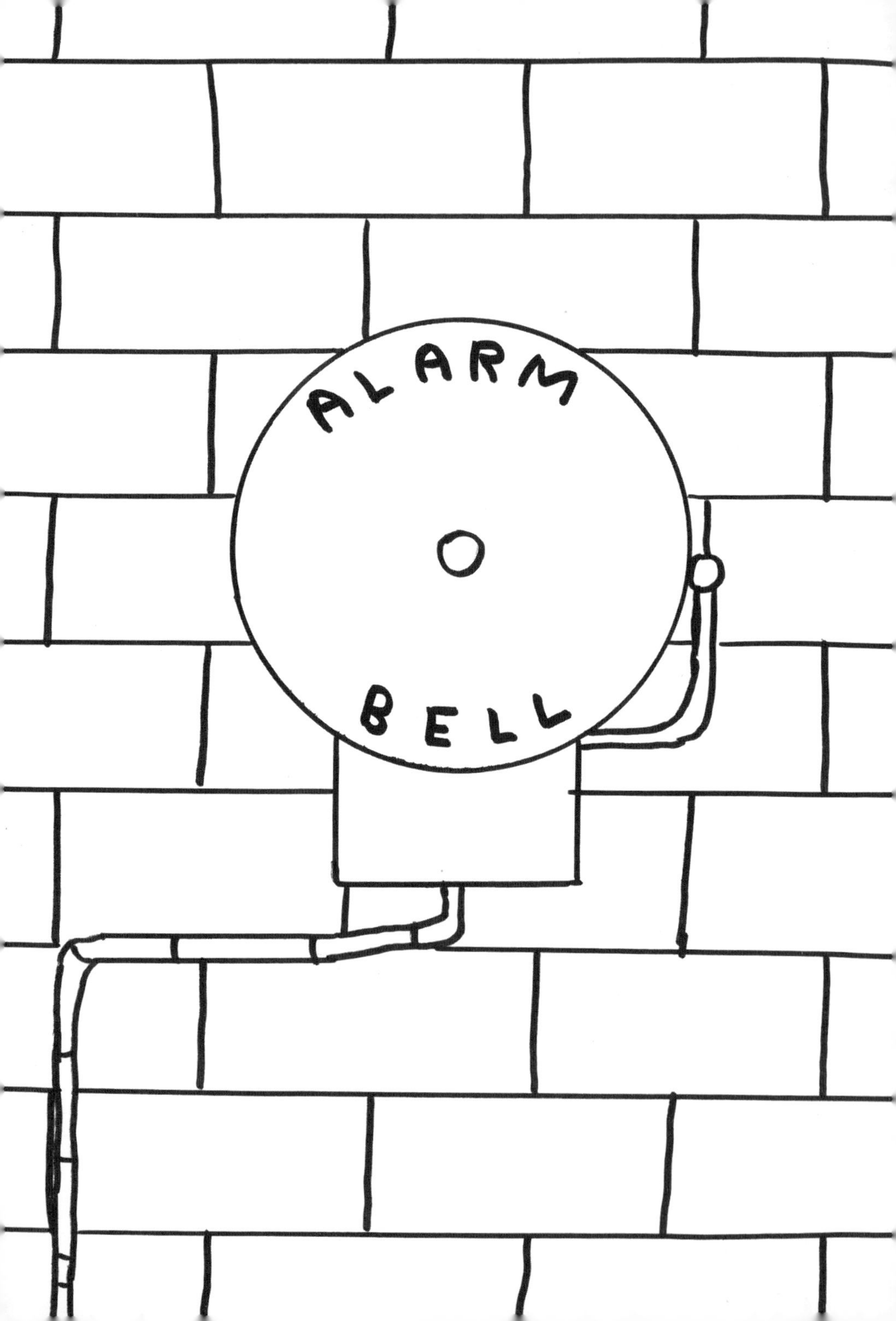

ALARM
BELL

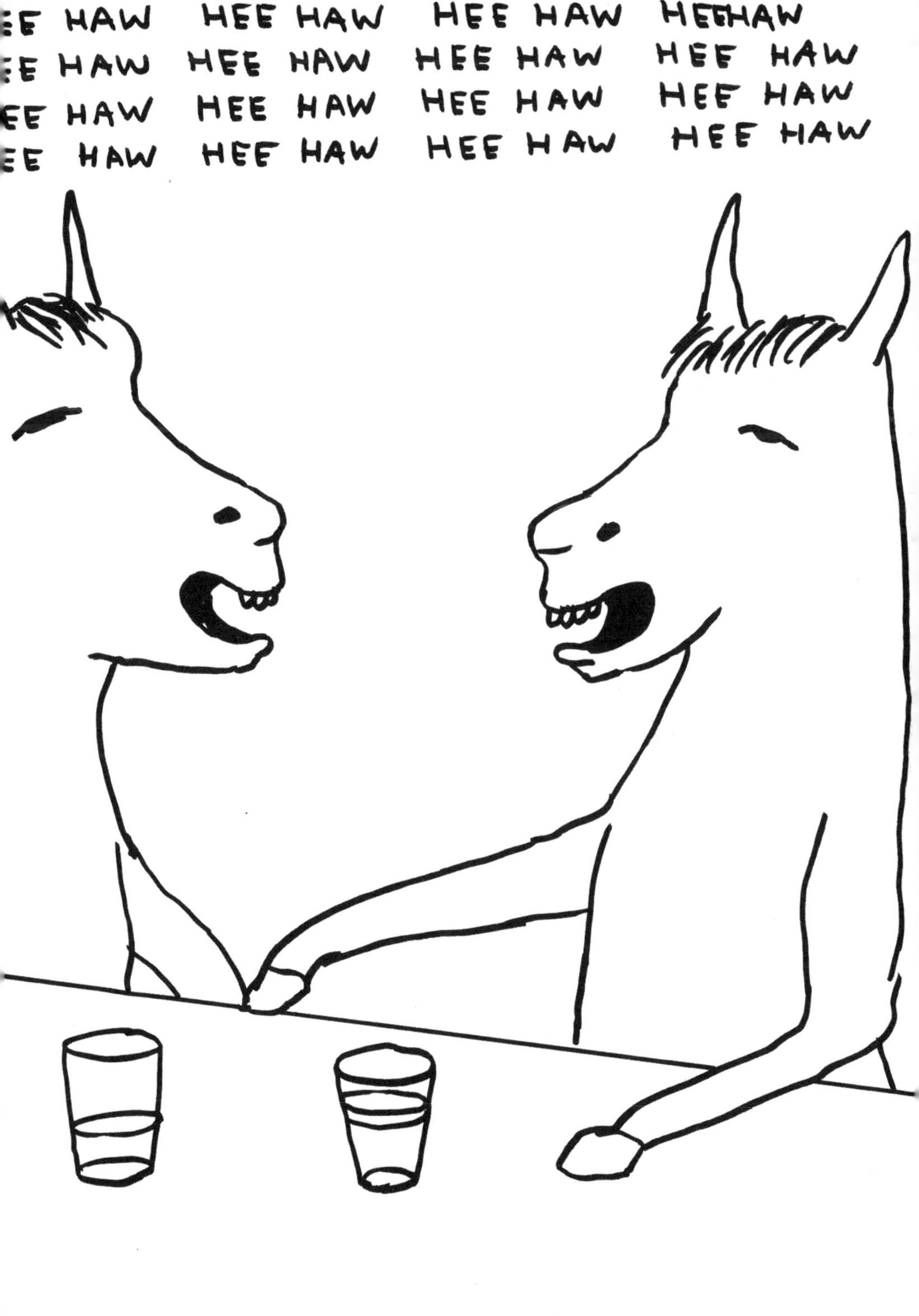

HEE HAW   HEE HAW   HEE HAW   HEEHAW
HEE HAW   HEE HAW   HEE HAW   HEE HAW
HEE HAW   HEE HAW   HEE HAW   HEE HAW
HEE HAW   HEE HAW   HEE HAW   HEE HAW

THE MEDIA

LIKE A SEWER
FULL OF RATS AND SHIT
BUT OTHERWISE IS A GOOD THING
AND MUST BE CHERISHED

STIMULUS:

PRODDING
AND **RESPONSE:**
SLIGHT MOVEMENT

POWER RELATIONSHIPS

HORSE: HE TAKES THE CART WHEREVE
HE WANTS
CART HAS NO SAY

POWER STRUCTURES

YOU ADMIRE THEM
YOU BUILD ONE IN YOUR GARDEN
THE AUTHORITIES FORCE YOU TO
TAKE IT DOWN
YOU REACT BADLY

THE STATE AND THE INDIVIDUA

STATE IS A BAT
INDIVIDUAL IS A BALL

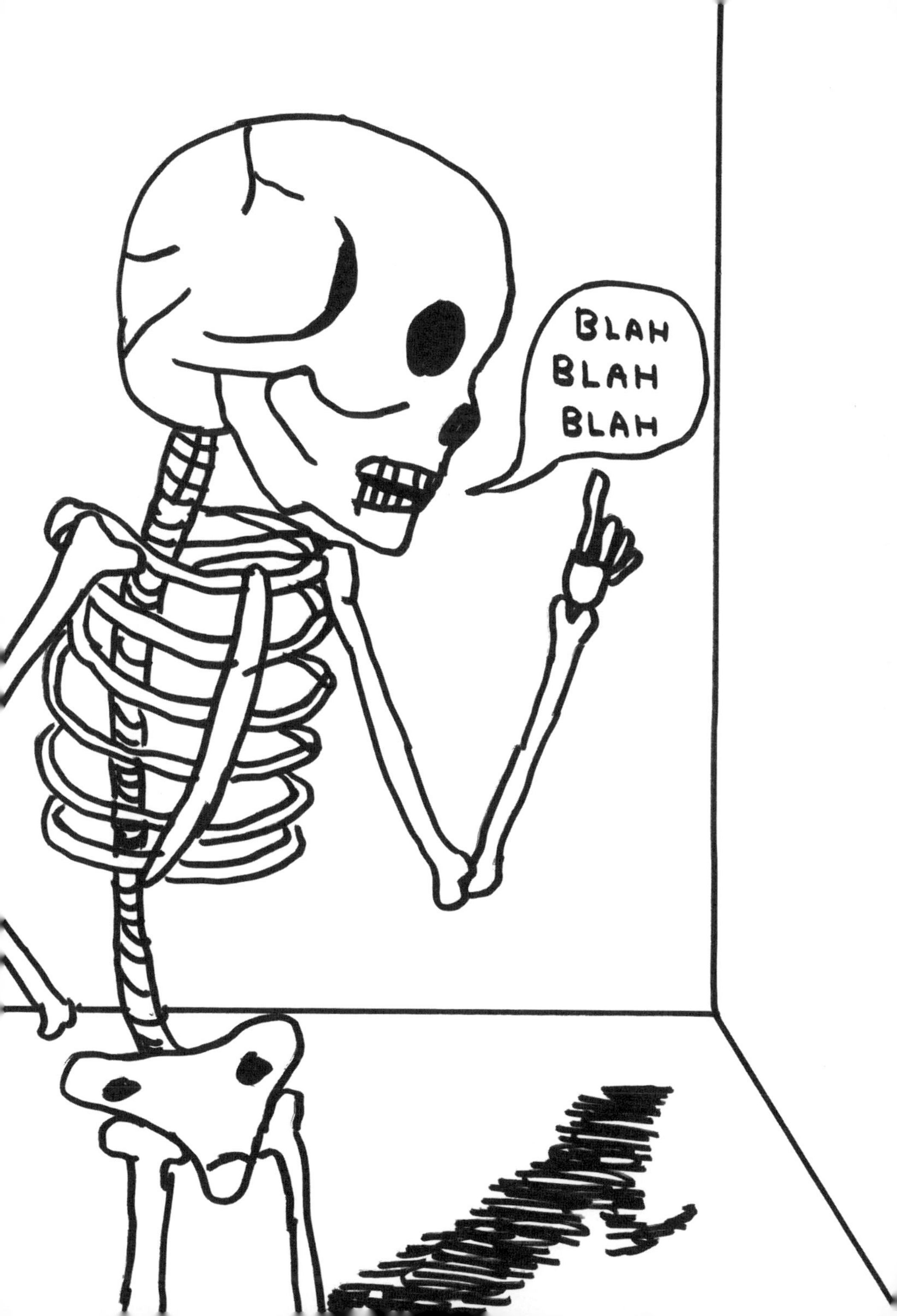

BLAH
BLAH
BLAH

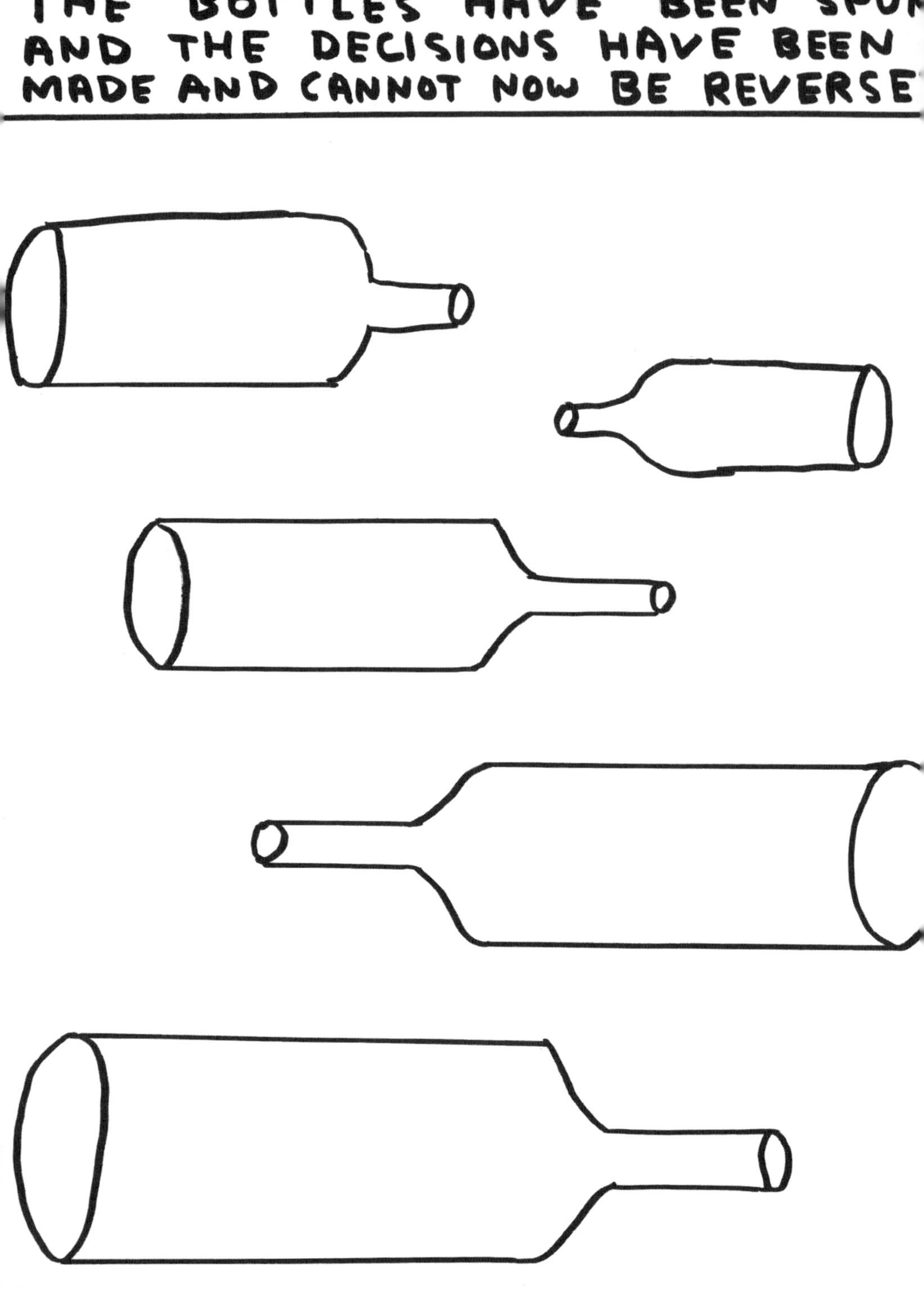

THE BOTTLES HAVE BEEN SPUN
AND THE DECISIONS HAVE BEEN
MADE AND CANNOT NOW BE REVERSE

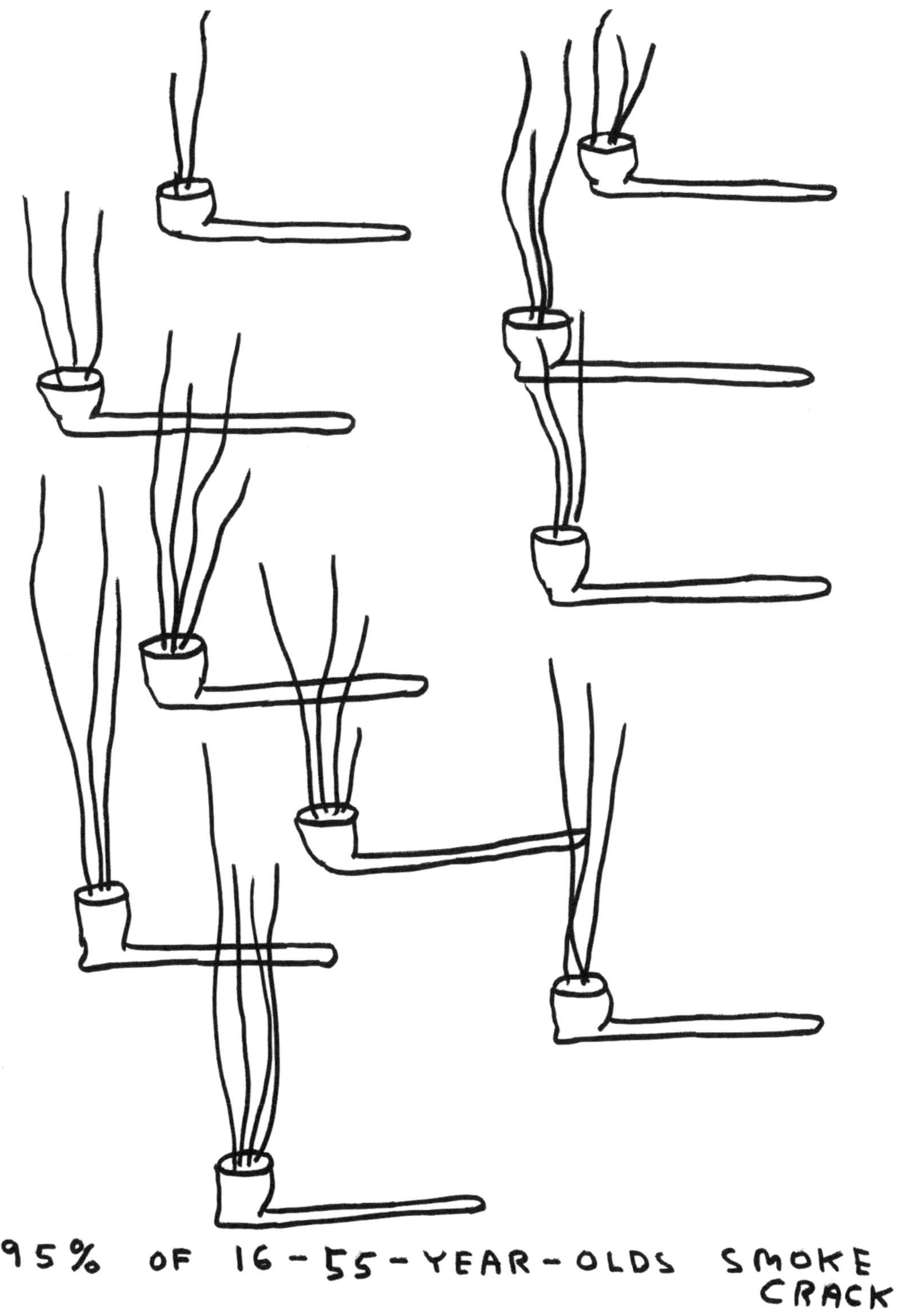

95% OF 16-55-YEAR-OLDS SMOKE CRACK

PROTECTING CITIZENS

AVOID LOCATING VULNERABLE CITIZENS
IN FROST-PRONE AREAS
THIN-SKINNED CITIZENS CAN BE
PROTECTED FROM THE ELEMENTS
WITH PLASTIC SHEETING
THOUGH CARE SHOULD BE TAKEN:
KEEP POLYTHENE FROM TOUCHING
THEM AS THIS CAN LEAD TO
CONDENSATION AND ROTTING.
USE THIS METHOD
ONLY IF FROSTS ARE FORECAST
AS MANY TEMPERATE INDIVIDUALS
NEED EXPOSURE TO COLD WEATHER
TO BREAK THIER SEASONAL DORMANC
AND POLLINATING INSECTS
NEED TO ACCESS THEM
DURING THE DAY

THINKING THE UNTHINKABL

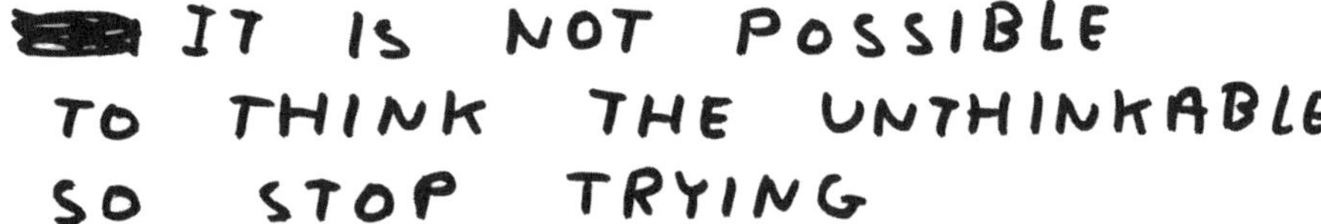

IT IS NOT POSSIBLE
TO THINK THE UNTHINKABLE
SO STOP TRYING

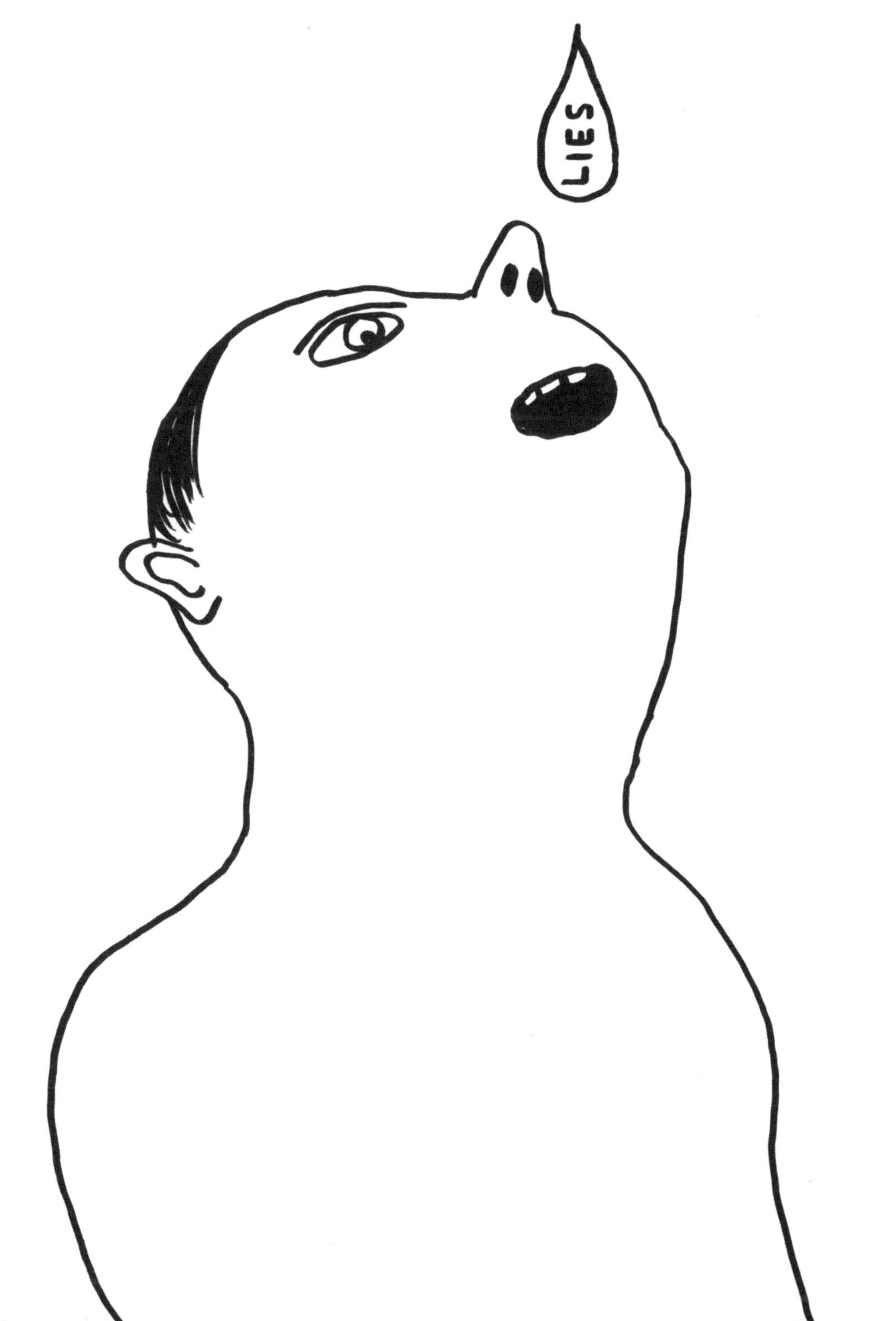

LIES

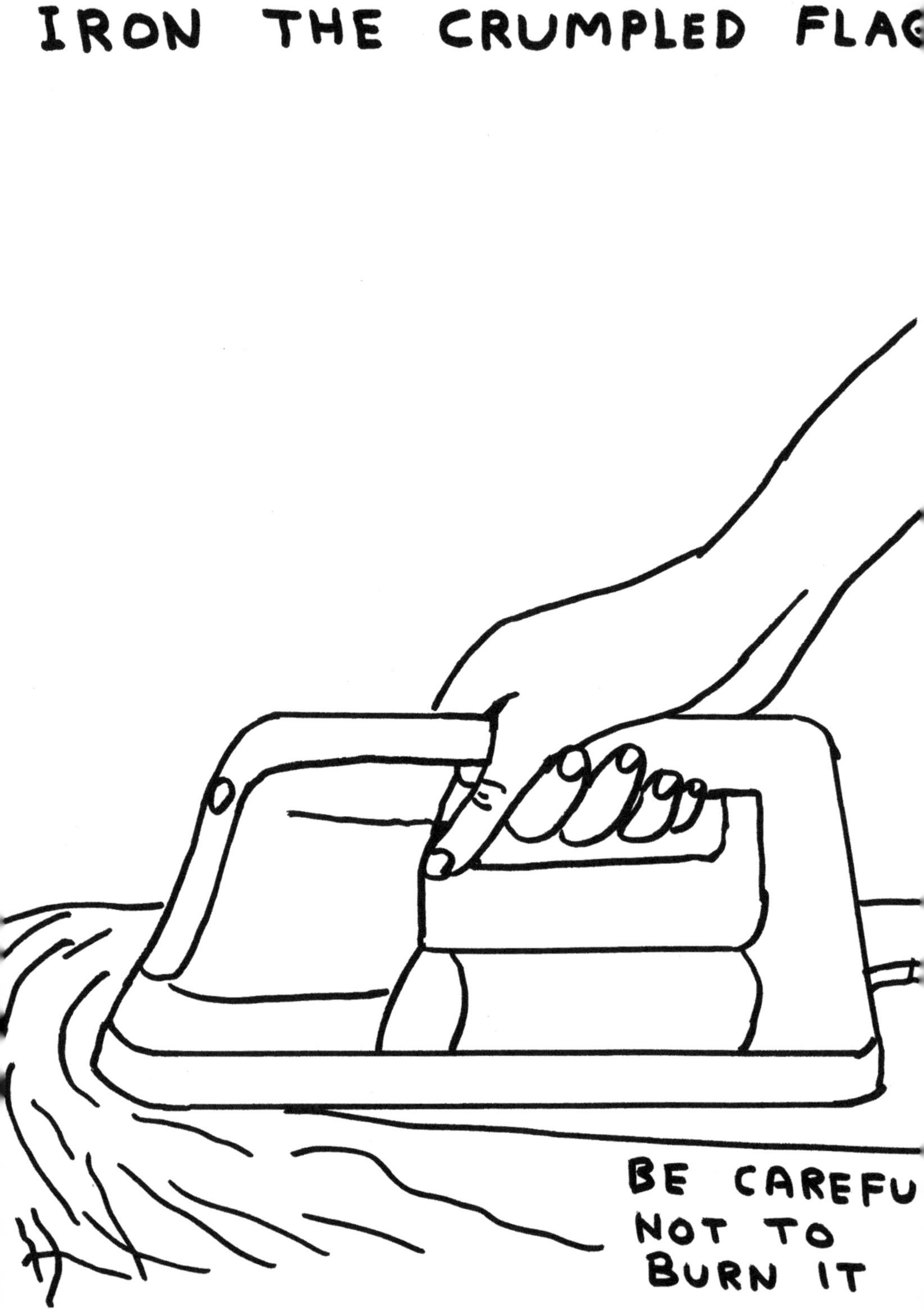

IRON THE CRUMPLED FLAG
BE CAREFUL NOT TO BURN IT

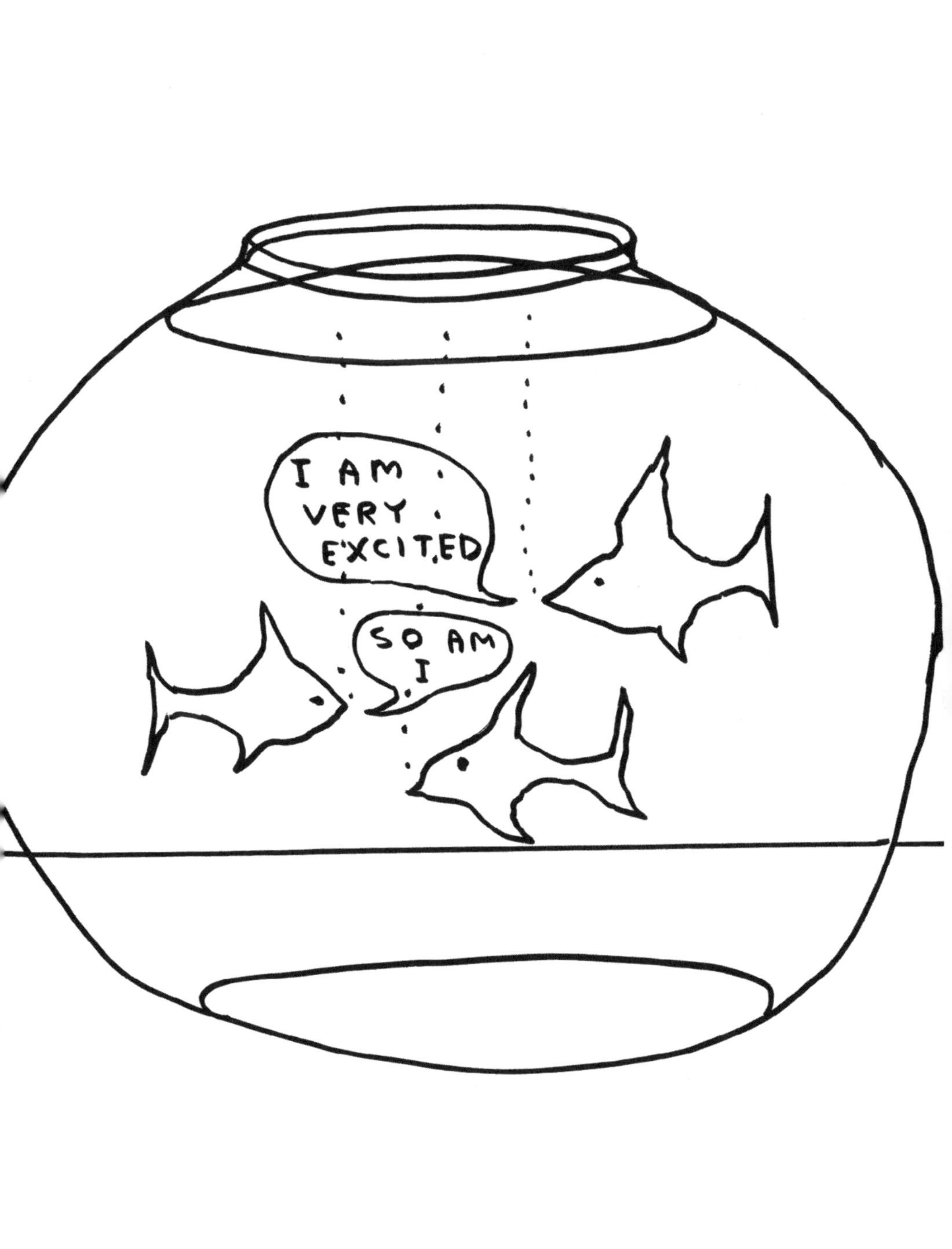

I AM VERY EXCITED
SO AM I

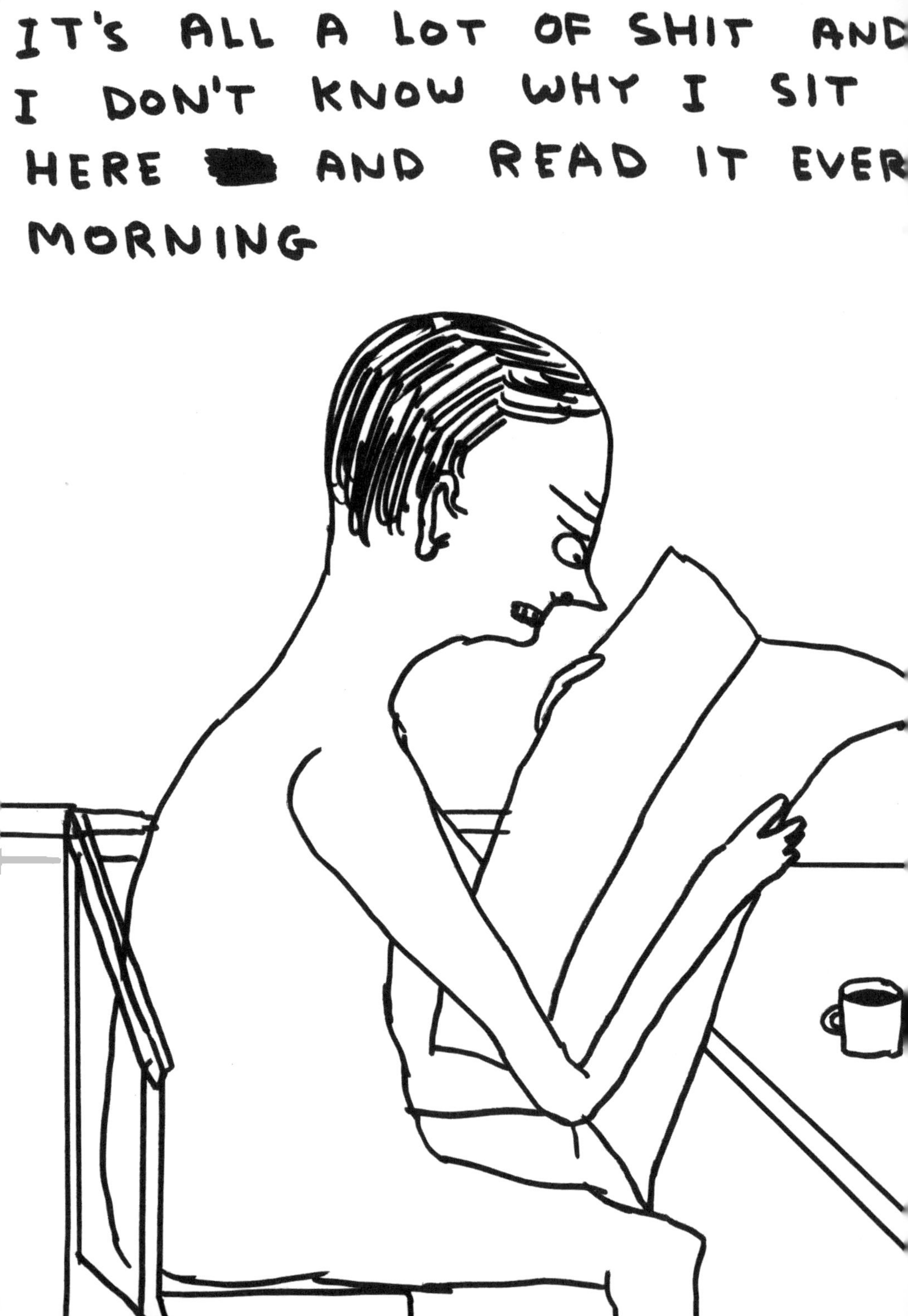
IT'S ALL A LOT OF SHIT AND
I DON'T KNOW WHY I SIT
HERE AND READ IT EVER
MORNING

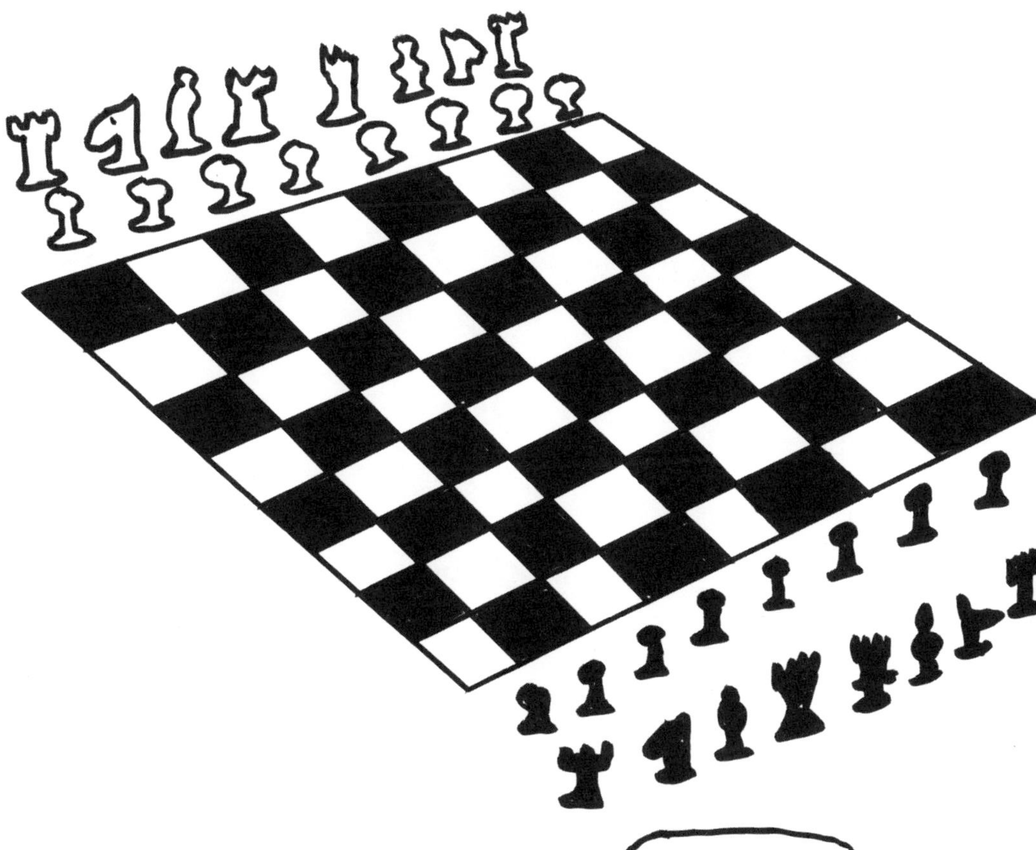

I DON'T KNOW HOW TO PLAY
I ALSO DON'T KNOW HOW TO PLAY

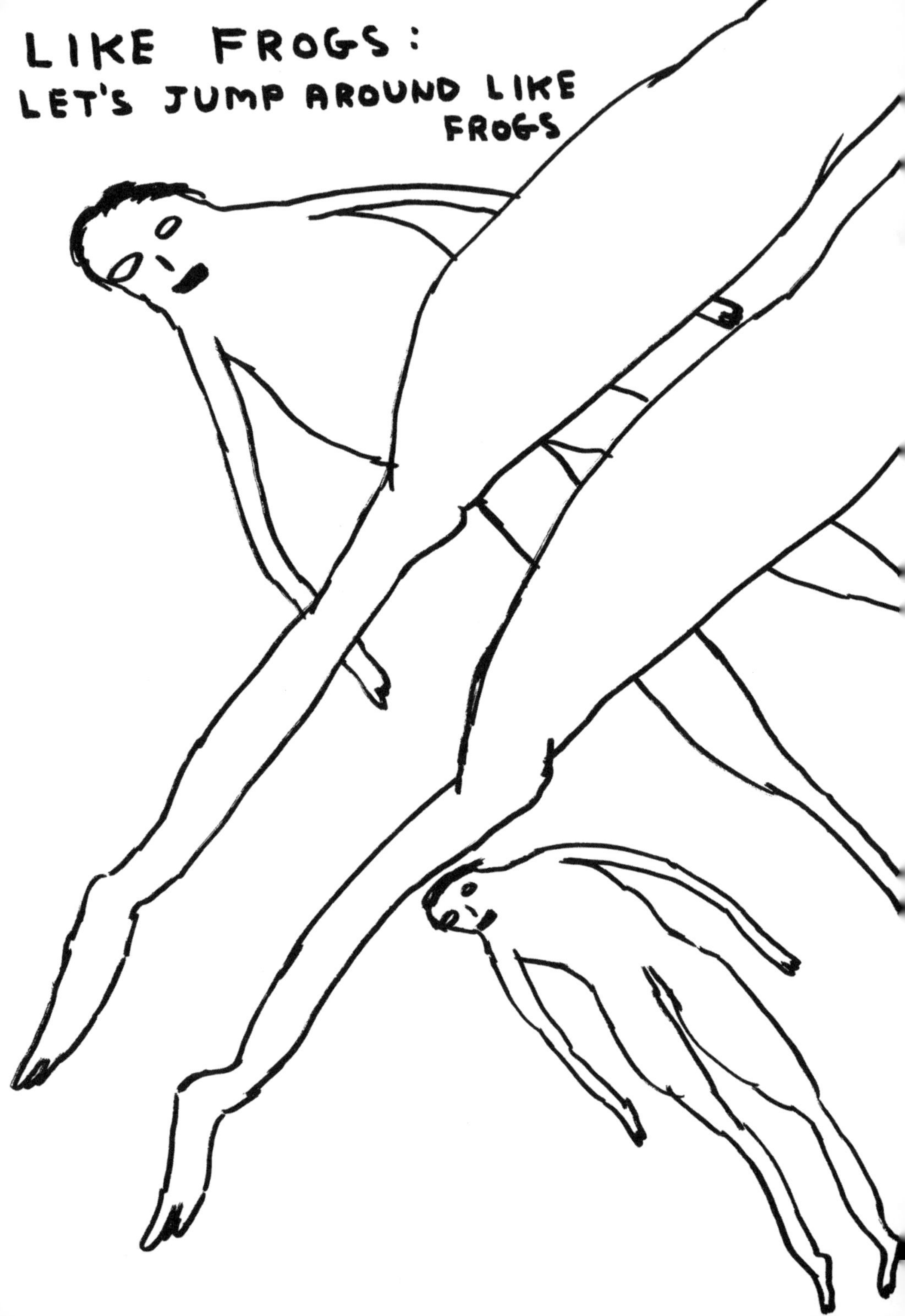
LIKE FROGS:
LET'S JUMP AROUND LIKE
FROGS

INTEGRATION

WE ARE OBLIGED TO INTEGRATE
LIKE VEGETABLES IN A STEW

ARBITRARY BORDERS

UNMANNED
TO KEEP OUT NO ONE IN PARTICULAR

STATISTICS

GATHERED BY A COMBINE HARVESTER
MADE INTO BALES
AND LEFT IN A FIELD
LIKE STRAW
WHEN WINTER COMES
ANIMALS WILL FEED ON THEM

EXCHANGE OF IDEAS

YOU GIVE ME AN IDEA:
A STRATEGY TO TACKLE INDIFFERENCE
I GIVE YOU AN IDEA:
THE WEATHER IS CONTROLLED BY
MY CAT'S THOUGHTS

TARGETS

ALL TARGETS ARE TO BE MADE BIGGER
AND BROUGHT CLOSER TO US
SO WE CAN ALL HIT THEM

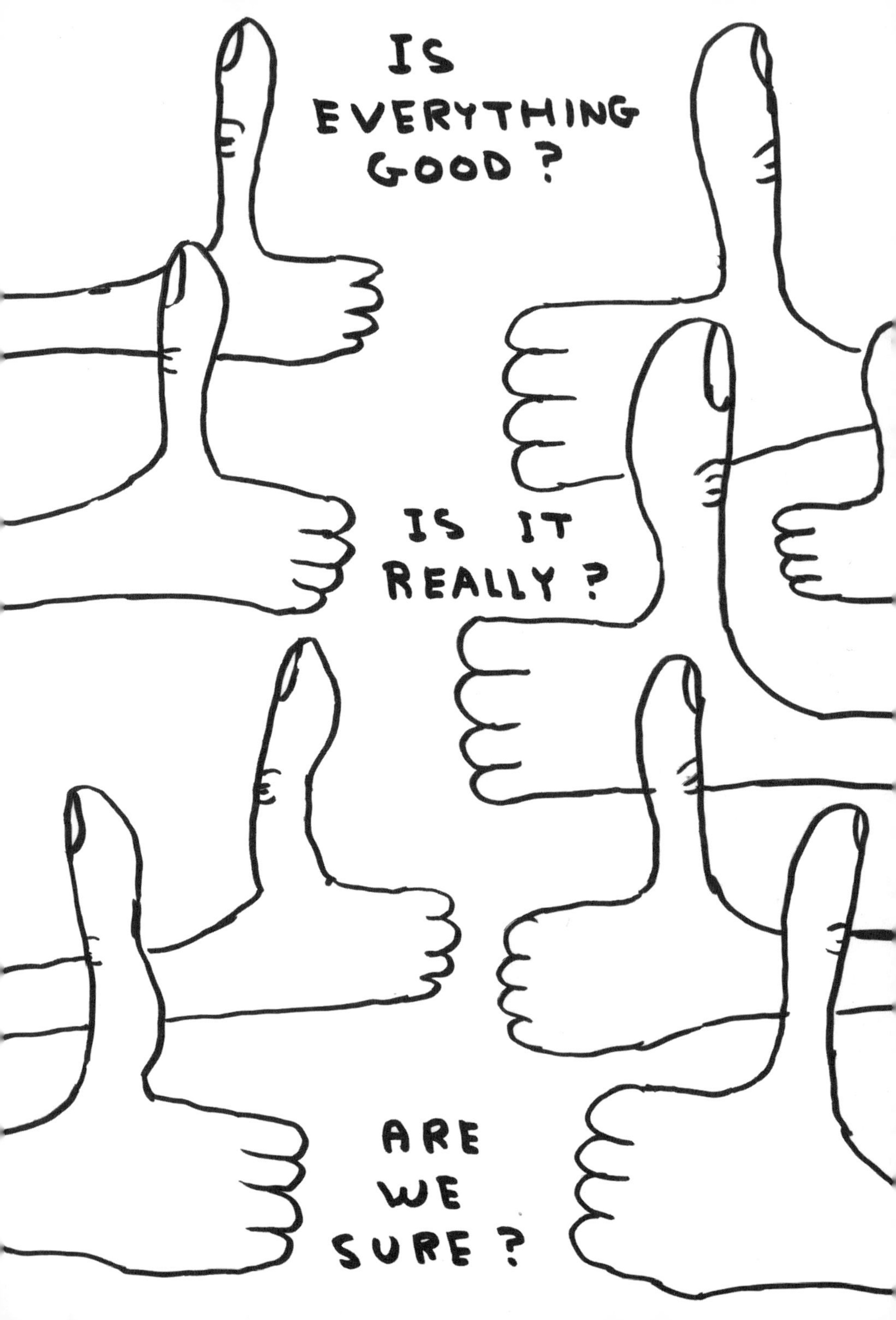

IS
EVERYTHING
GOOD ?
IS IT
REALLY ?
ARE
WE
SURE ?

F YOU NEED ME I SHALL
E AT THE BOTTOM OF
HE WELL

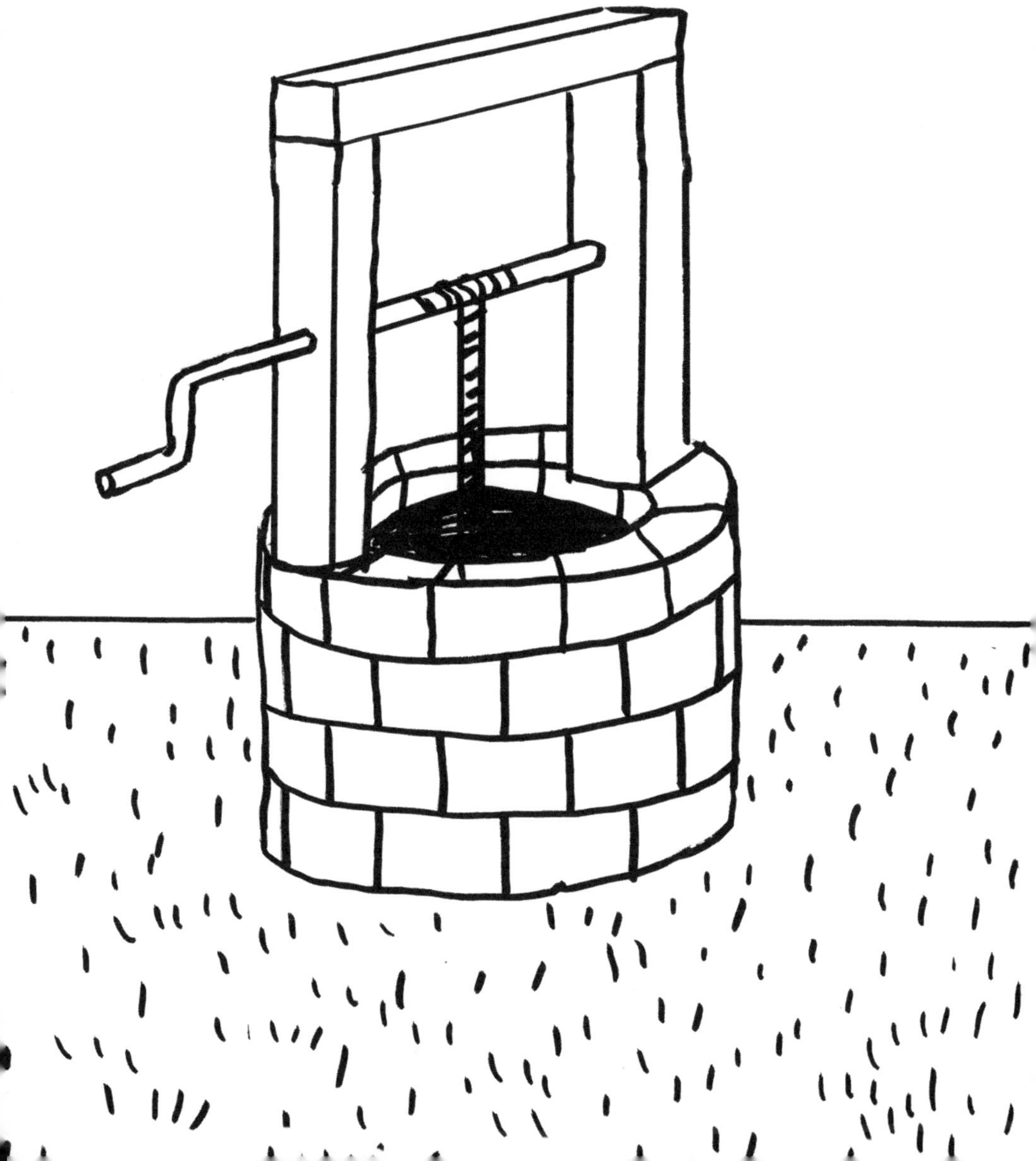

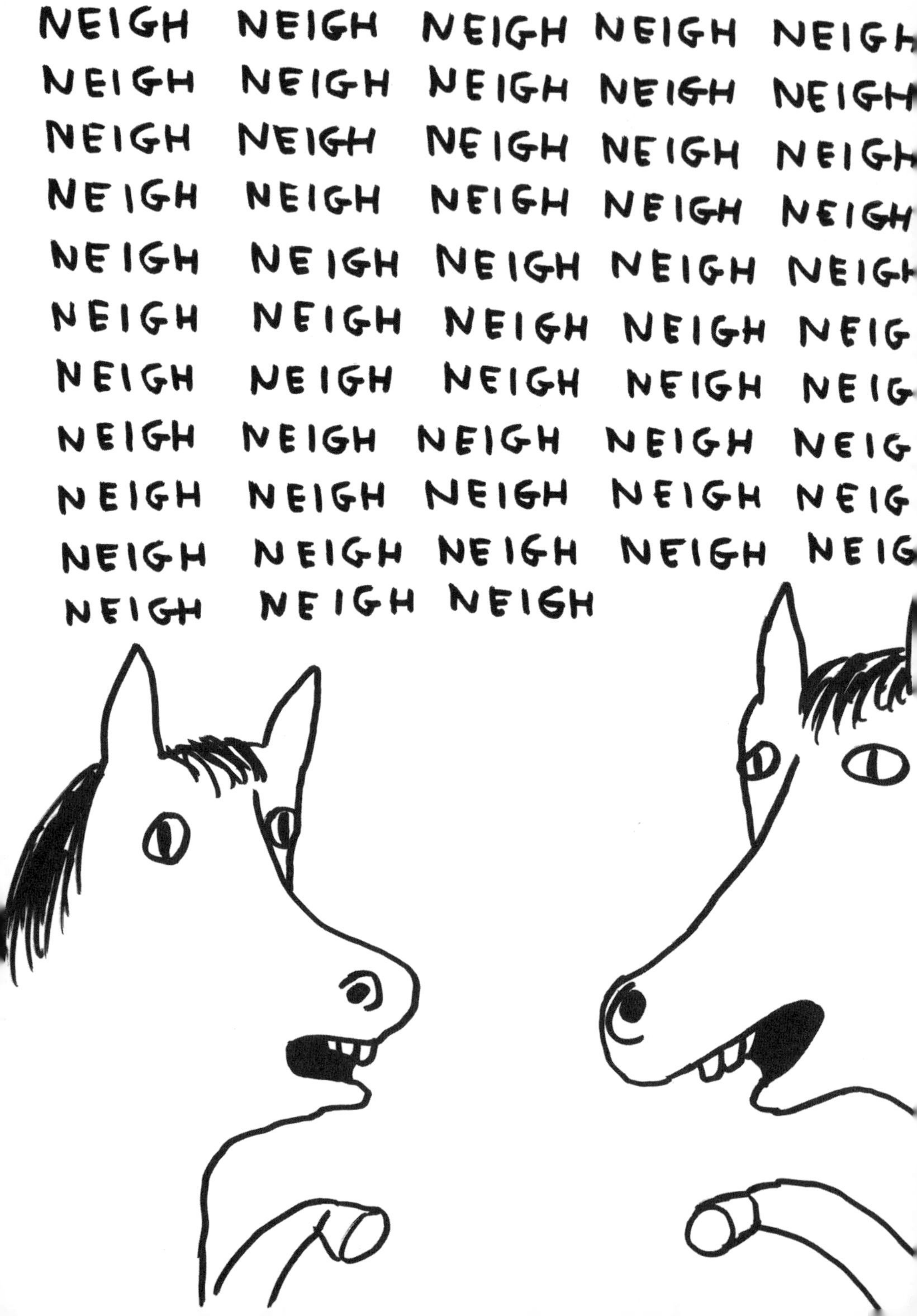

NEIGH NEIGH NEIGH NEIGH NEIGH
NEIGH NEIGH NEIGH NEIGH NEIGH
NEIGH NEIGH NEIGH NEIGH NEIGH
NEIGH NEIGH NEIGH NEIGH NEIGH
NEIGH NEIGH NEIGH NEIGH NEIGH
NEIGH NEIGH NEIGH NEIGH NEIG
NEIGH NEIGH NEIGH NEIGH NEIG
NEIGH NEIGH NEIGH NEIGH NEIG
NEIGH NEIGH NEIGH NEIGH NEIG
NEIGH NEIGH NEIGH NEIGH NEIG
NEIGH NEIGH NEIGH

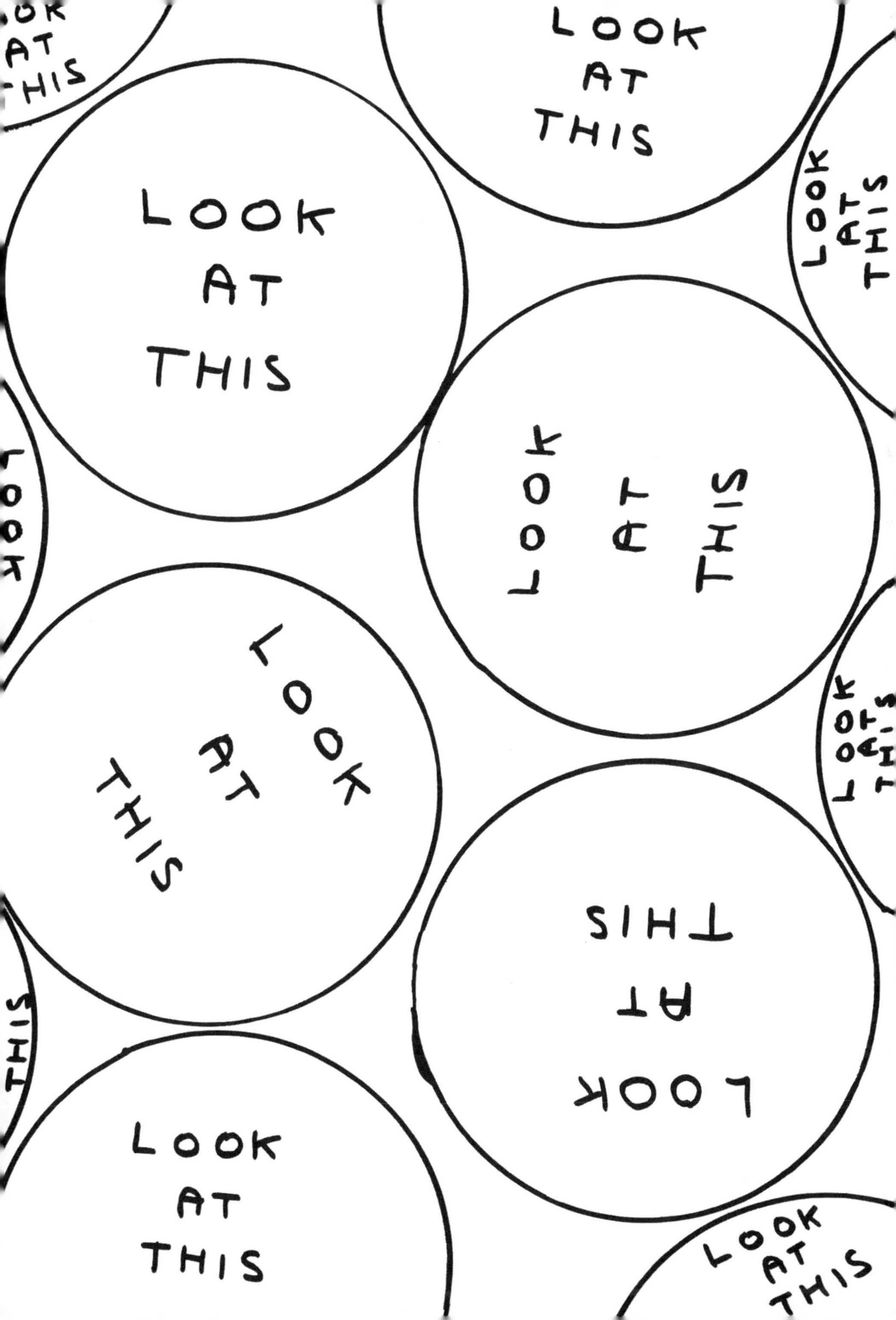

LOOK AT THIS
LOOK AT THIS
LOOK AT THIS
LOOK AT THIS
LOOK AT THIS
LOOK AT THIS
LOOK AT THIS
LOOK AT THIS
LOOK AT THIS
LOOK AT THIS
LOOK AT THIS

HEADLESS BASTARDS

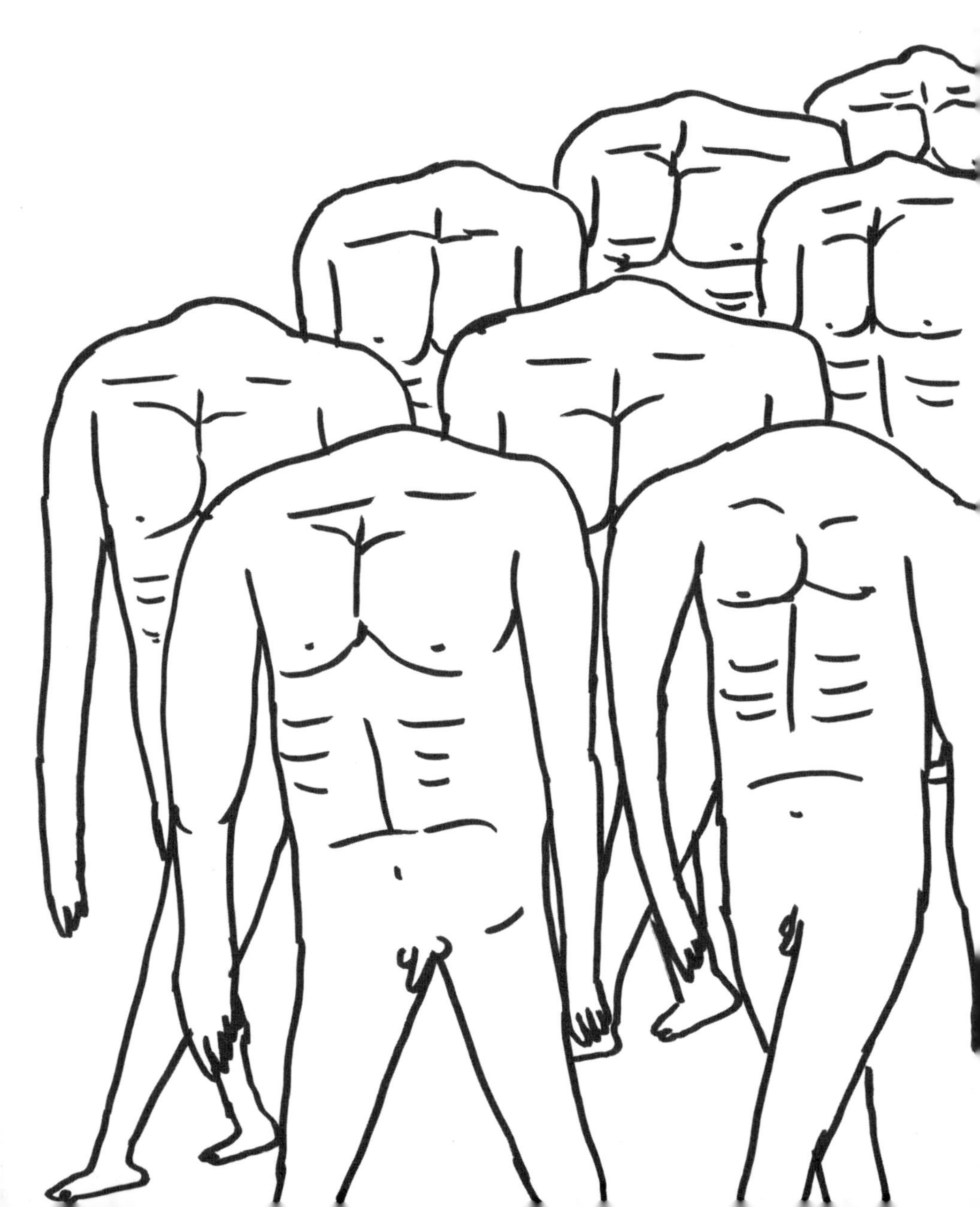

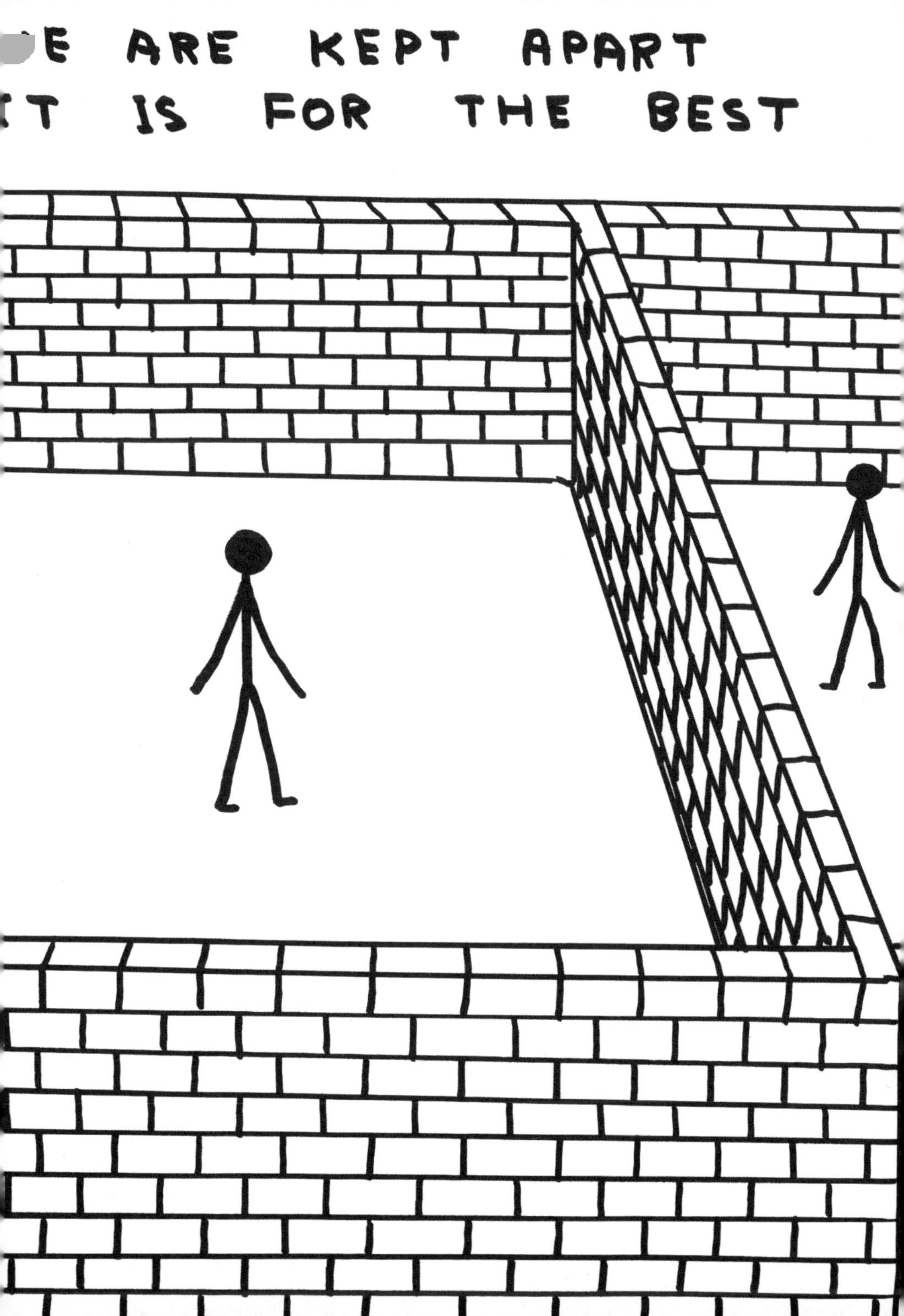

E ARE KEPT APART
T IS FOR THE BEST

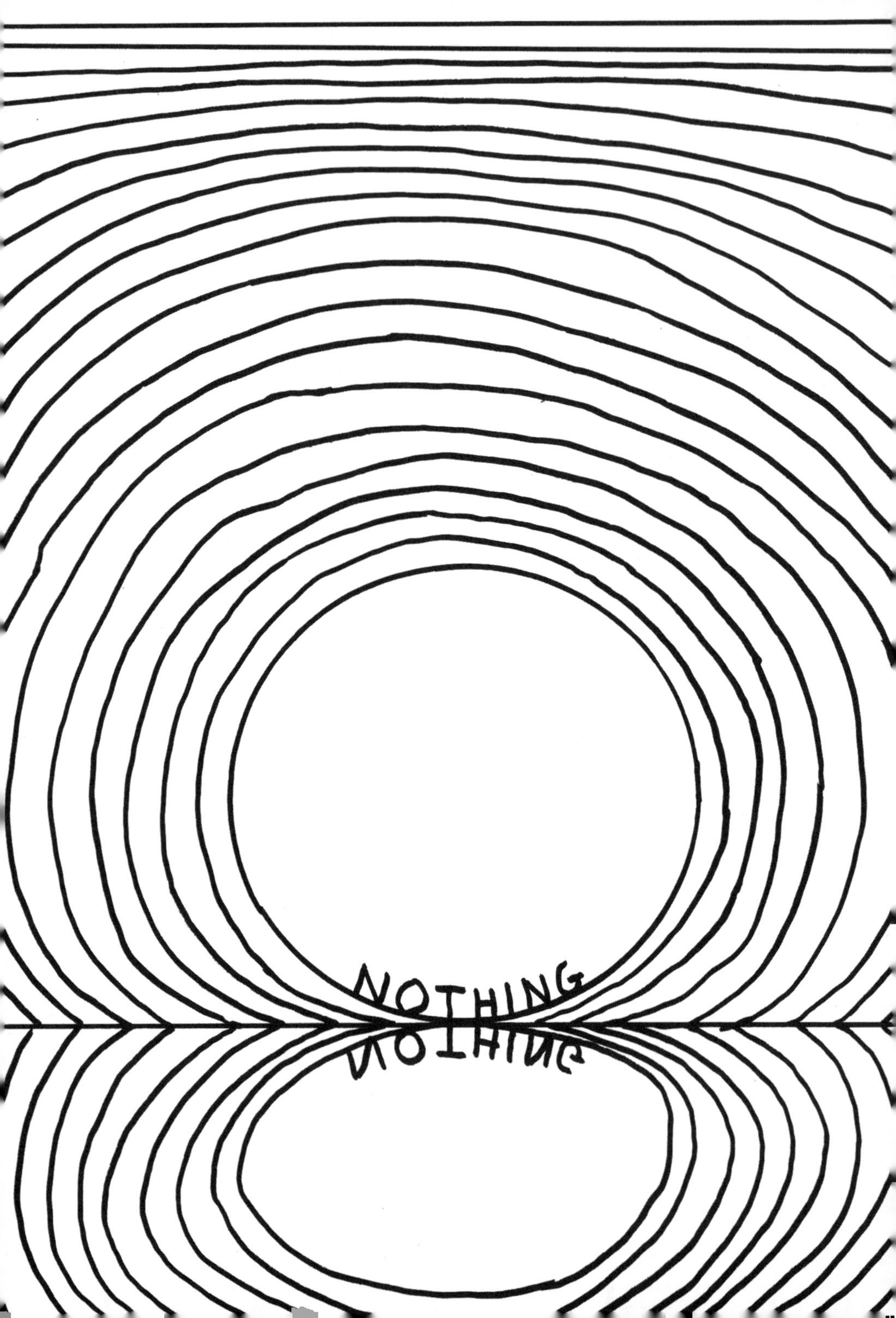

NOTHING

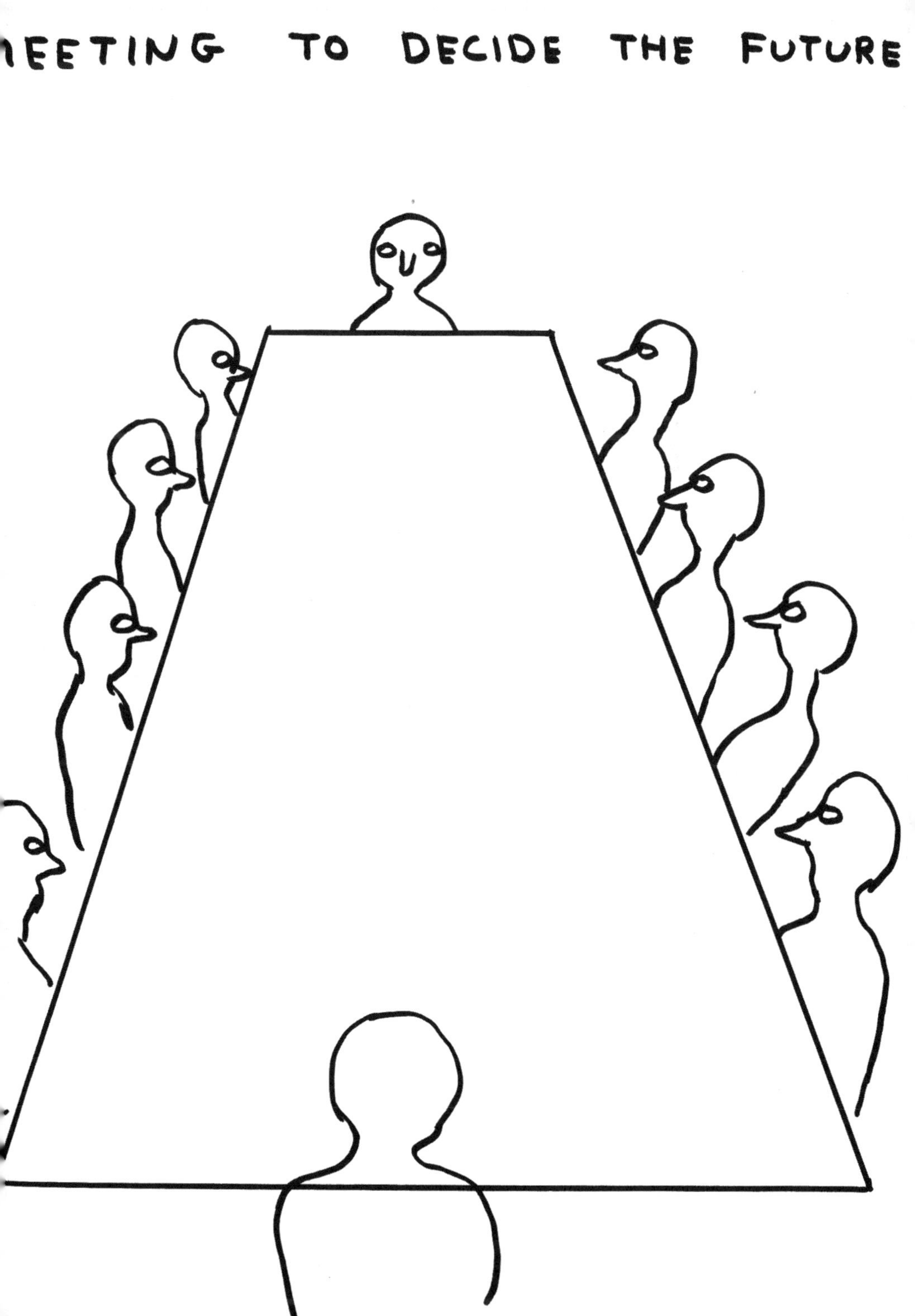
MEETING TO DECIDE THE FUTURE

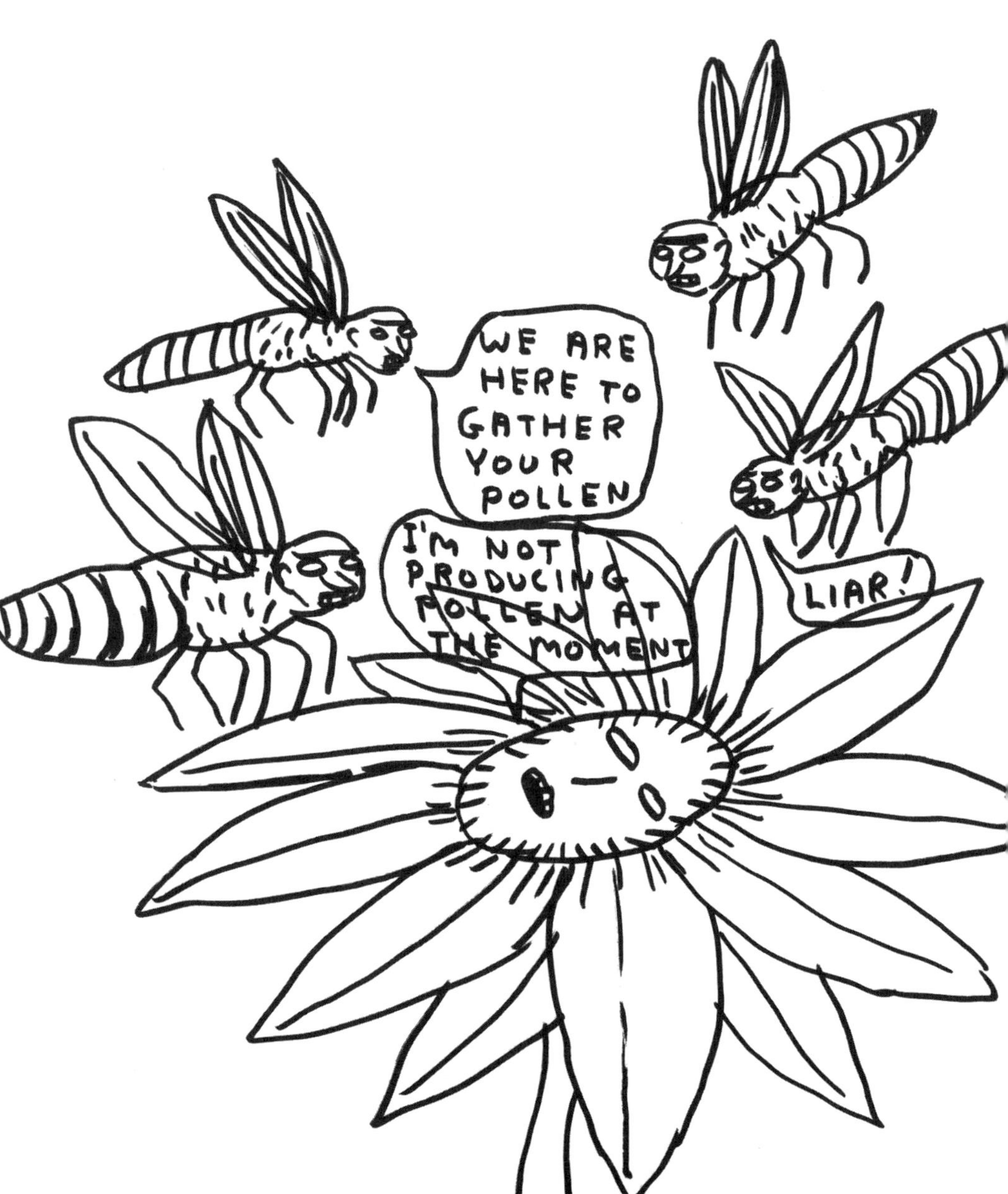

WE ARE HERE TO GATHER YOUR POLLEN
I'M NOT PRODUCING POLLEN AT THE MOMENT
LIAR!

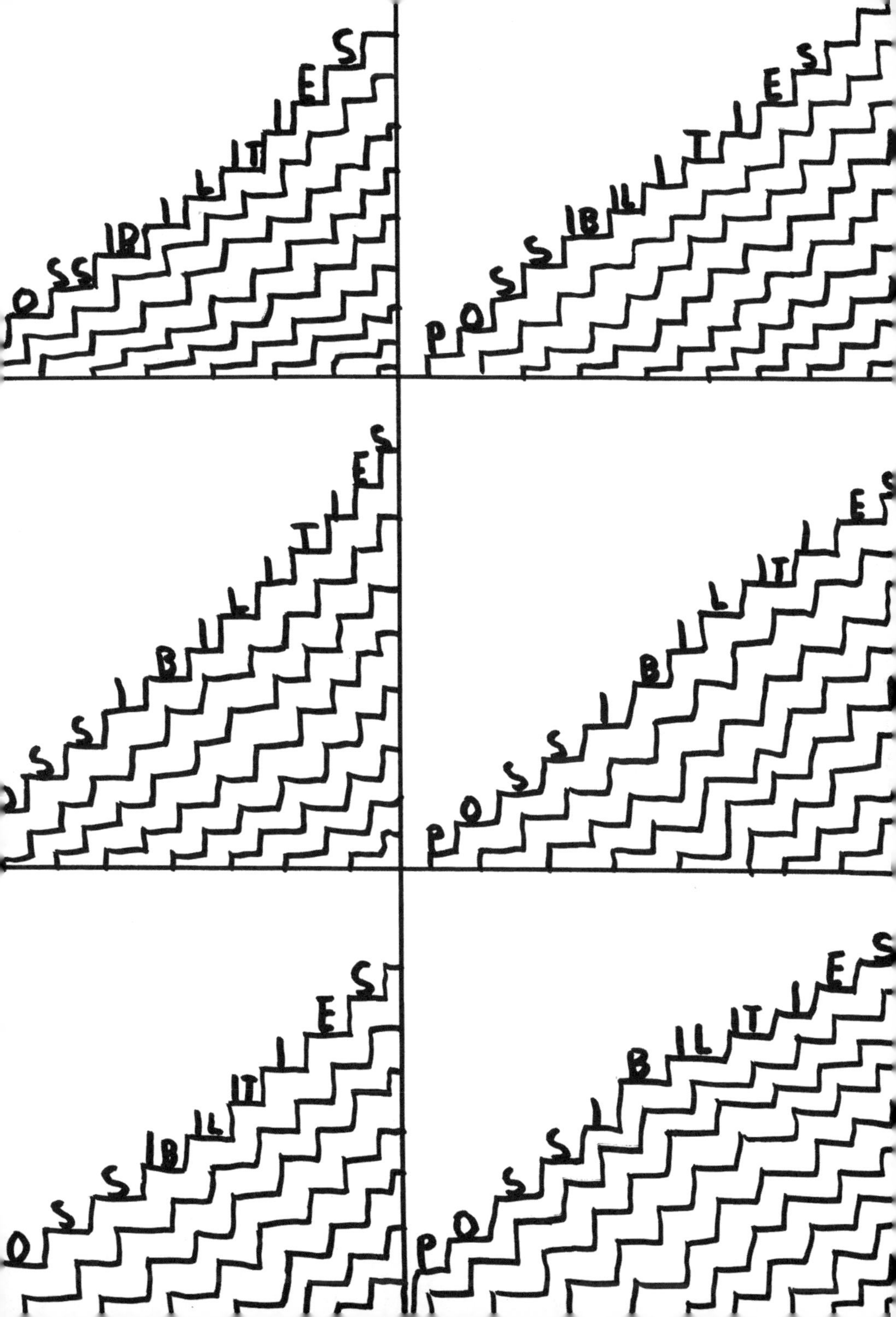

POSSIBILITIES
POSSIBILITIES
POSSIBILITIES
POSSIBILITIES
POSSIBILITIES
POSSIBILITIES

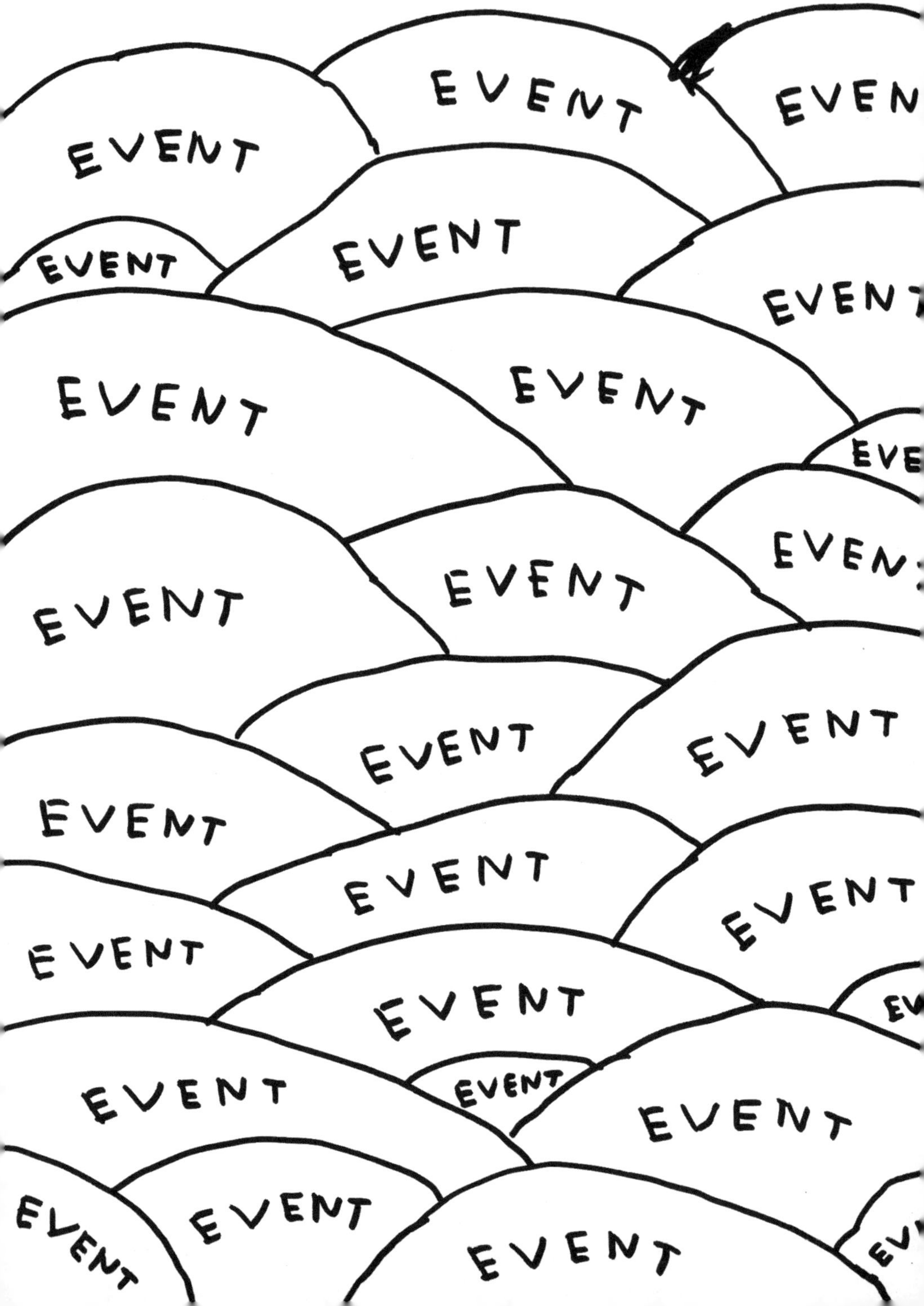

EVENT
EVENT
EVENT
EVENT
EVENT
EVENT
EVENT
EVE
EVENT
EVEN
EVENT
EVENT
EVENT
EVENT
EVENT
EVENT
EVENT
EVENT
EVENT
EVENT
EVENT
EVENT
EVENT
EV
EVENT
EV

CONVERSATIONS

LAH LAH LAH LAH LAH	TALK TALK TALK TALK TALK TALK TALK TALK TALK TALK	BLAB BLAB BLAB BLAB BLAB
AK YAK AK YAK AK YAK AK YAK	CHITTY CHATTY CHITTY CHATTY CHITTY	YADDA YADDA YADDA ~~────~~ YADDA
ITCH MOAN BITCH MOAN BITCH	BLAH BLAH BLAH BLAH BLAH	BLAB BLAB BLAB BLAB BLAB
WOOF WOOF WOOF WOOF WOOF	YAK YAK YAK YAK YAK YAK YAK YAK	NER NER NER NER NER NER NER NER

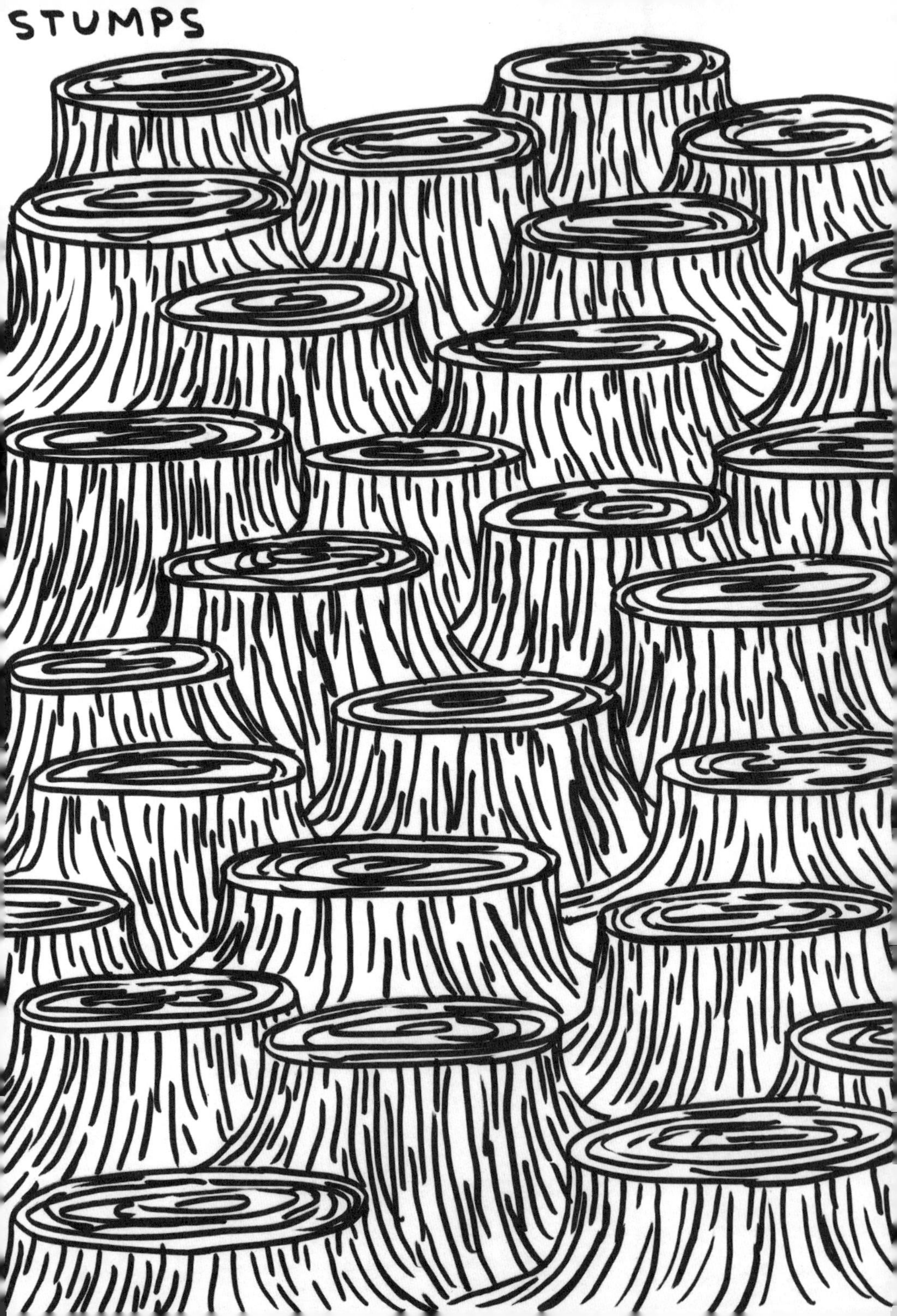
STUMPS

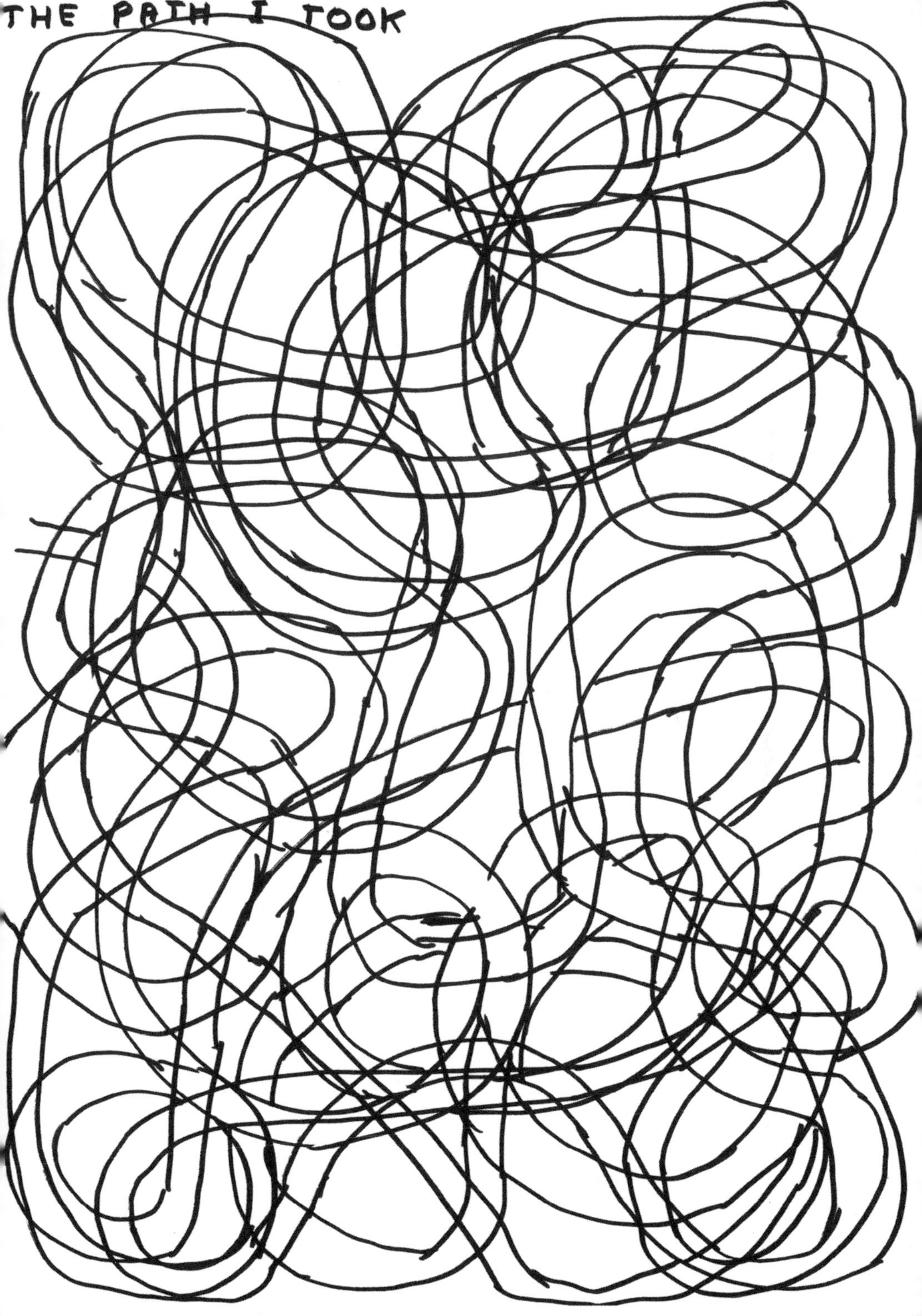
THE PATH I TOOK

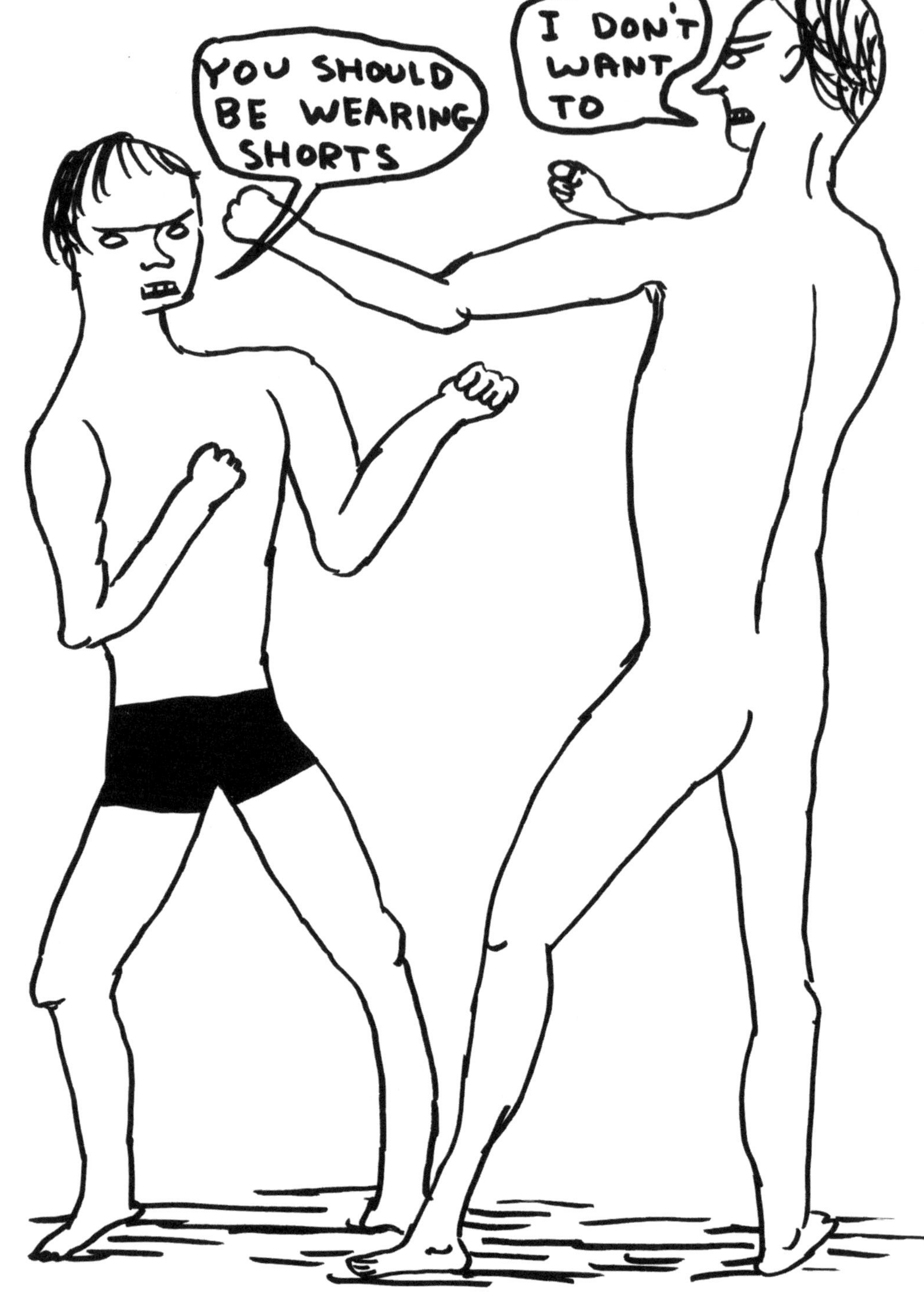

YOU SHOULD BE WEARING SHORTS
I DON'T WANT TO

PUPPETS

THEIR RIGHTS MUST BE RESPECTED

CRUST OF SOCIETY

EVENTUALLY IT WILL FALL OFF
AND A NEW ONE WILL FORM IN ITS PLACE

BRUISES

BRUISES OCCUR
WHEN YOU BANG A PART OF YOUR BODY
AGAINST SOMETHING HARD
LIKE A WALL
OR A DOOR
OR AN ANVIL
BRUISES CAN BE REMOVED
WITH A PENCIL ERASER
NOT MANY PEOPLE KNOW THIS
BUT IT REALLY WORKS

INSPECTION TIME

WE DID AN INSPECTION
WE INSPECTED YOU
WHILE YOU WERE ASLEEP
YOU APPEAR TO BE IN GOOD ORDER
WE WERE IMPRESSED
WE WILL INSPECT YOU AGAIN
IN ABOUT A YEAR

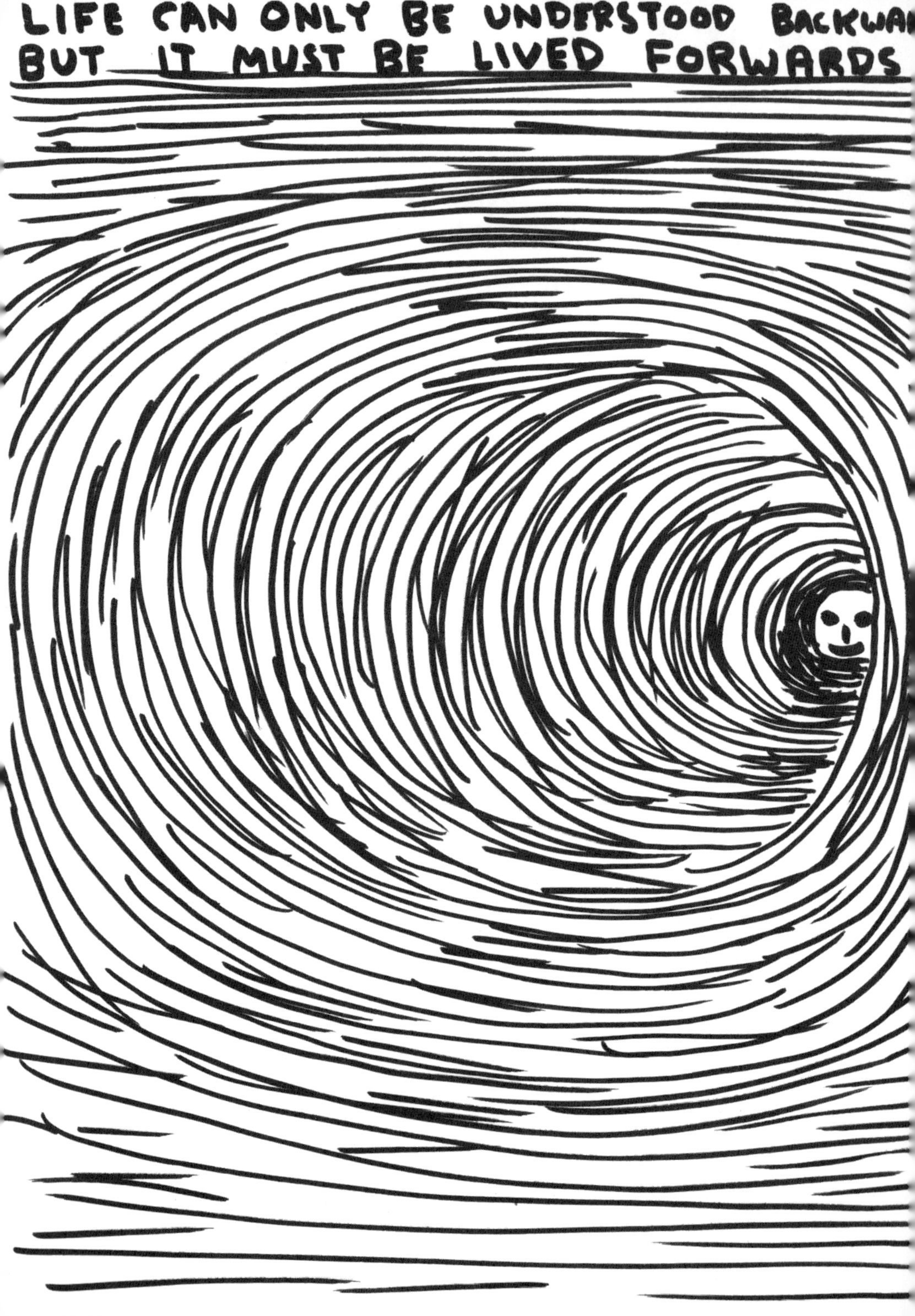

LIFE CAN ONLY BE UNDERSTOOD BACKWARDS
BUT IT MUST BE LIVED FORWARDS

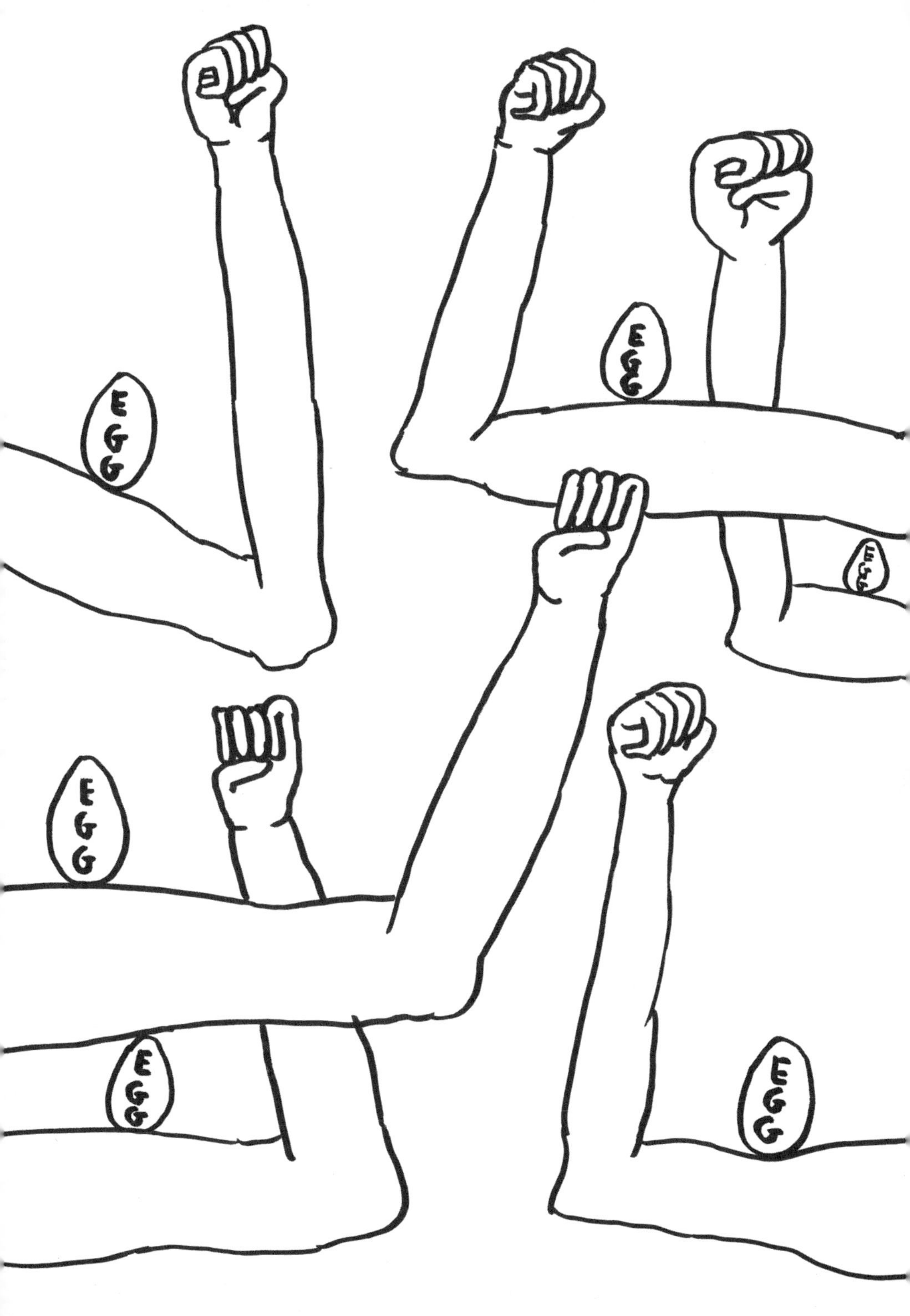

EGG
EGG
EGG
EGG
EGG
EGG

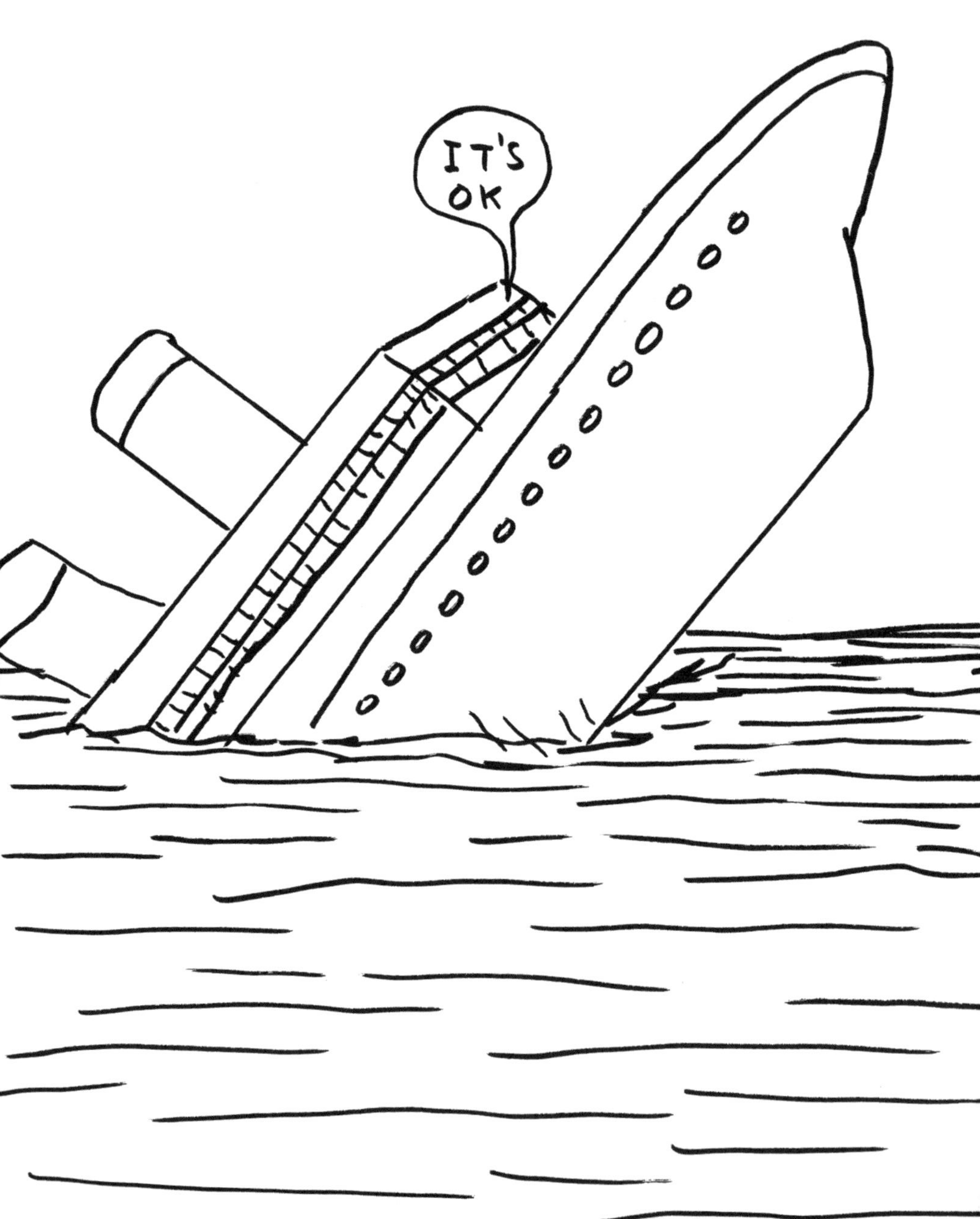
IT'S
OK

CHAPTER EIGHT
SOCIAL STRATIFICATION

SOCIAL STRATIFICATION
THE CREAM RISES TO THE TOP
THE CRUD STAYS AT THE BOTTOM
THE CROUTONS STAY IN THE MIDDLE
THE CROUTONS ARE MADE OF STALE BRE

THE GAP BETWEEN THE RICH AND POOR
THE RICH ARE ON THE ROOF OF A TALL
BUILDING ONTOP OF A MOUNTAIN
THE POOR ARE ALSO ON THE ROOF OF
A TALL BUILDING ON TOP OF A MOUNTAI
BUT THE MOUNTAIN IS ON THE
OTHER SIDE OF THE PLANET

DISTRIBUTION OF RESOURCES
BY SMALL PEOPLE ON ELECTRIC CARTS

DISTRIBUTION OF MARBLES
IT COULD BE IMPROVED
IT WILL BE IMPROVED

SCARCE RESOURCES
SPARKLING WATER

EVEN-HANDEDNESS
BOTH HANDS MUST BE EVEN:
SIMILAR SIZES, ETC.

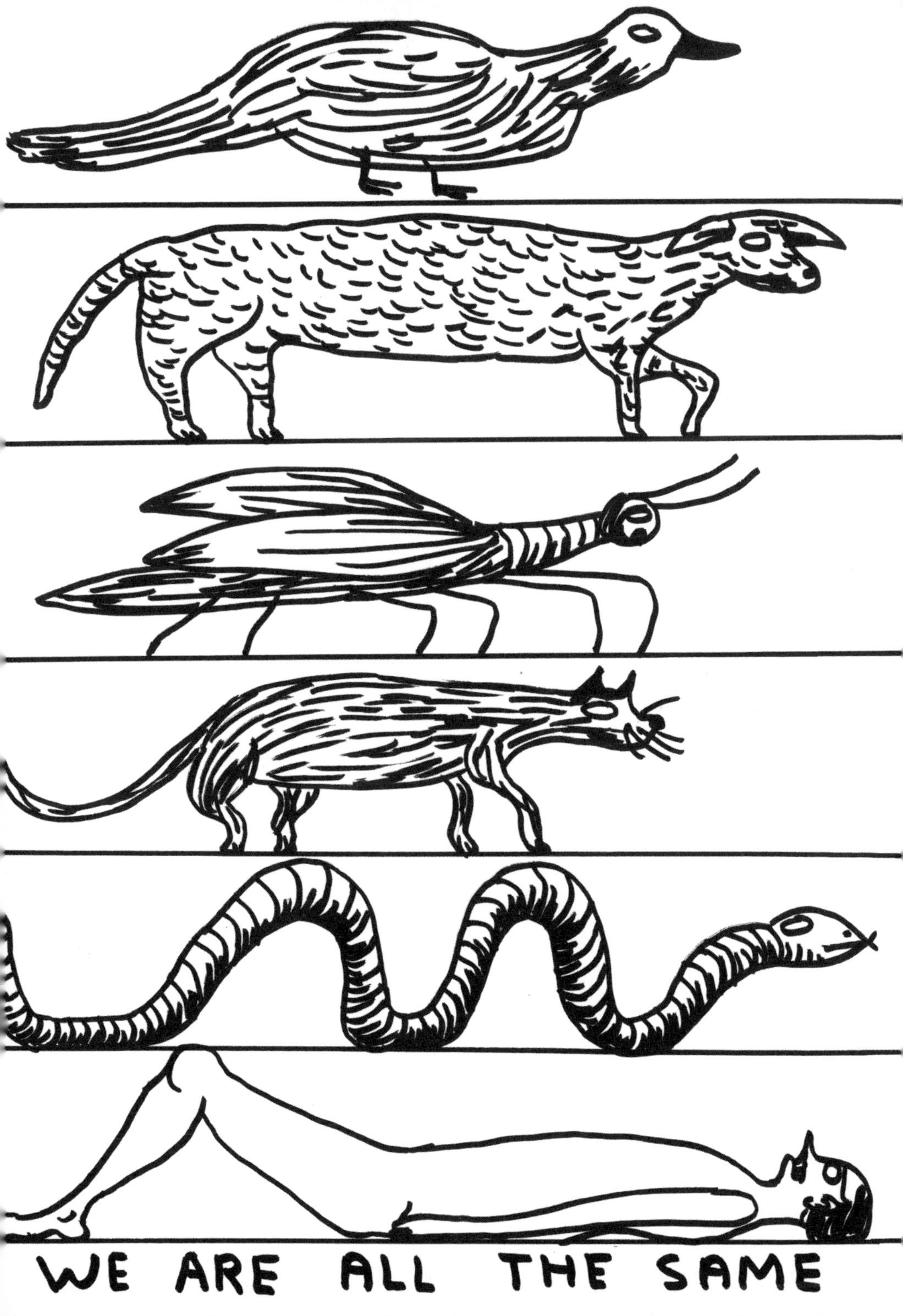

WE ARE ALL THE SAME

BACK-SCRATCHER

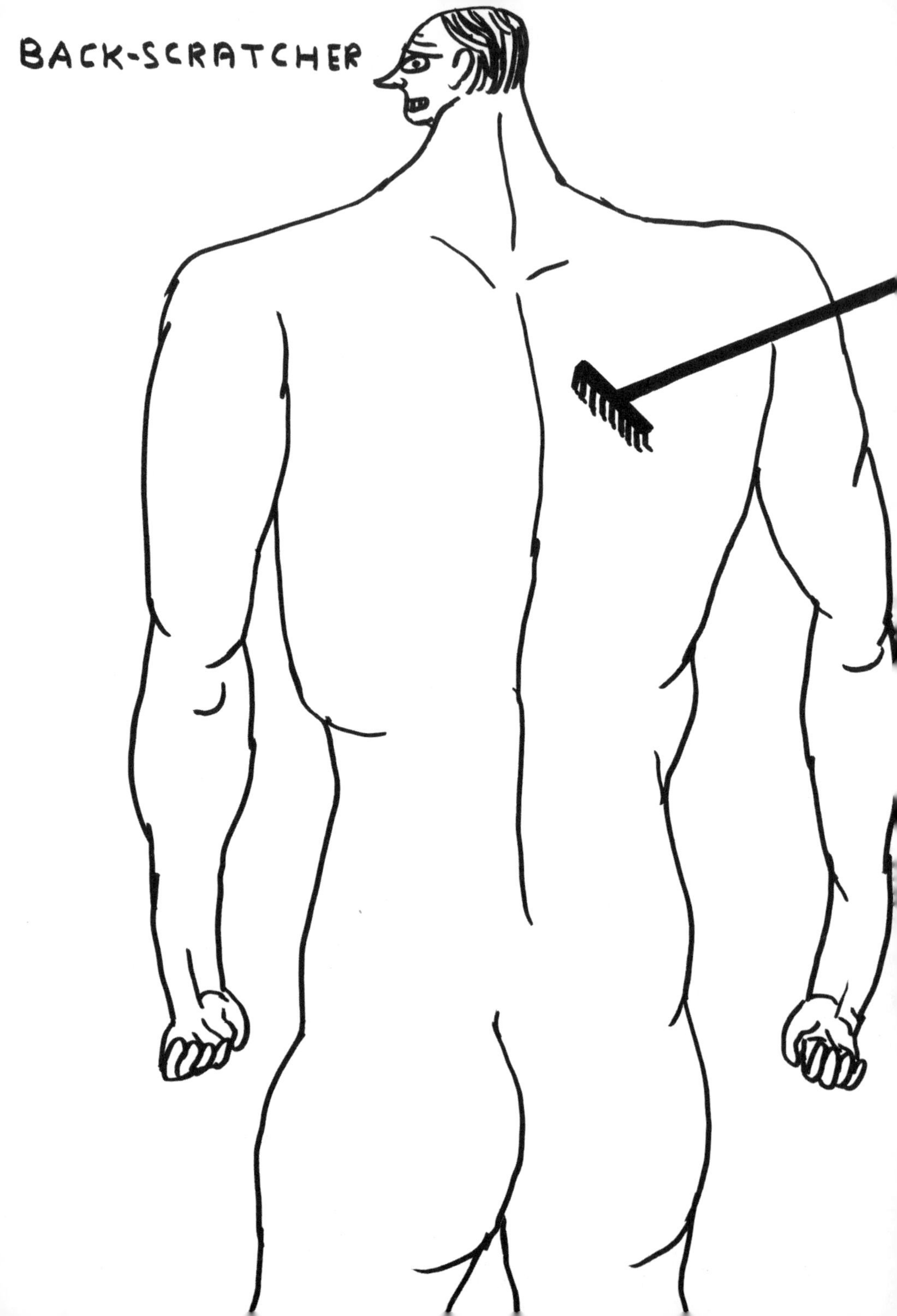

IN THE CONTROL ROOM

YOU THINK THAT YOU ARE IN
THE CONTROL ROOM
BUT YOU ARE NOT REALLY IN
THE CONTROL ROOM
YOU DON'T REALLY CONTROL ANYTHING
YOU DON'T EVEN CONTROL
YOUR OWN THOUGHTS

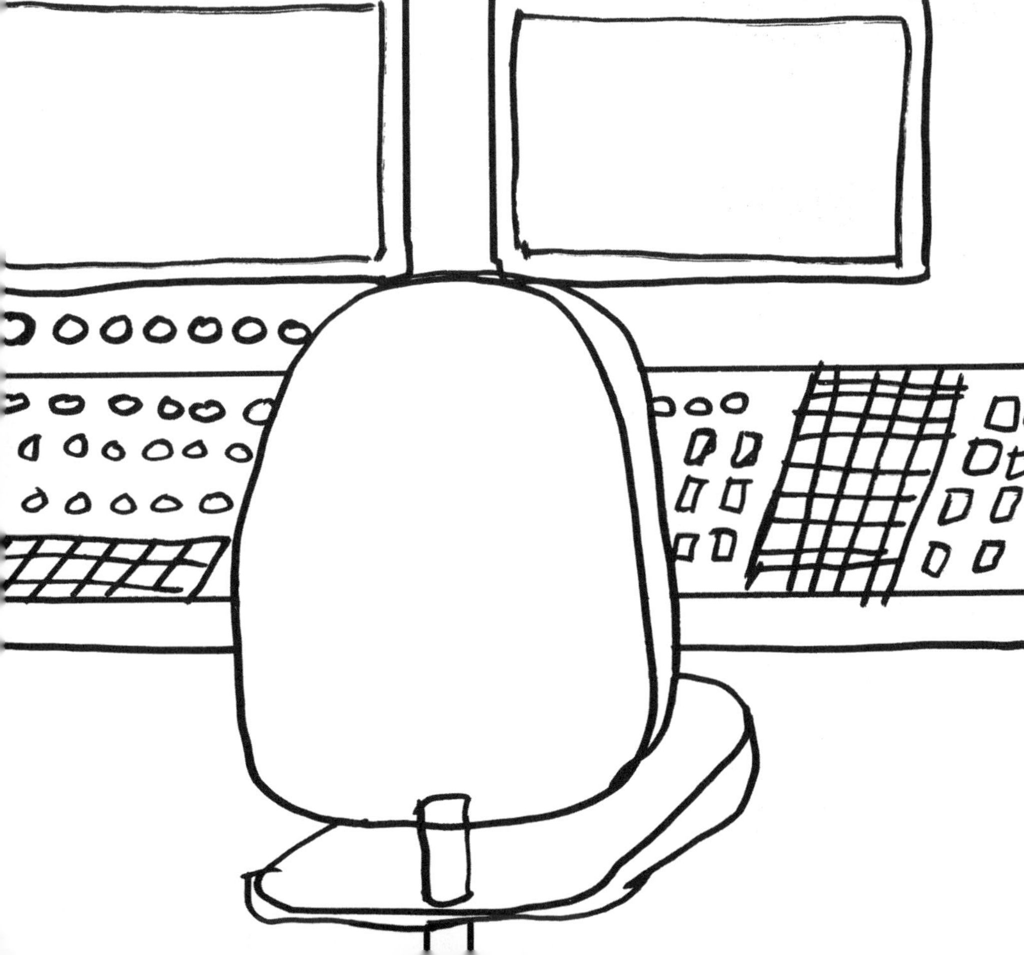

SYSTEM OF UNEQUAL REWARDS

YOU GIVE ME A LAPTOP COMPUTER
I GIVE YOU AN EGG CUP
YOU GIVE ME A GOLD WATCH
I GIVE YOU A WOOLLY HAT
YOU GIVE ME A MOTOR CAR
I GIVE YOU SOME SOUP
IT IS NOT FAIR
IT IS NOT AT ALL FAIR
BUT I DID NOT INVENT THE SYSTEM
IT WAS A PRE-EXISTING THING

STEPS ON THE STAIRCASE

GO CAREFULLY
UP THE STEPS
EACH STEP
EMITS A DIFFERENT CREAK

THE WIND

THE WIND WILL BLOW YOU AROUND
BECAUSE YOU ARE A LEAF

WILD ANIMALS

ALSO: CHILDREN

SHOULD HOUSEHOLD PETS BE ALLOWED TO VOTE?

YES.

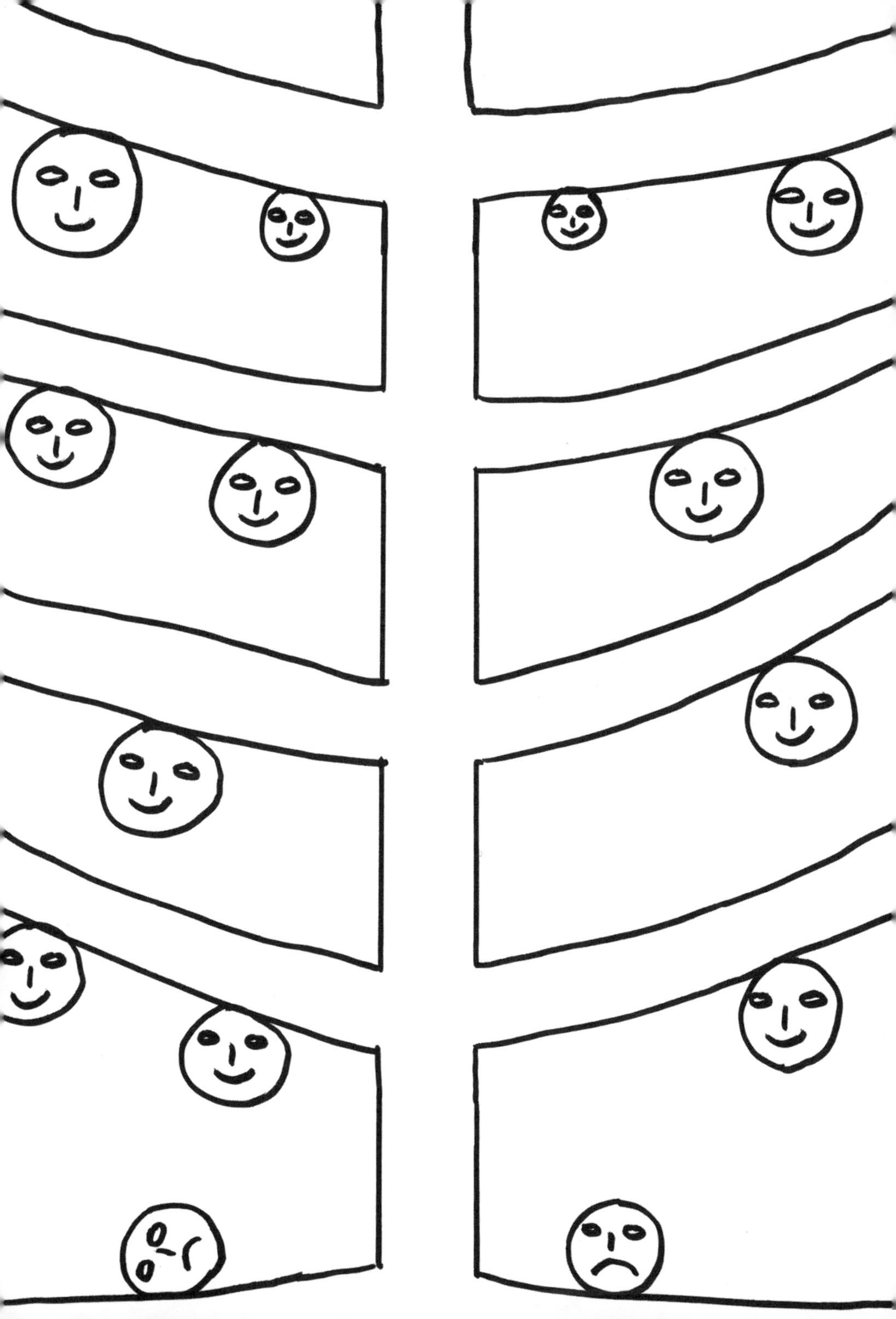

DRIVE FAST THROUG[H]
DEPRAVED AREA TO
AVOID DEGENERATES

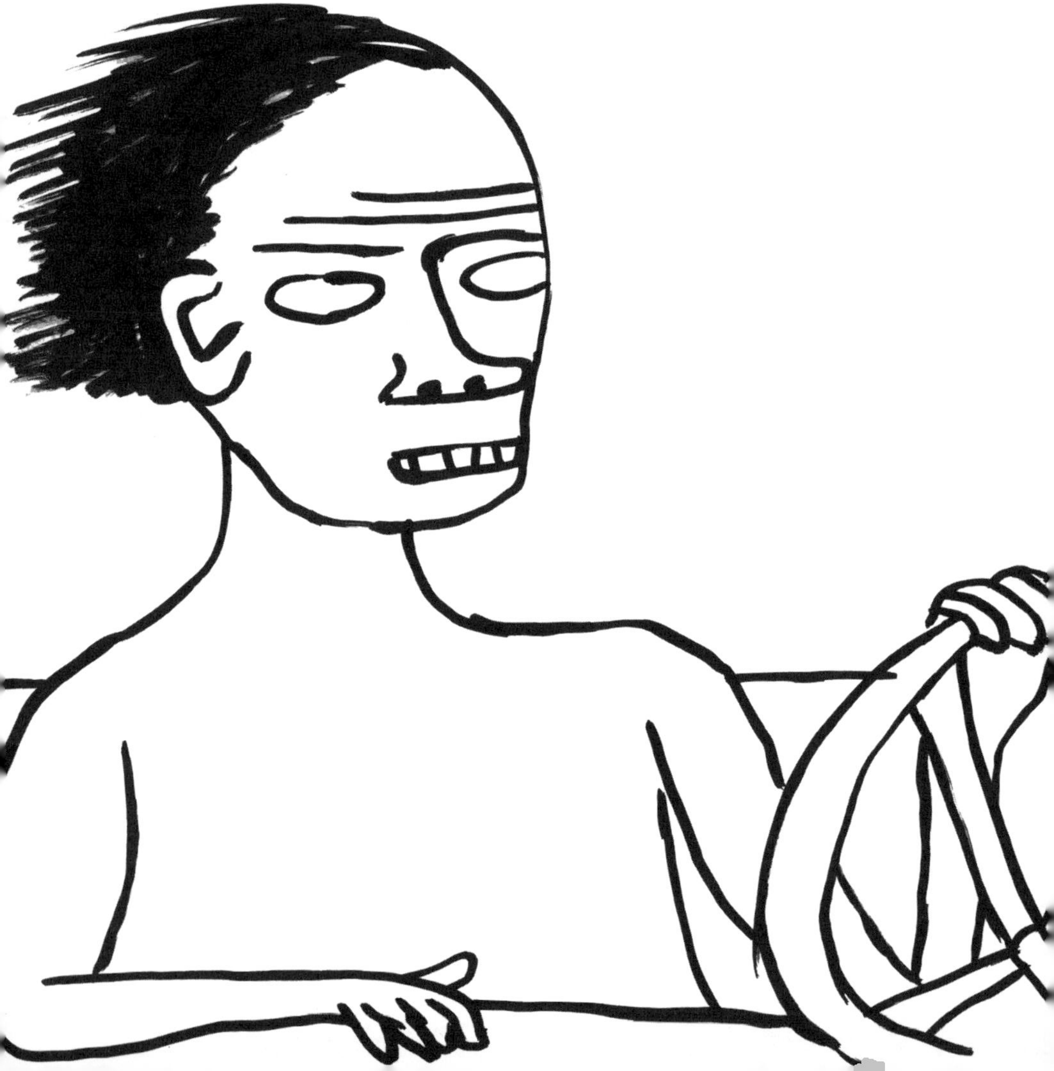

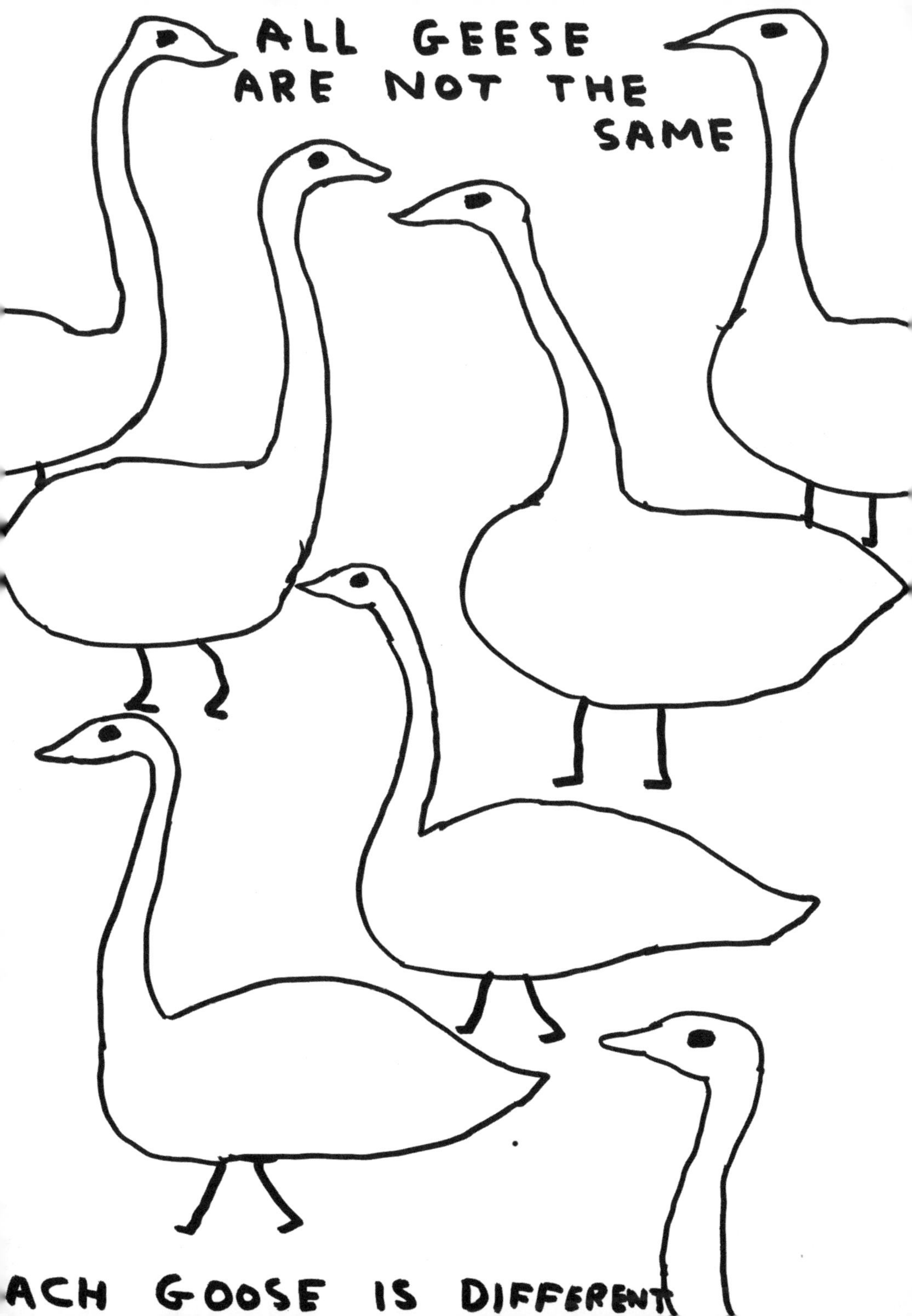

ALL GEESE
ARE NOT THE
SAME
ACH GOOSE IS DIFFERENT

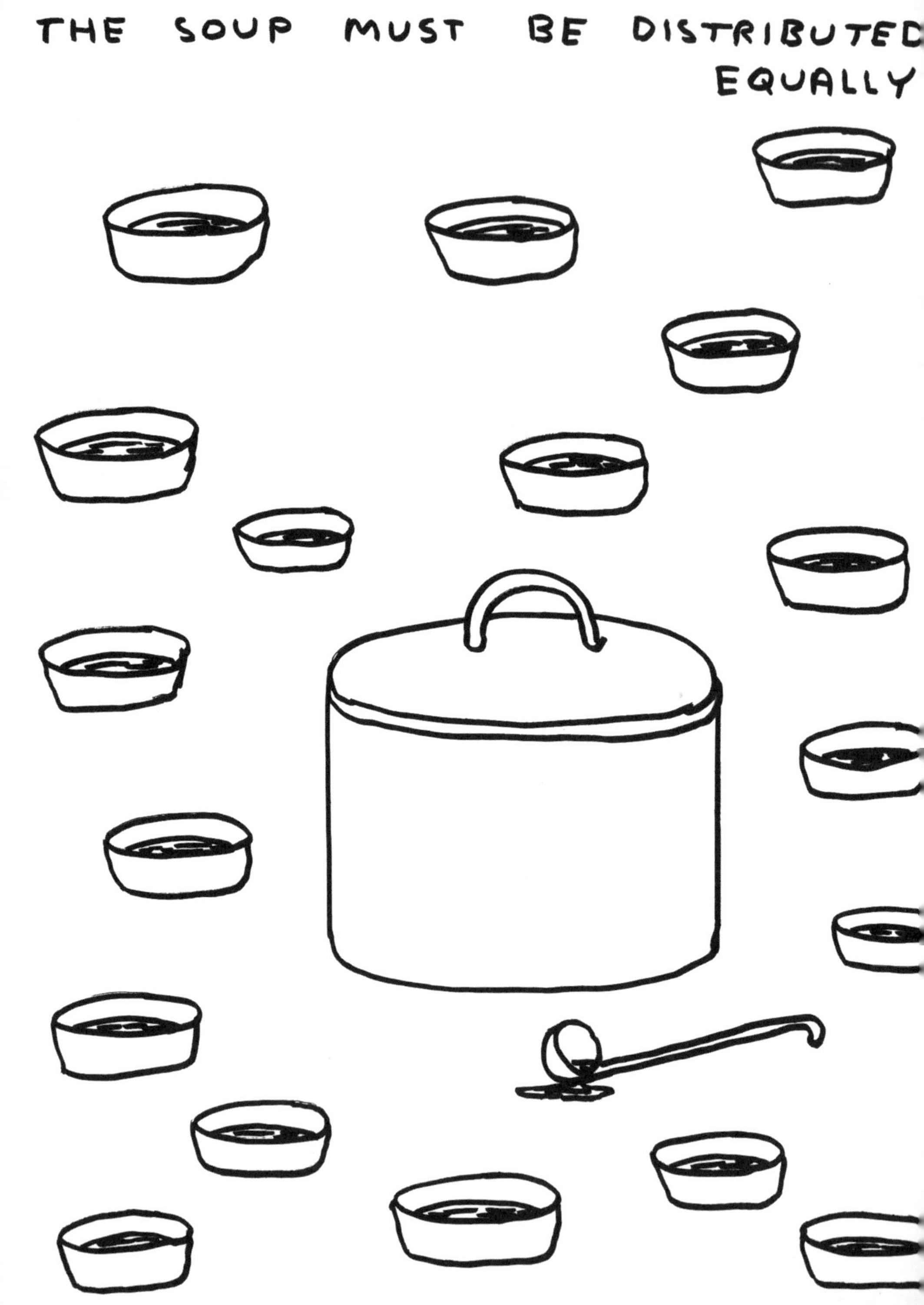

THE SOUP MUST BE DISTRIBUTED EQUALLY

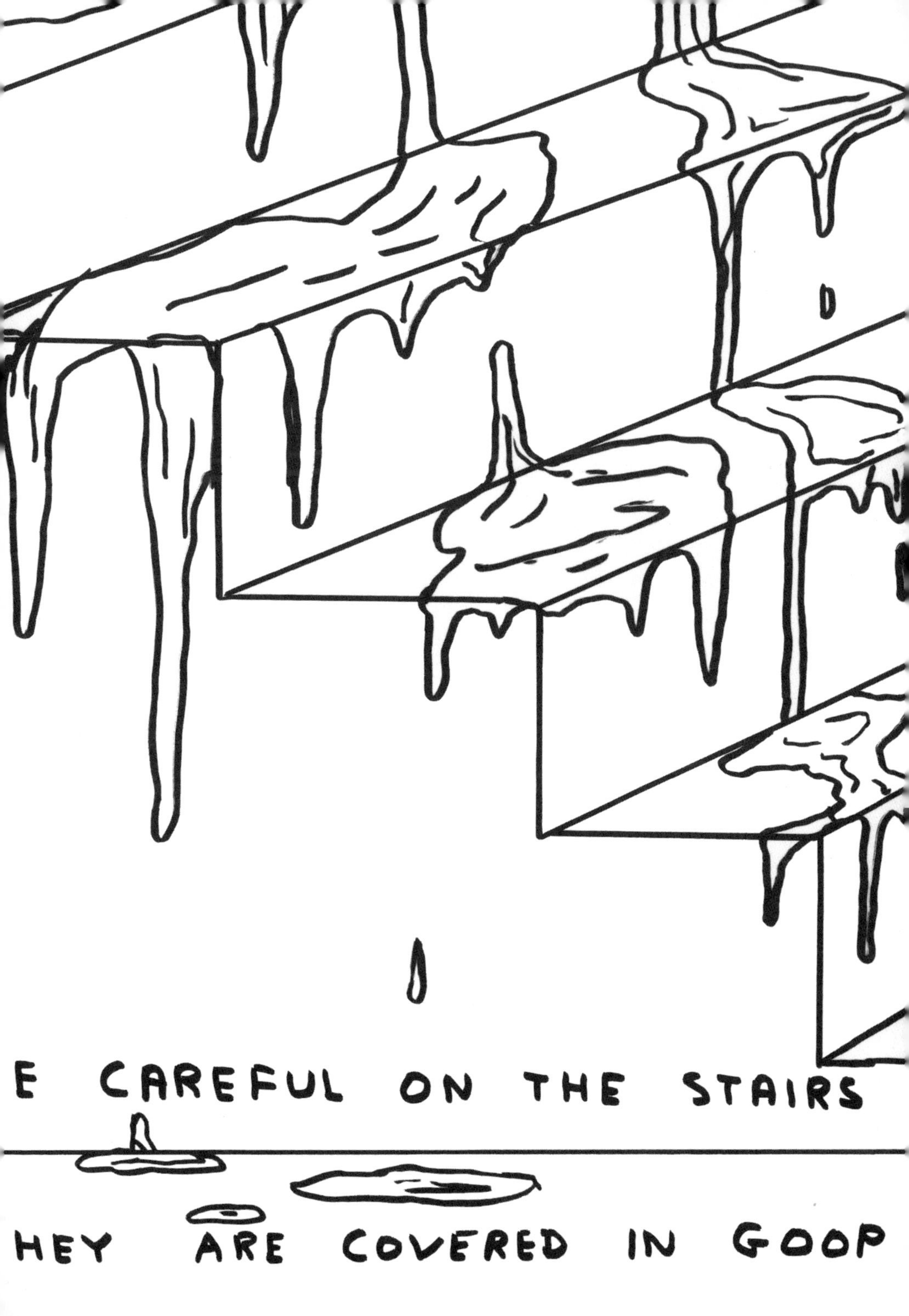
E CAREFUL ON THE STAIRS
HEY ARE COVERED IN GOOP

I BLEW THE BIGGEST
BUBBLE IN THE WORLD AND
THEN I DID NOTHING FO
THE REST OF MY LIFE

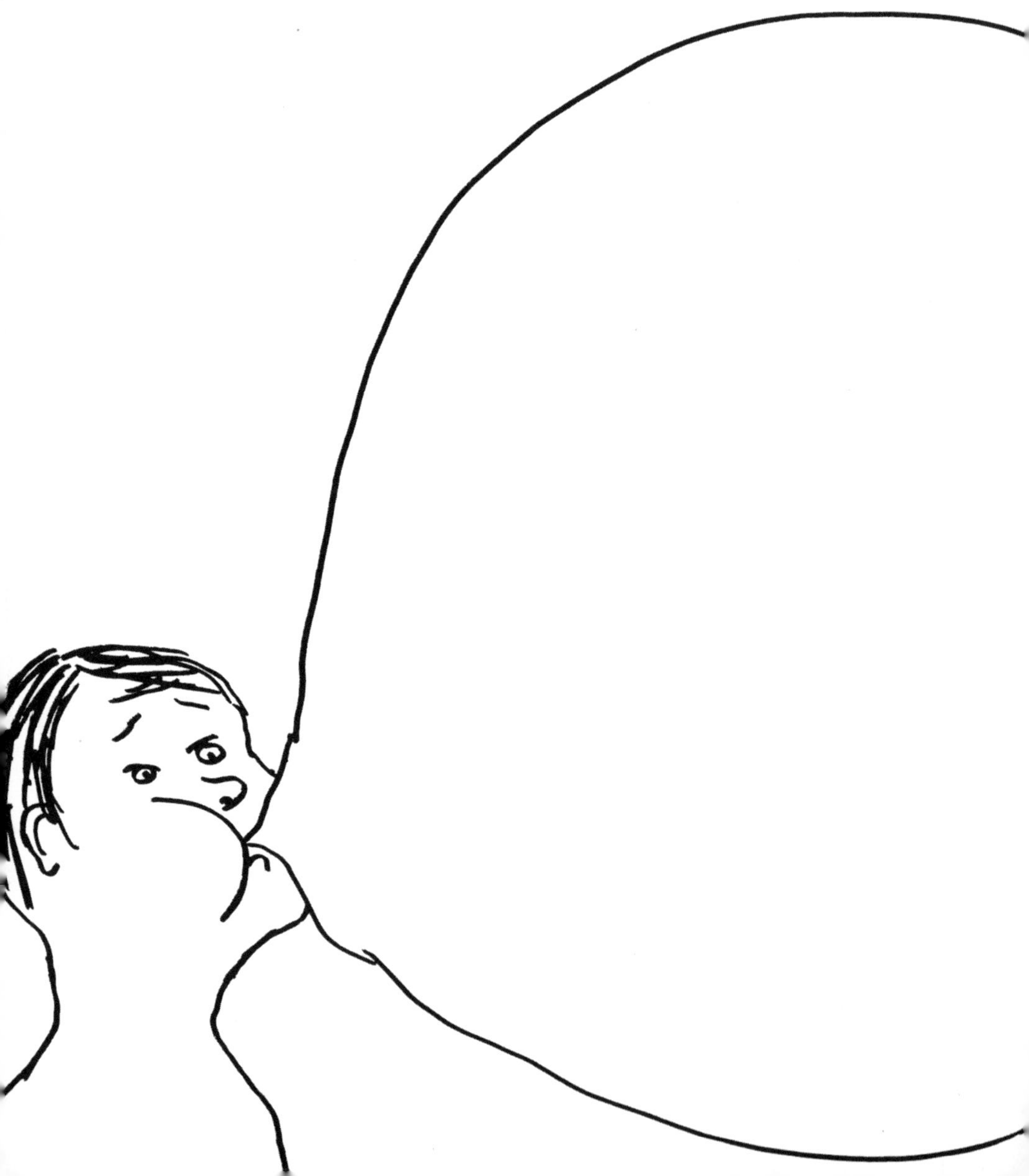

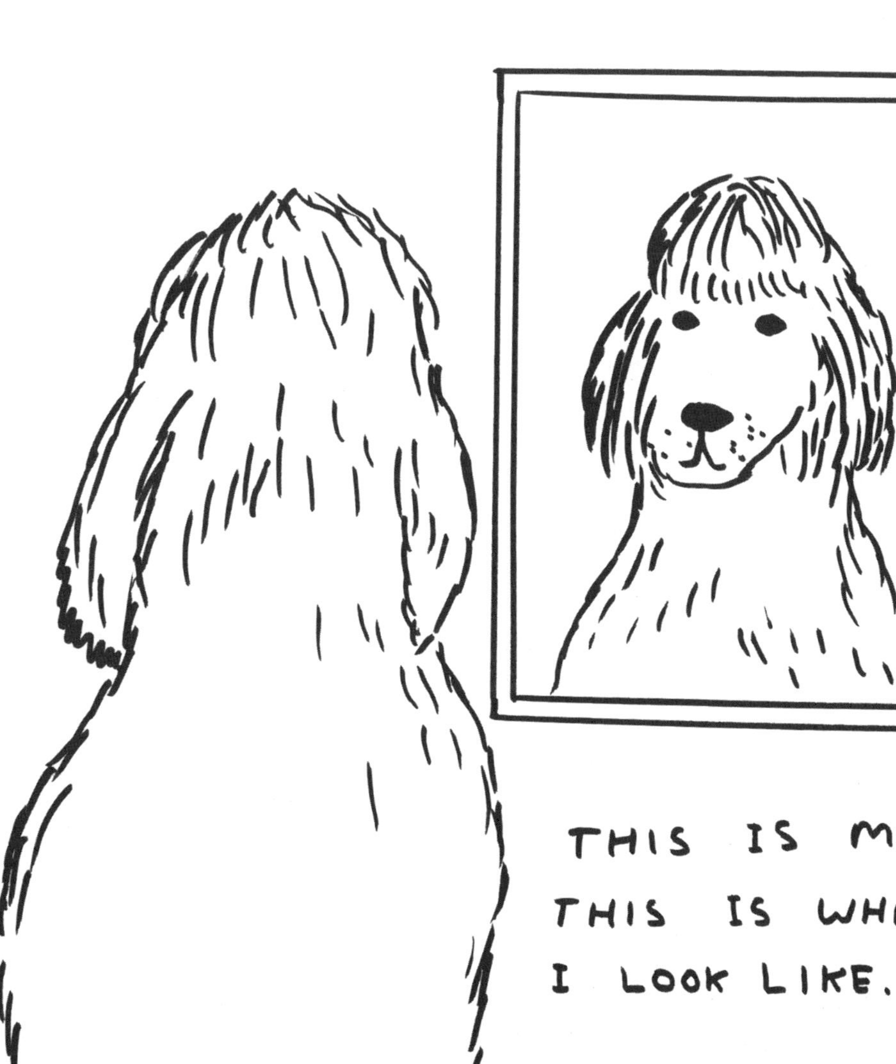
THIS IS ME.
THIS IS WHAT I LOOK LIKE.

THE PEOPLE

A LIST OF ALL MEMBERS OF SOCIETY
(INCLUDING HOUSEHOLD PETS)
HANDWRITTEN IN GOTHIC SCRIPT
BY THE PRIME MINISTER
THERE IS A FILM OF HIM/HER DOING IT

SOCIALIZATION

IS IMPORTANT BECAUSE
IT IS THE MECHANISM
FOR TRANSFERRING
THE ACCEPTED NORMS AND VALUES
OF SOCIETY
TO THE MORONS WITHIN THE SYSTEM

PRIMARY SOCIALIZATION

LEARNING NOT TO SWEAR, HIT, BITE, ETC.

SECONDARY SOCIALIZATION

LEARNING HOW TO DRIVE A LORRY

YOU MIGHT SAY

" HIS HIGH-PITCHED VOICE ANNOYS ME
I MAY PUNCH OR KICK HIM "

YOU SHOULD SAY

" HIS HIGH-PITCHED VOICE ANNOYS ME
I WILL NOT PUNCH OR KICK HIM "

CRAWLING PHASE

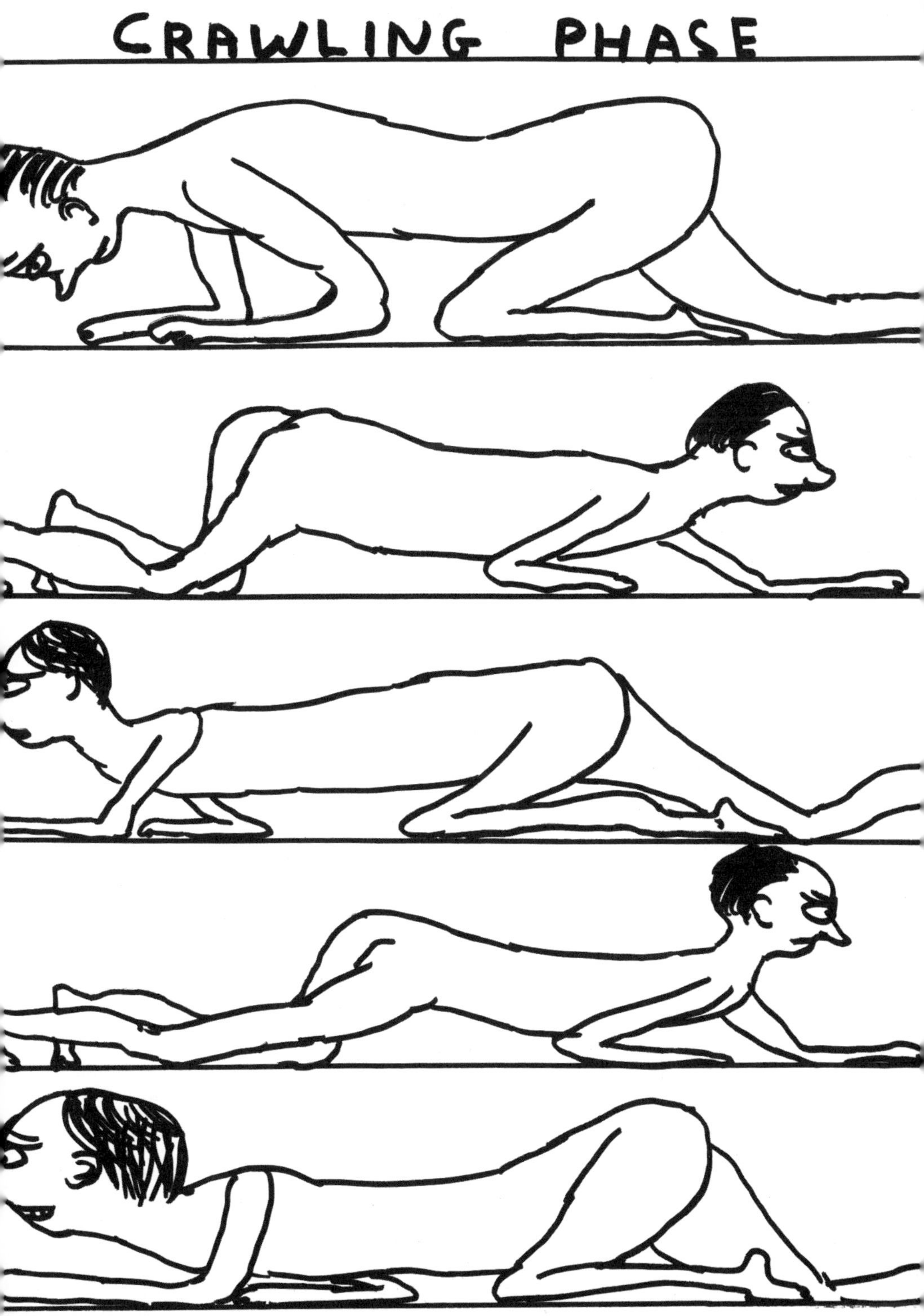

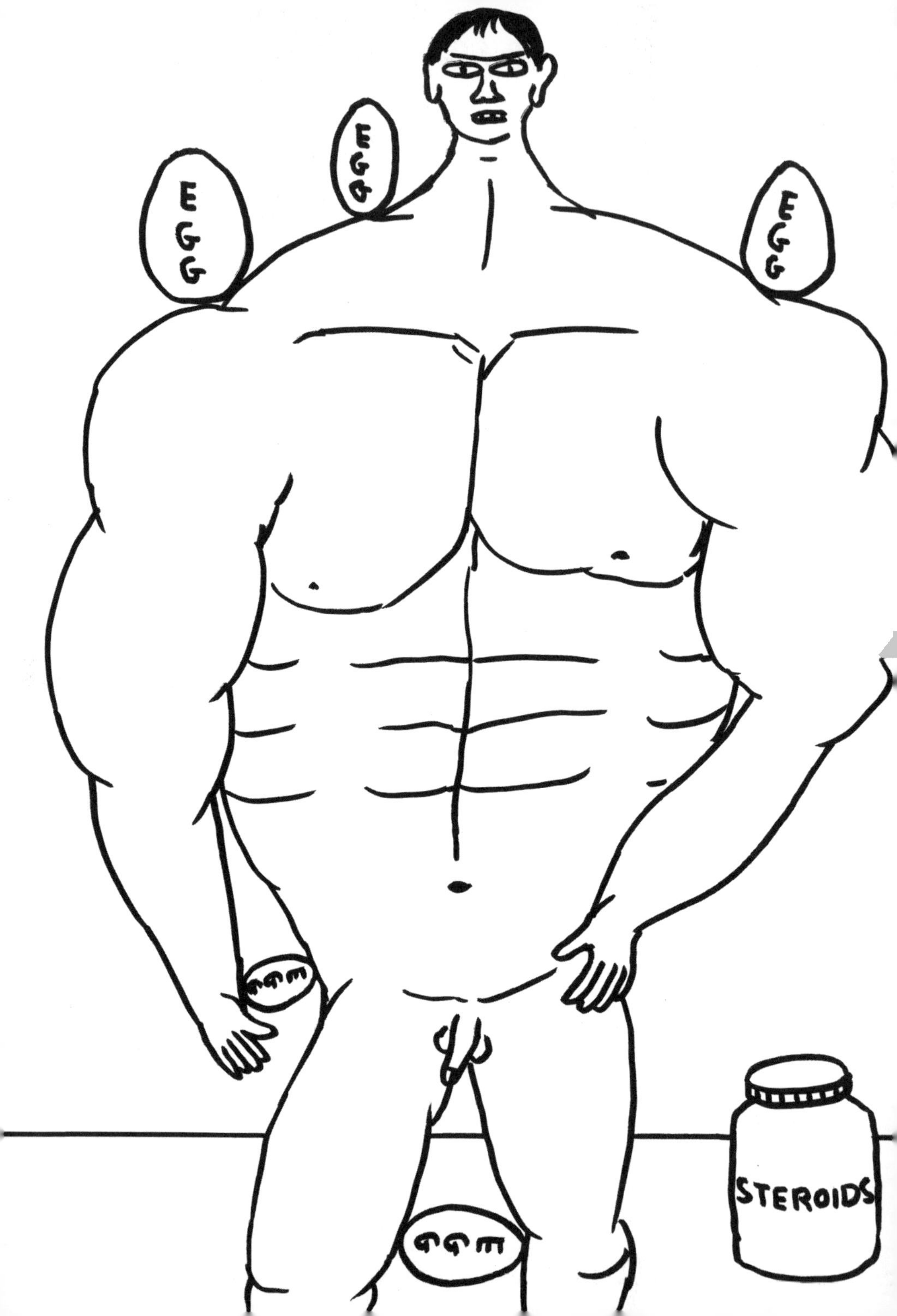

EGG
EGG
EGG
STEROIDS

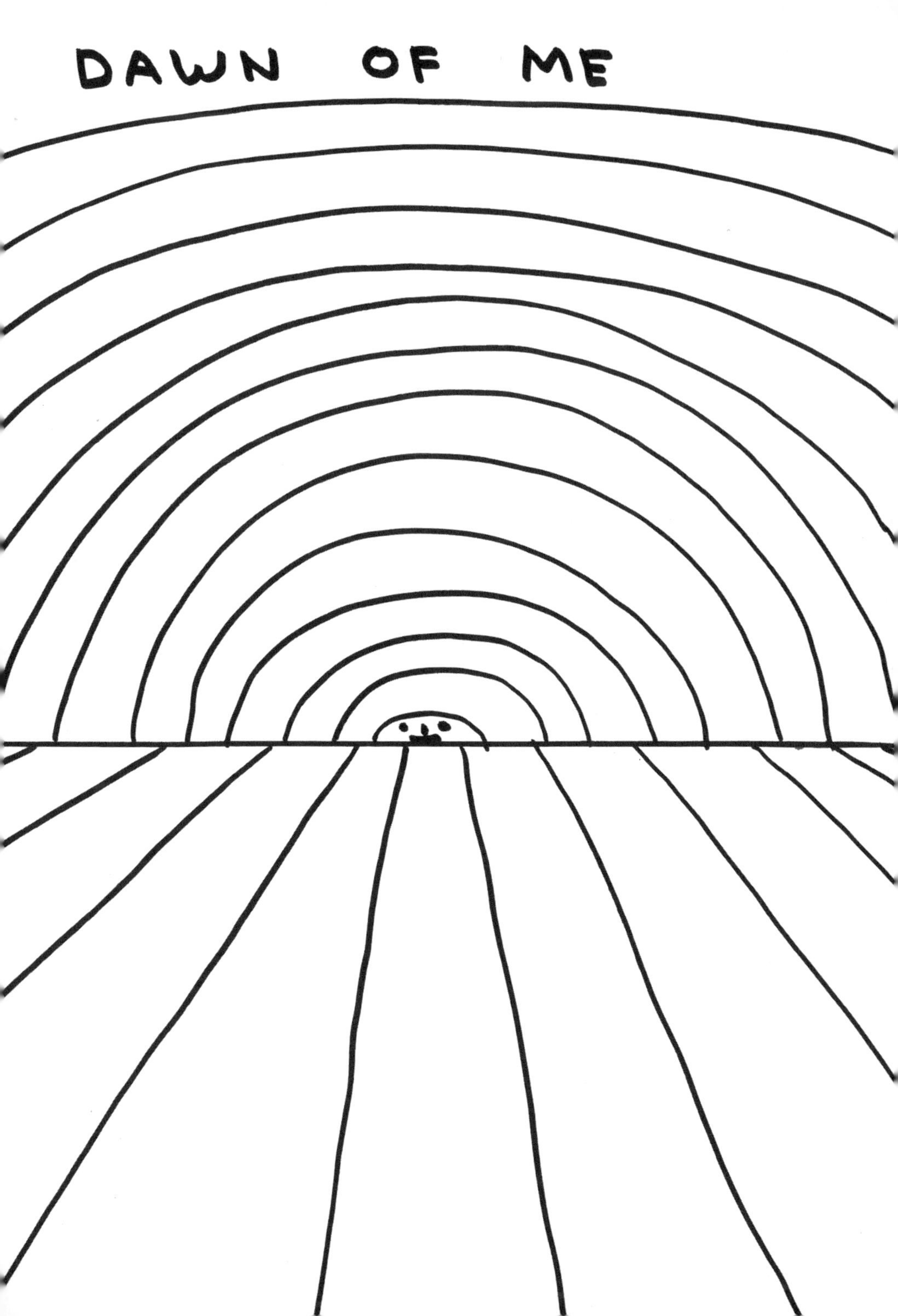

DAWN OF ME

SOCIAL CHIMNEY

IN THE SOCIAL WINTER
WHEN THE SOCIAL FIRE IS LIT
THE SOCIAL SMOKE
GOES UP THE SOCIAL CHIMNEY
THE ZOMBIES CAN SEE THAT
WE ARE HERE
THEY FIND IT MADDENING
AND THEIR GROANING BECOMES AUDIBL
FROM AFAR

DIABOLICAL LIBERTY

MY BICYCLE WAS TAKEN
AND RIDDEN AROUND THE TOWN

ACTION:

AN INSECT BIT ME
ON THE PALM OF MY HAND
NOW IT ITCHES
AND I SCRATCH IT OFTEN

REACTION / SOLUTION:

I DO NOT KNOW WHAT TO DO

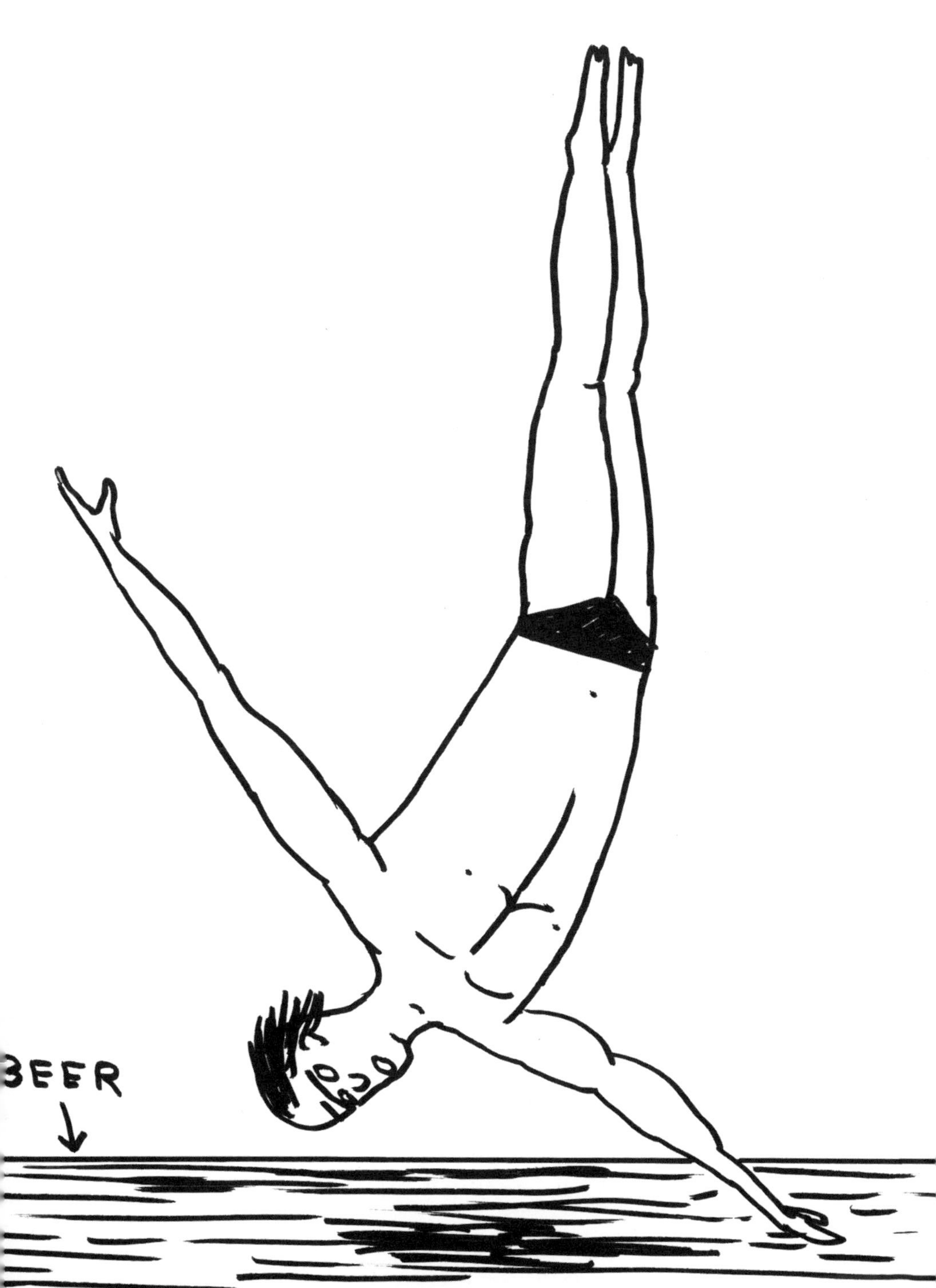

BEER

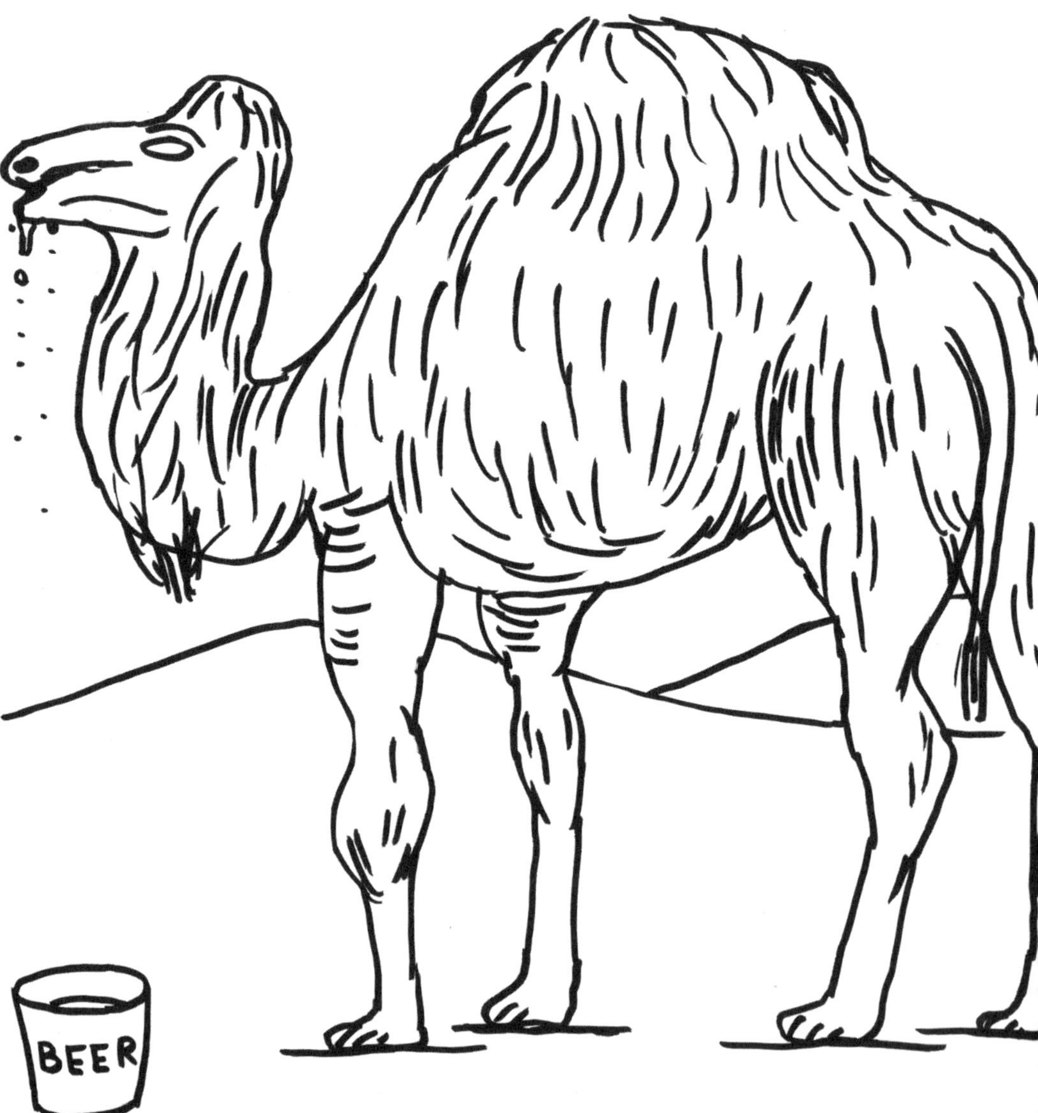
BEER

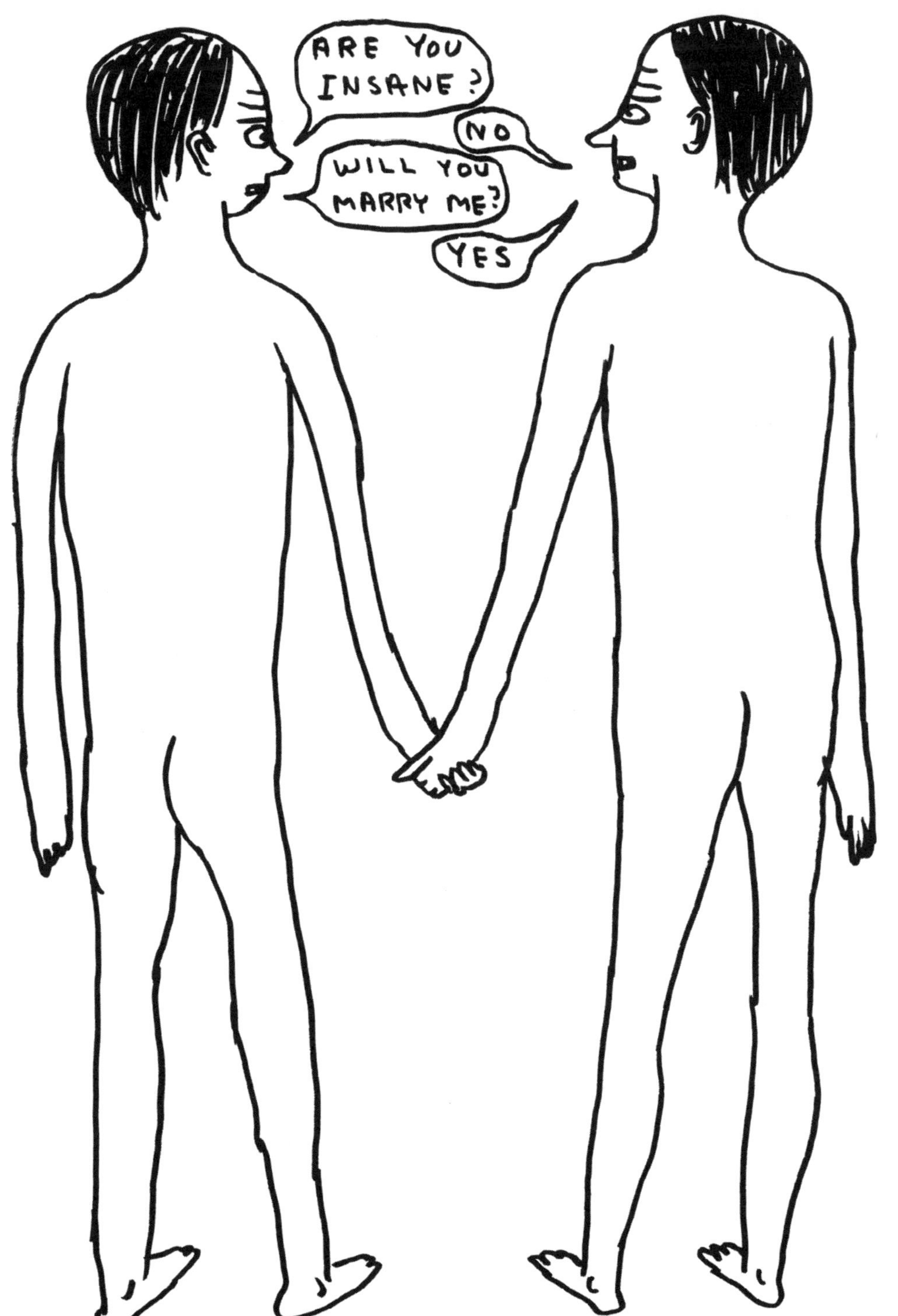

ARE YOU INSANE?
NO
WILL YOU MARRY ME?
YES

CONFORMISTS

CONFORMISTS ACCEPT SOCIETY'S GOALS
AND THE SOCIALLY ACCEPTABLE MEANS
OF ACHIEVING THEM
THEIR NAMES OFTEN BEGIN WITH THE
LETTER J : JOHN, JIM , JANE , JEAN, ETC.

RIOTING

THIS IS NORMAL BEHAVIOUR
A SCHEDULE OF FORTHCOMING RIOTS
IS AVAILABLE ON THE GOVERNMENT'S
WEB SITE

SINISTER FORCES AT WORK

MAKING US FORGET THINGS
HIDING OUR KEYS
GETTING US DRUNK EVERY NIGHT

AN EXPLOSION
IN THE ENCLOSED SPACE
OF YOUR BRAIN

DRINKING A SUGARY BEVERAGE
DRIVES YOU FORWARD
MAKES YOU POWERFUL
NOW YOU ARE A PRODUCTIVE CITIZEN
VERY GOOD

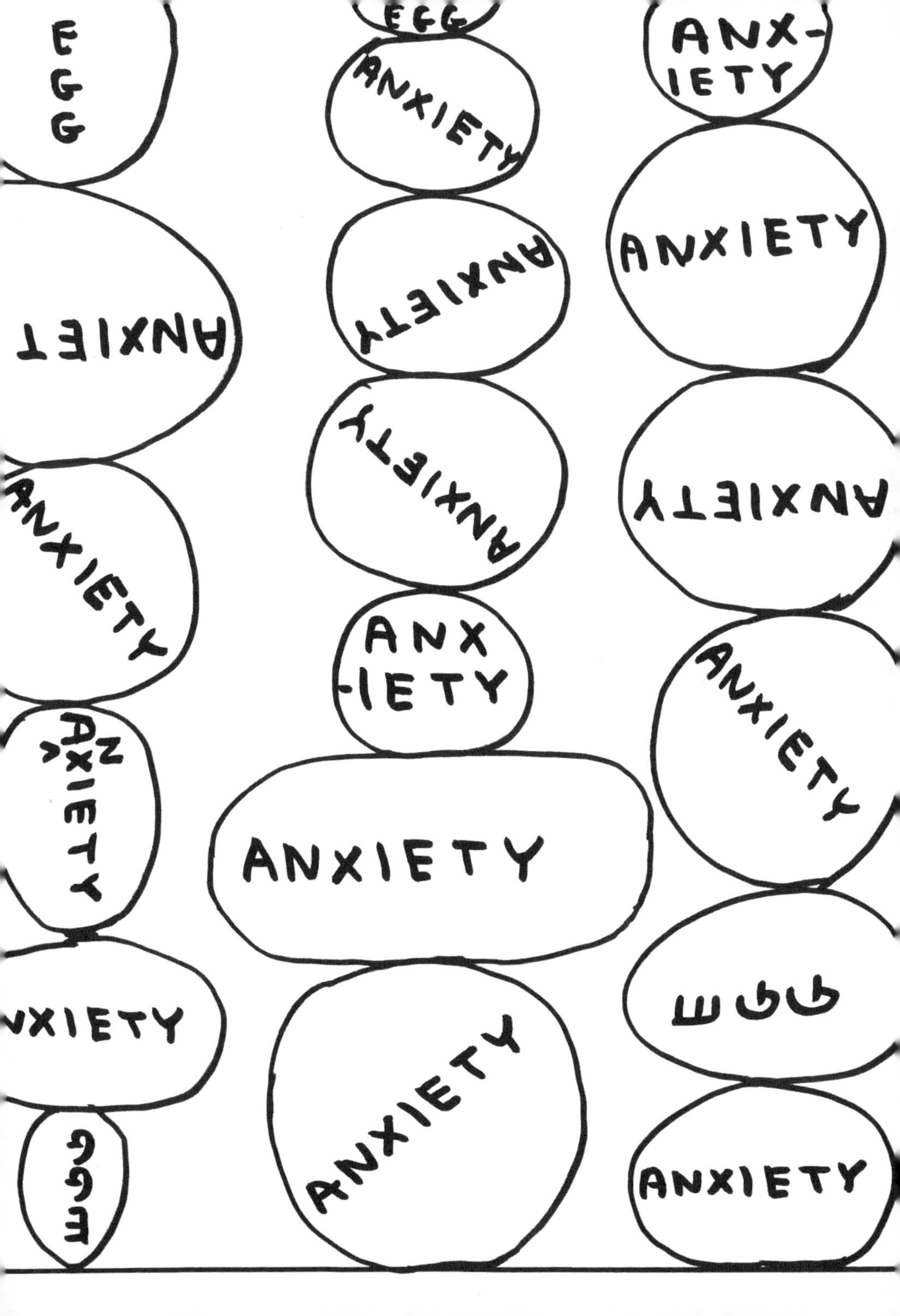

EGG
ANXIETY
ANXIETY
ANXIETY
IETY
ANXIETY
ANXIETY
ANXIETY
ANXIETY
ANXIETY
ANXIETY
ANX-IETY
ANXIETY
ANXIETY
ANXIETY
EGG
ANXIETY
ANXIETY
ANXIETY

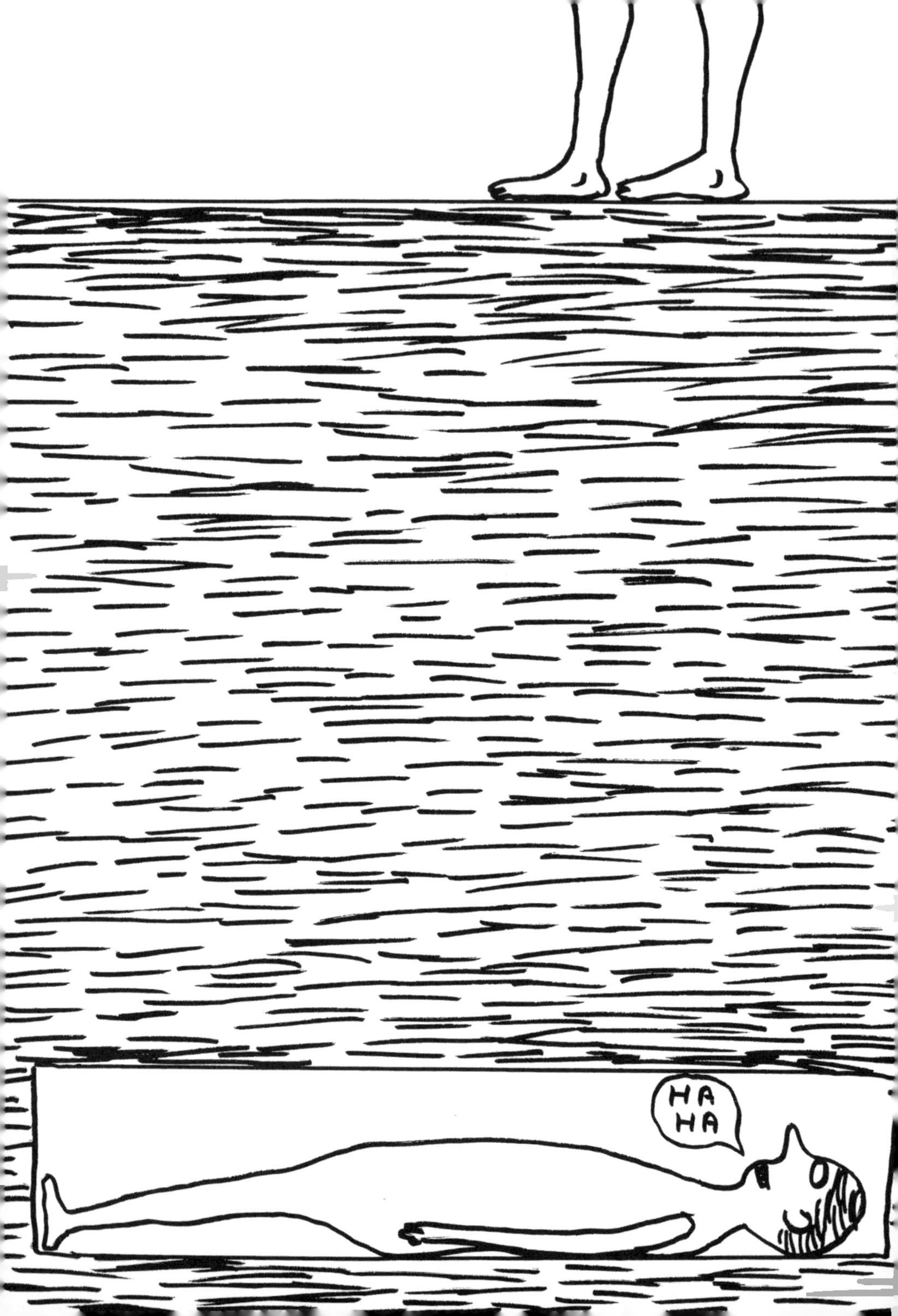

HA
HA

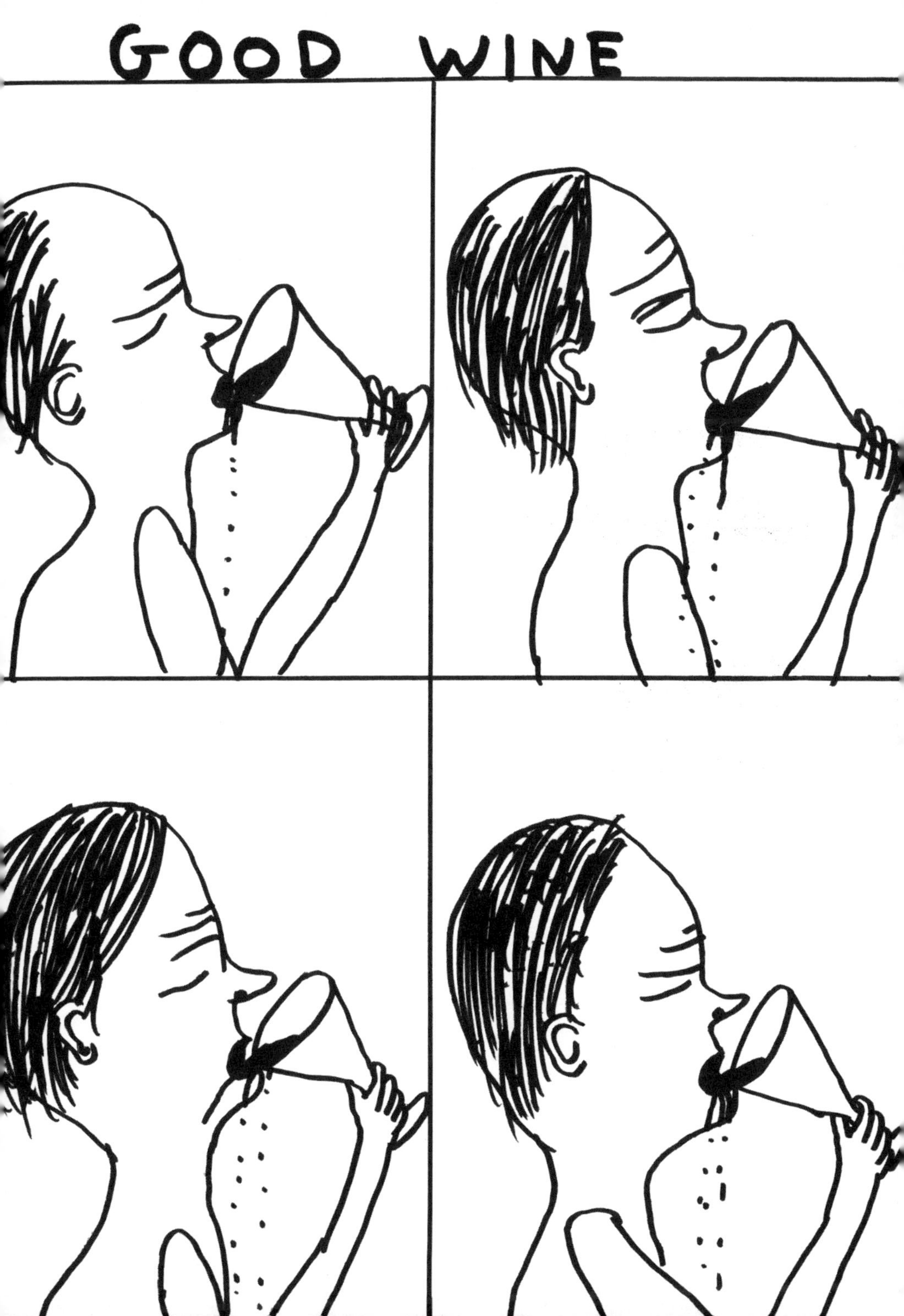
GOOD WINE

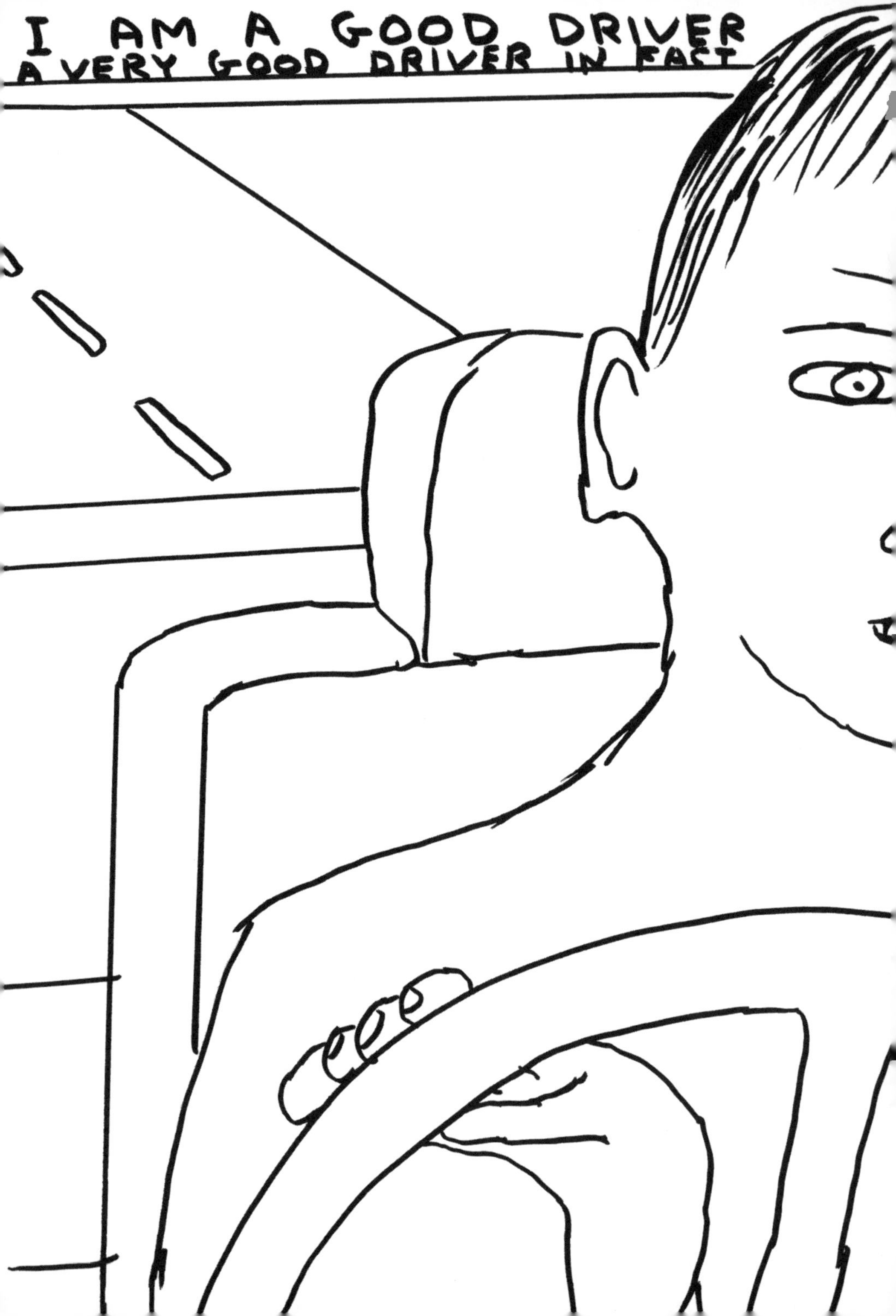
I AM A GOOD DRIVER
A VERY GOOD DRIVER IN FACT

ACTIONS OF GROUPS

TEND TO BE LARGELY WITHOUT REASON
CAN BE PREDICTED SOMETIMES
ACCORDING TO AIR TEMPERATURE

PEOPLE MOVING AROUND AT RANDOM

SOMETIMES THEY BUMP INTO EACH OTHER
SOMETIMES THEY FALL OVER
WE OBSERVE THEM
FROM OUR HIGH VANTAGE POINT
WE INVENT NAMES FOR THEM
IT IS DISRESPECTFUL BUT
IT AMUSES US
WE ARE BORED
AND WE MUST FIND WAYS
TO ENTERTAIN OURSELVES

KINDNESS

YOU HAVE TO BE CRUEL TO BE KIND
BE CRUEL TO PEOPLE
WHEN YOU FIRST MEET THEM
SLAP THEM
THROW GARBAGE ON THEM
THEY WILL LIKE YOU
AND THEY WILL BECOME YOUR FRIEND

PUBLIC VS PRIVATE SPACE

PUBLIC SPACES:
PARKS
RUNWAYS
THE SEA
THE TOP OF THE HEAD
PRIVATE SPACES:
HANDBAGS
TROUSER POCKET
SECRET COMPARTMENT
BEHIND THE EAR

THINGS THAT PREVENT US FROM BEING OUR TRUE SELVES

ALMOST EVERYTHING
BUT ESPECIALLY:
MASKS
CLOAKS
HATS

HYPER-INDIVIDUALISM

HE SAYS:
"I DO NOT CARE ABOUT SOCIETY
I JUST CARE ABOUT MYSELF"
WE SAY:
"WE WILL THROW HIM OFF A CLIFF"

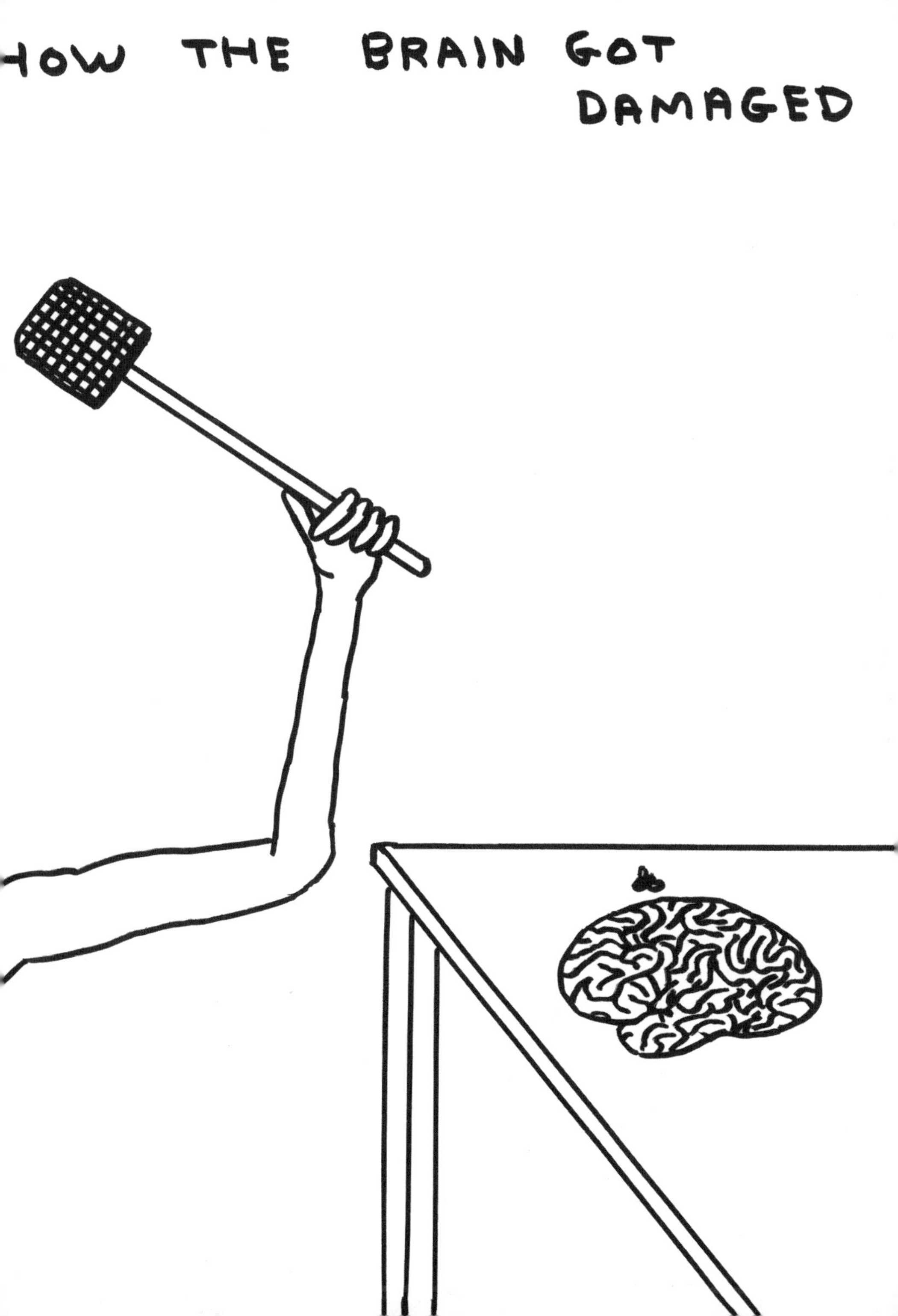

HOW THE BRAIN GOT DAMAGED

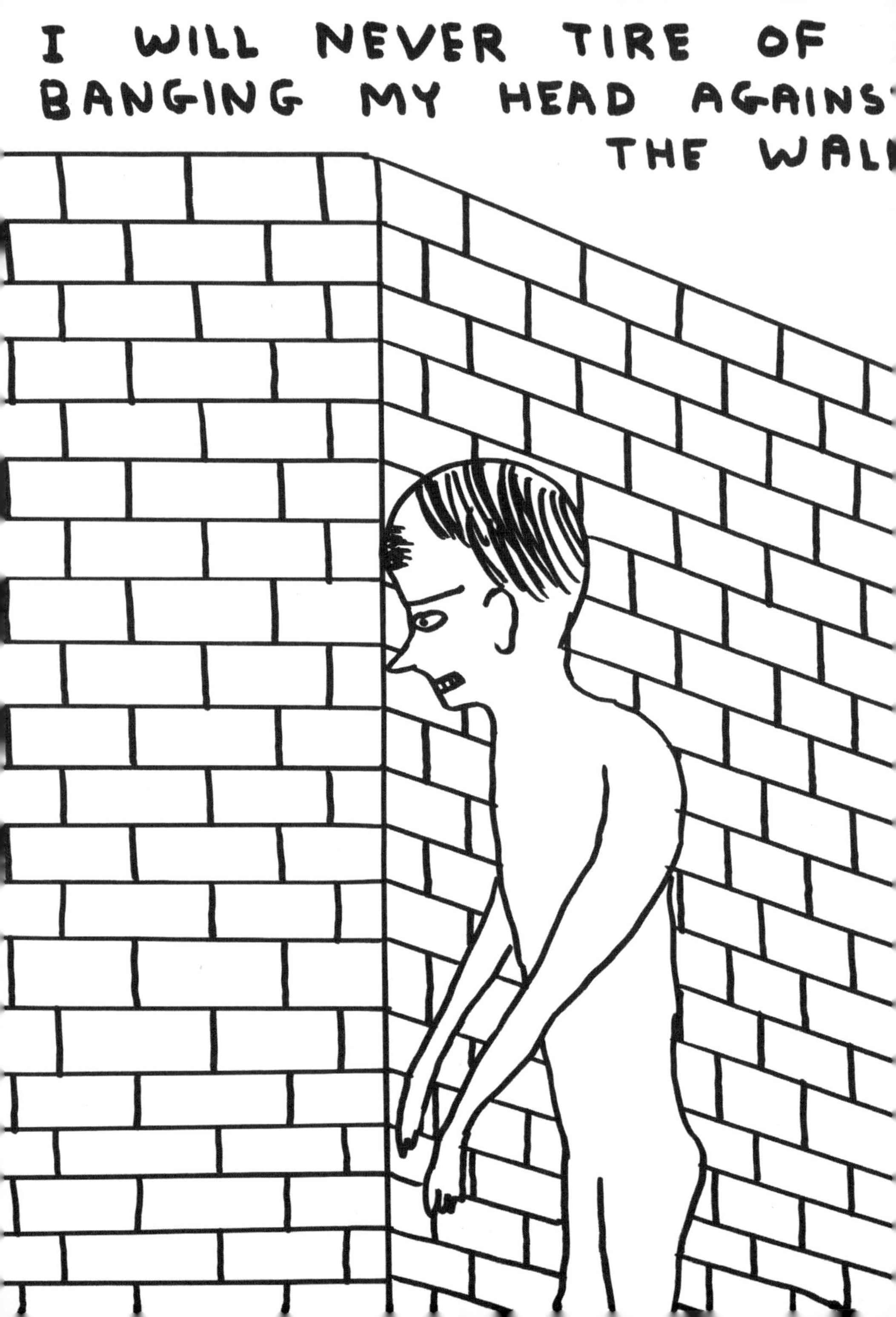

I WILL NEVER TIRE OF BANGING MY HEAD AGAINST THE WALL

9 CUPS OF COFFEE

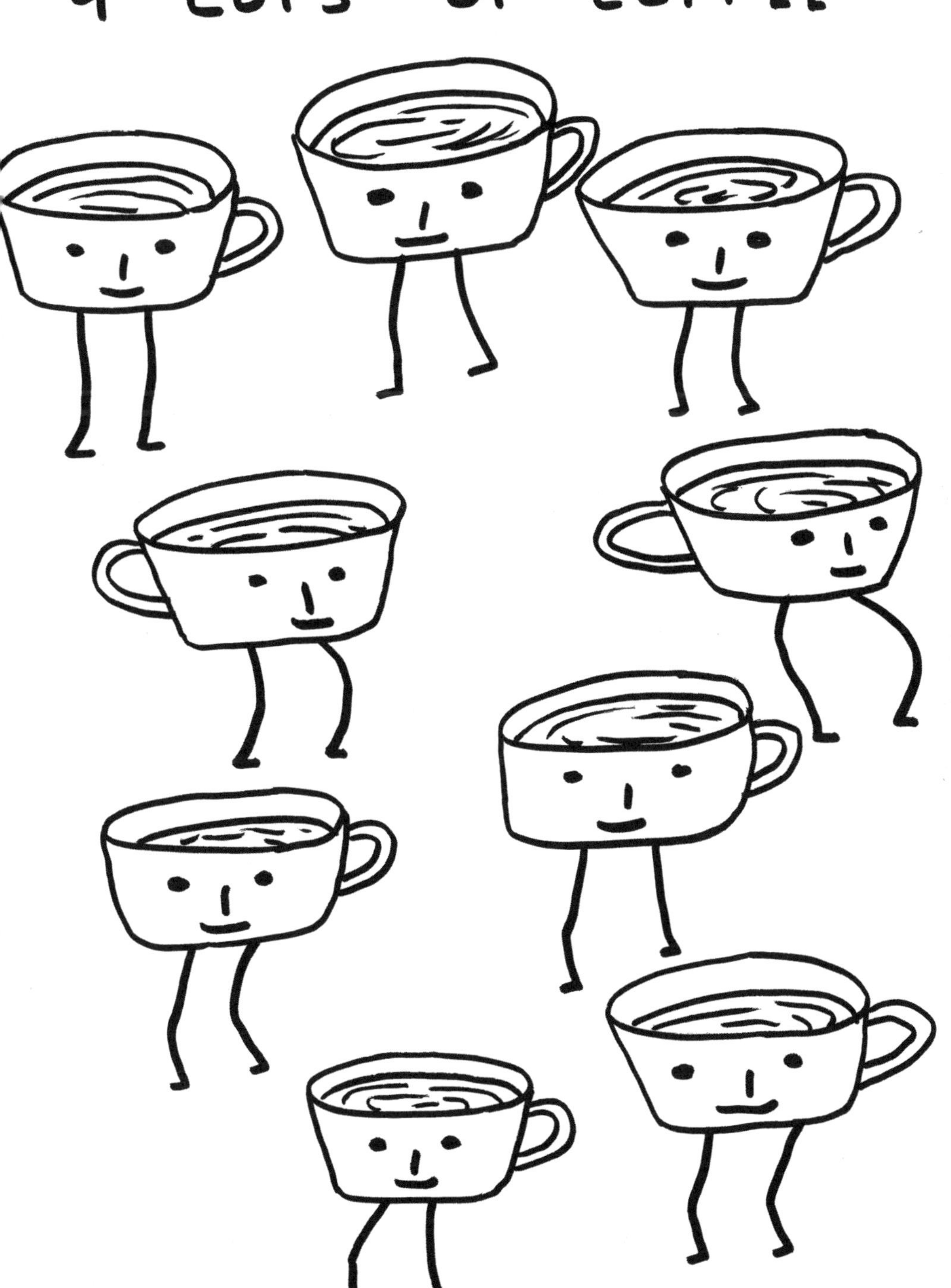

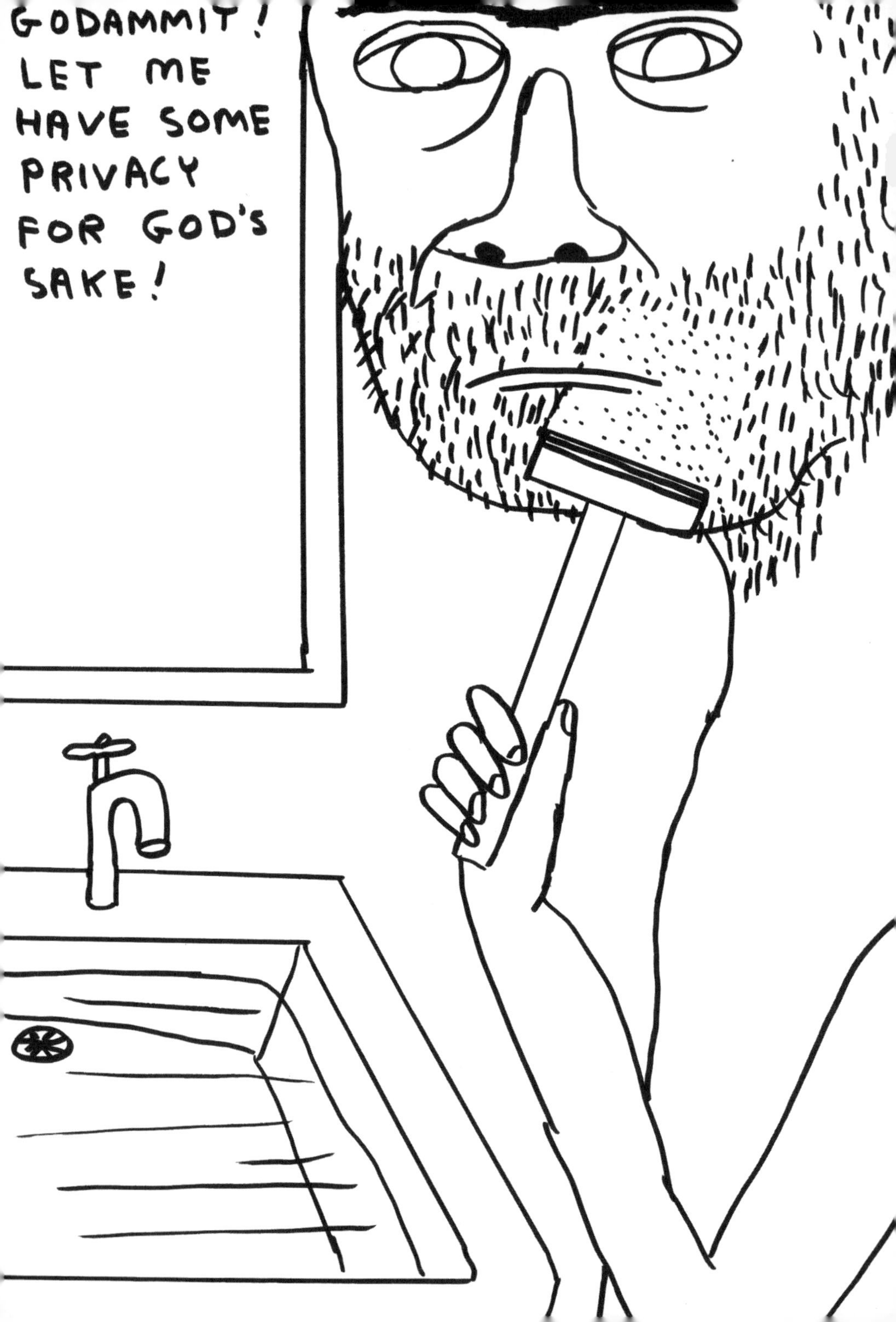

GODAMMIT!
LET ME
HAVE SOME
PRIVACY
FOR GOD'S
SAKE!

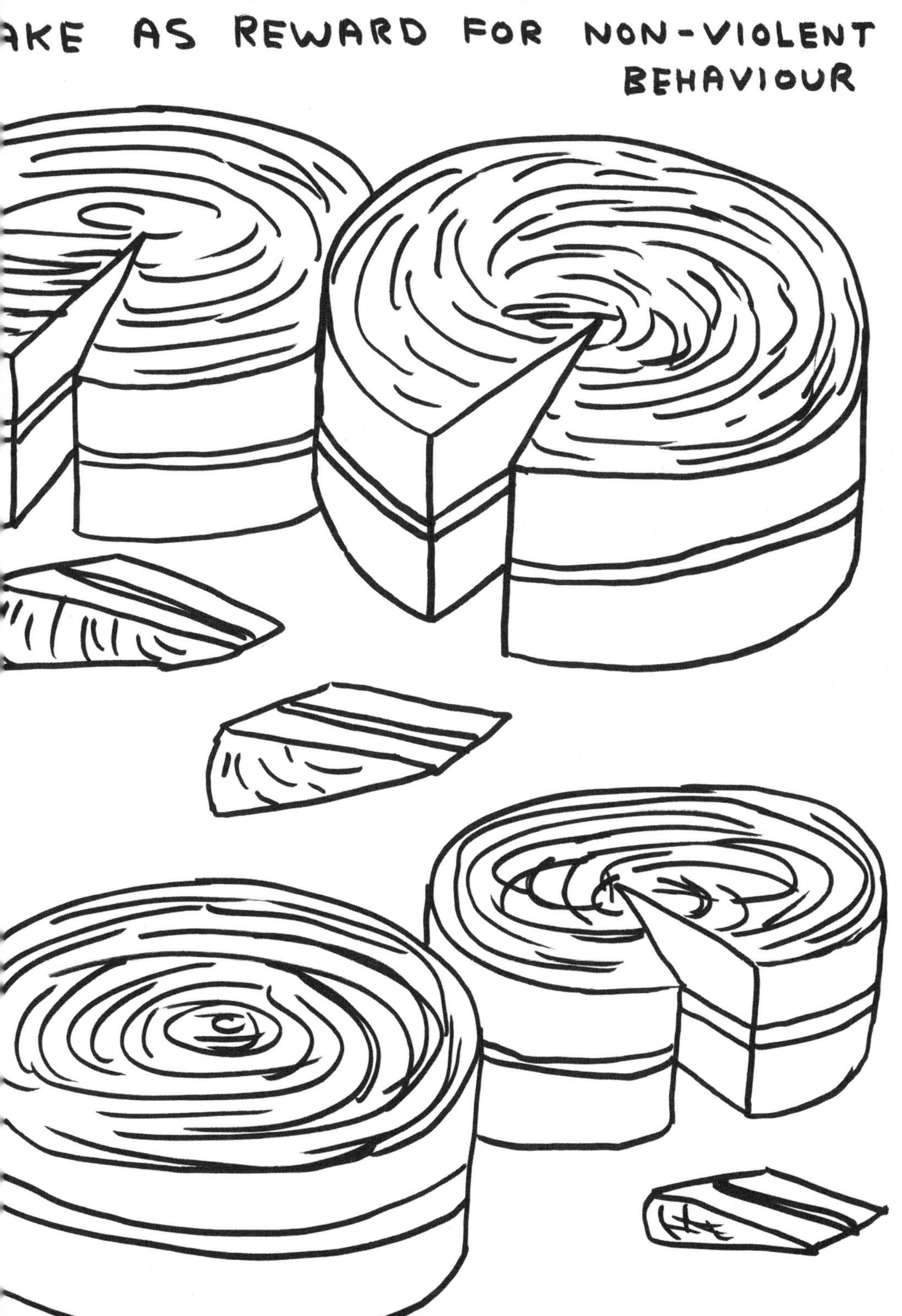

AKE AS REWARD FOR NON-VIOLENT
BEHAVIOUR

LIFE

PLANT LIFE
TRYING TO GROW
ANIMALS
TRYING TO BREED
ALL THIS MADE DIFFICULT
BY YOU
AND YOUR PUBLIC ART PROJECT

SOCIAL BARRIERS

YOU DRESS IN A STRANGE COSTUME
AND YOU WEAR MAKE UP
IT IS A BARRIER BETWEEN US
IT IS A BARRIER THAT YOU HAVE ERECTE
IT IS NOT A BARRIER THAT I HAVE ERECTE

GENERAL HEALTH

DRINK A TANKARD
OF BOILING WATER
IN THE MORNING

FALSE VISIONS

I SAW A BAT
FLYING AROUND THE SUPERMARKET

EFRIEND THE DEGENERATES

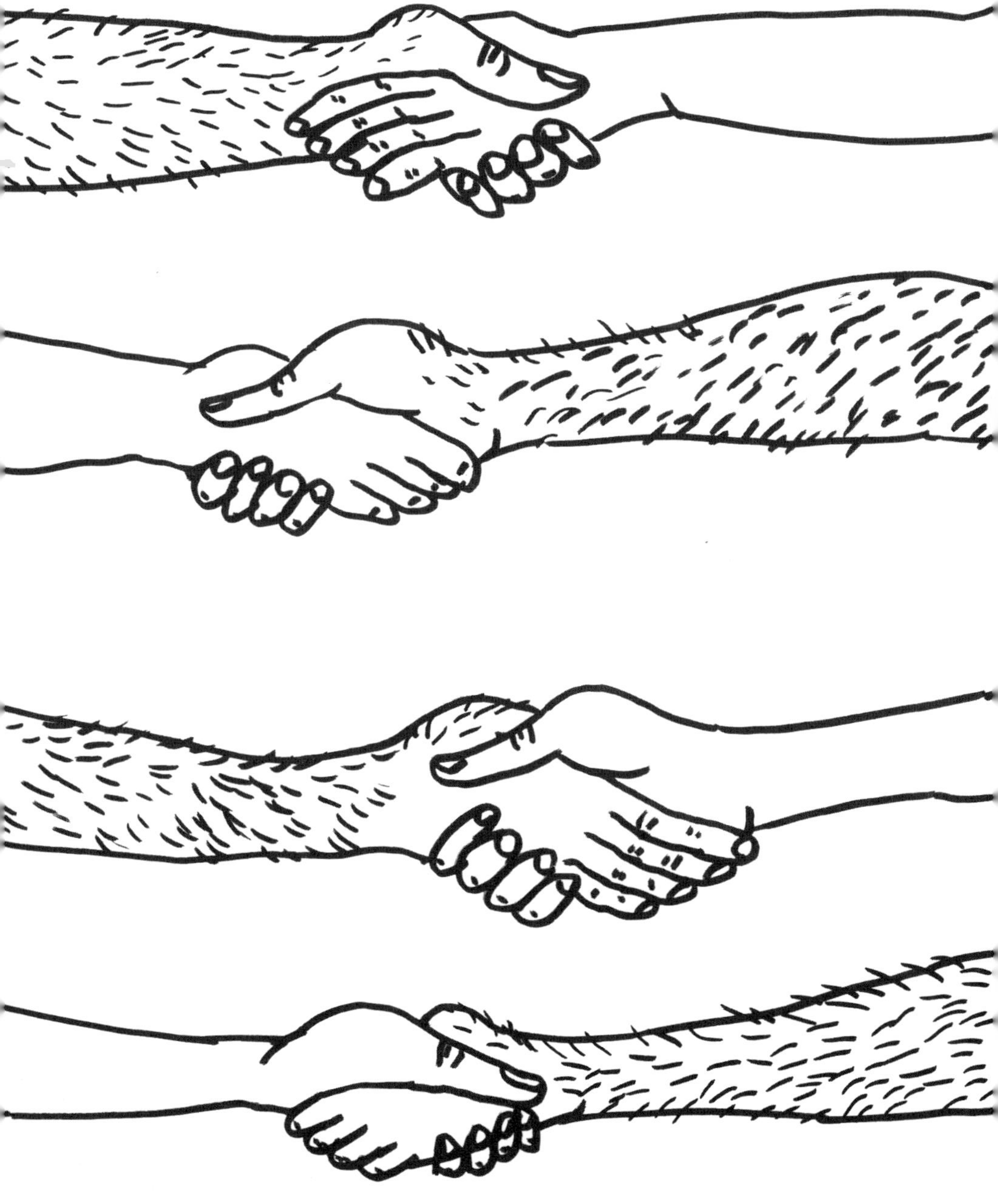

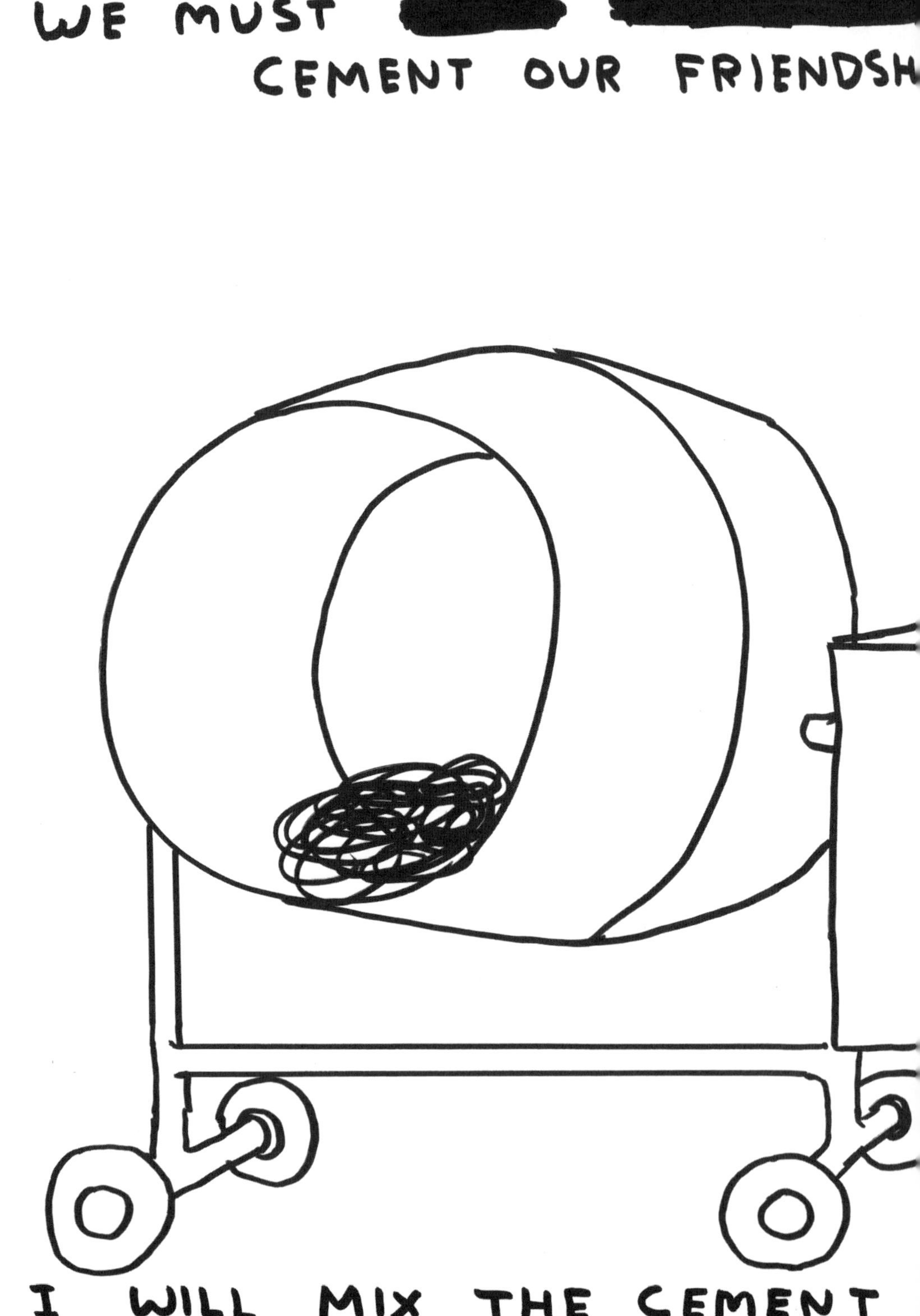

WE MUST ████ ████
CEMENT OUR FRIENDSH
I WILL MIX THE CEMENT

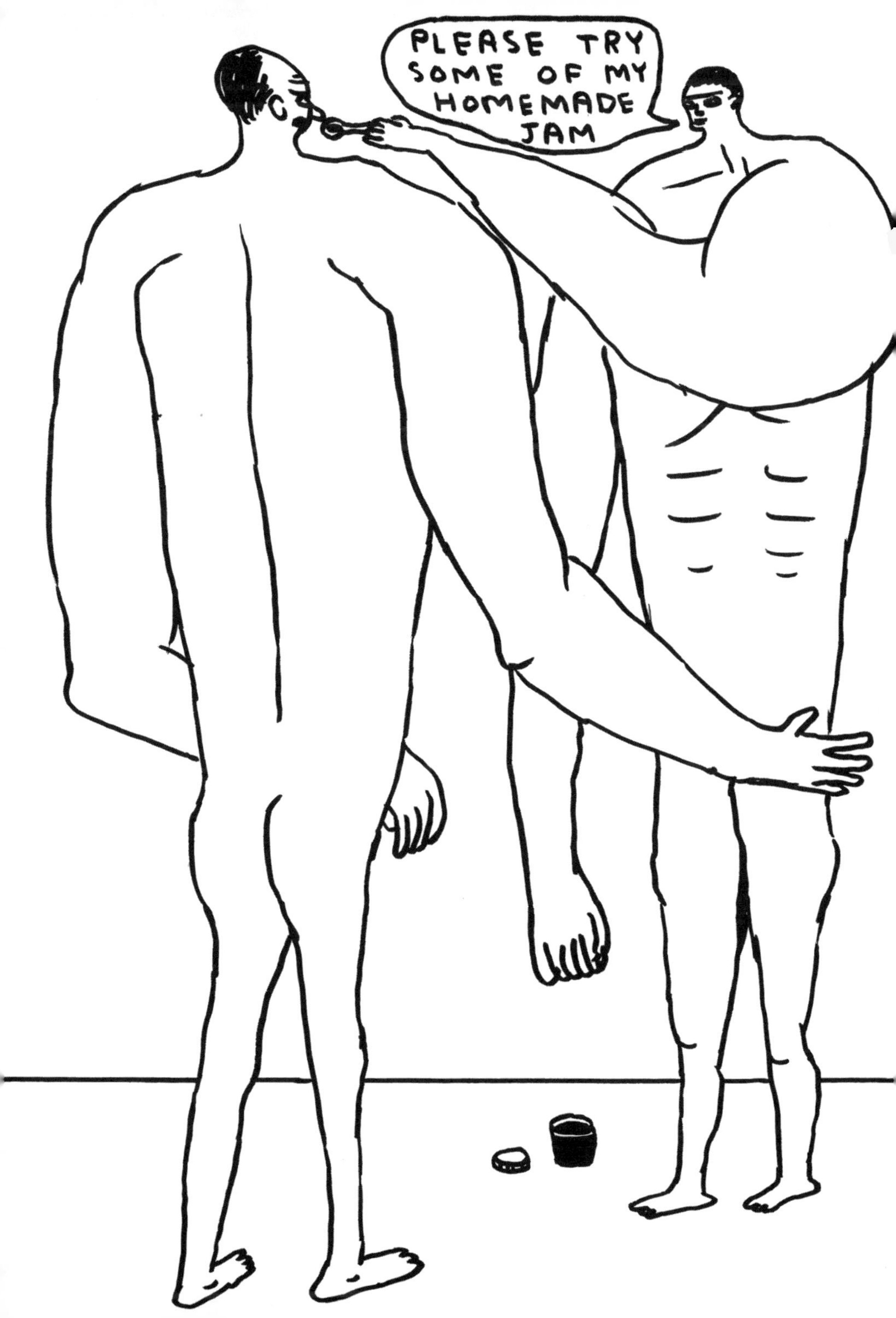

PLEASE TRY SOME OF MY HOMEMADE JAM

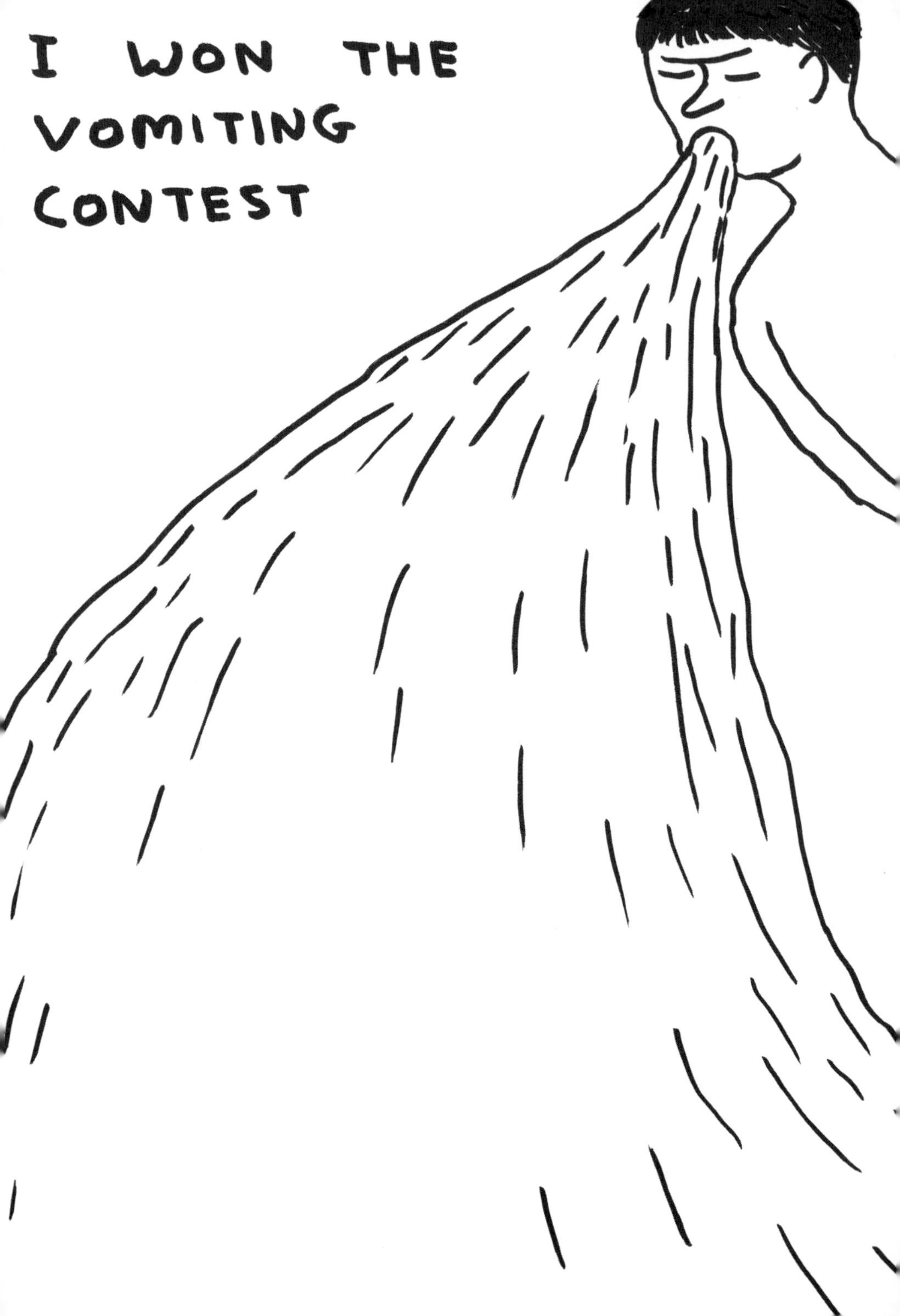
I WON THE
VOMITING
CONTEST

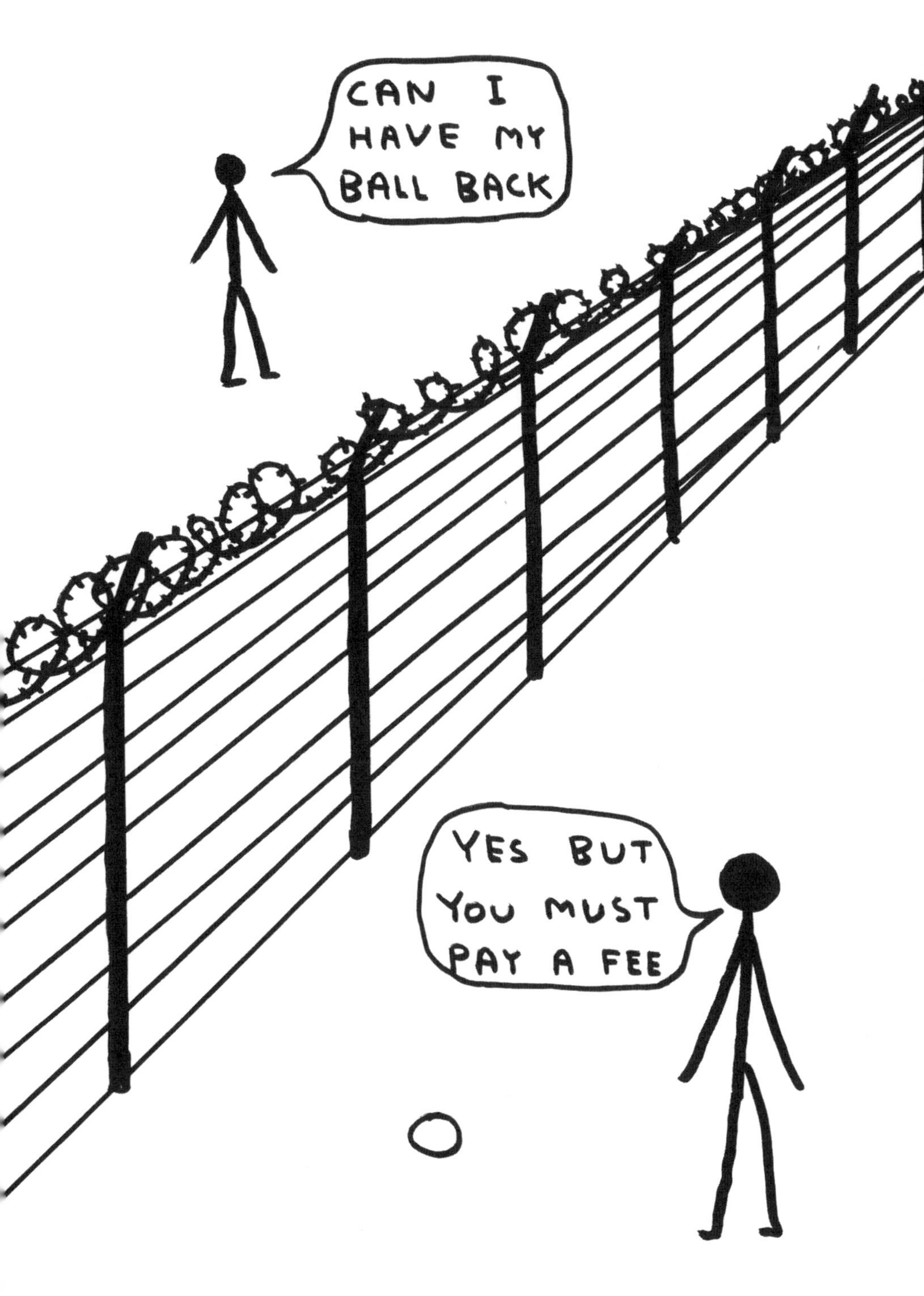

CAN I HAVE MY BALL BACK
YES BUT YOU MUST PAY A FEE

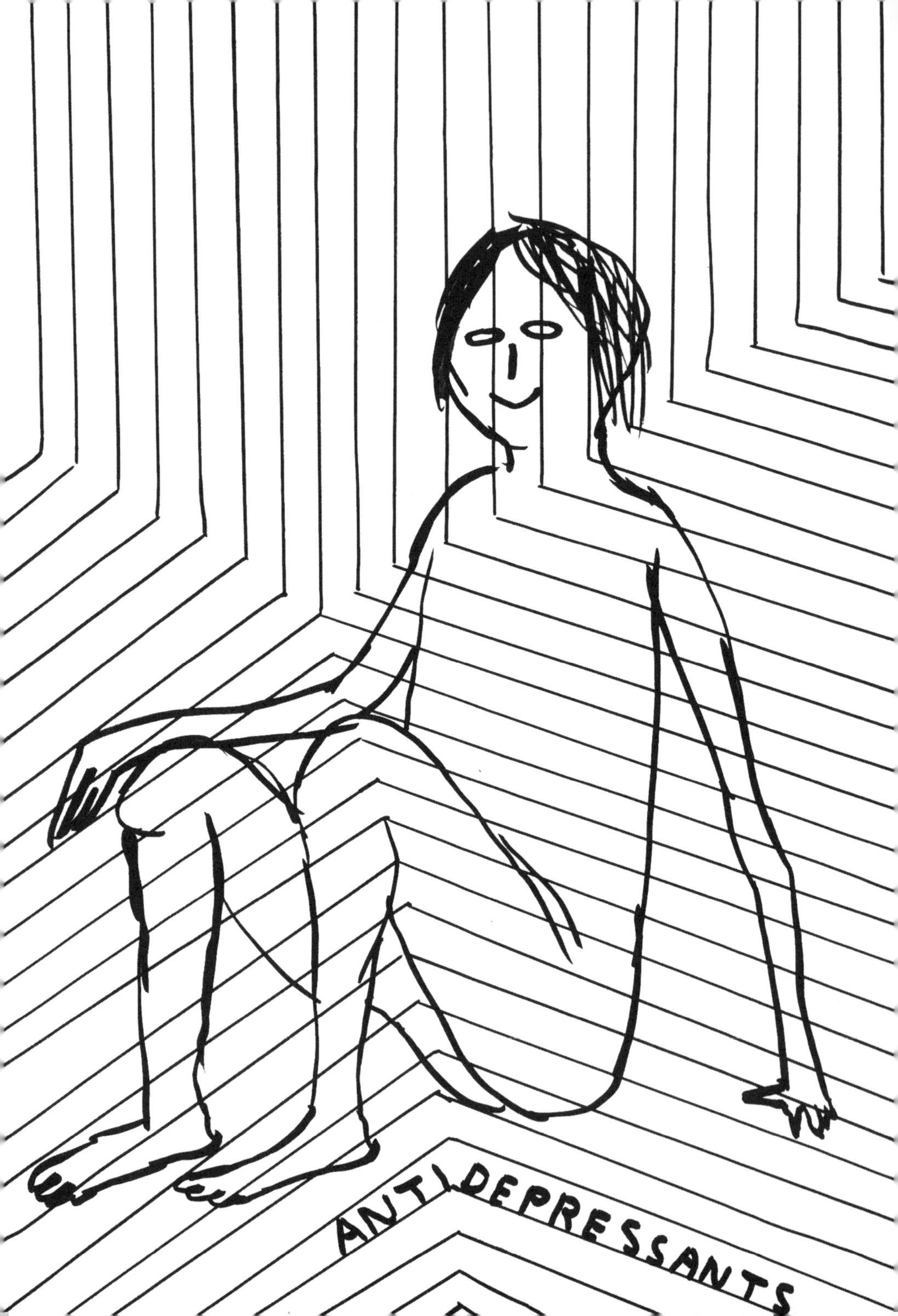

ANTIDEPRESSANTS

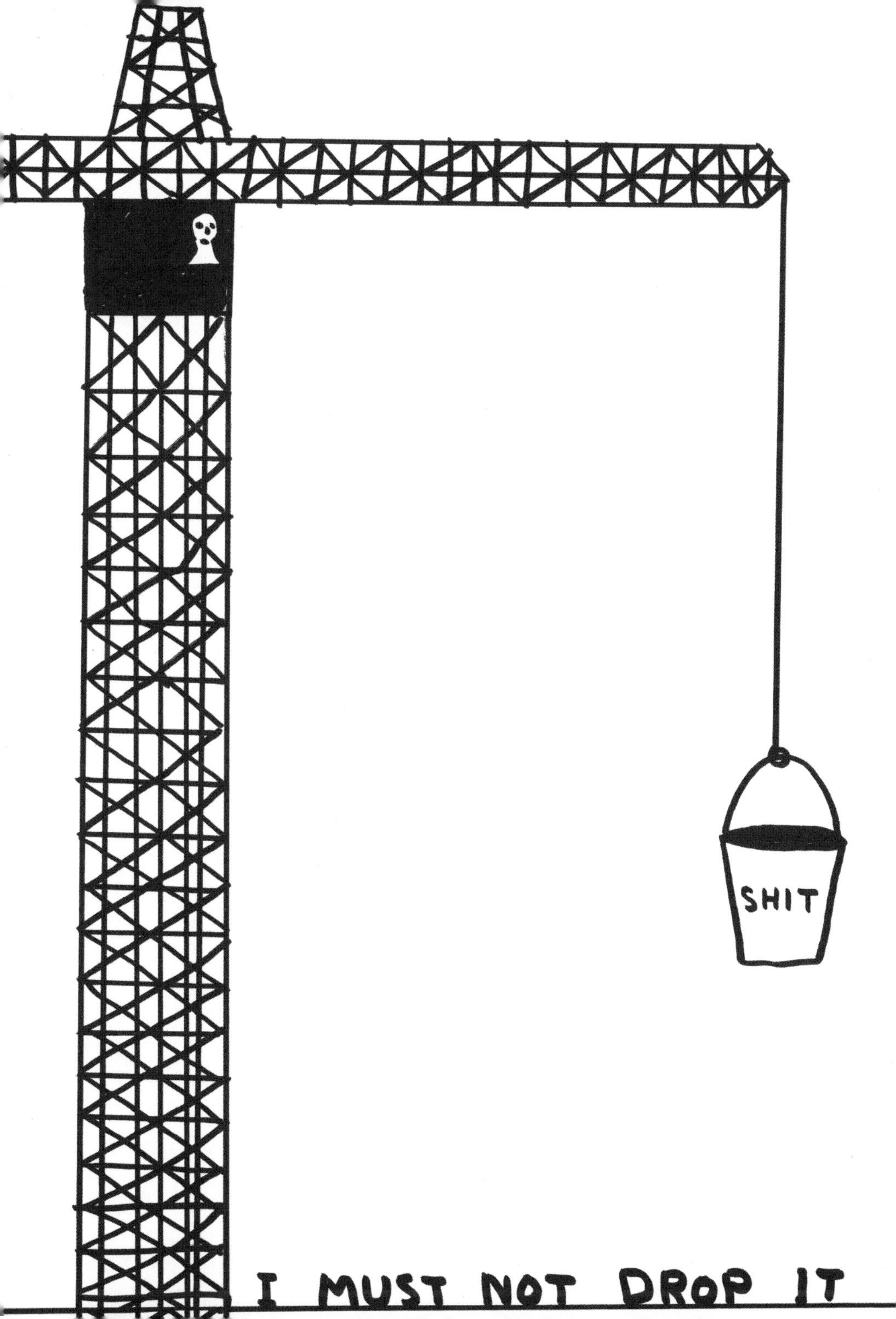

SHIT
I MUST NOT DROP IT

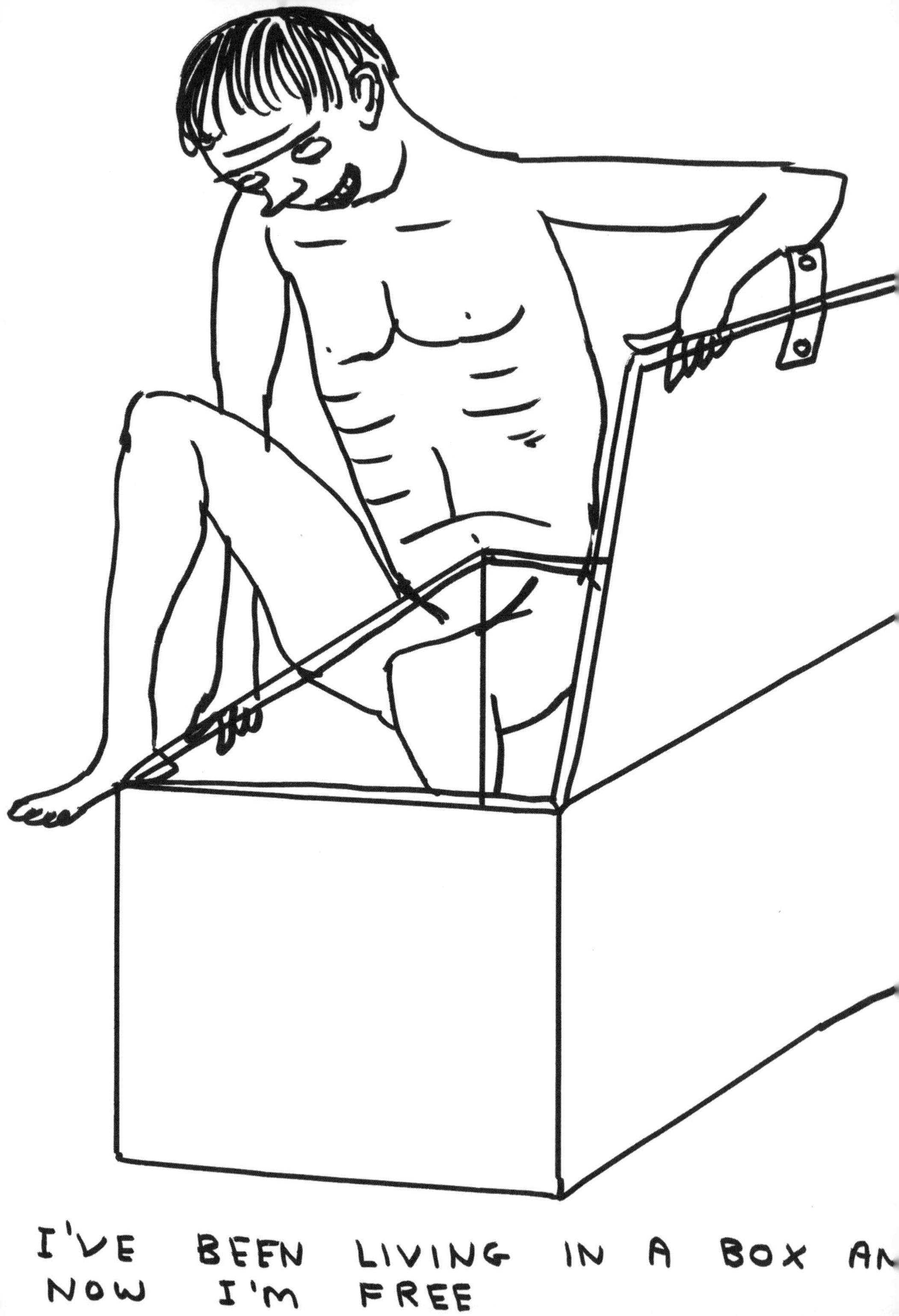

I'VE BEEN LIVING IN A BOX AN
NOW I'M FREE

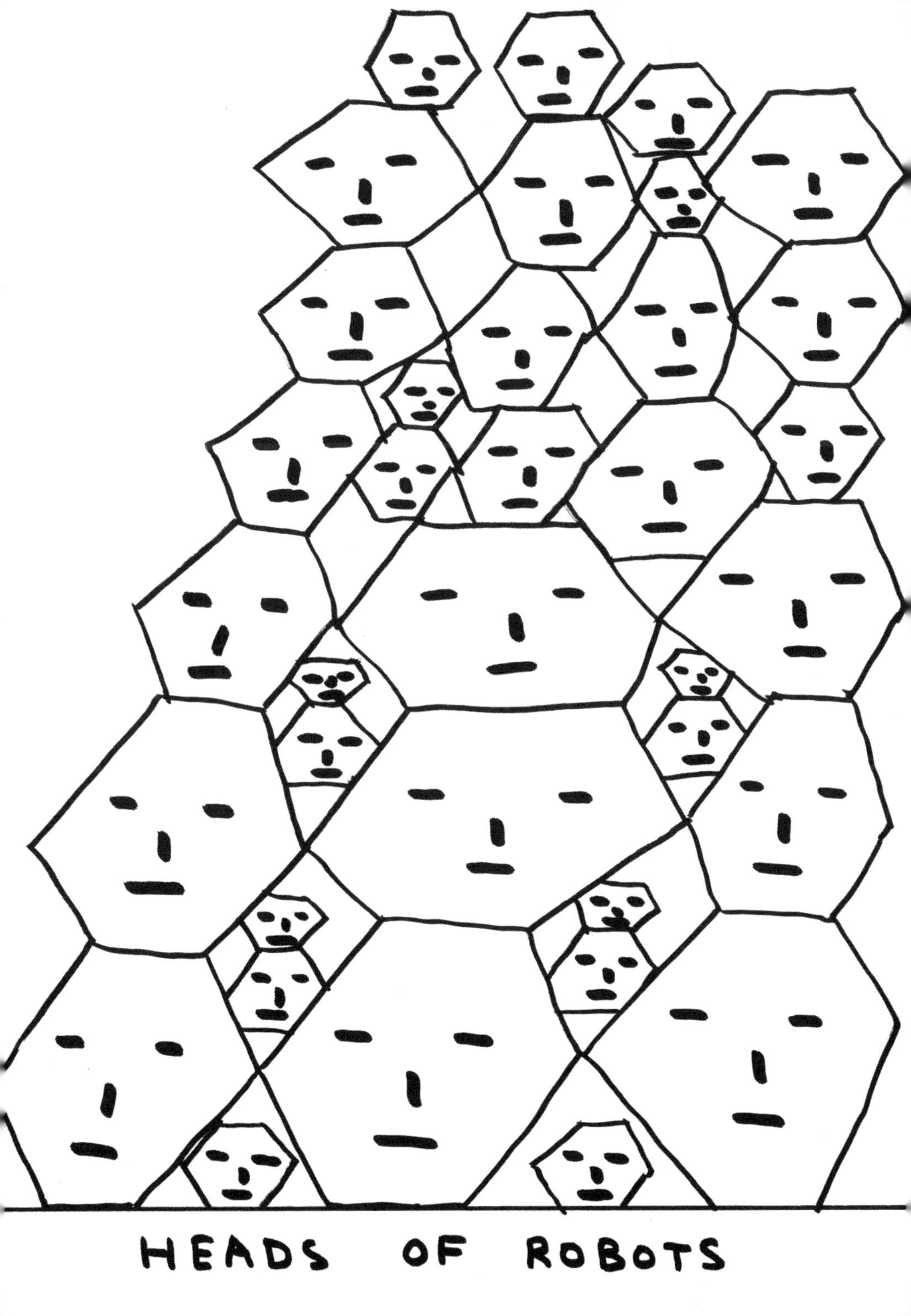

HEADS OF ROBOTS

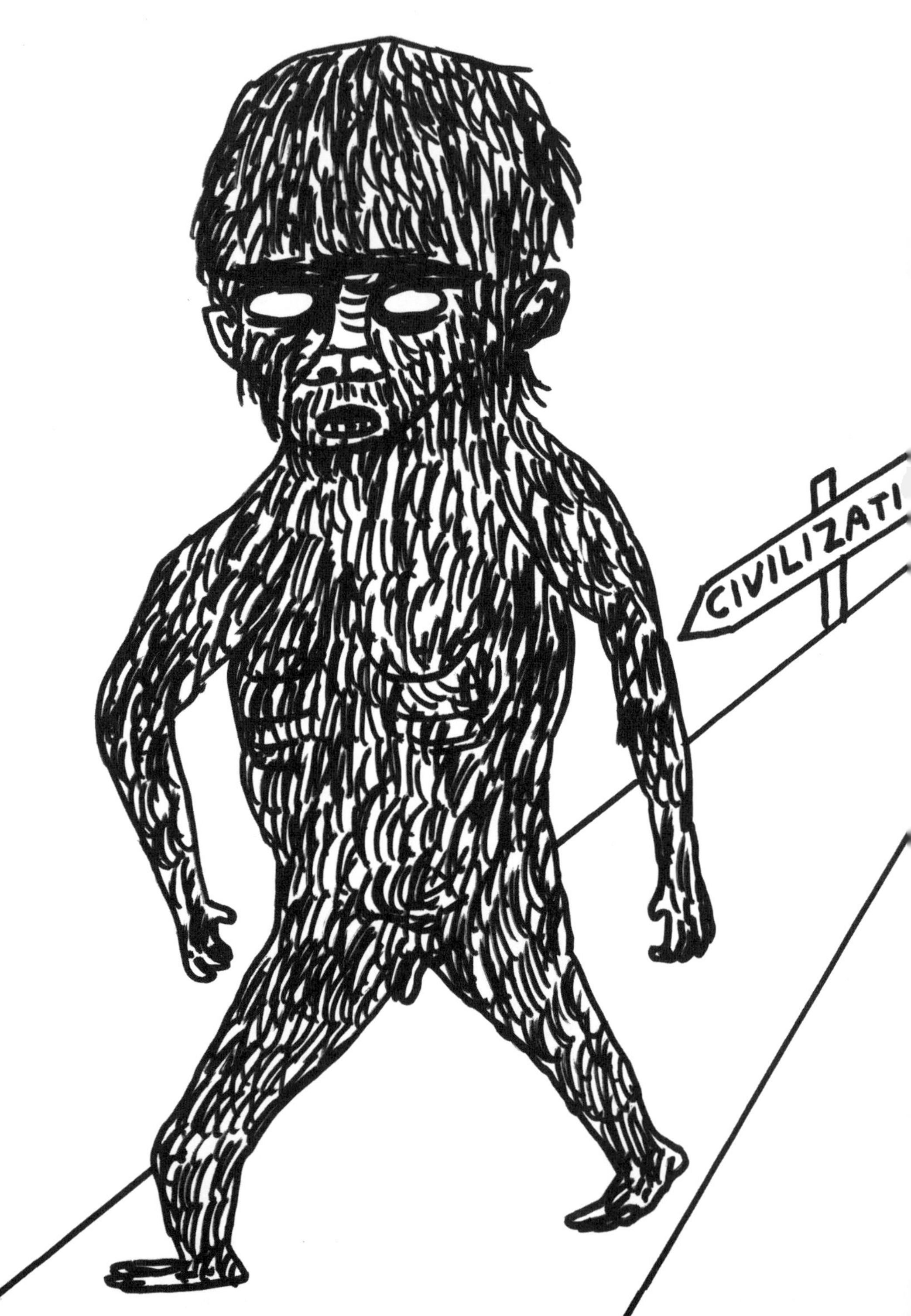

CIVILIZATI

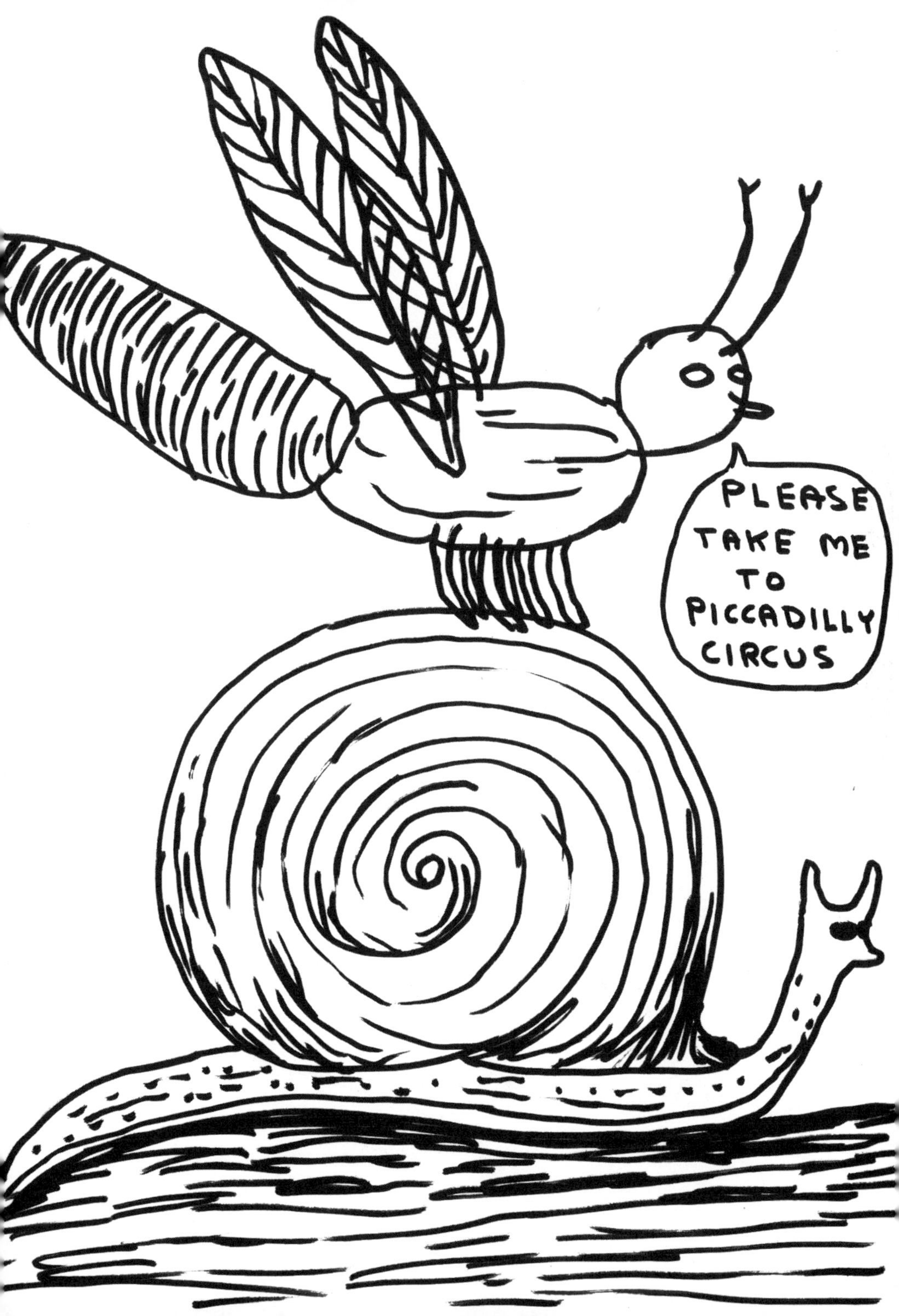

PLEASE
TAKE ME
TO
PICCADILLY
CIRCUS

NO POEM TODAY

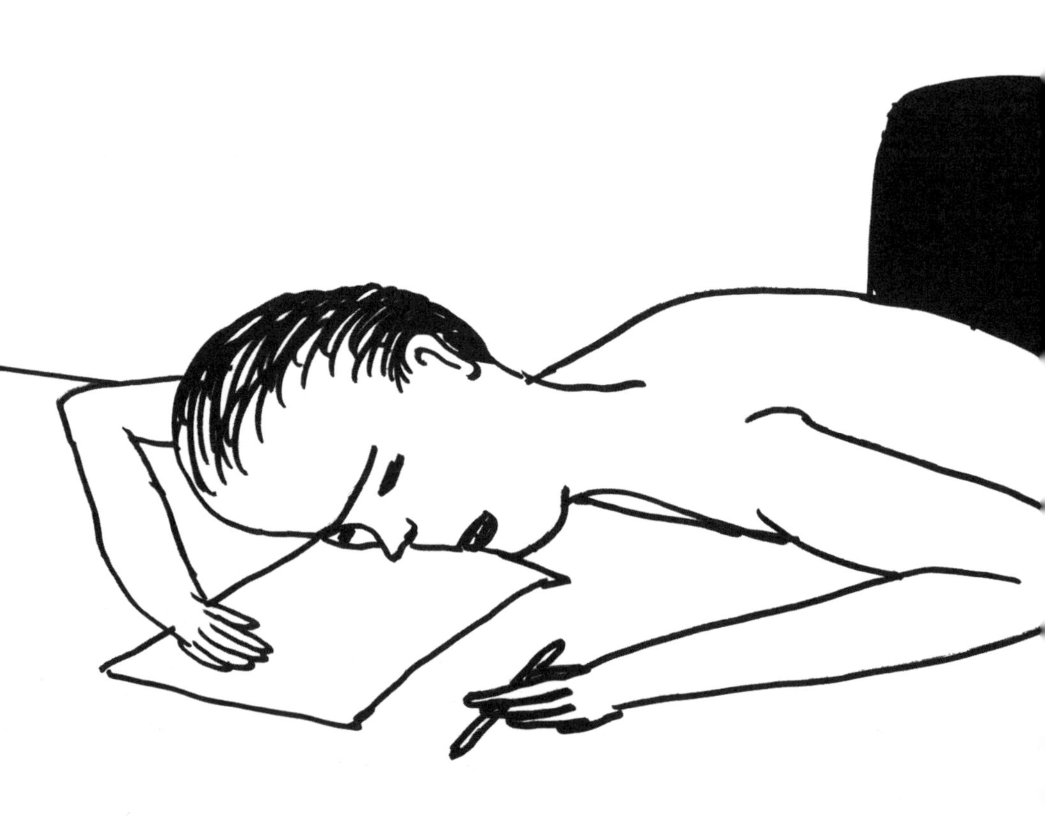

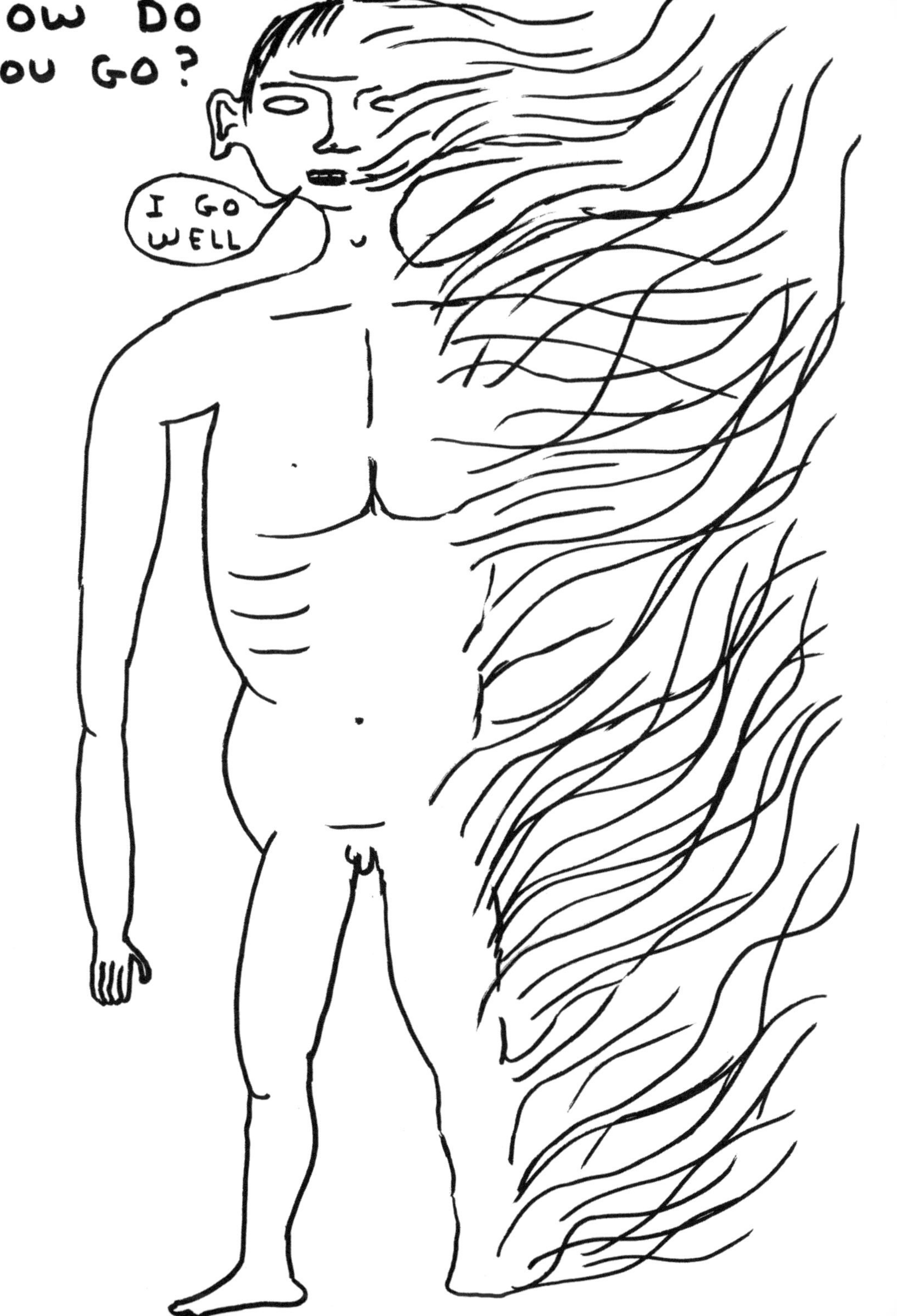
HOW DO
YOU GO?
I GO
WELL

SAFE INSIDE MY FORTRESS

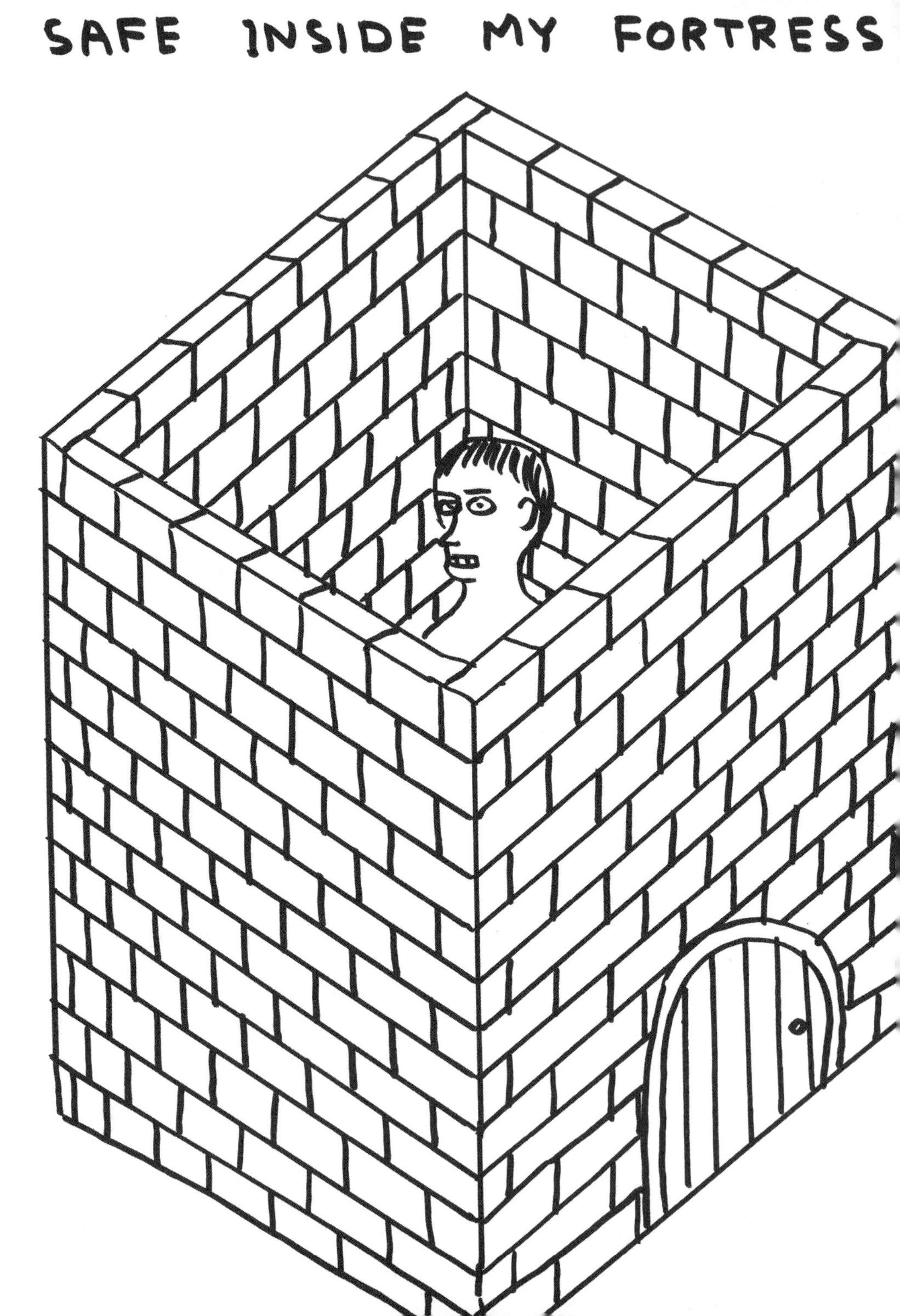

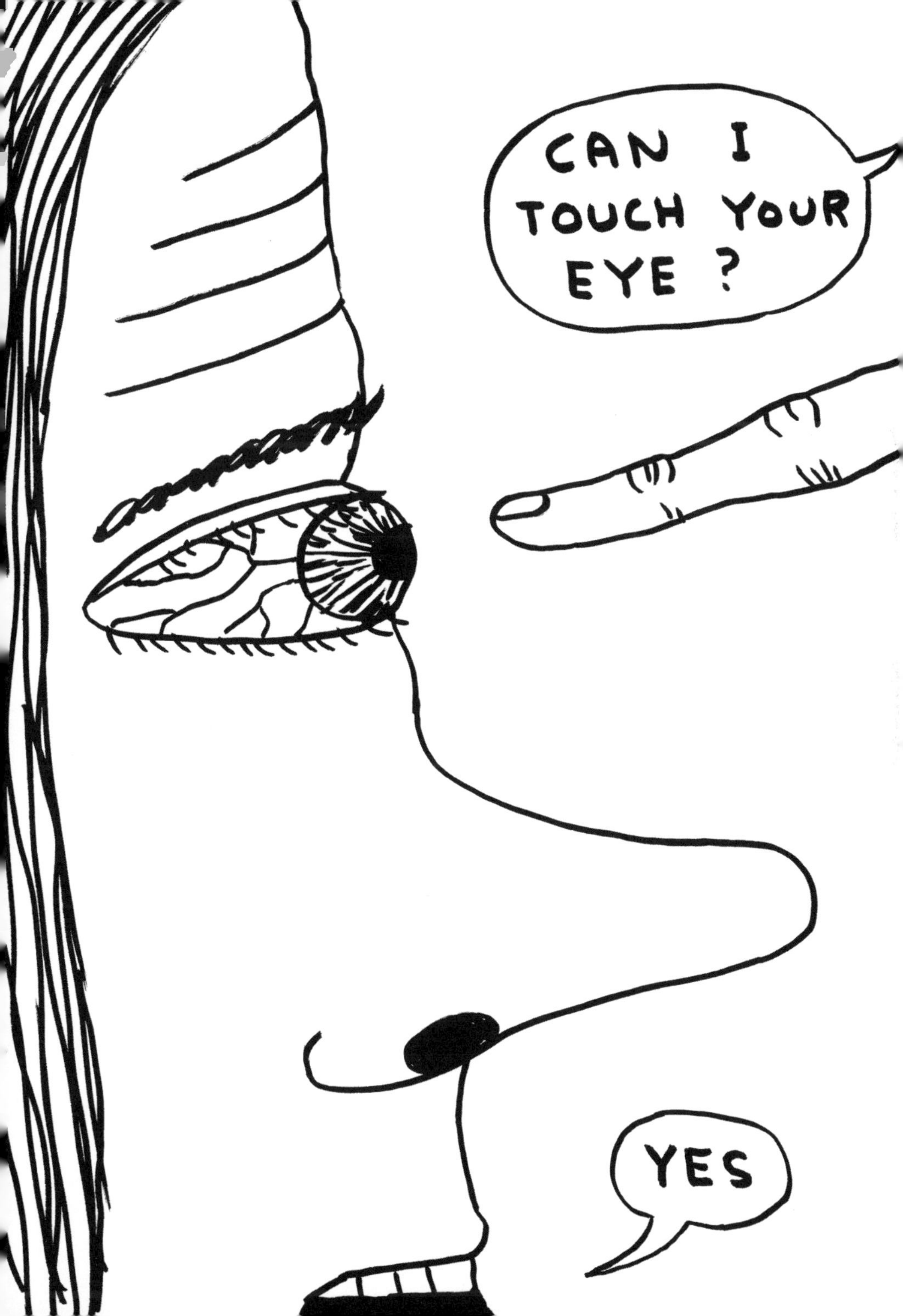

CAN I TOUCH YOUR EYE ?
YES

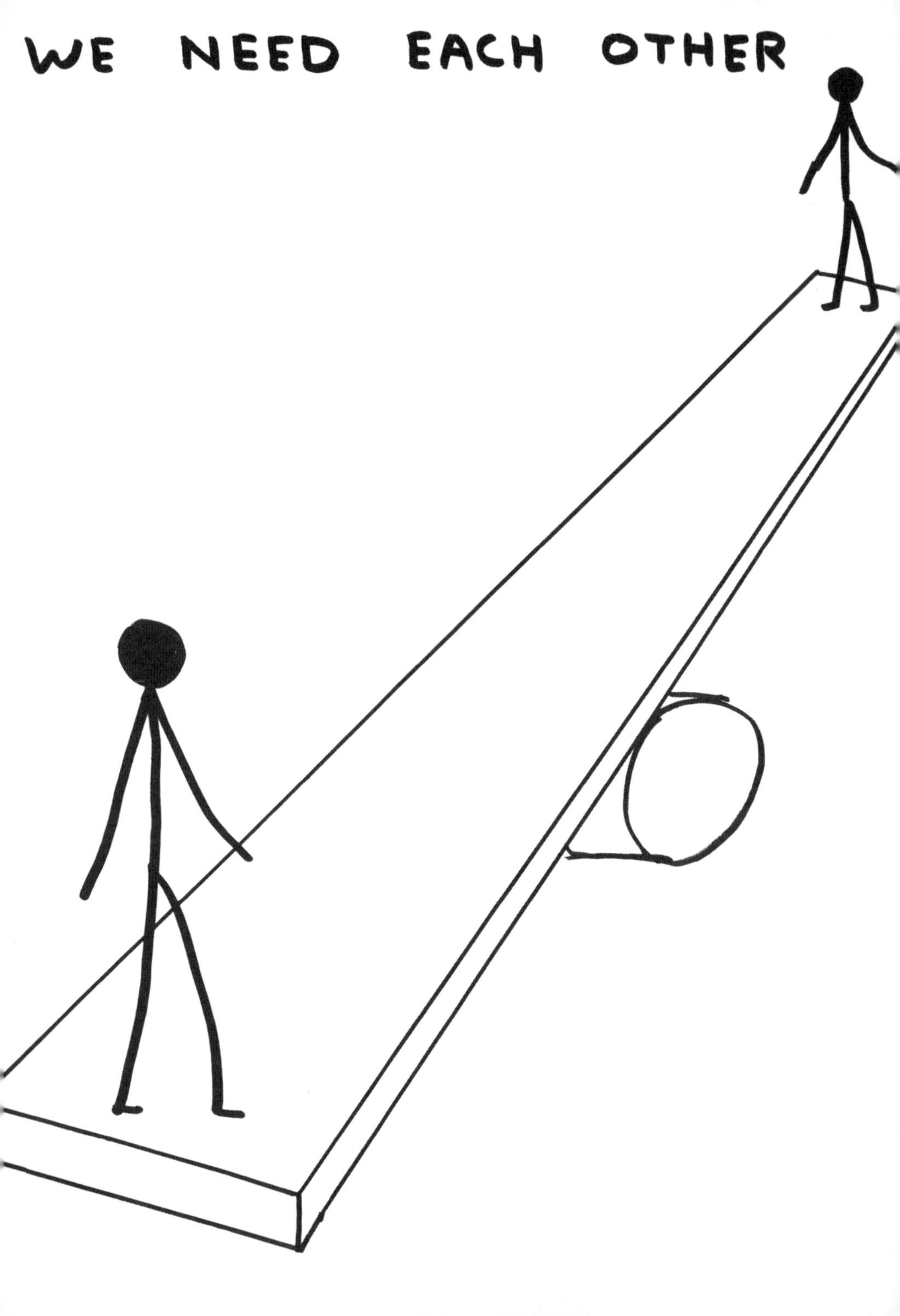

WE NEED EACH OTHER

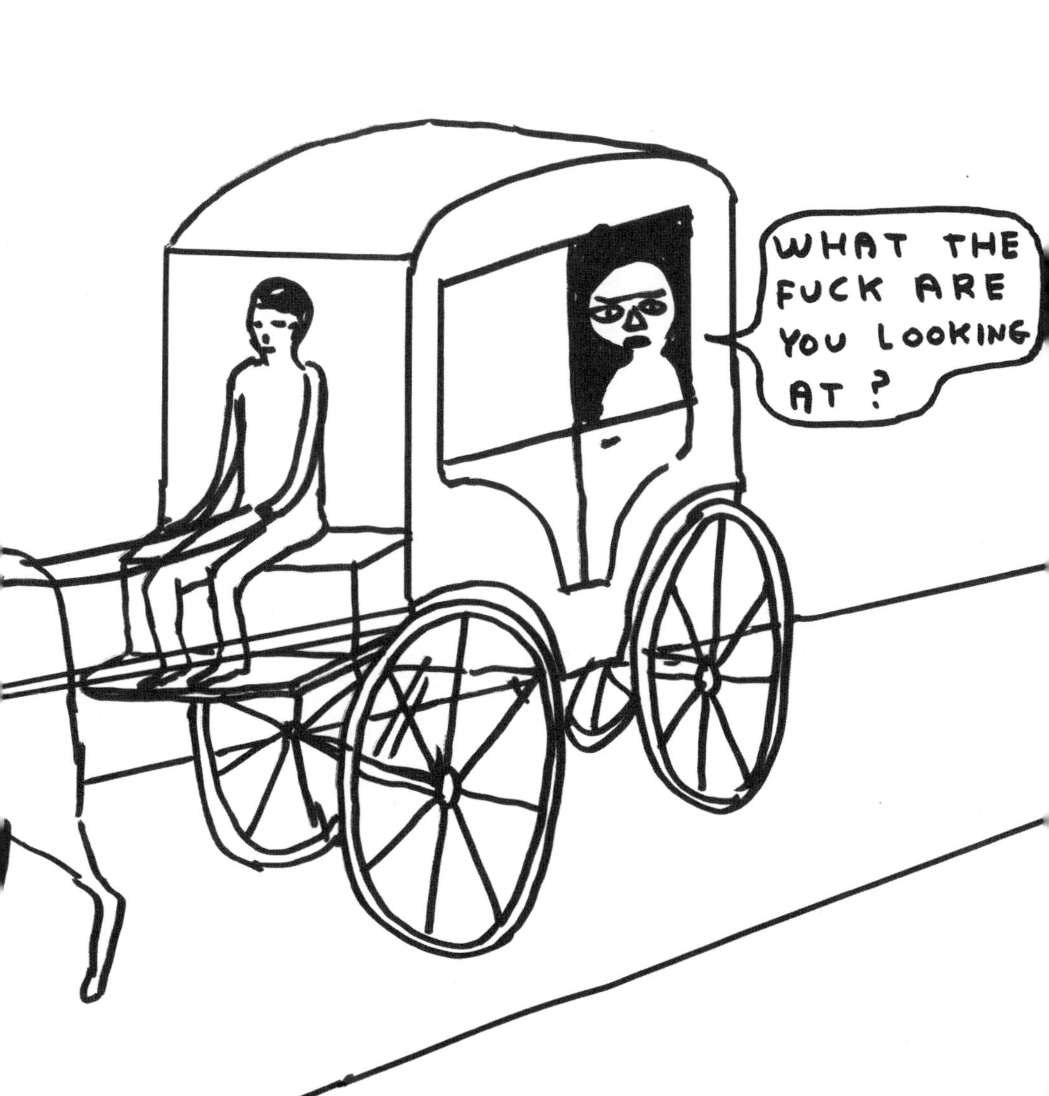

WHAT THE
FUCK ARE
YOU LOOKING
AT ?

I WROTE A WONDERFUL SONG AN
EVERYONE LOVED IT BUT THEN
BECAME TIRED OF IT AND I
STOPPED PLAYING IT AND IF
PEOPLE ASKED ME TO PLAY IT
I BECAME ANGRY AND NOW I
WILL NEVER EVER PLAY IT
AGAIN. NEVER.

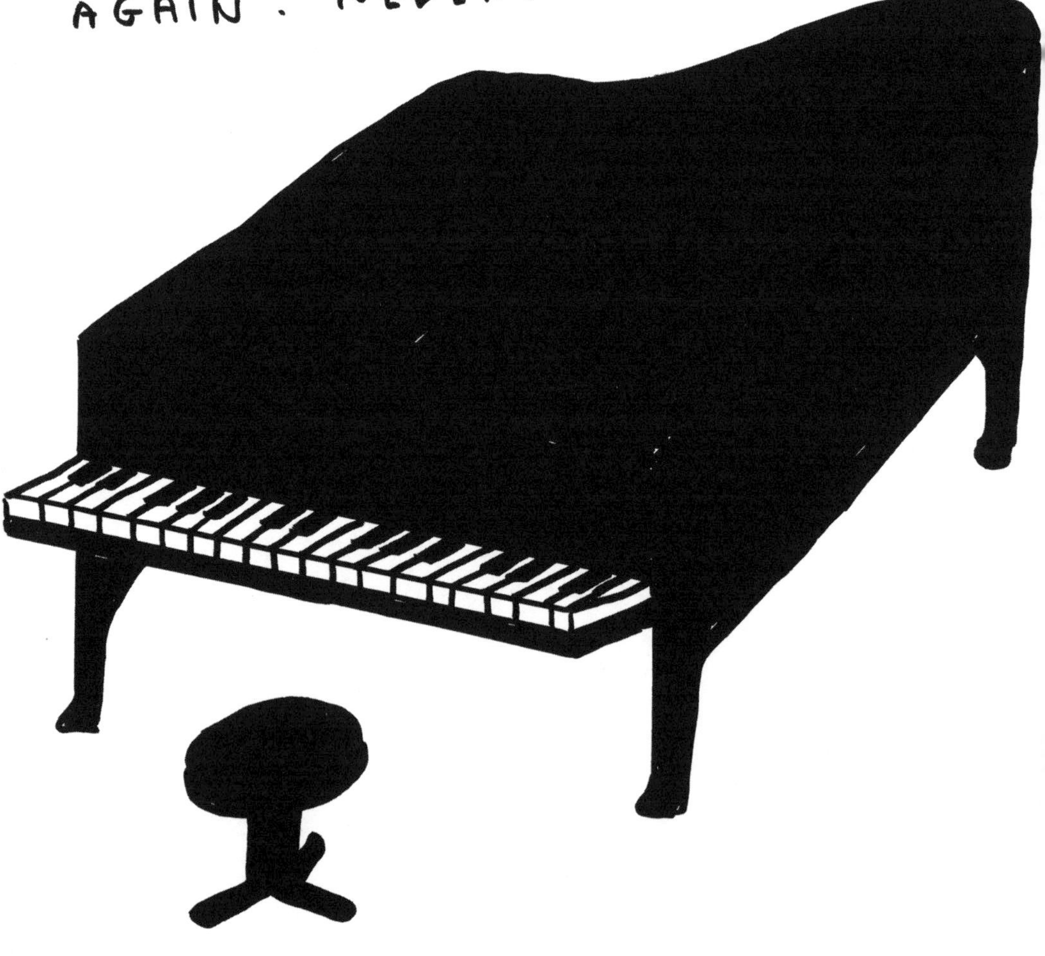

Y NEIGHBOUR HAS GROWN A
EAUTIFUL FLOWER AND I VERY
MUCH ENJOY LOOKING AT IT

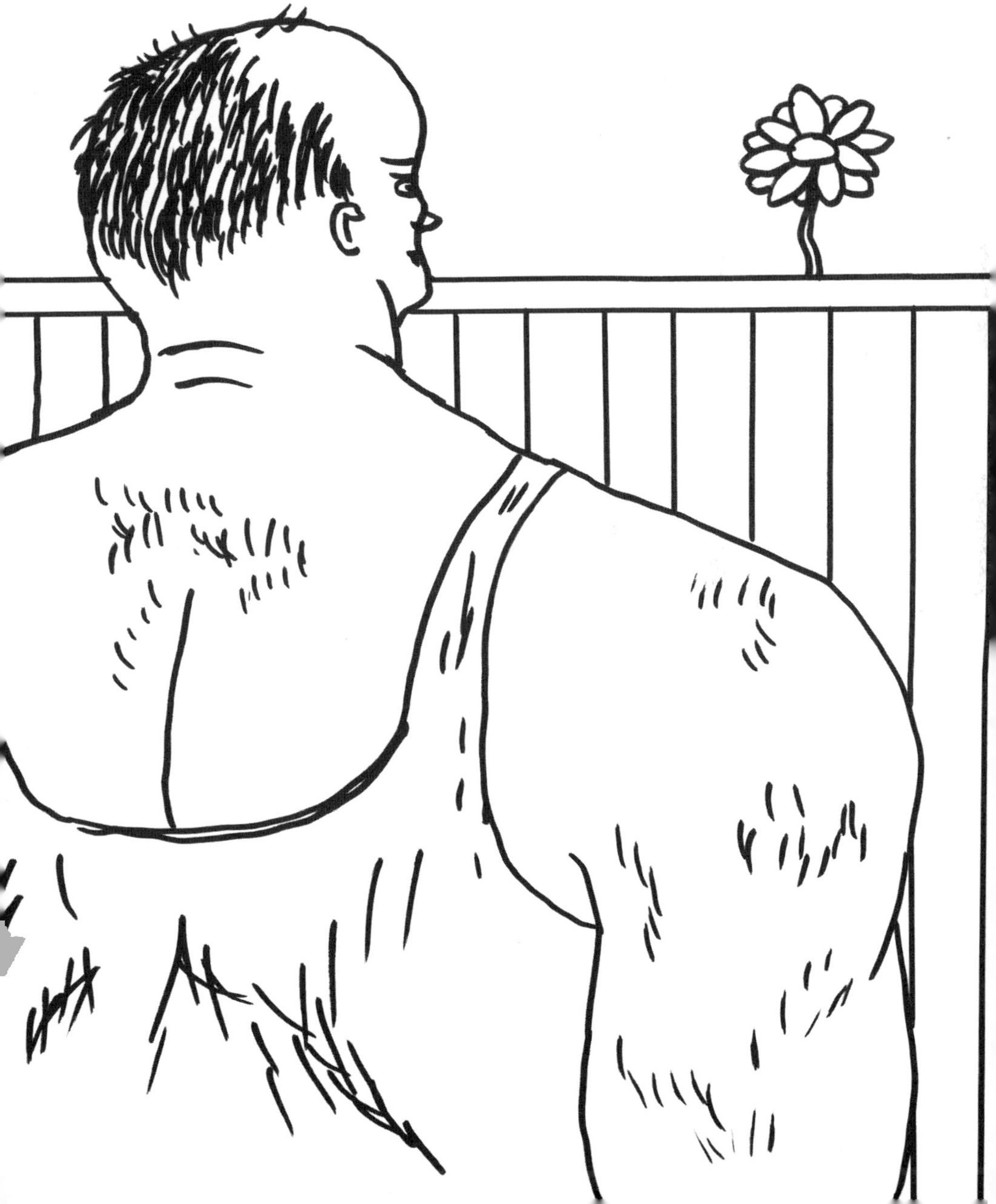

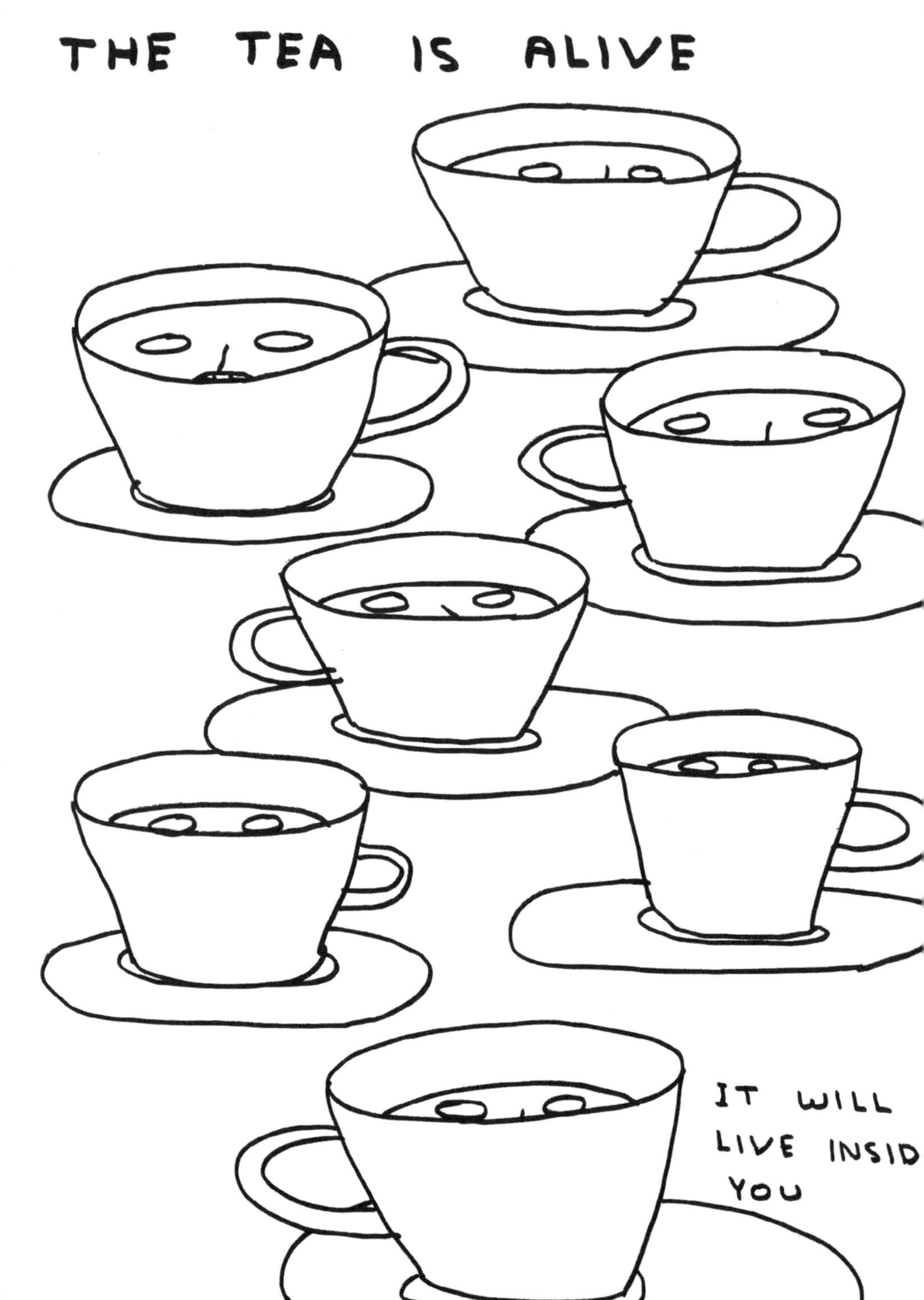

THE TEA IS ALIVE
IT WILL LIVE INSID YOU

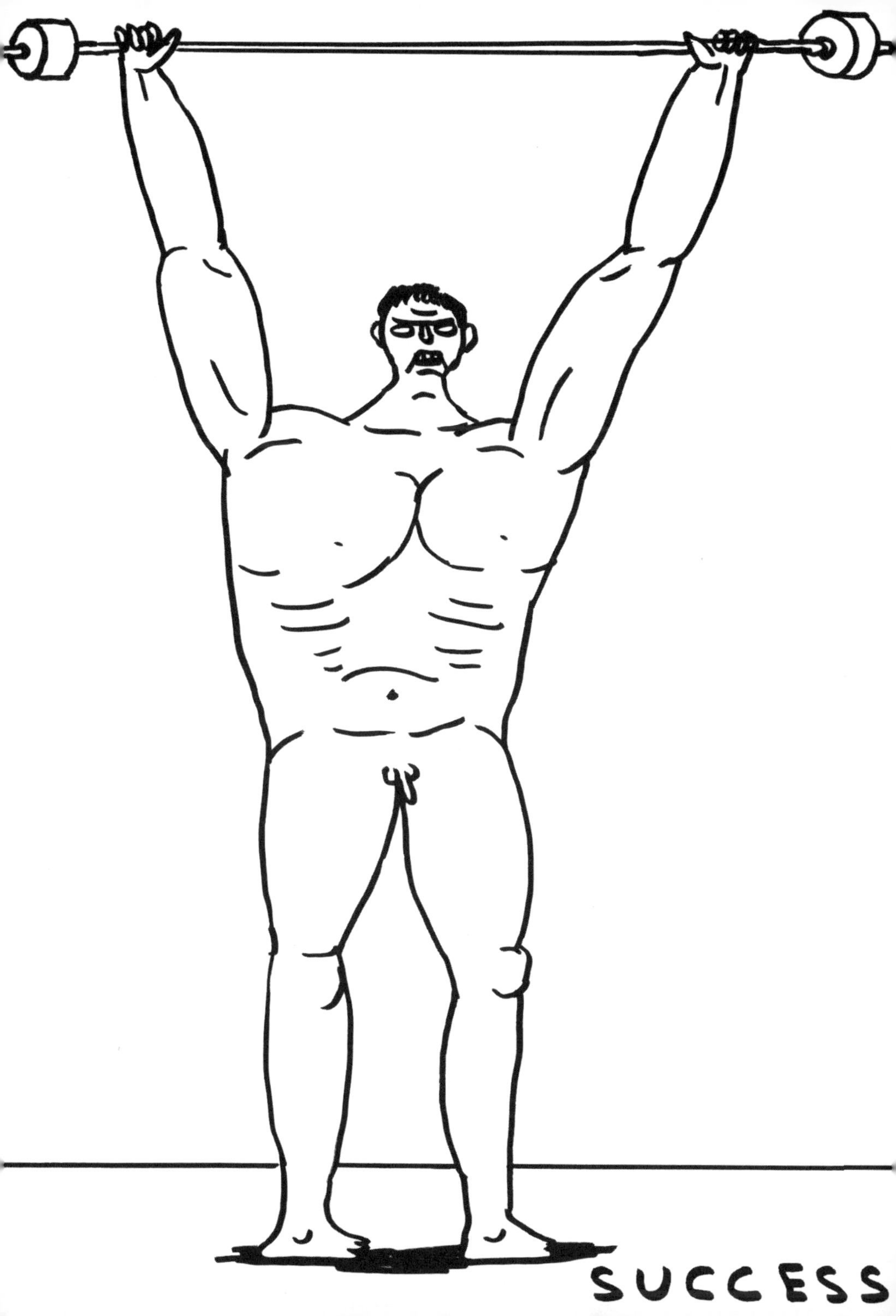

SUCCESS

BREAKING DOWN BARRIERS THROUGH SOCIAL CONTACT

FACE ON A SCREEN
TALKING TO ME
TELLING ME ABOUT THINGS
I DO NOT TRUST IT
I TRY TO SWITCH IT OFF
IT IS A MIRROR
OH DEAR

MICROAGGRESSIONS

STABBING WITH A PIN
GRIT PLACED IN THE SANDWICH
GRIT ALSO PLACED IN THE MILKSHAKE
SMALL AMOUNTS OF GLUE IN YOUR HAIR

THE DIAMOND-ENCRUSTED SKULL

I WANT THAT FUCKING THING
I WANT IT SO BADLY
GIVE IT TO ME
OR I'M GOING TO COME OVER
AND TAKE IT FROM YOU

LABELLING THEORY

"YOU ARE A DEGENERATE"
YES, I AM A DEGENERATE
I AM SORRY

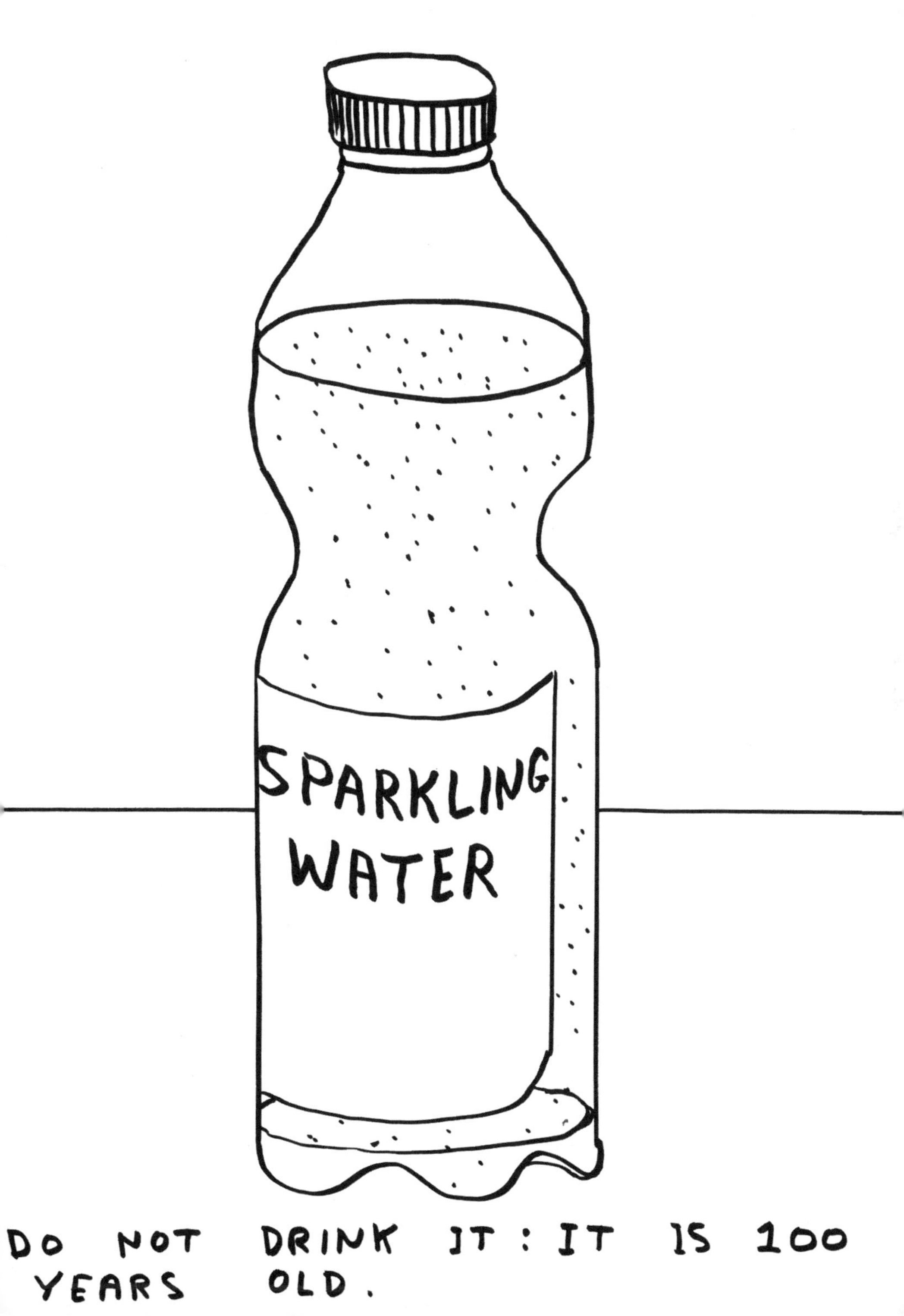

DO NOT DRINK IT : IT IS 100 YEARS OLD.

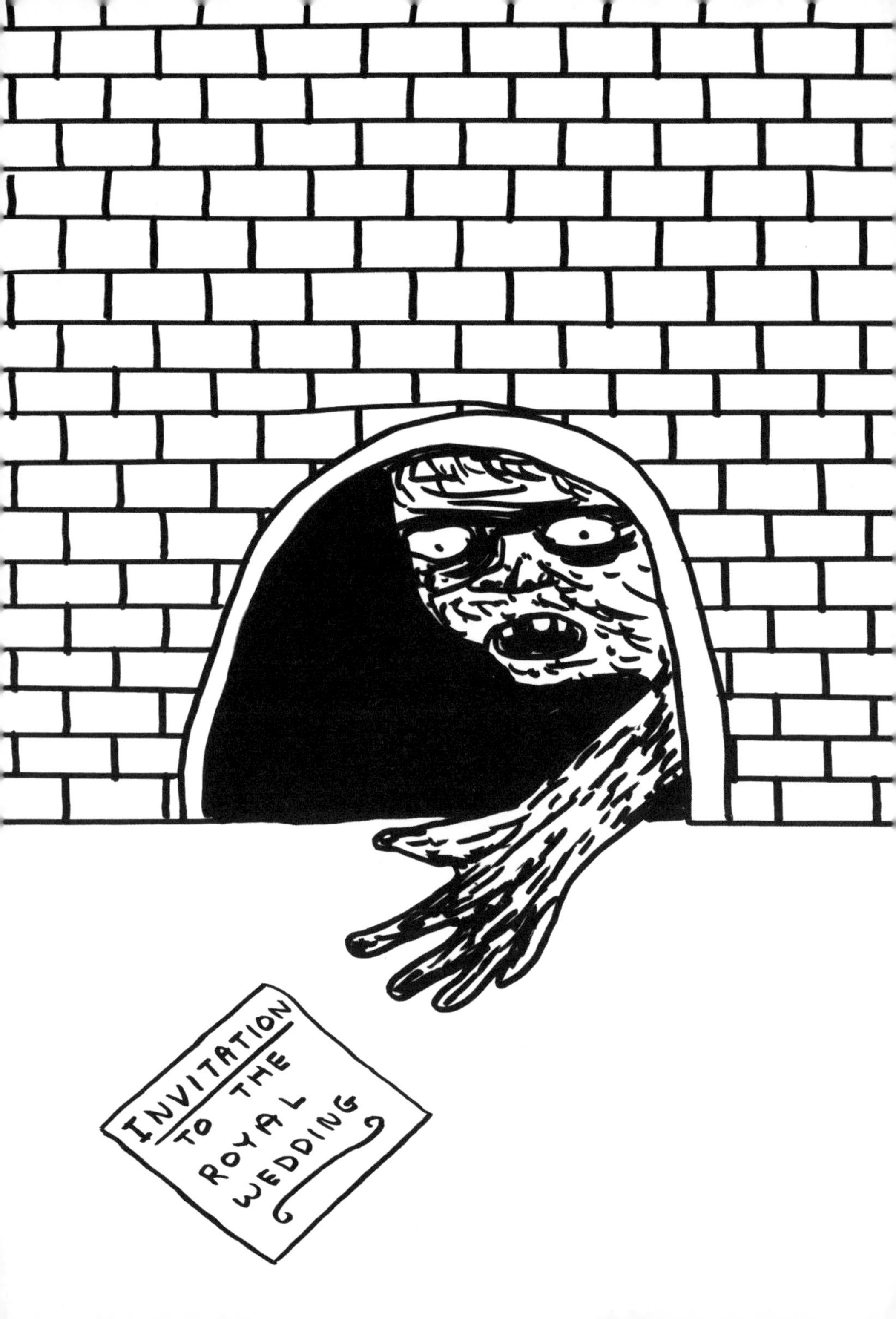

INVITATION TO THE ROYAL WEDDING

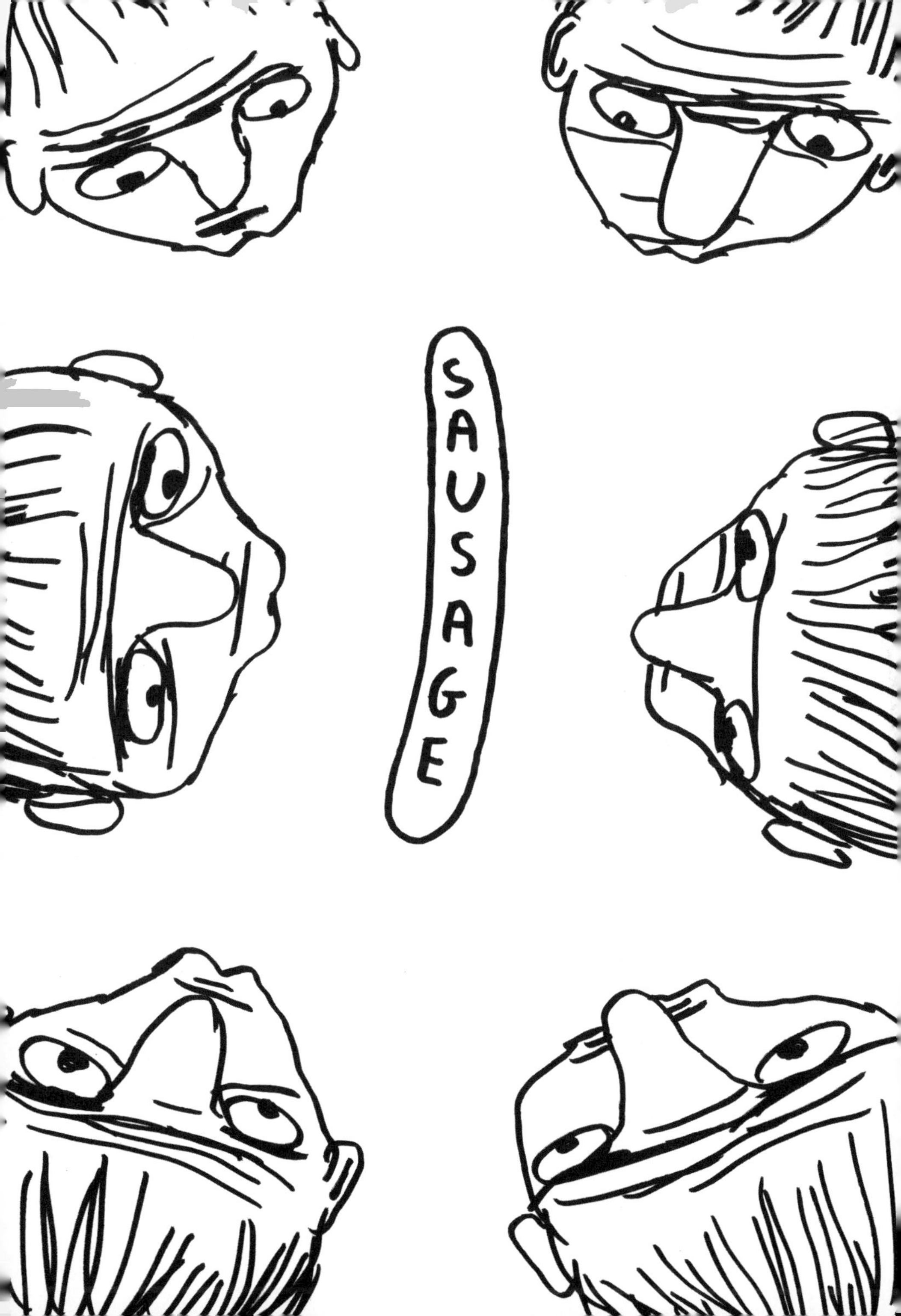

SAUSAGE

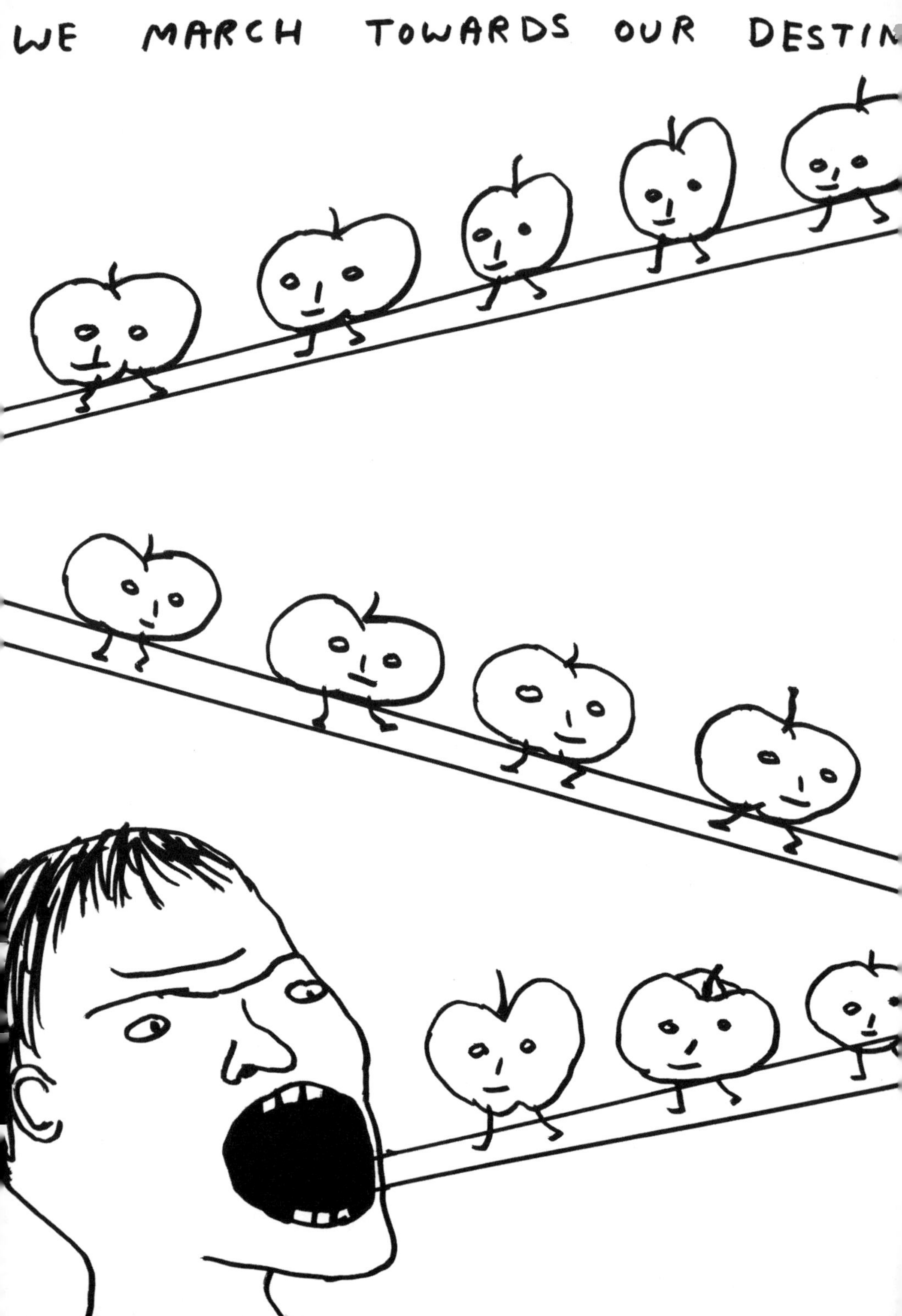

WE MARCH TOWARDS OUR DESTIN

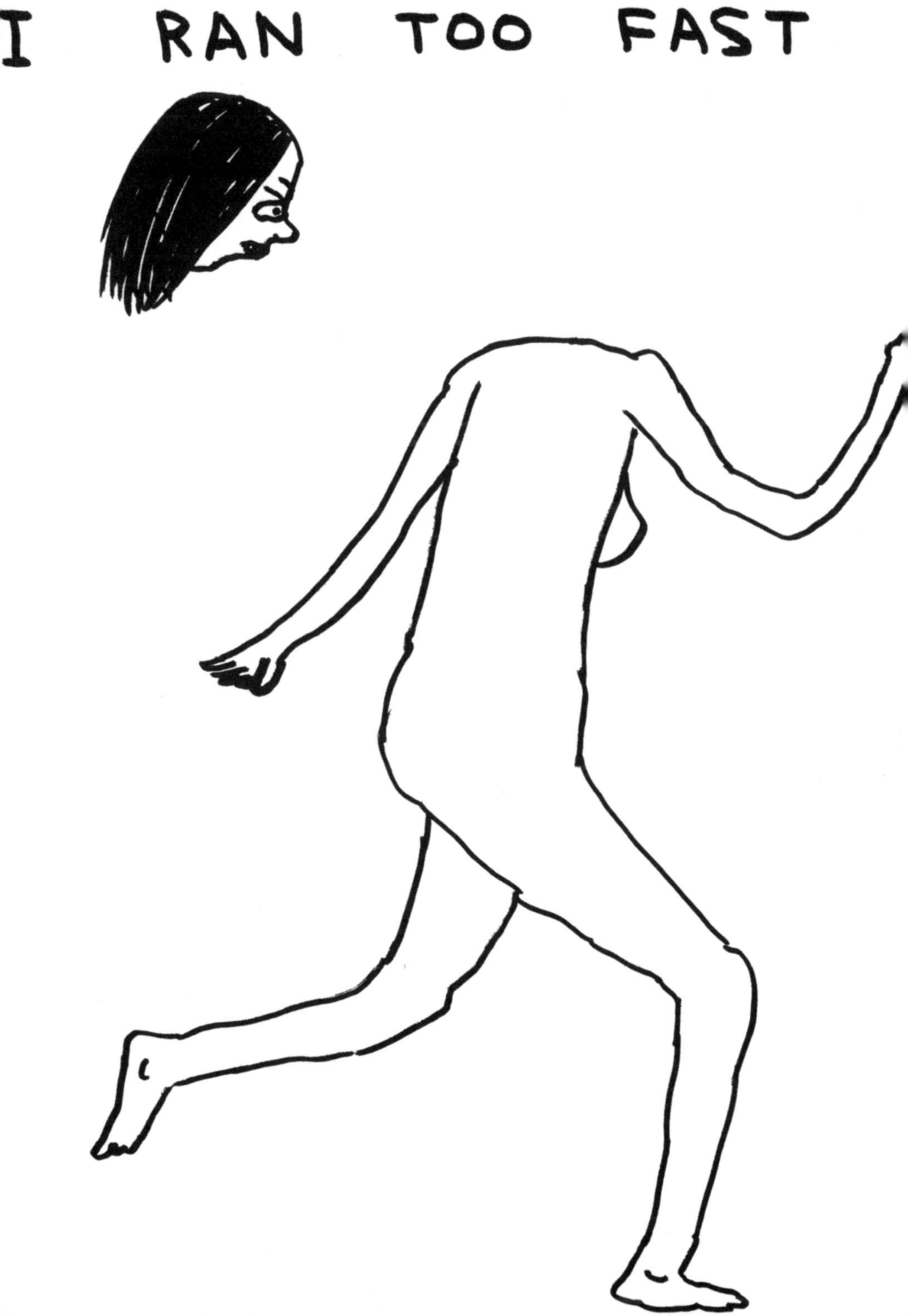
I RAN TOO FAST

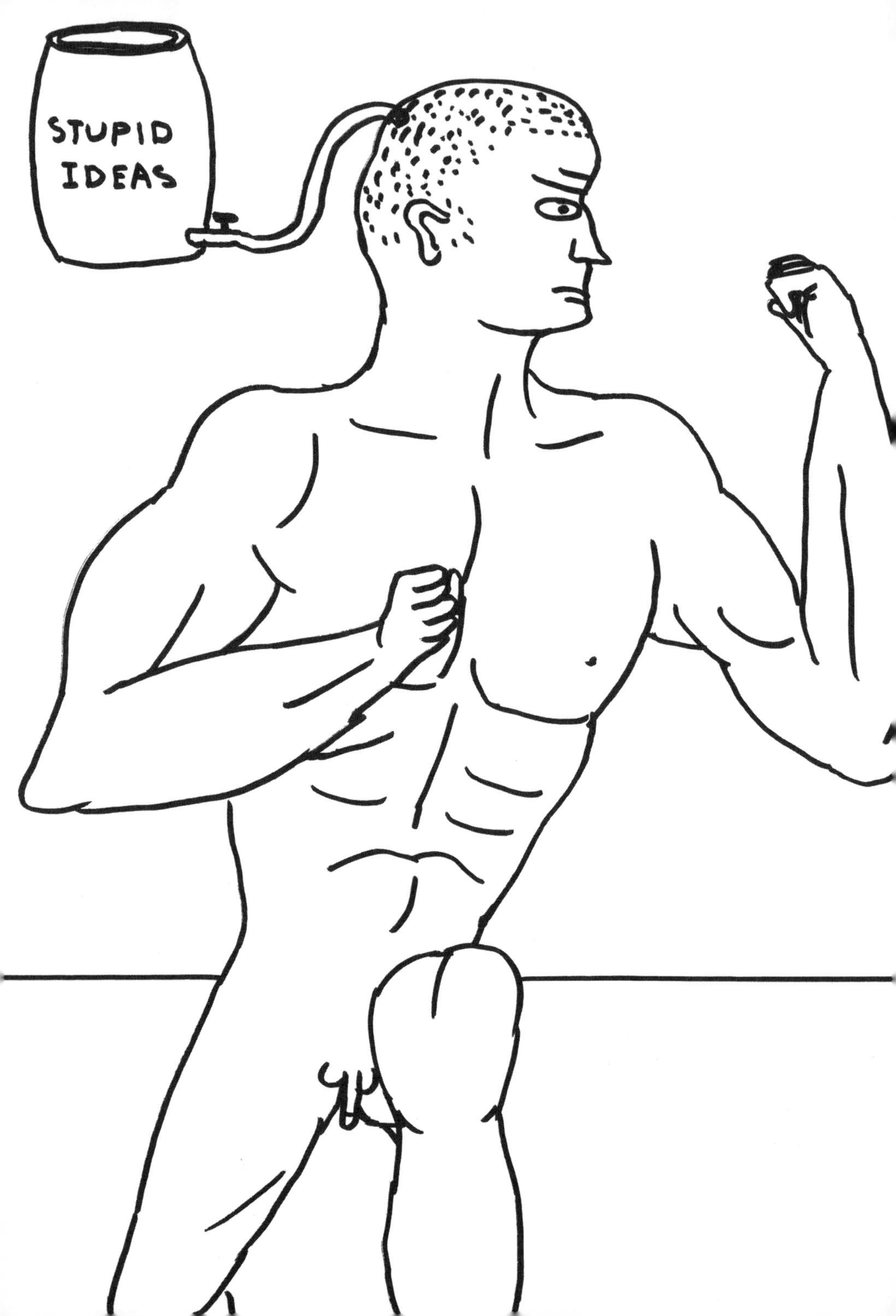

STUPID
IDEAS

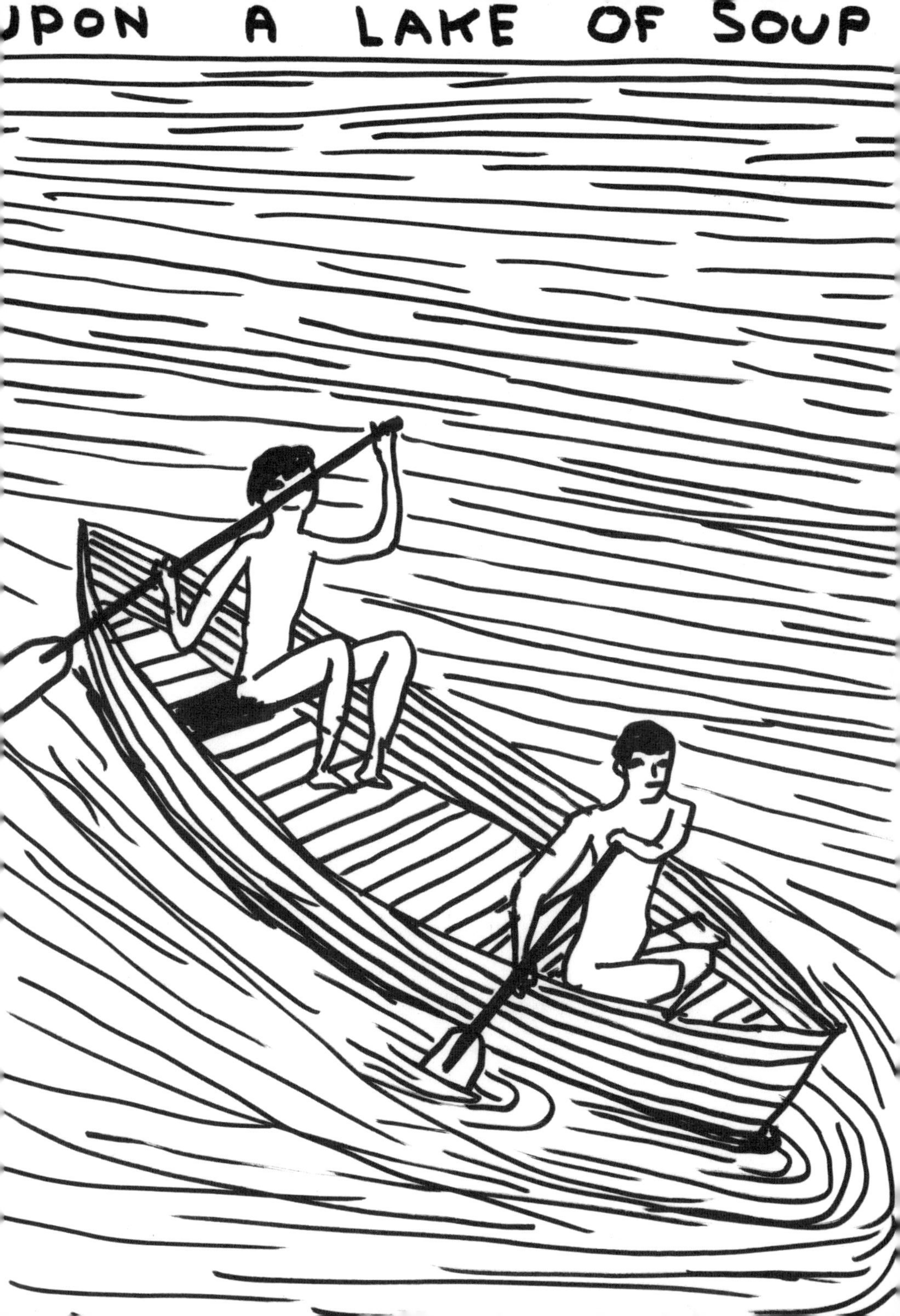
UPON A LAKE OF SOUP

THE FAMILY UNIT

DADDY
MUMMY
YOU
BABY
EVIL SPIRIT
CAT

HEROES / HEROINES AND THEIR DEEDS

I MADE AN OMELETTE

SOLUTIONS TO PROBLEMS

PROBLEMS CAN BE SOLVED
THROUGH DISCUSSION
AND THROUGH DUELS

WINDOW VS MIRROR

YOU MUST CHOOSE
WE MUST CHOOSE

LOOKING THROUGH THE PRISM

THINGS LOOK THE SAME THROUGH IT
IT IS A NEUTRAL PRISM
IT IS MADE OF PLASTIC

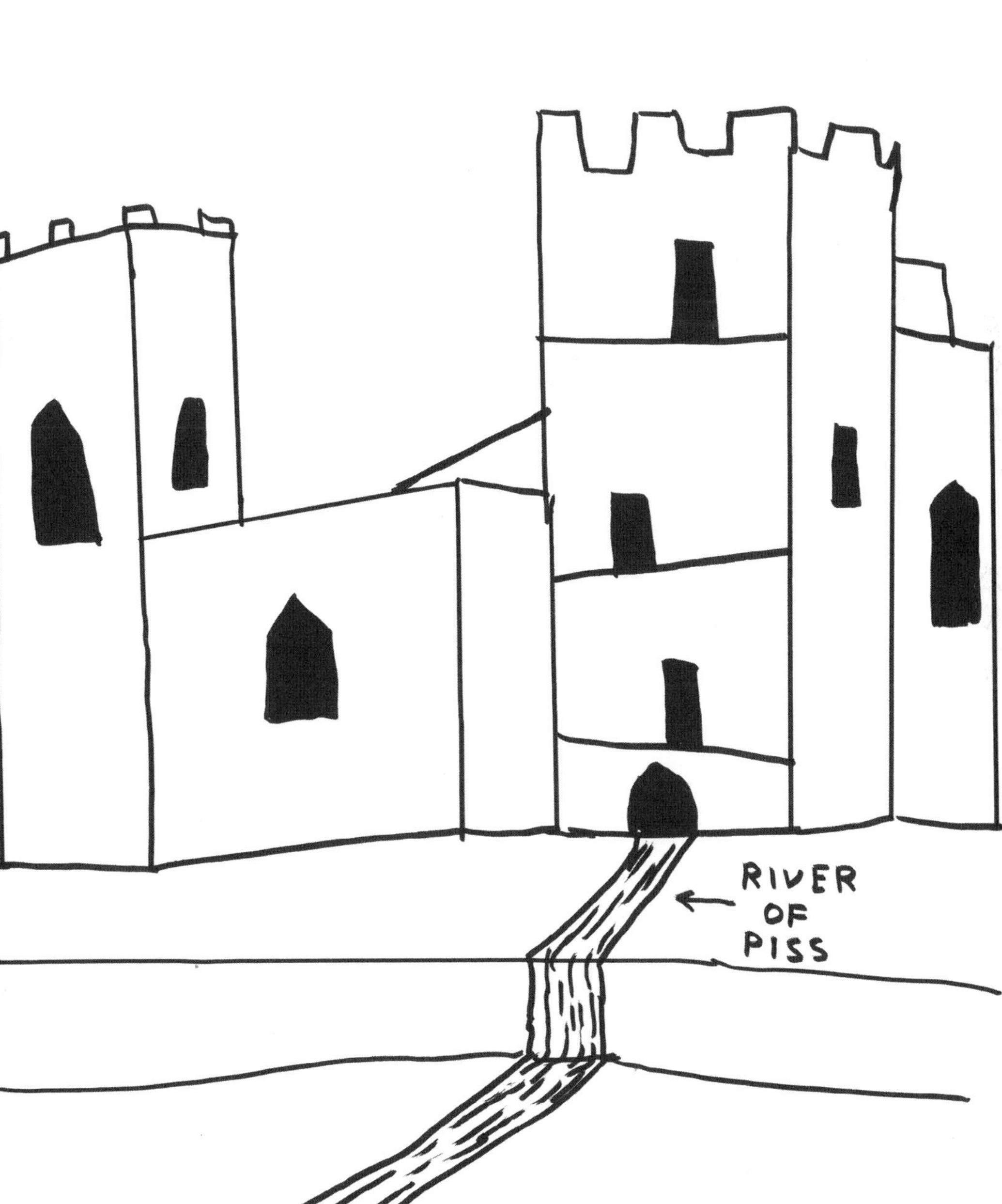
RIVER
OF
PISS

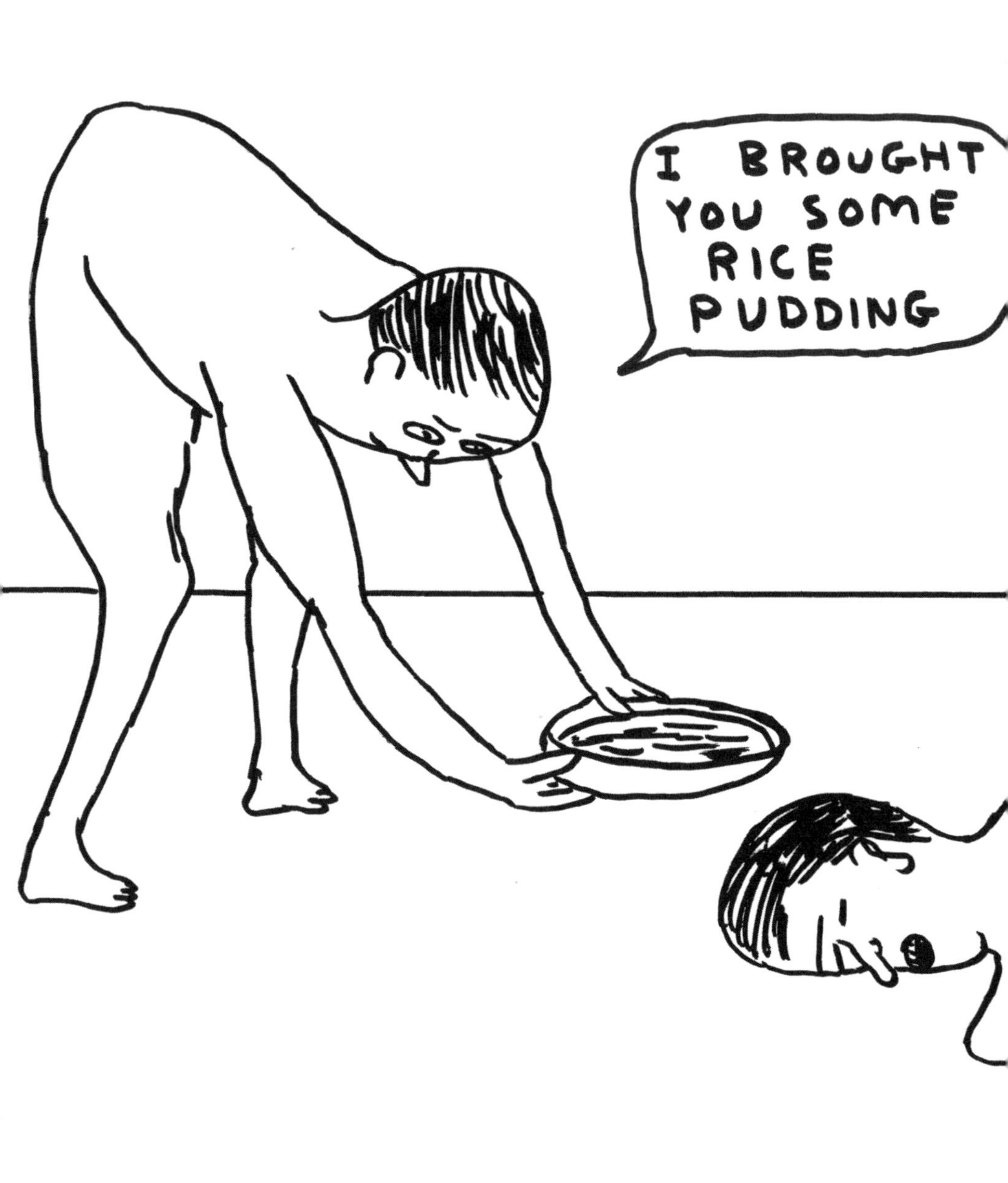

I BROUGHT YOU SOME RICE PUDDING

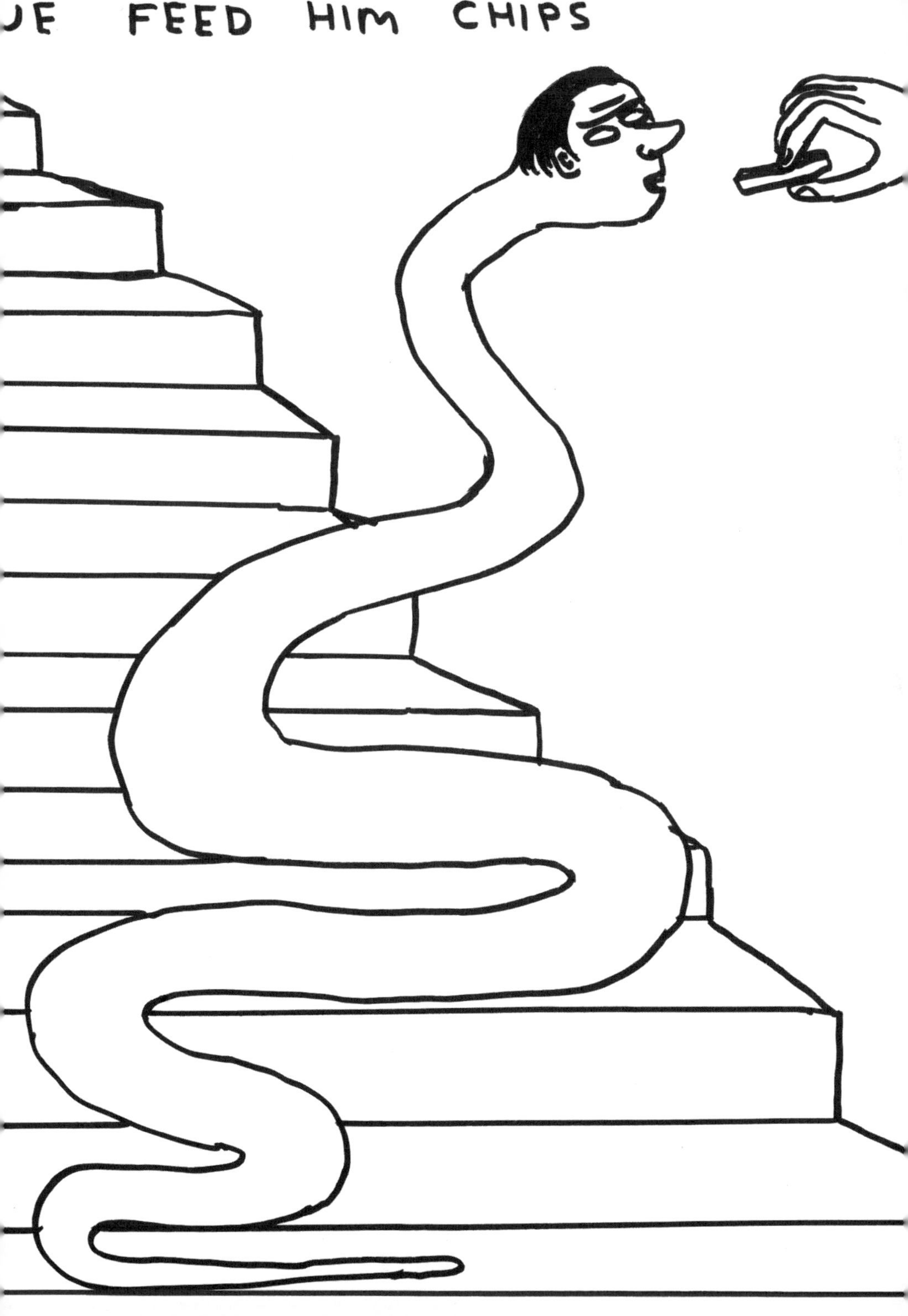
JE FEED HIM CHIPS

THOUGHTS

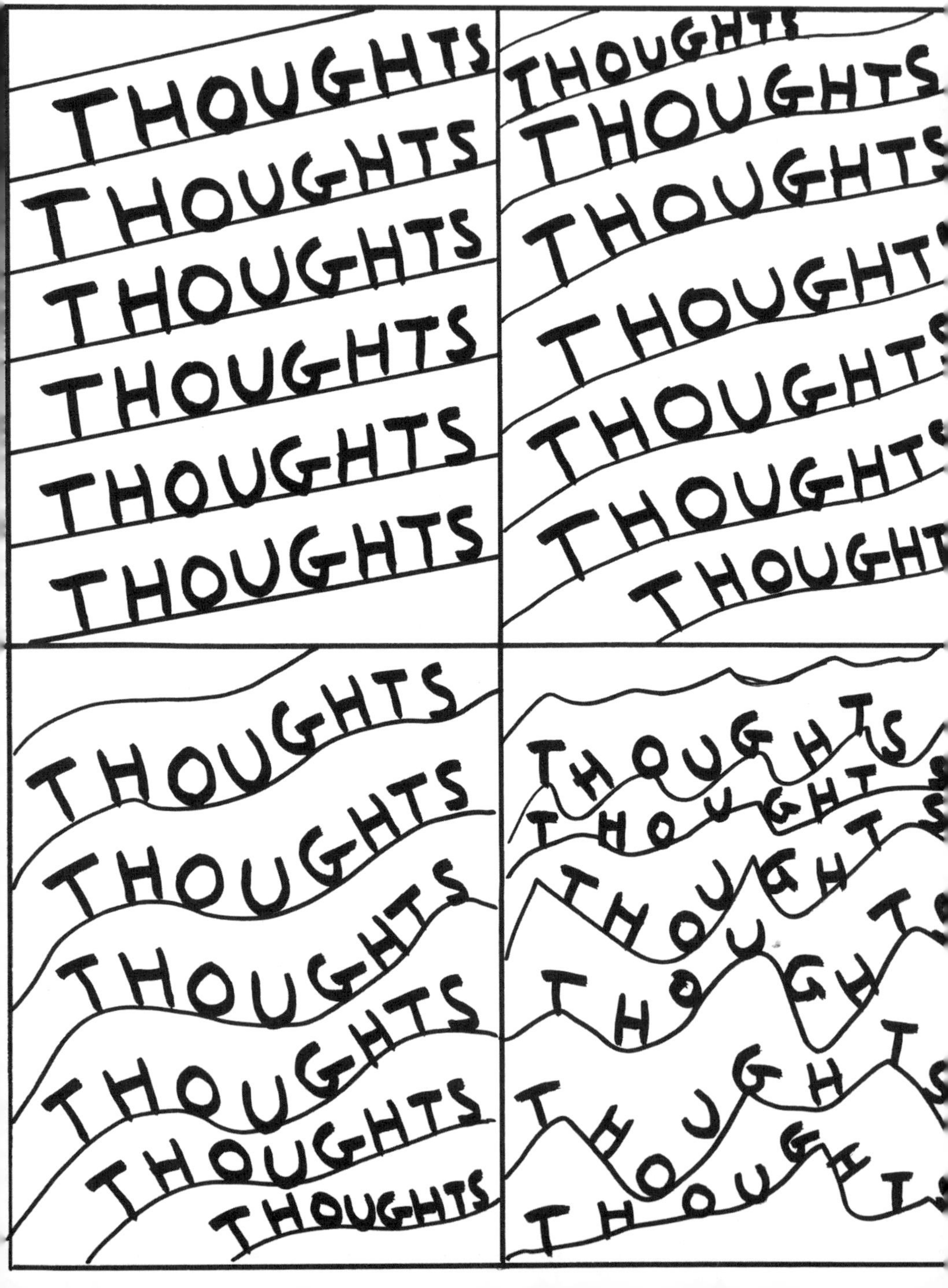

THOUGHTS
THOUGHTS
THOUGHTS
THOUGHTS
THOUGHTS
THOUGHTS

THOUGHTS
THOUGHTS
THOUGHTS
THOUGHTS
THOUGHTS
THOUGHTS
THOUGHT

THOUGHTS
THOUGHTS
THOUGHTS
THOUGHTS
THOUGHTS
THOUGHTS

THOUGHTS
THOUGHTS
THOUGHTS
THOUGHTS
THOUGHTS
THOUGHTS

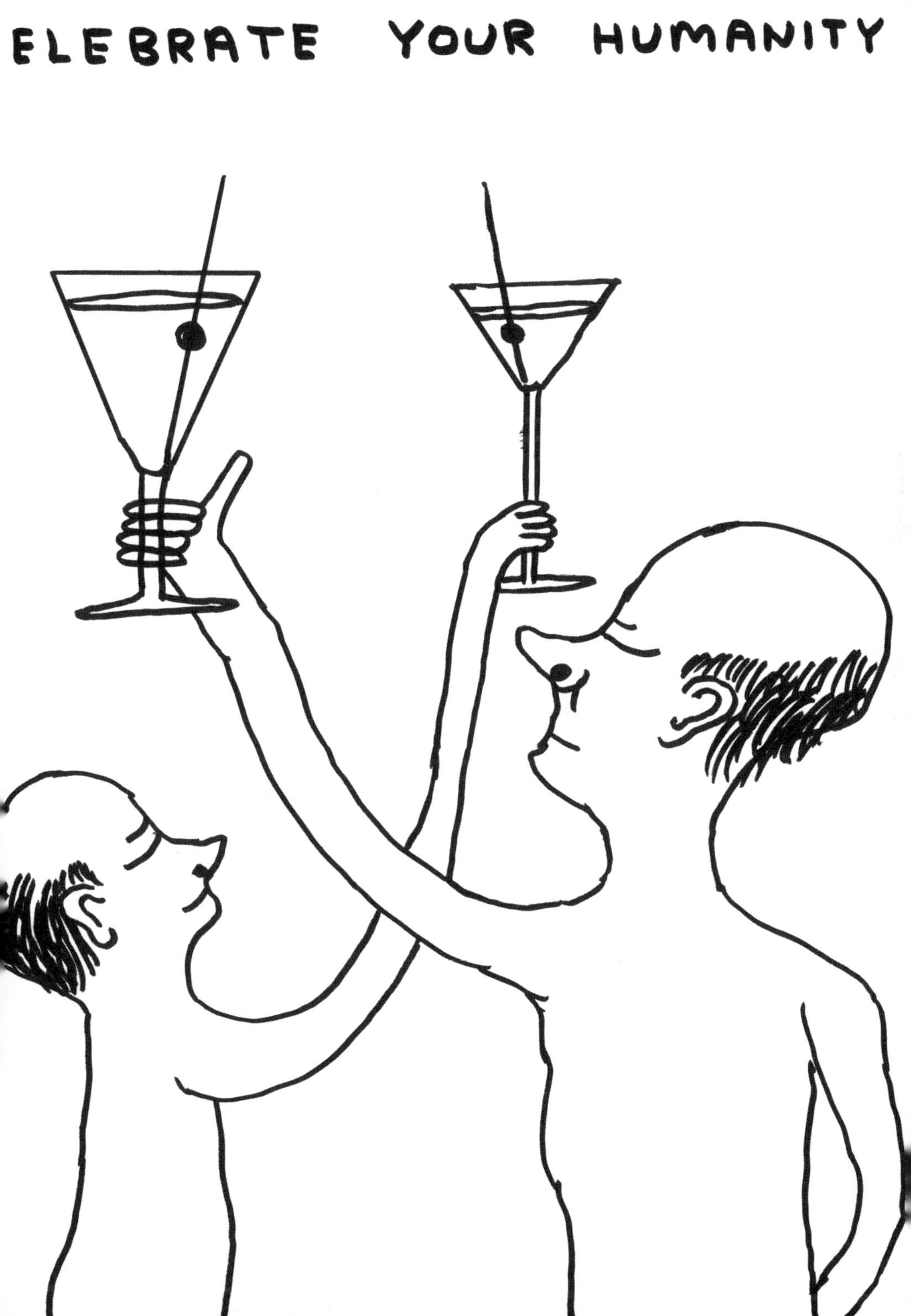
ELEBRATE YOUR HUMANITY

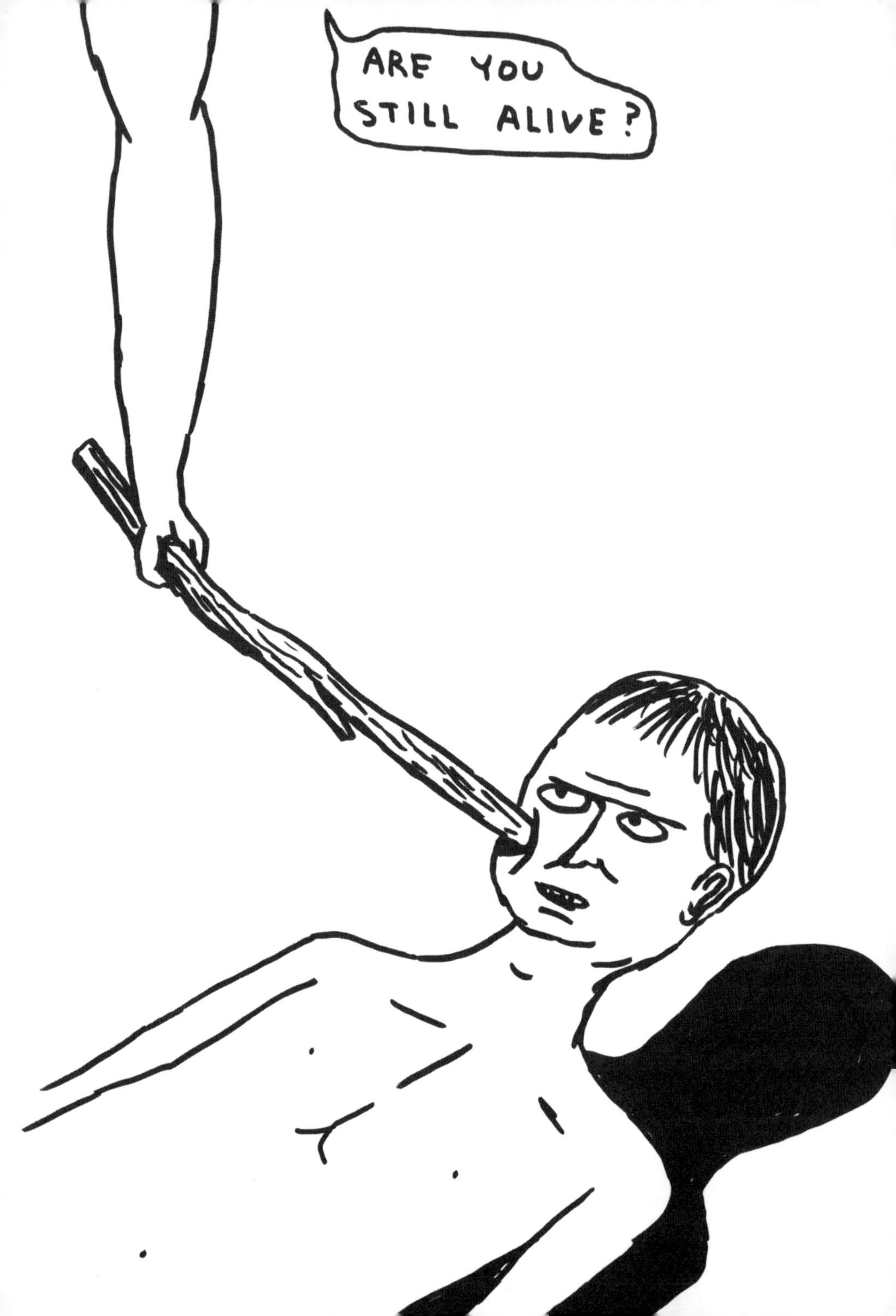

ARE YOU STILL ALIVE ?

CHAPTER TEN
DIRT AND SOCIETY

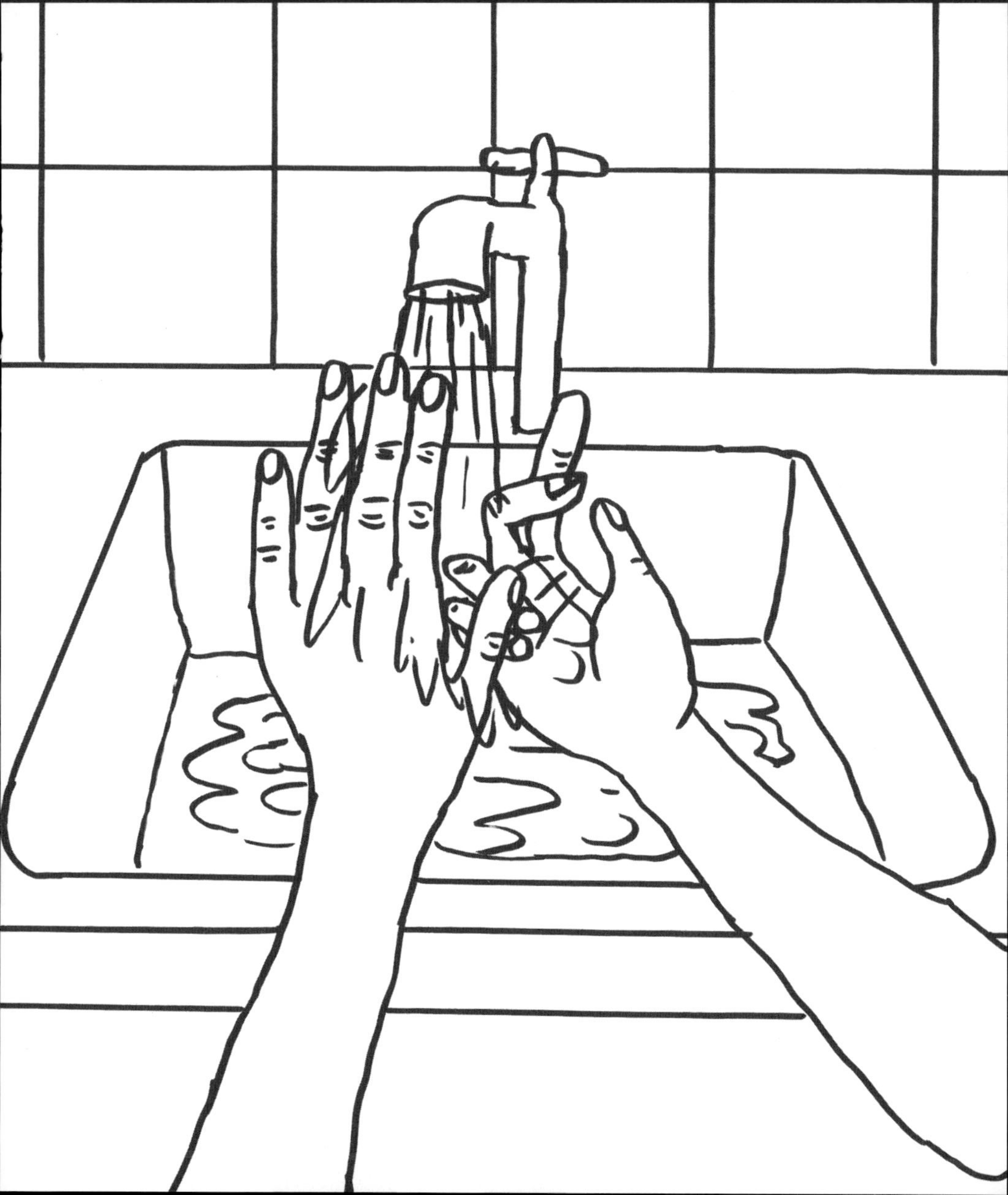

DIRT

DIRT
WHERE?
IN THE TEMPLE
SHOULD WE CLEAN IT UP?
NO
WHY?
IT IS HOLY DIRT
SO?
ONLY A PRIEST CAN CLEAR IT UP
IS THERE NOTHING WE CAN DO?
WE CAN PRAY

MORE DIRT

THE DIRT
OH
THE DIRT
I AM KING OF IT
I HAVE POWER
OVER IT
IT MUST YIELD
TO ME
I COLLECT IT
AND REMOVE IT
FROM YOUR HOUSE
IT IS MY JOB

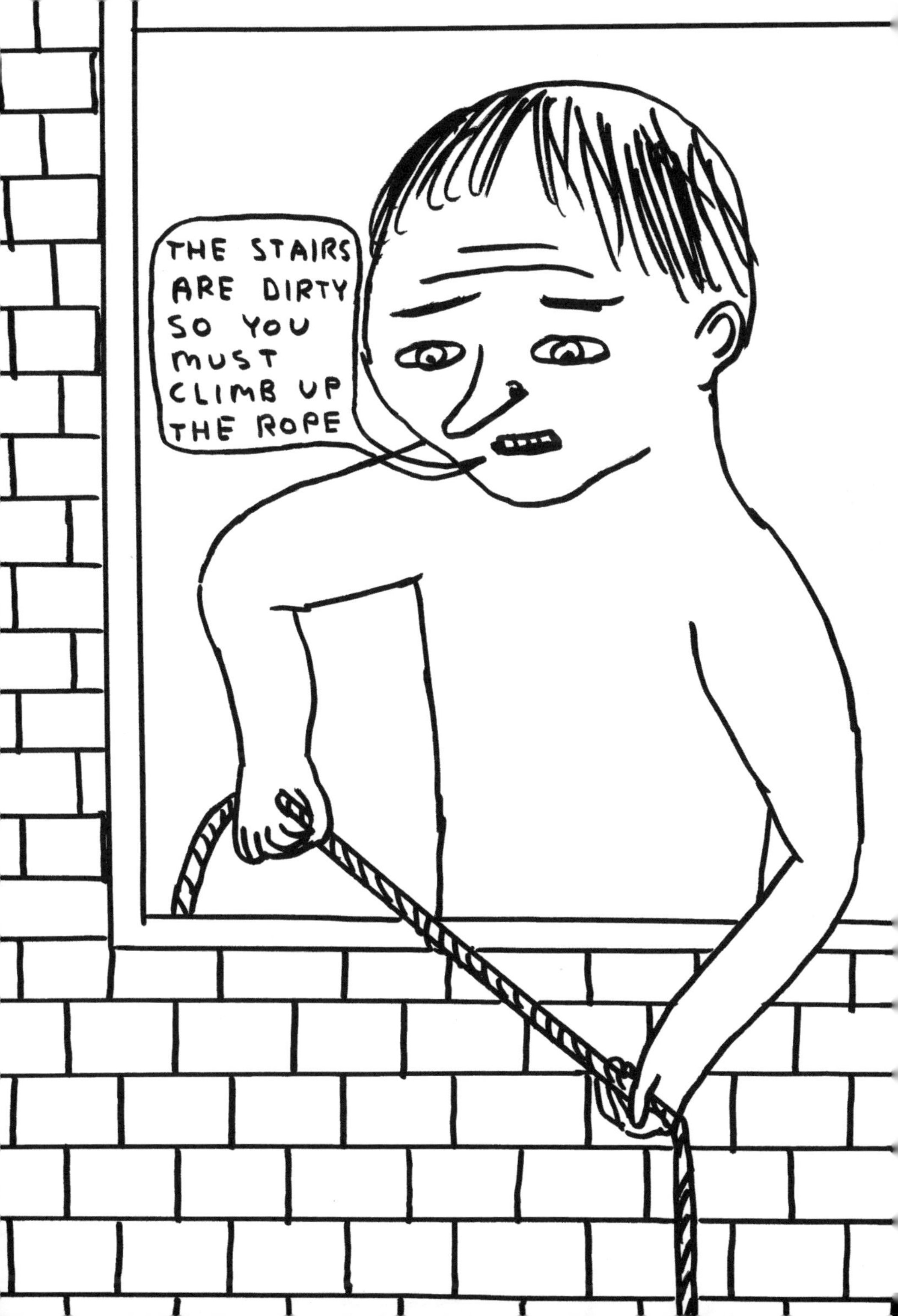

THE STAIRS ARE DIRTY SO YOU MUST CLIMB UP THE ROPE

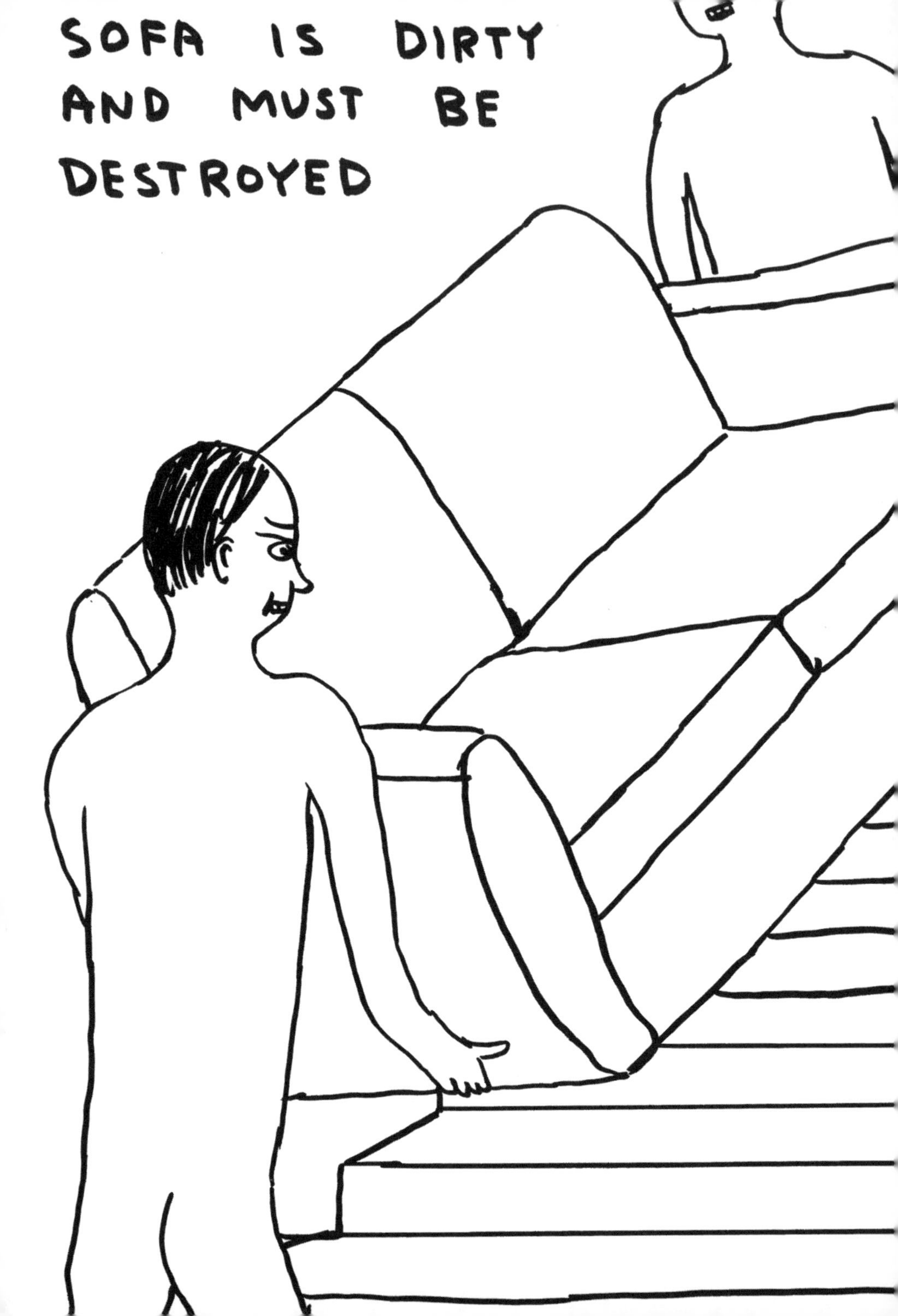
SOFA IS DIRTY
AND MUST BE
DESTROYED

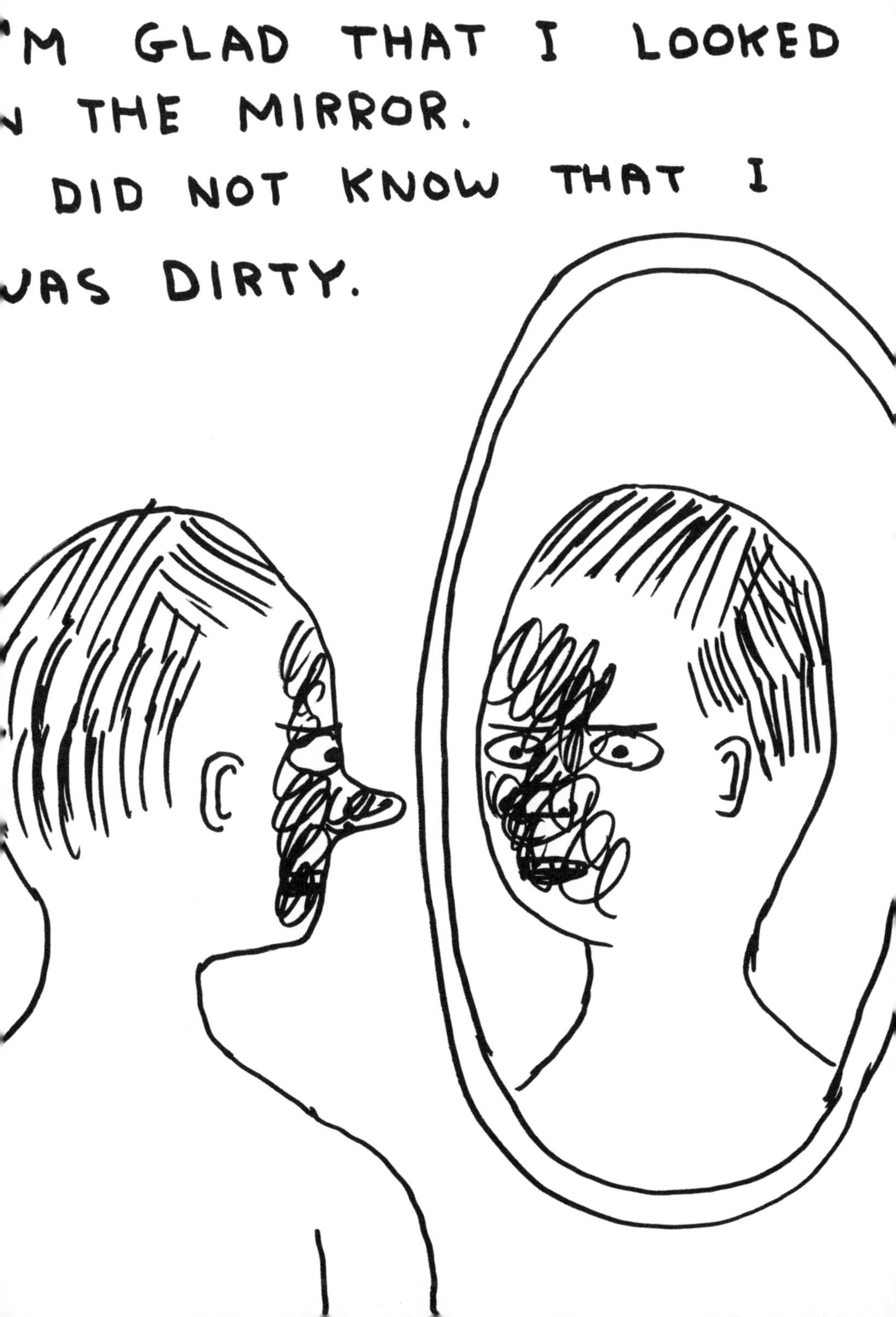

'M GLAD THAT I LOOKED
N THE MIRROR.
DID NOT KNOW THAT I
JAS DIRTY.

FILTH PILES UP WITHOUT
YOU NOTICING AT FIRST BU
THEN EVENTUALLY YOU
NOTICE AND YOU ARE SHOCKE
YOU ARE OH SO SHOCKED
AT ALL THE FILTH THAT
HAS PILED UP

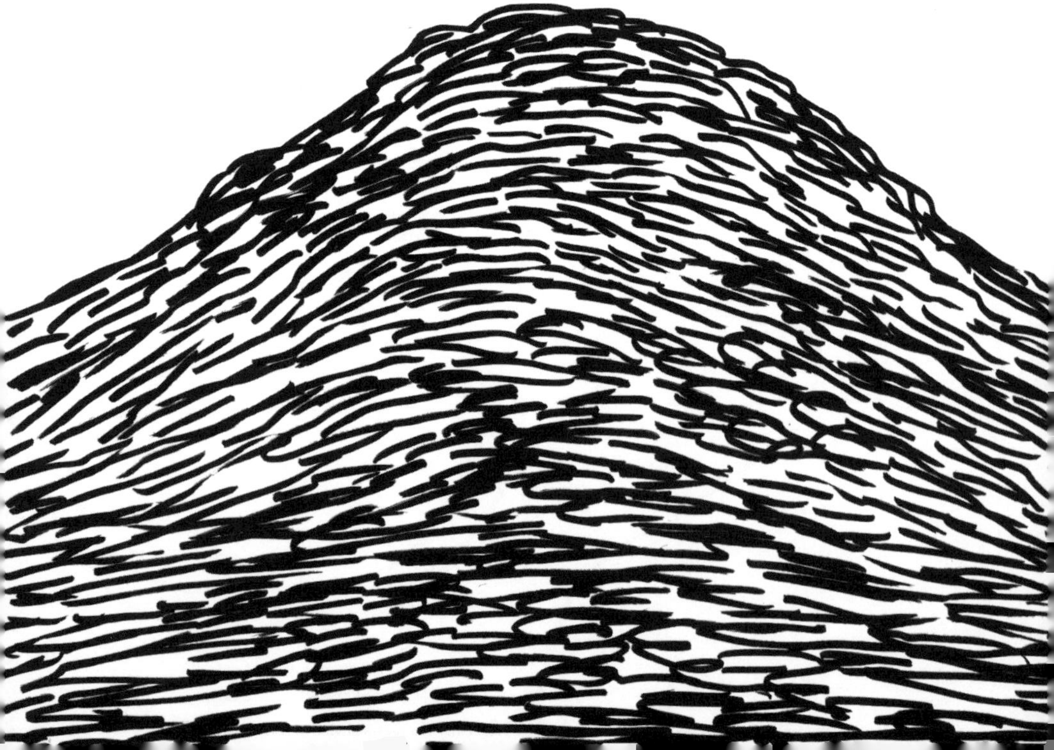

EXAMINE THE BUGS
LEARN FROM THE BUGS
THE BUGS CAN BE YOUR TEACHER

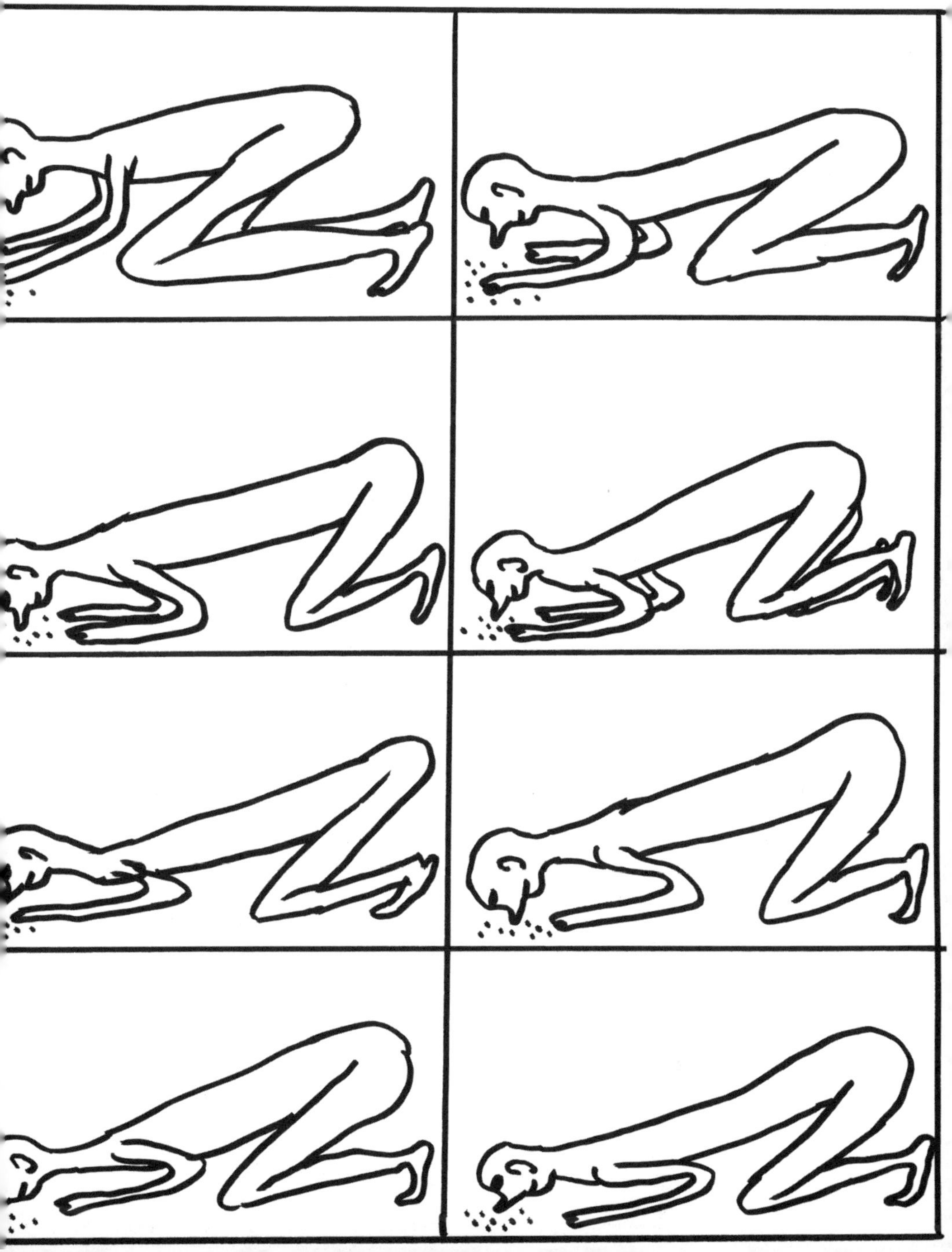

FILTHY HAND

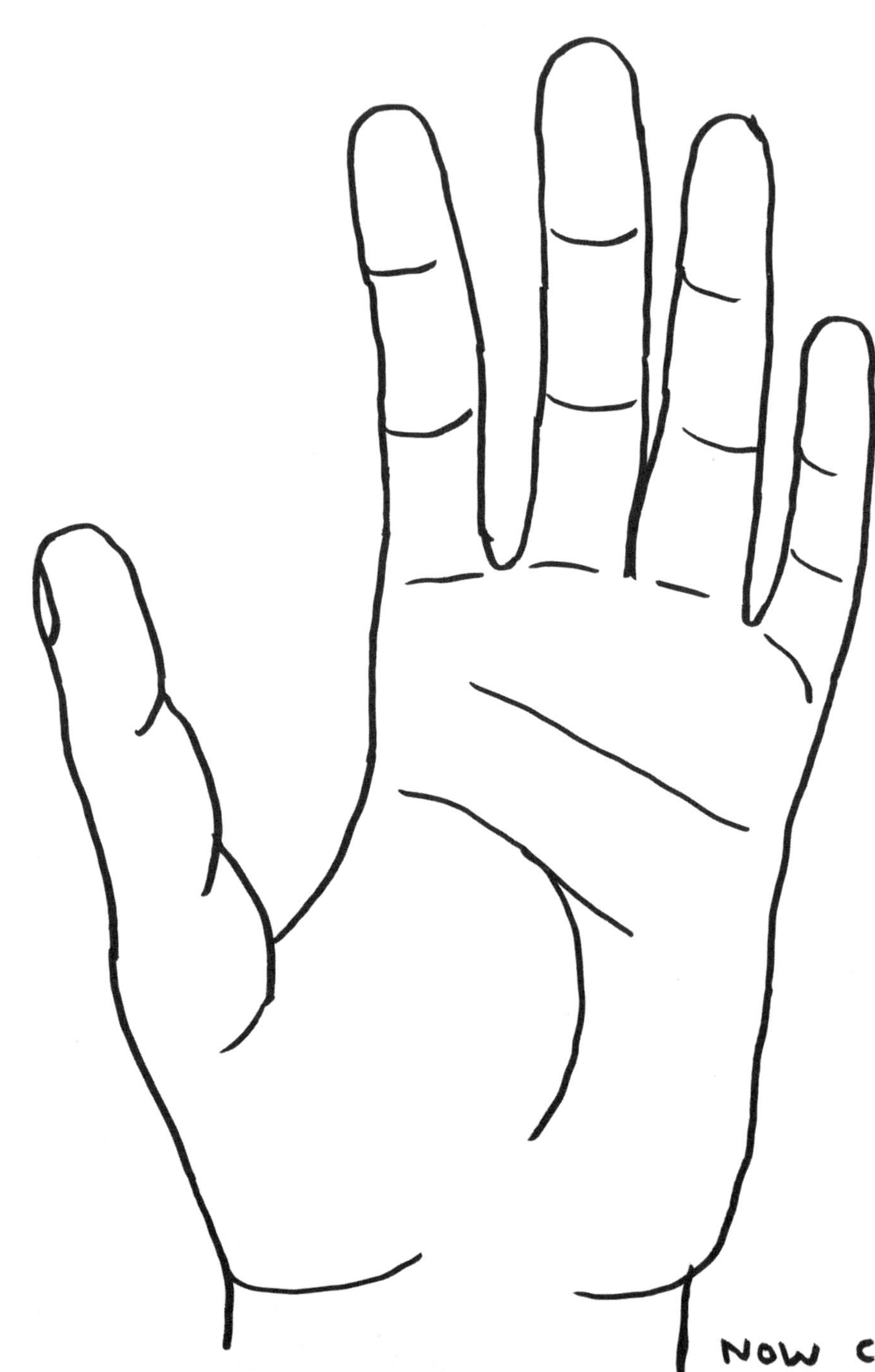

NOW CLEA

CHAPTER ELEVEN

CONCLUSIONS

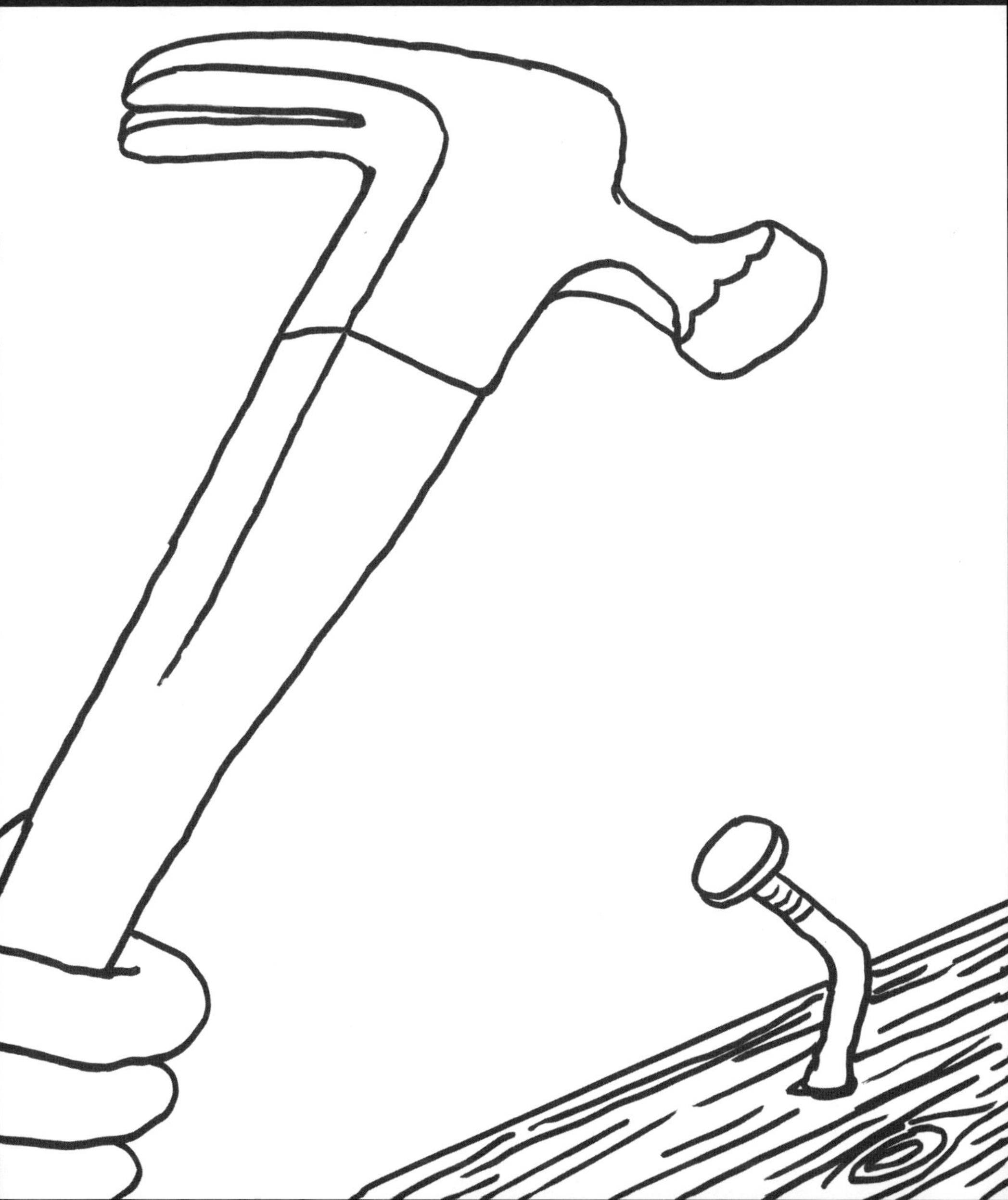

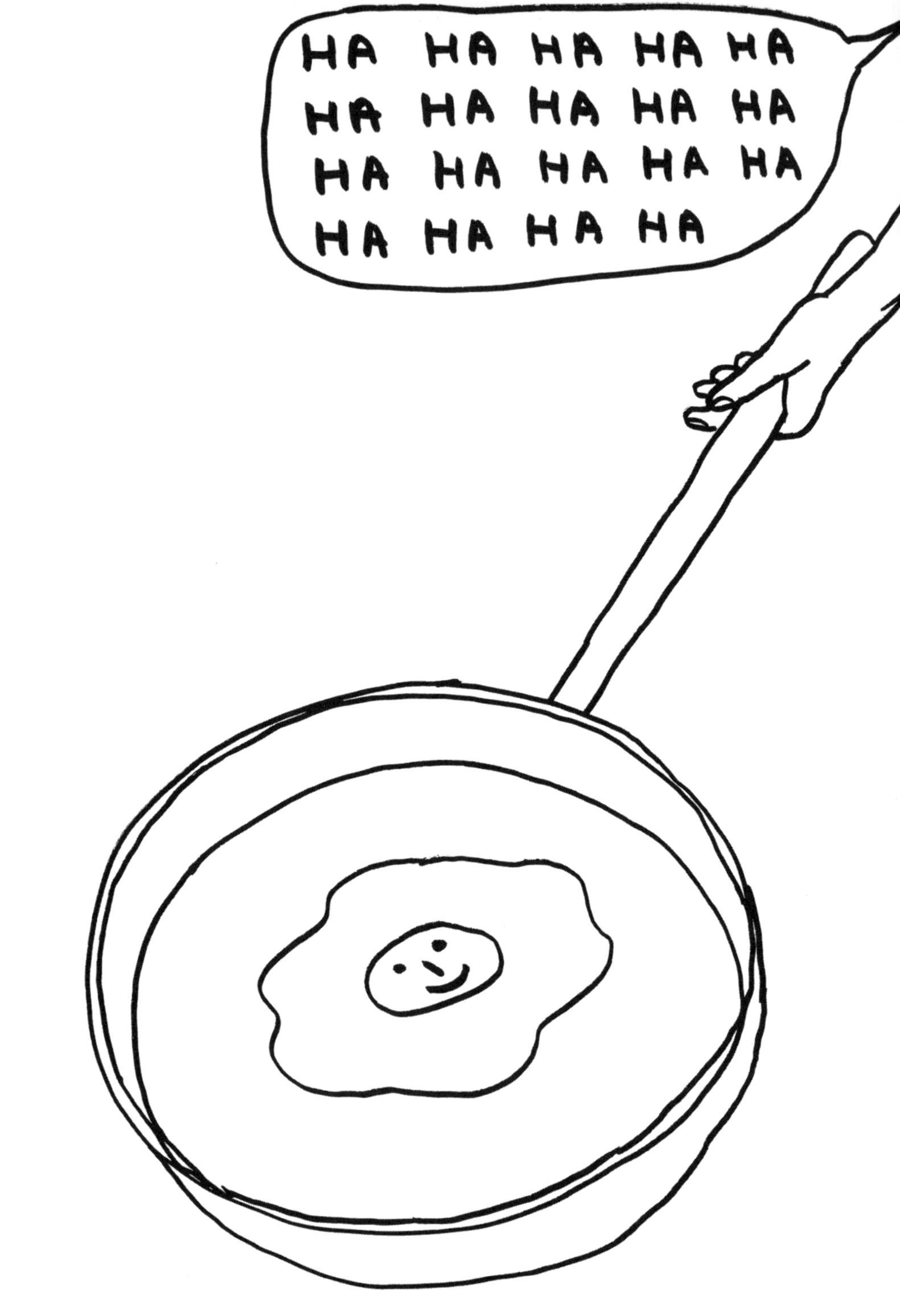
HA HA HA HA HA
HA HA HA HA HA
HA HA HA HA HA
HA HA HA HA

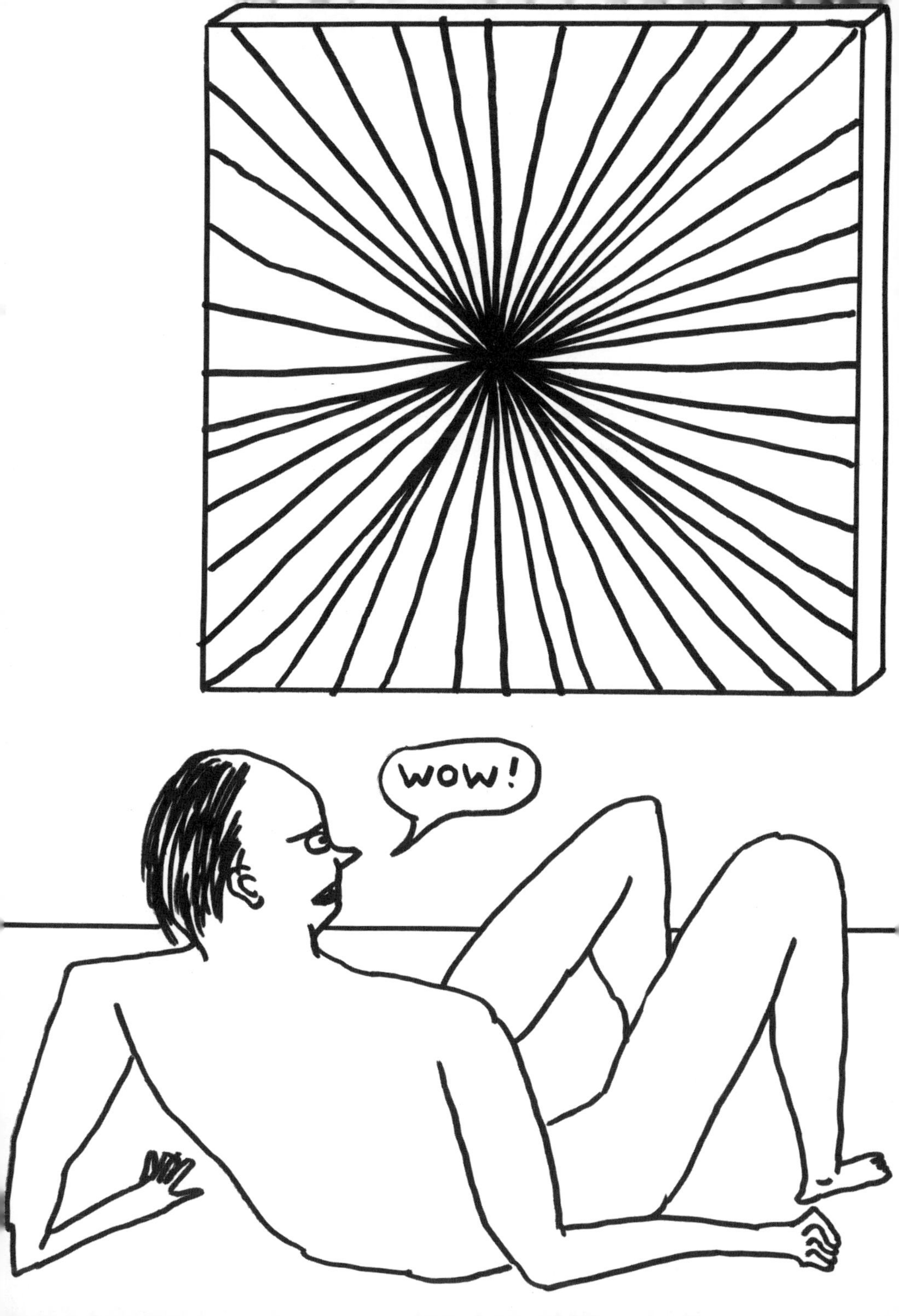WOW!

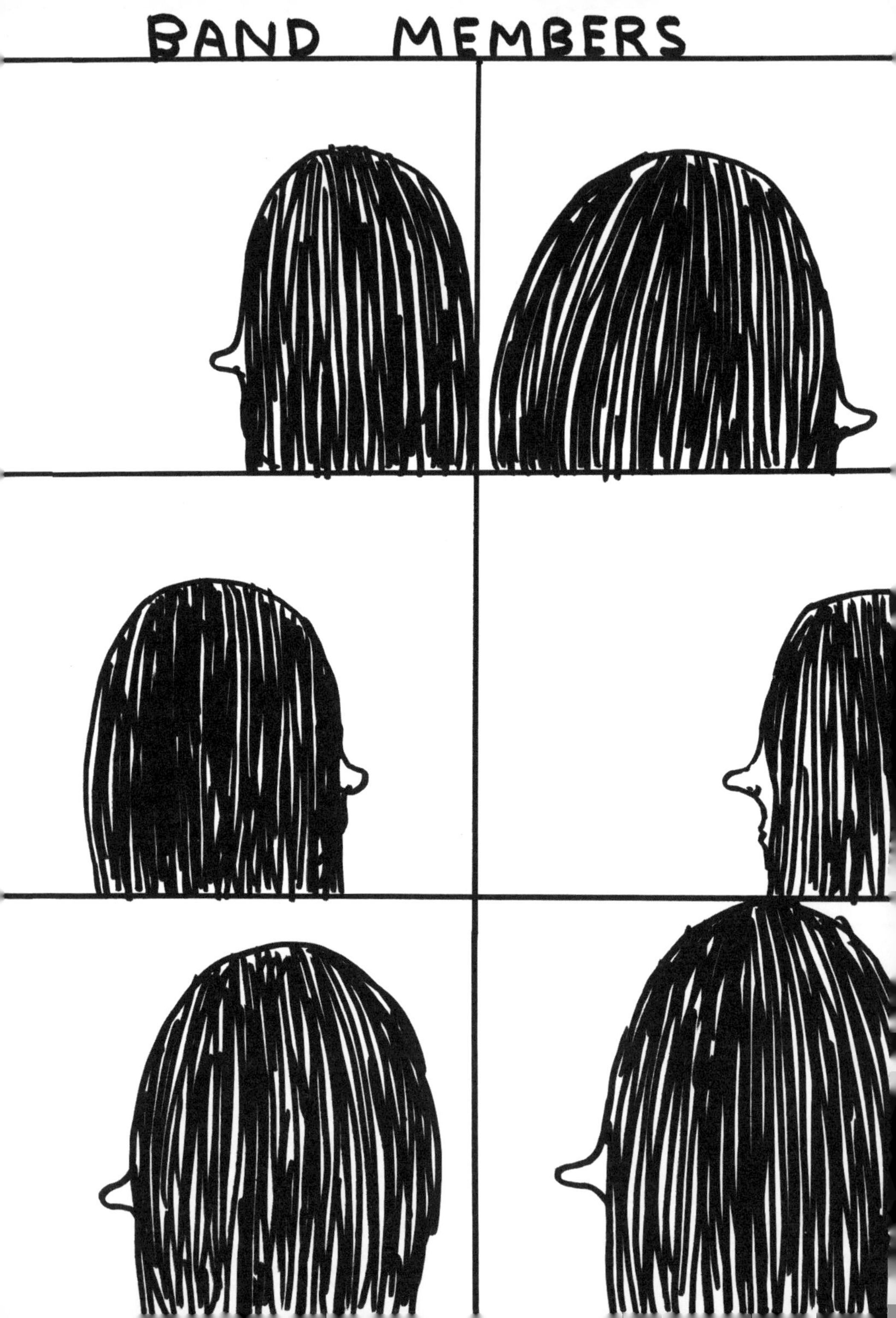
BAND MEMBERS

A RAT

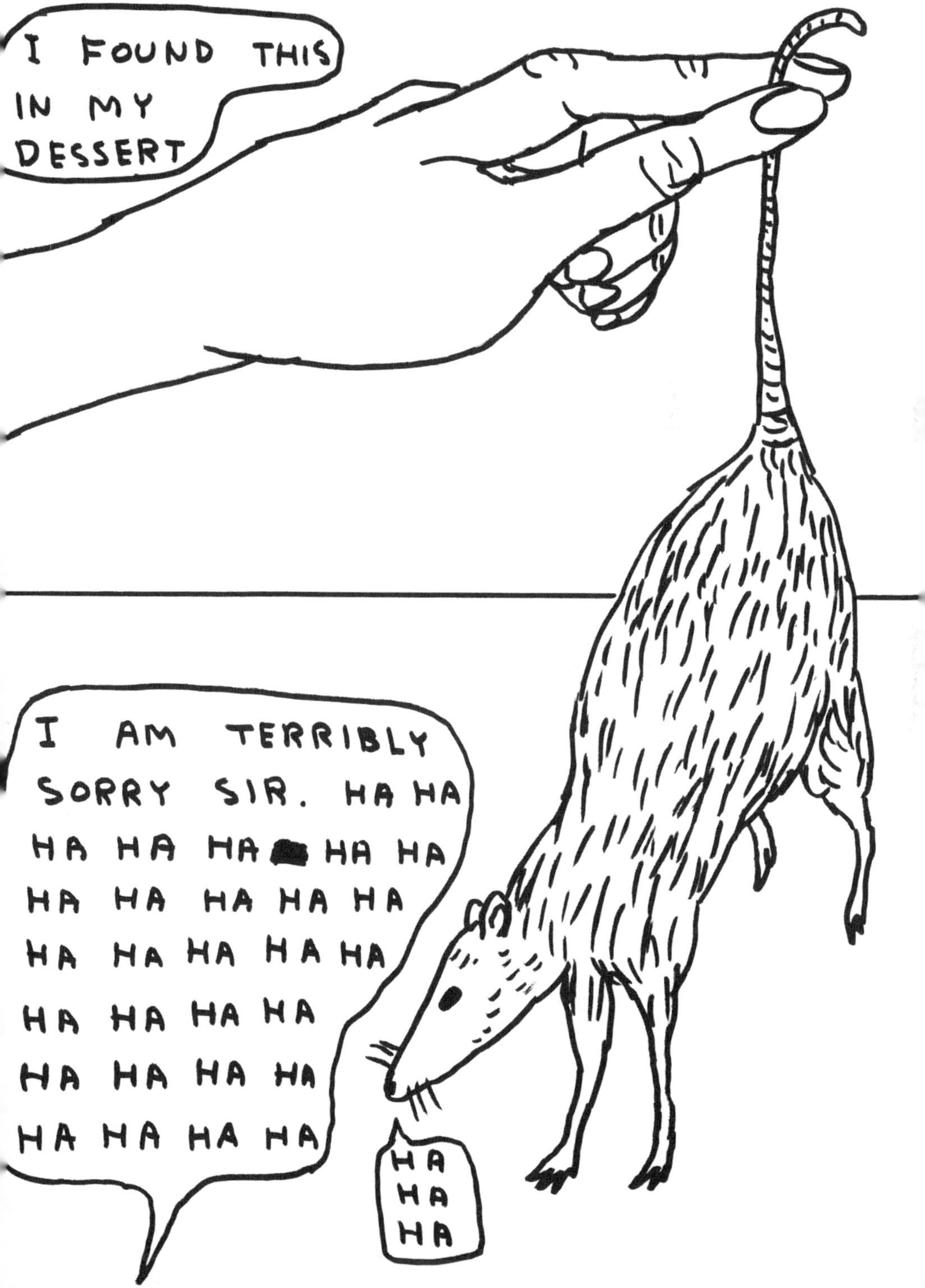

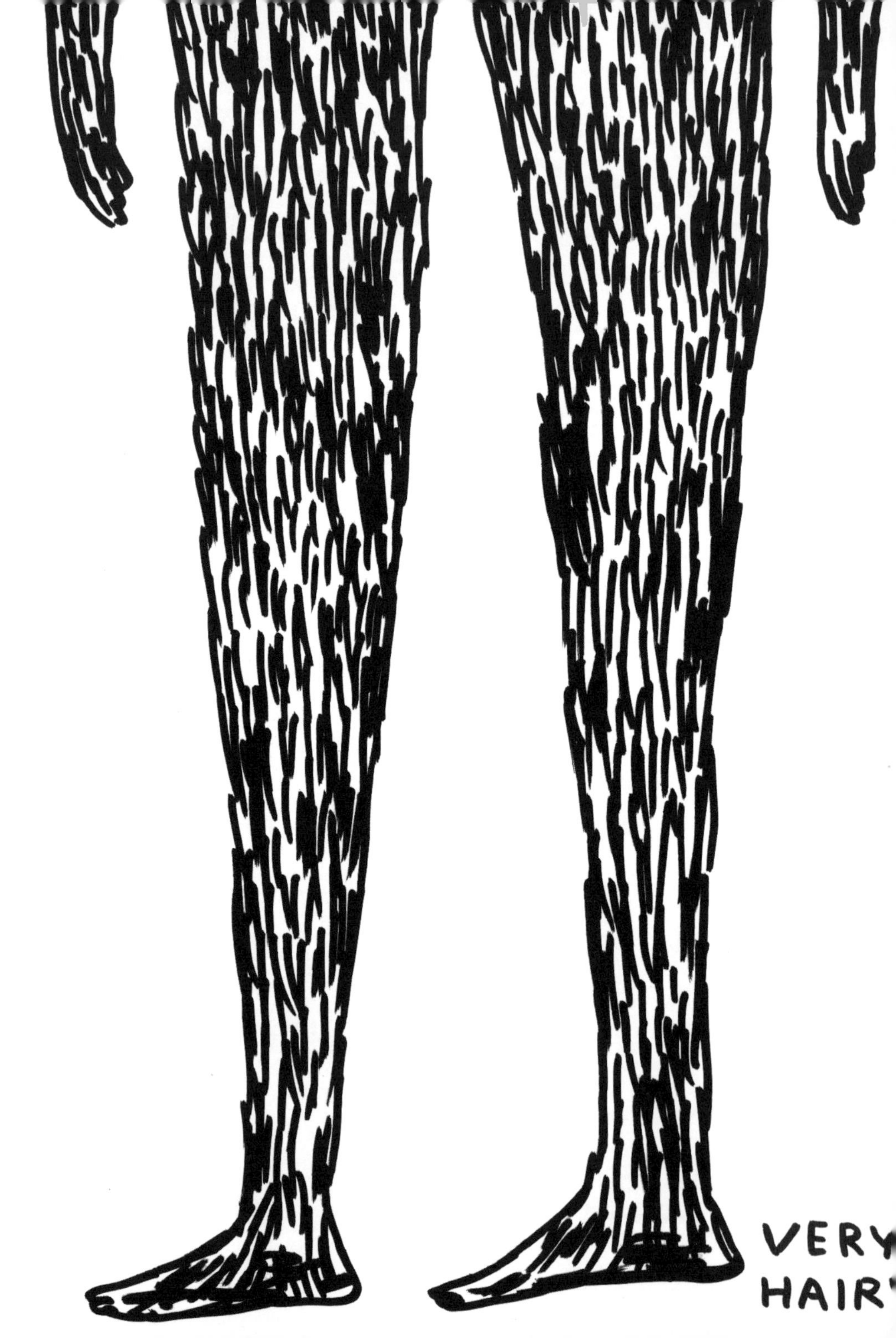
VERY
HAIRY

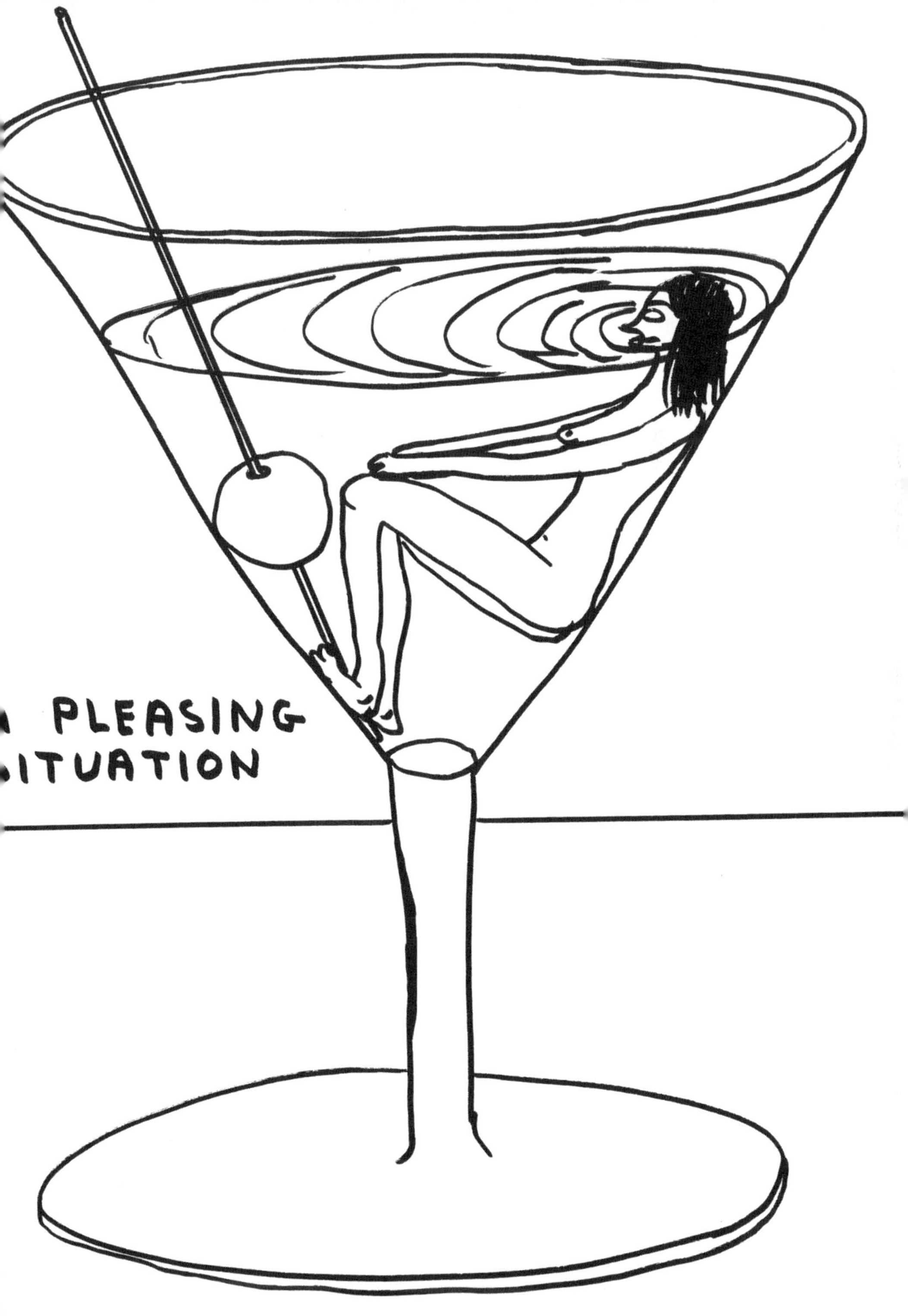

PLEASING
SITUATION

COOKING NOTHING

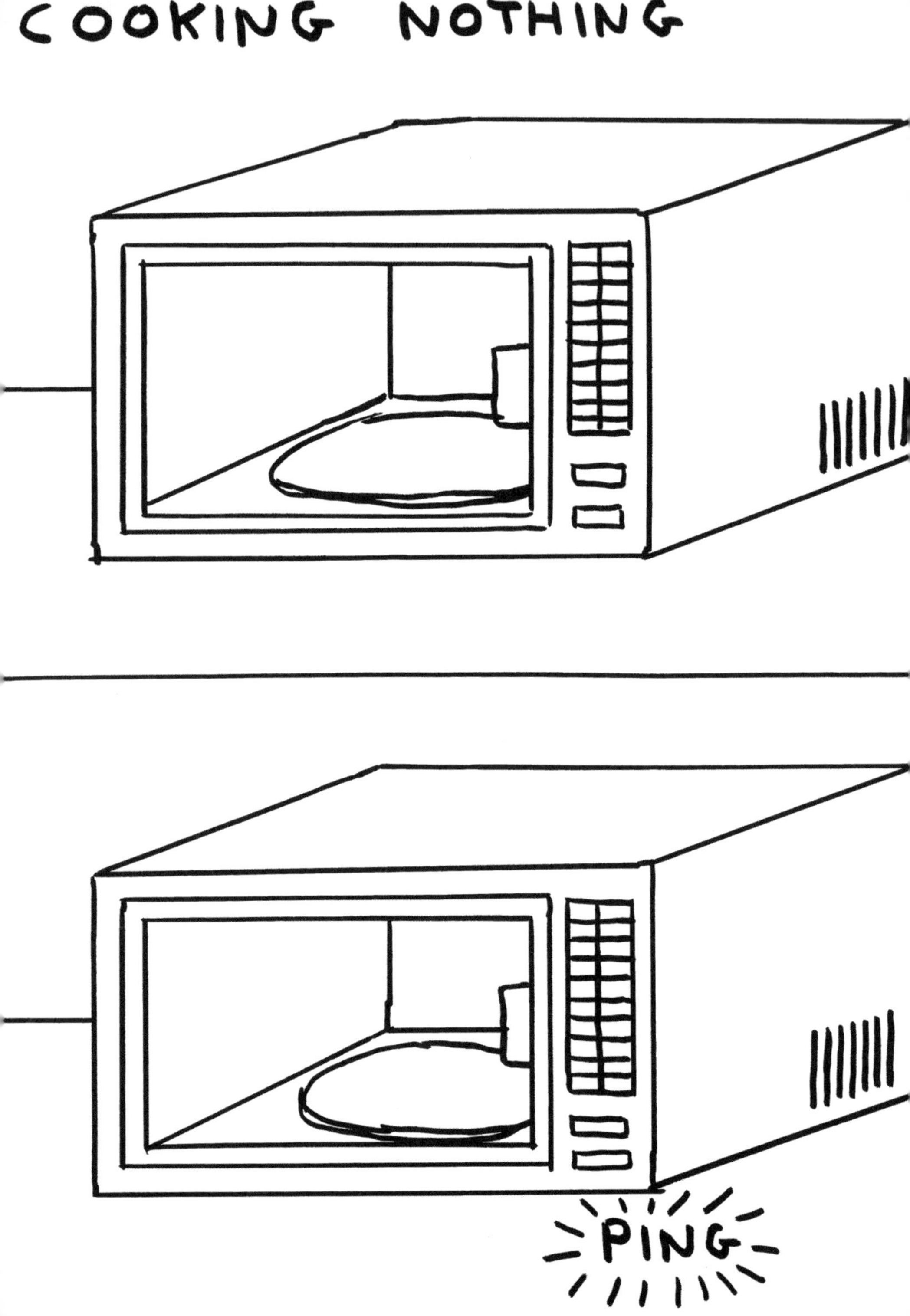

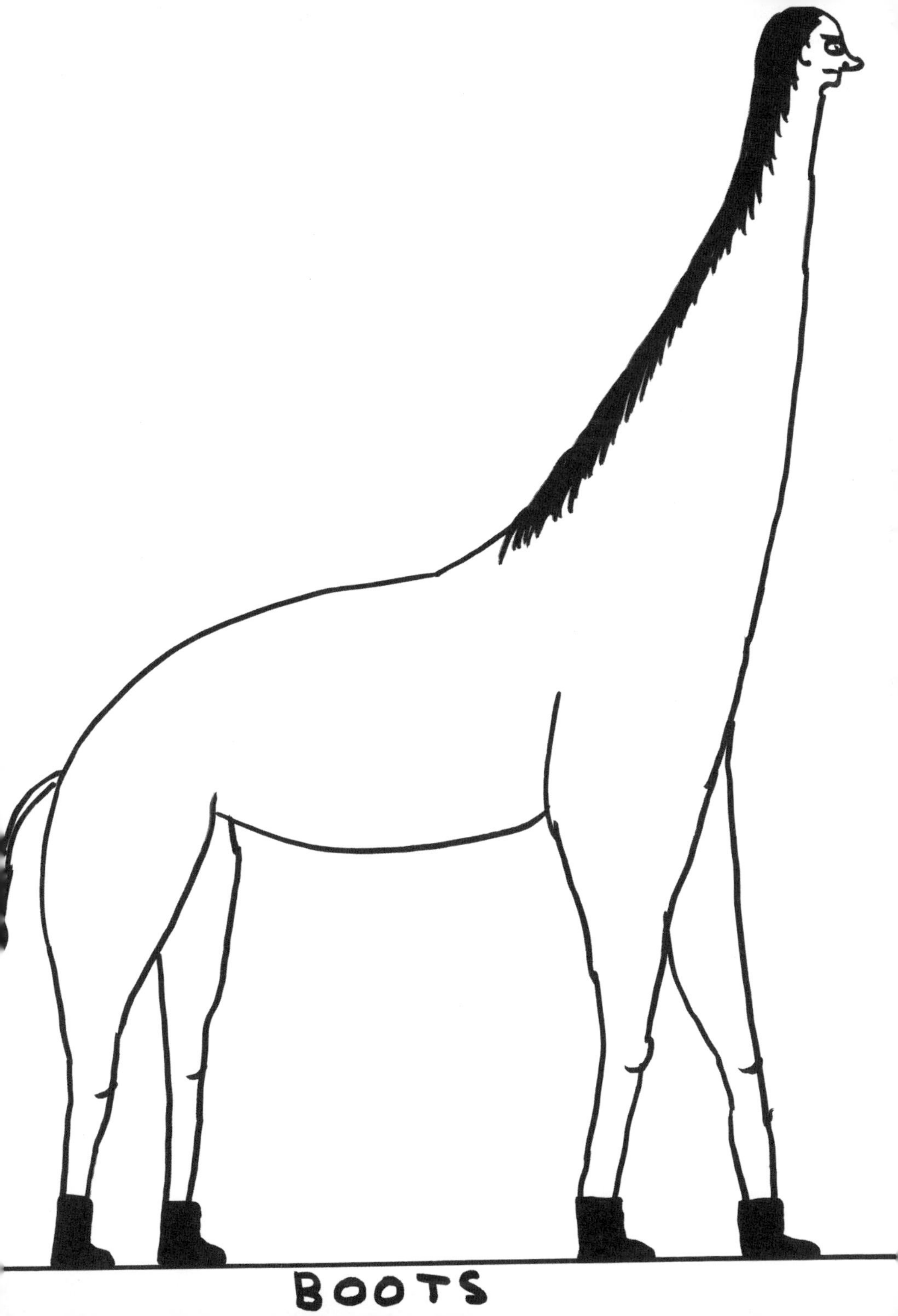

BOOTS

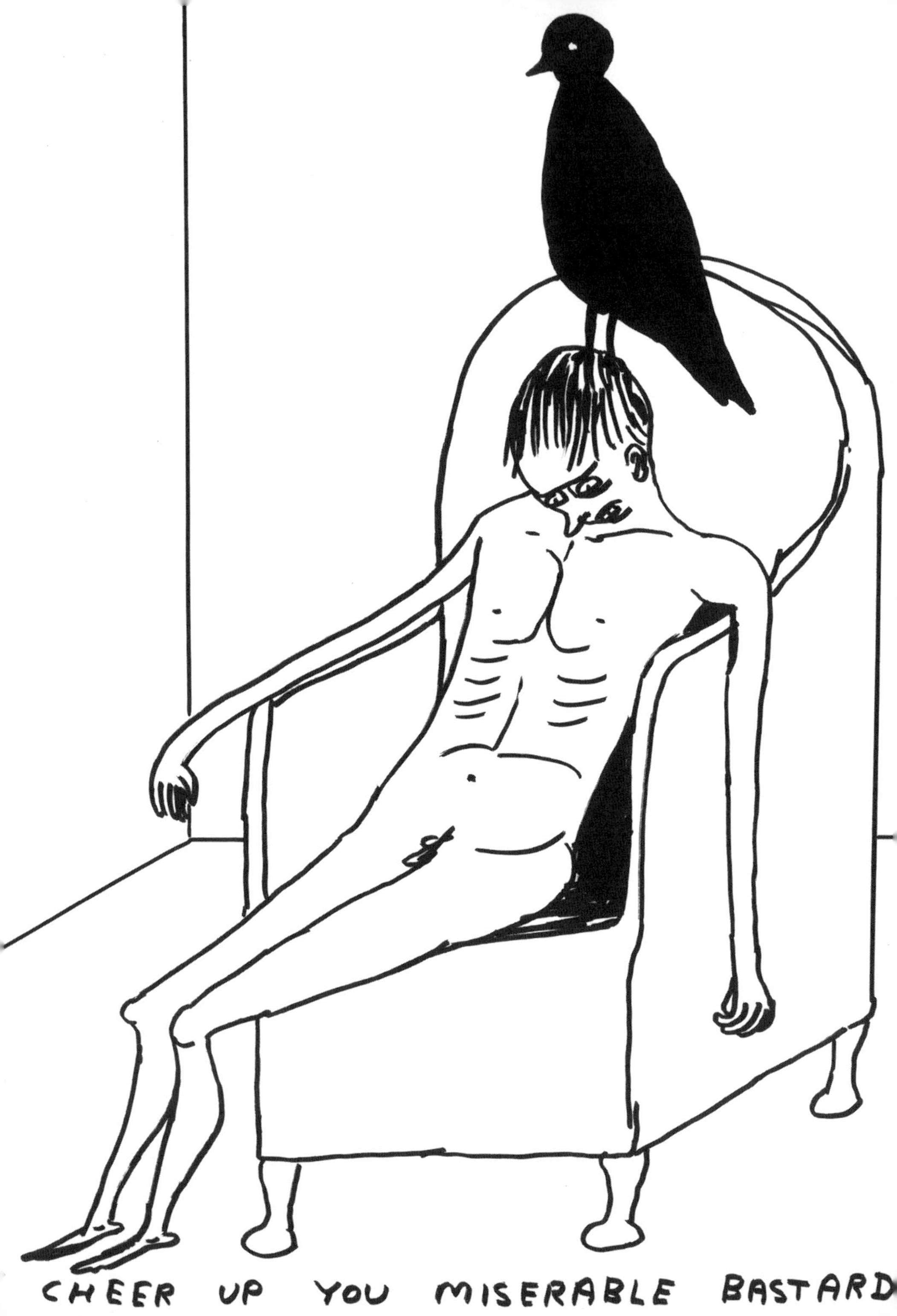

CHEER UP YOU MISERABLE BASTARD

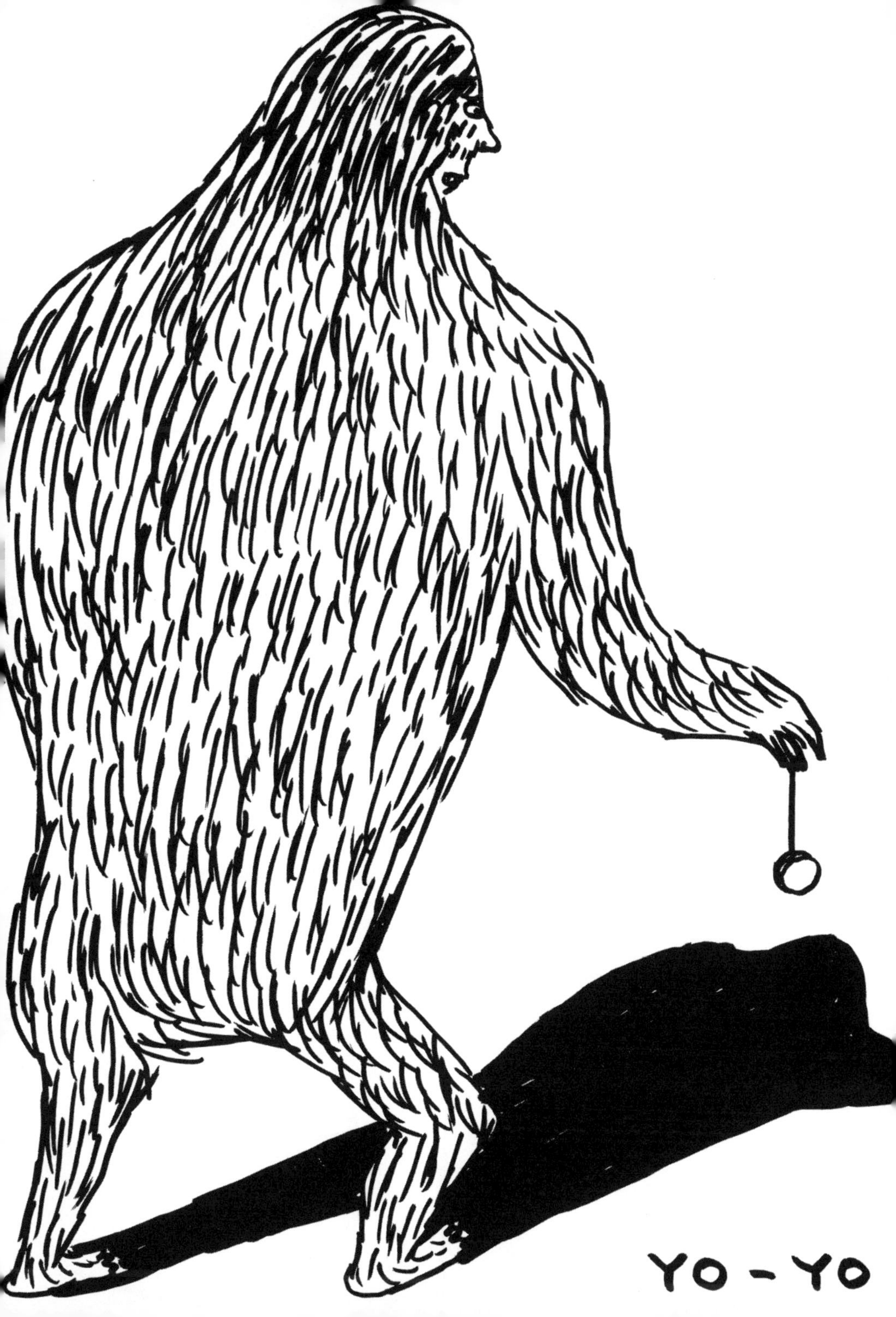

YO - YO

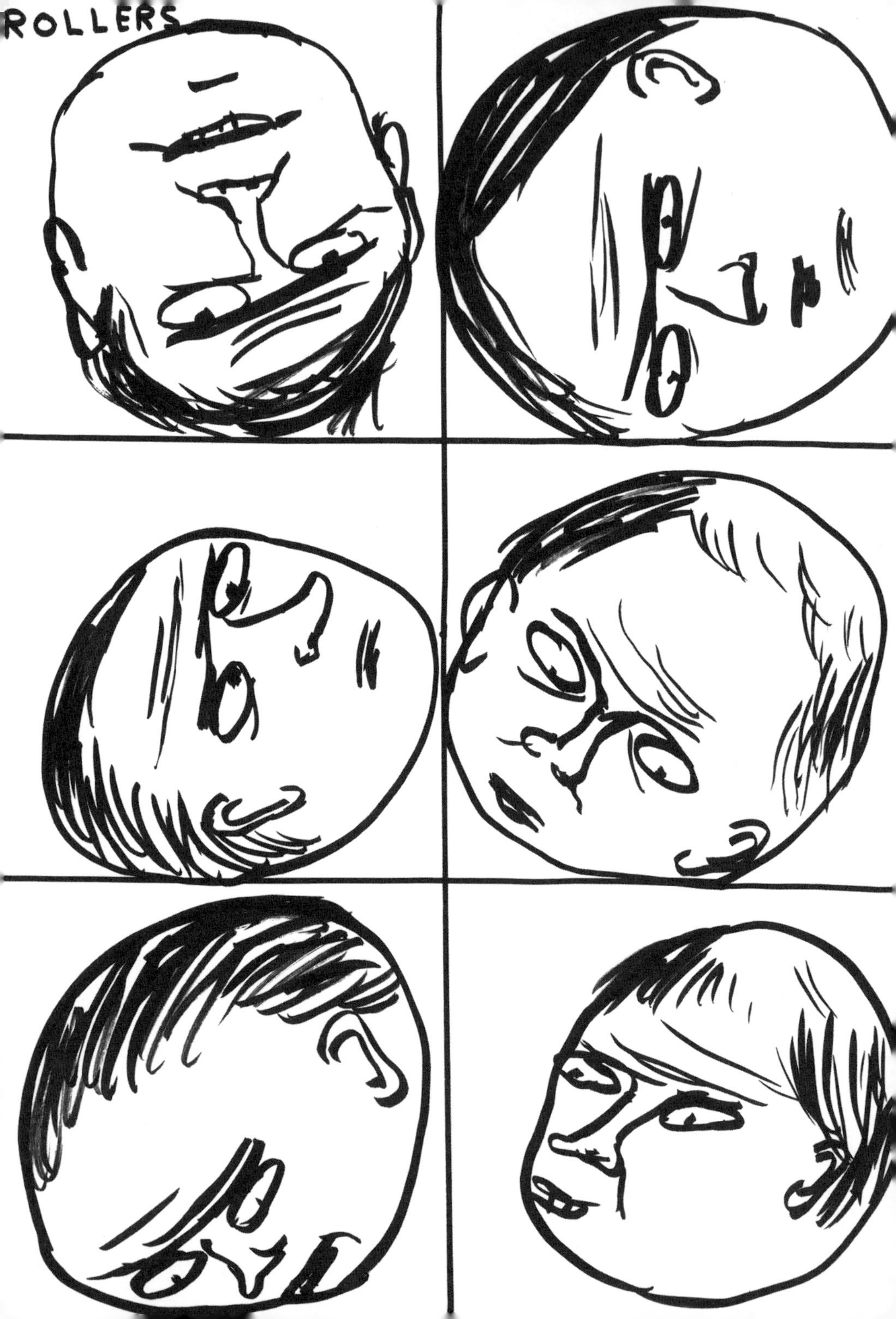
ROLLERS

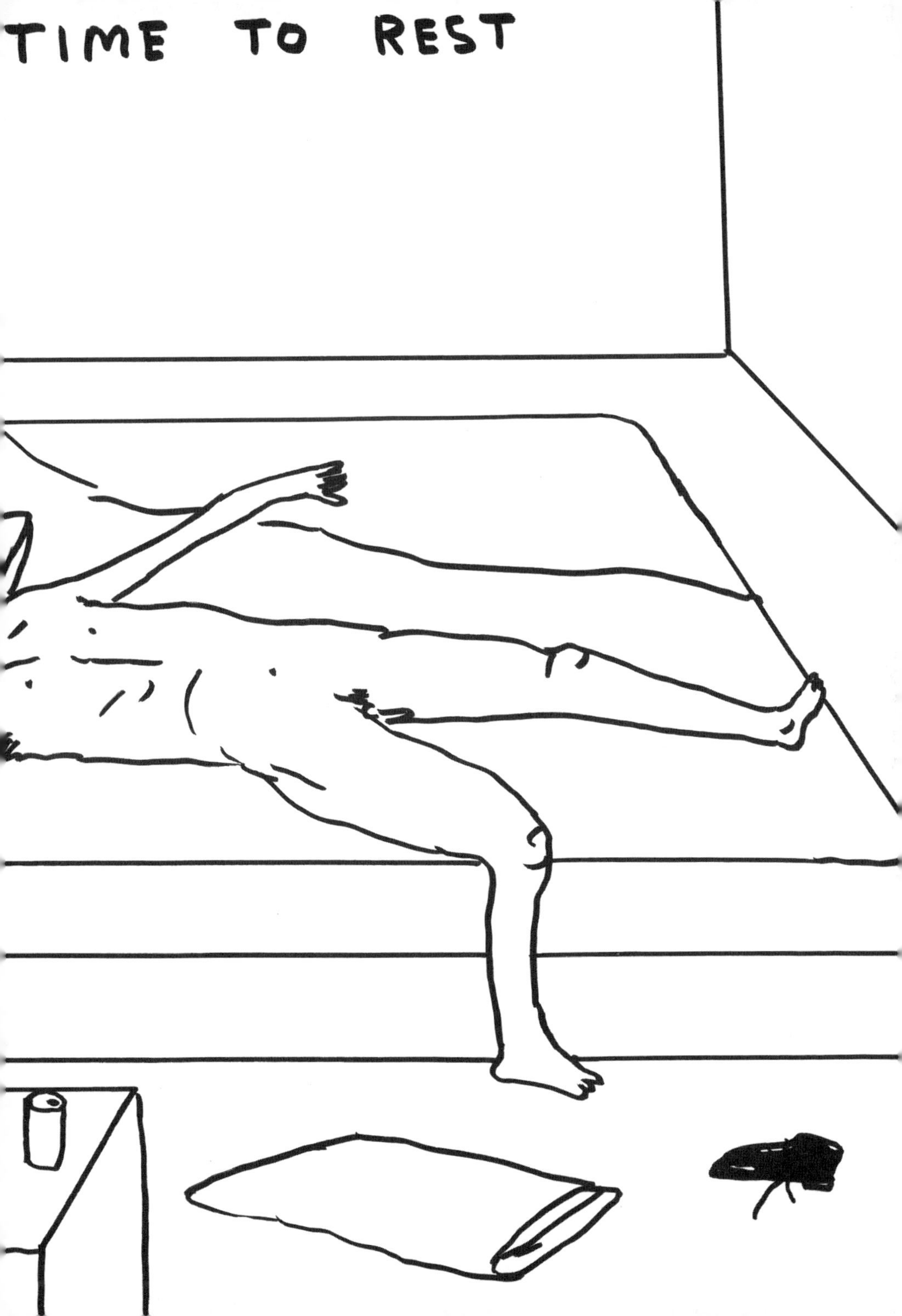

TIME TO REST

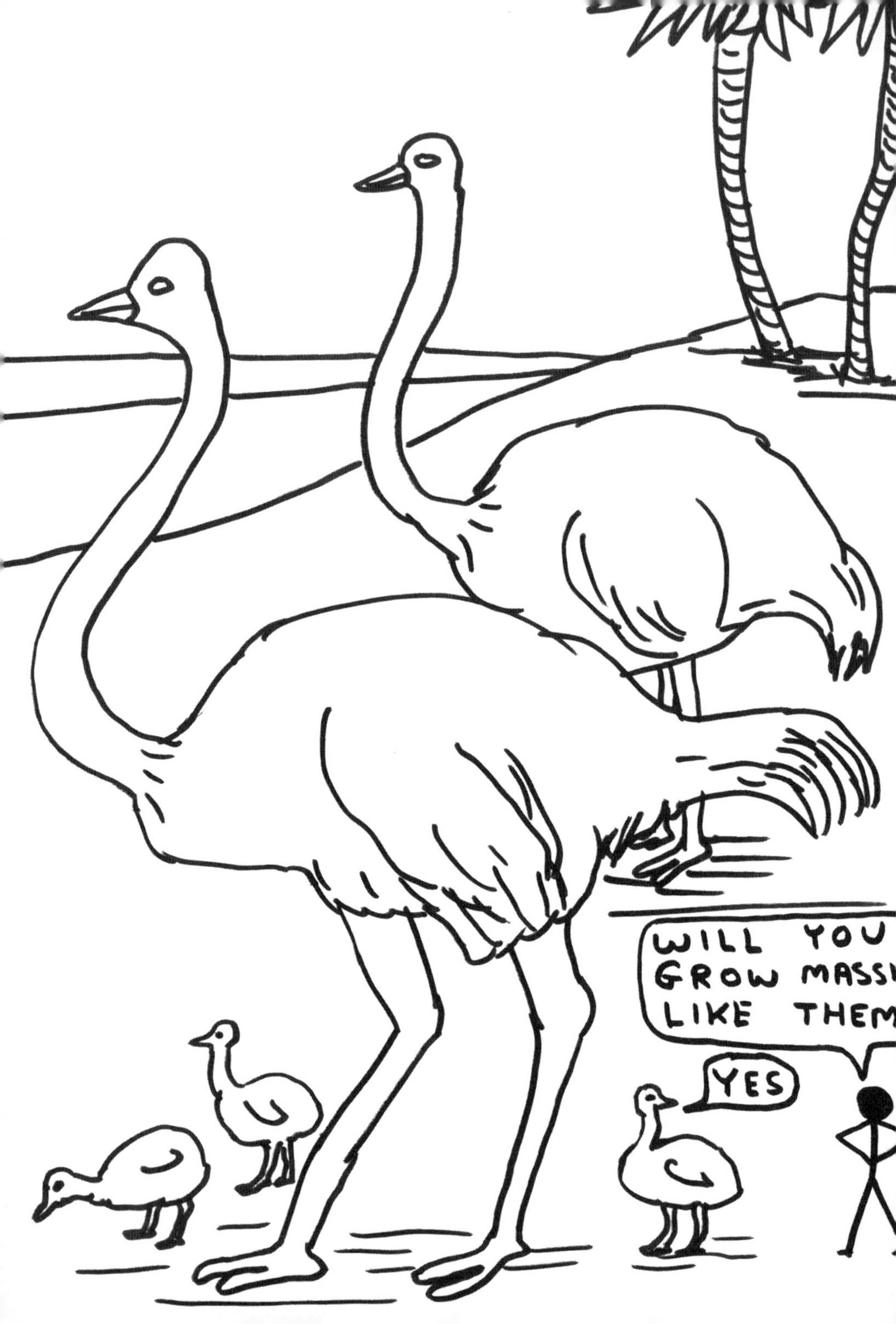
WILL YOU GROW MASSIVE LIKE THEM
YES

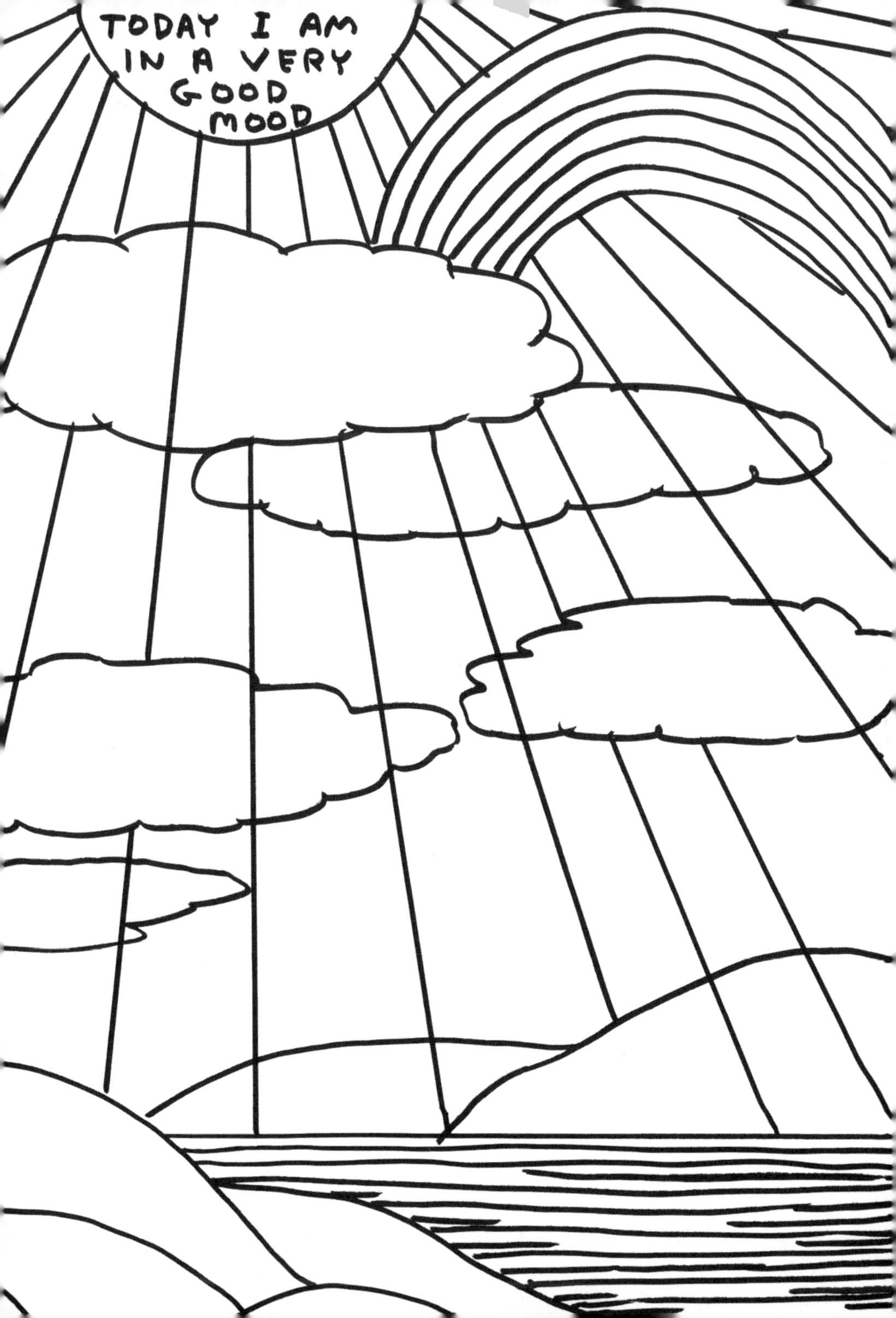

TODAY I AM
IN A VERY
GOOD
MOOD

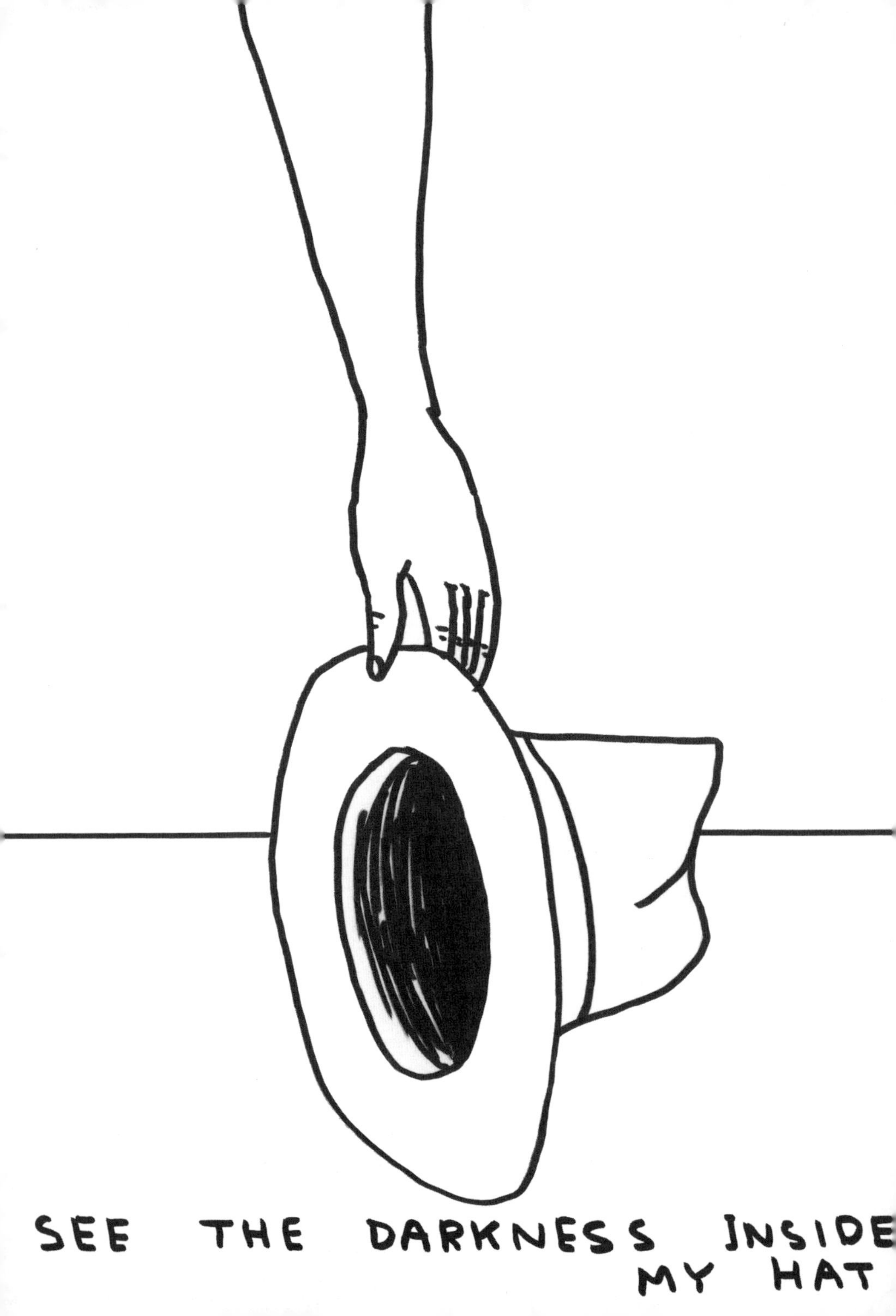
SEE THE DARKNESS INSIDE
MY HAT

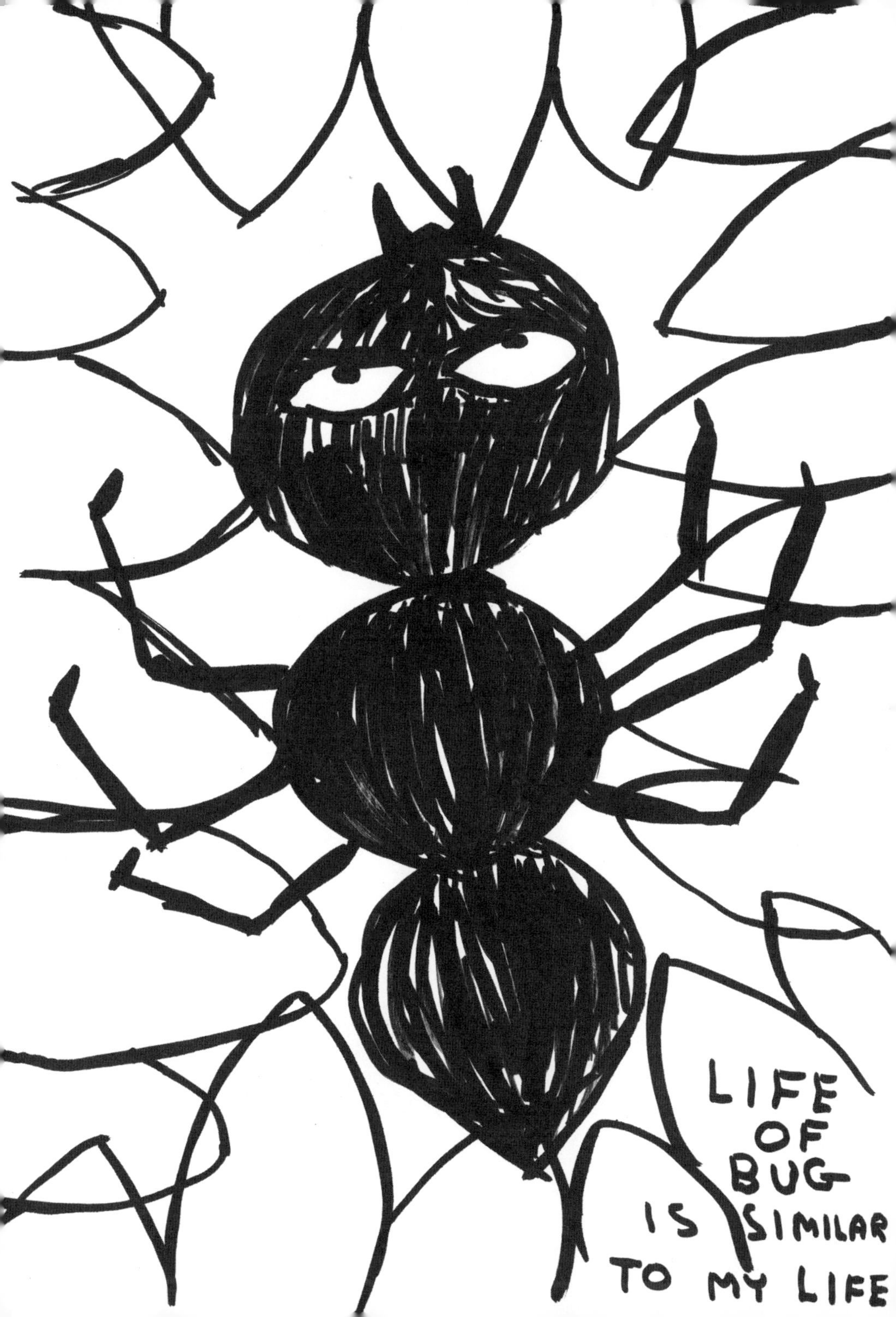

LIFE
OF
BUG
IS SIMILAR
TO MY LIFE

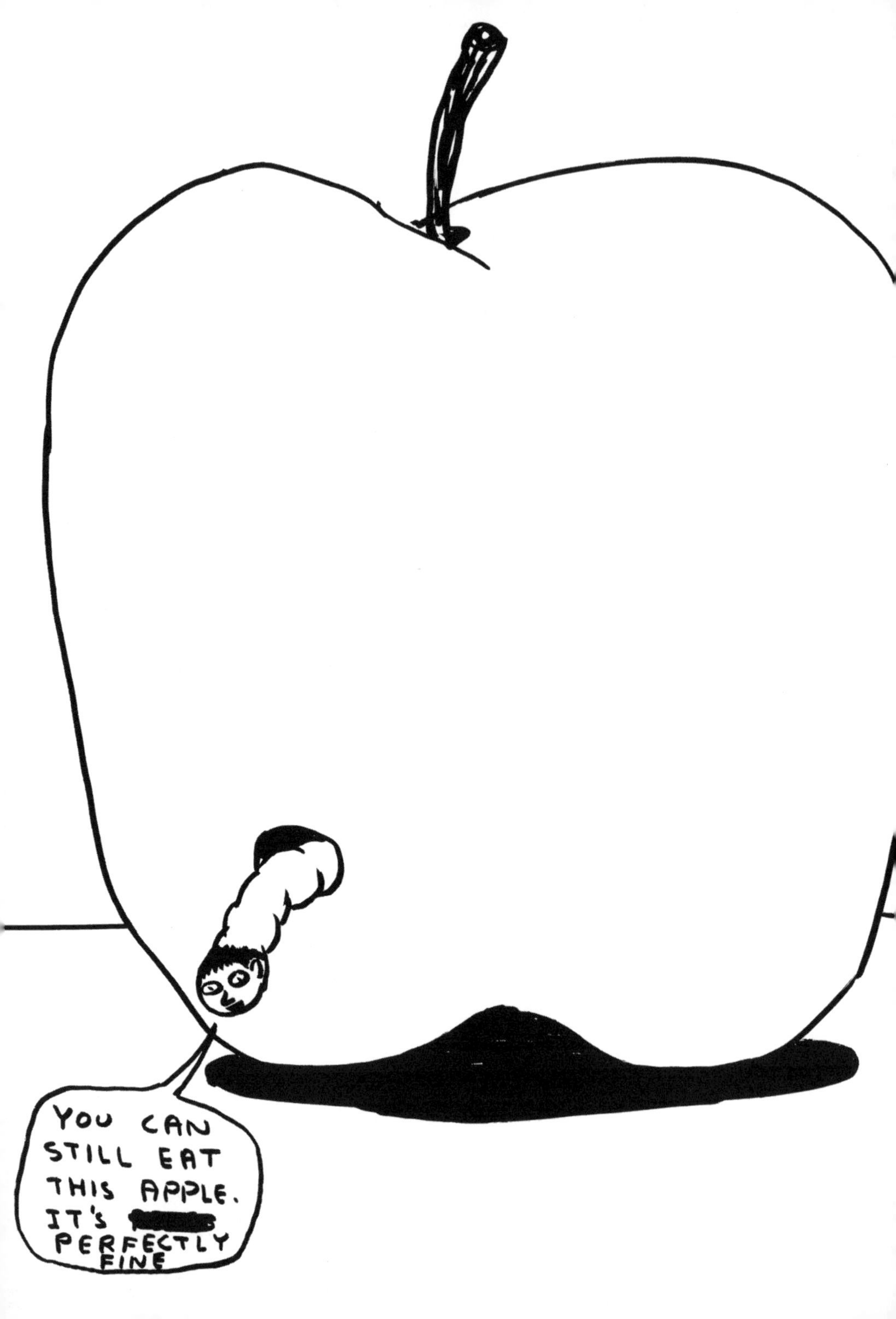

YOU CAN STILL EAT THIS APPLE. IT'S PERFECTLY FINE

HEADS IN THE CLOUDS

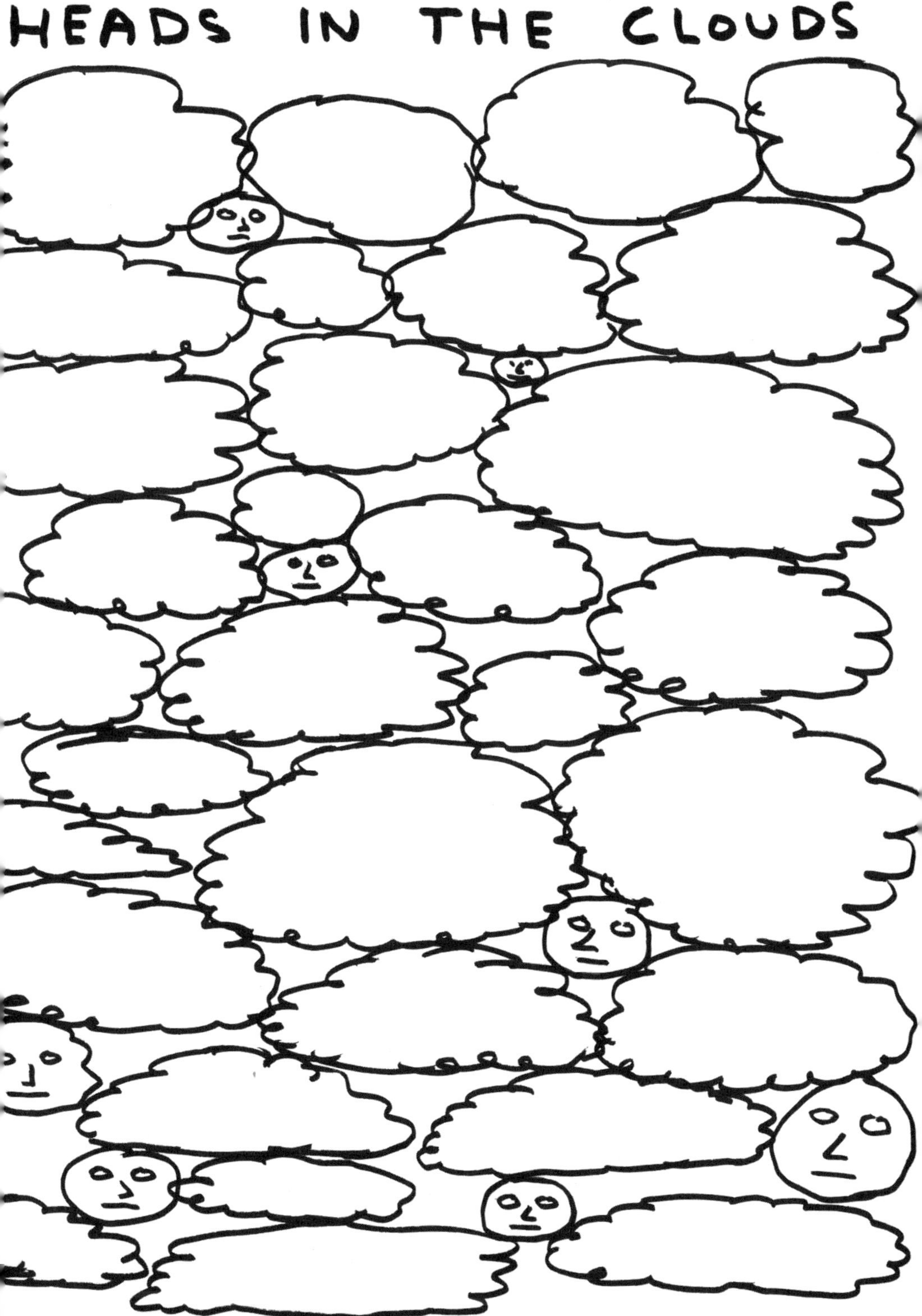

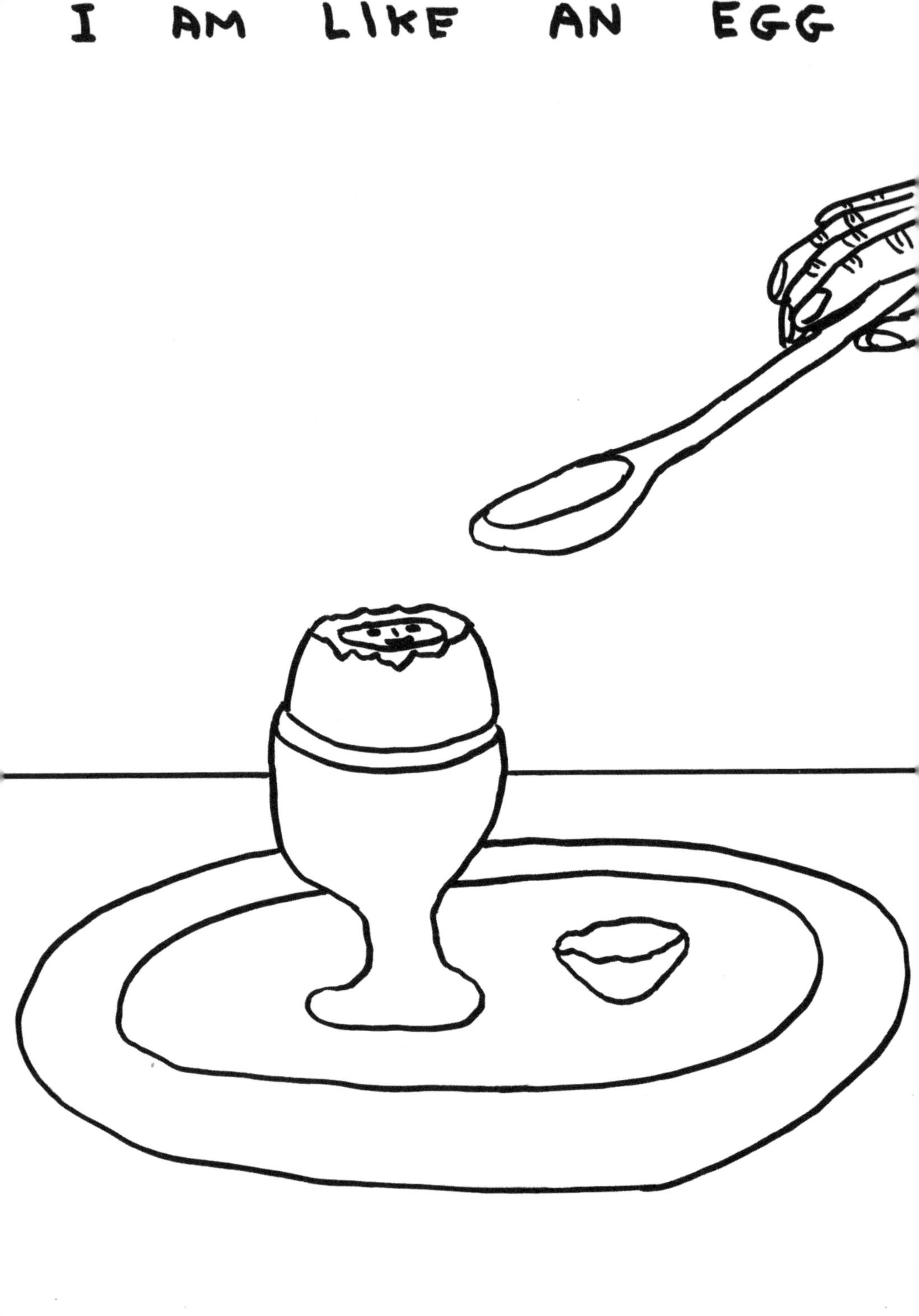

I AM LIKE AN EGG

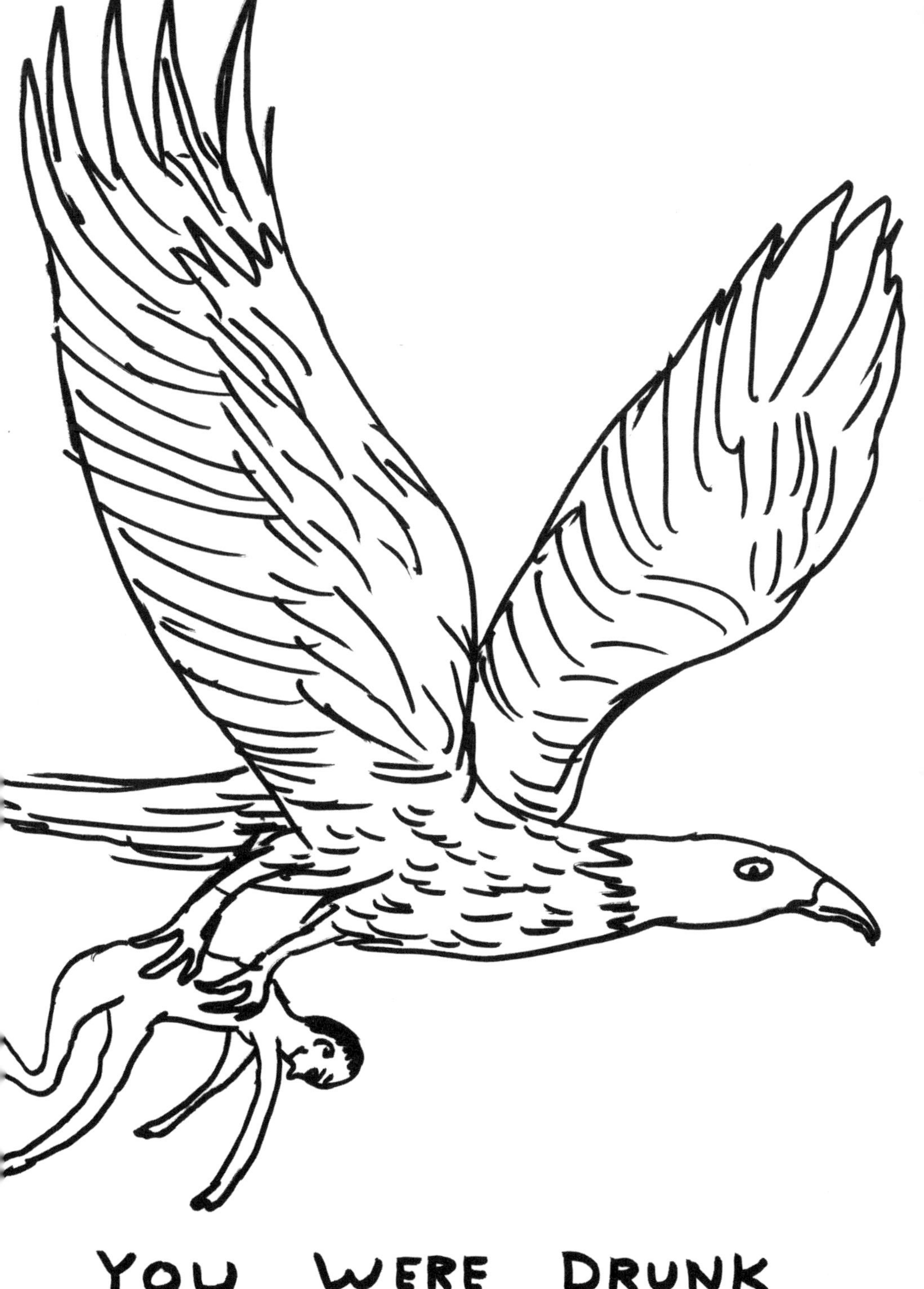

YOU WERE DRUNK

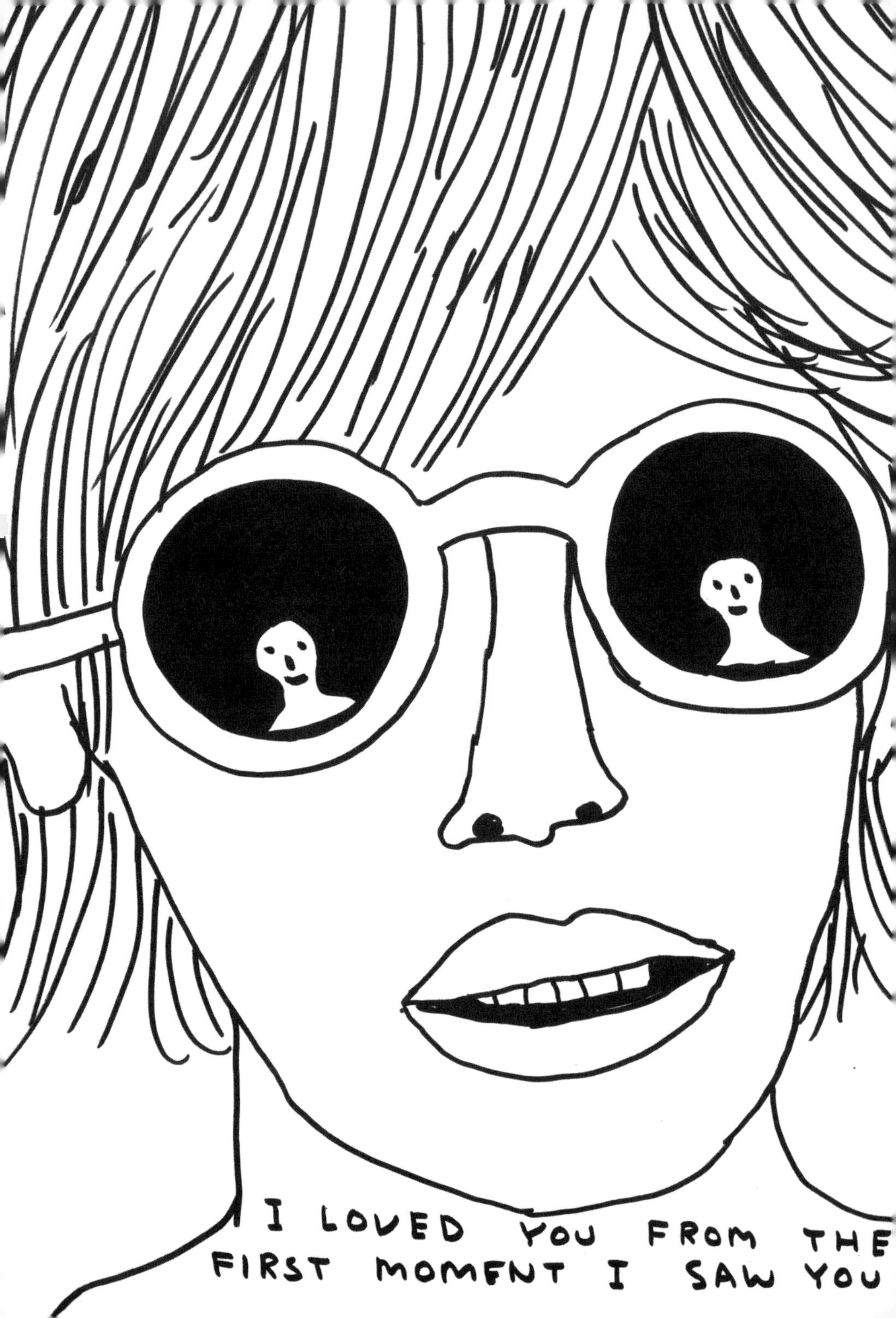

I LOVED YOU FROM THE FIRST MOMENT I SAW YOU

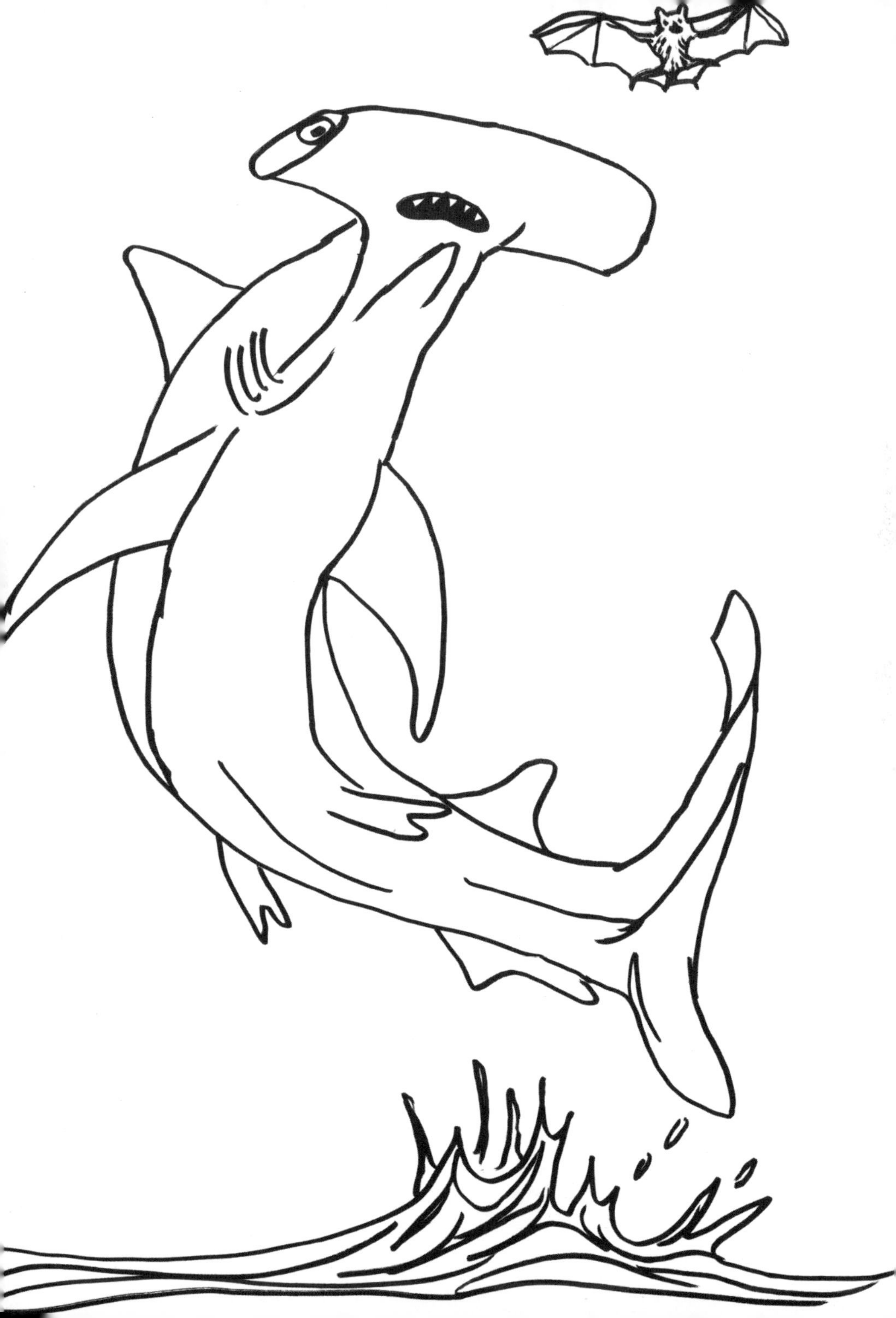

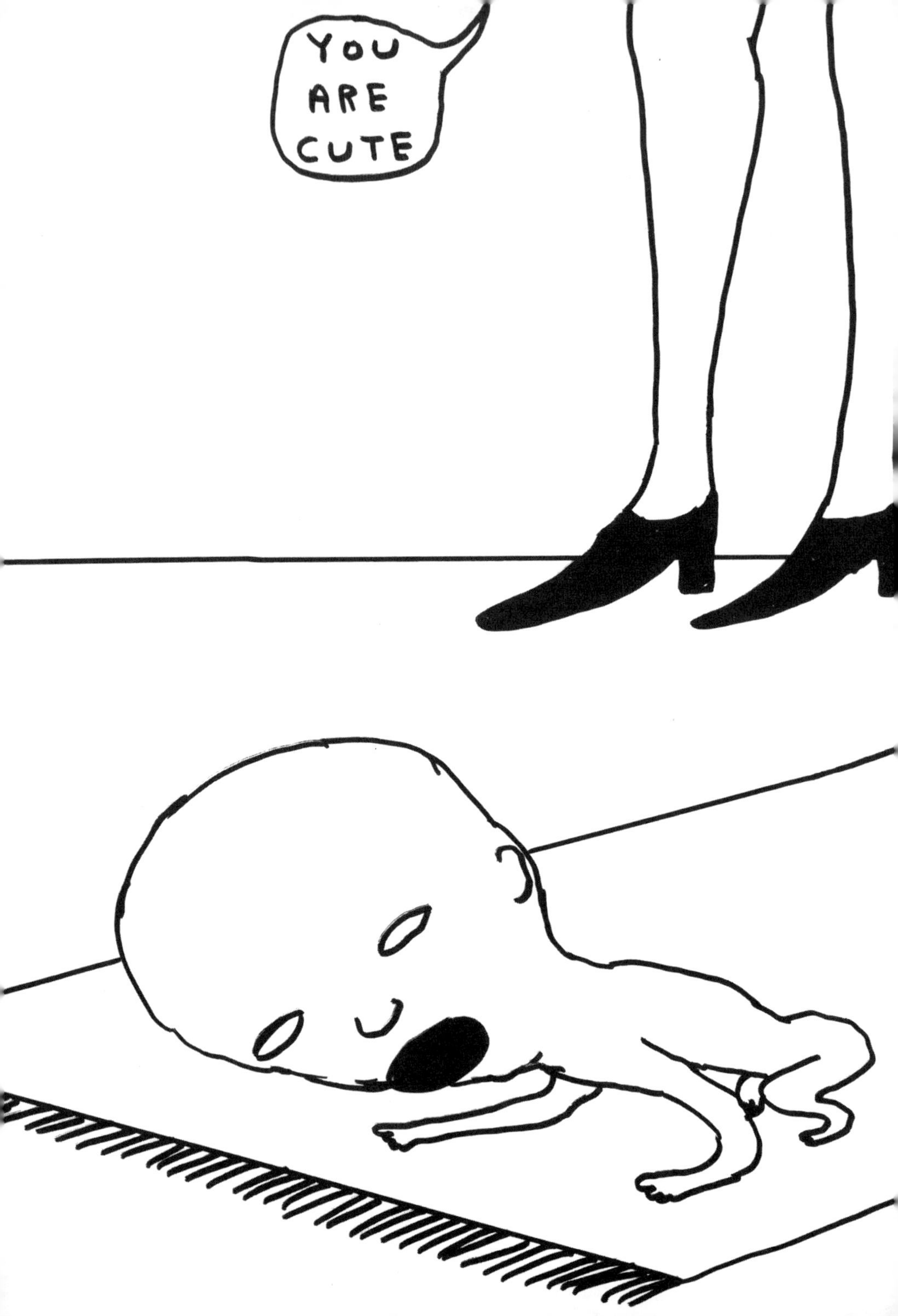

YOU
ARE
CUTE

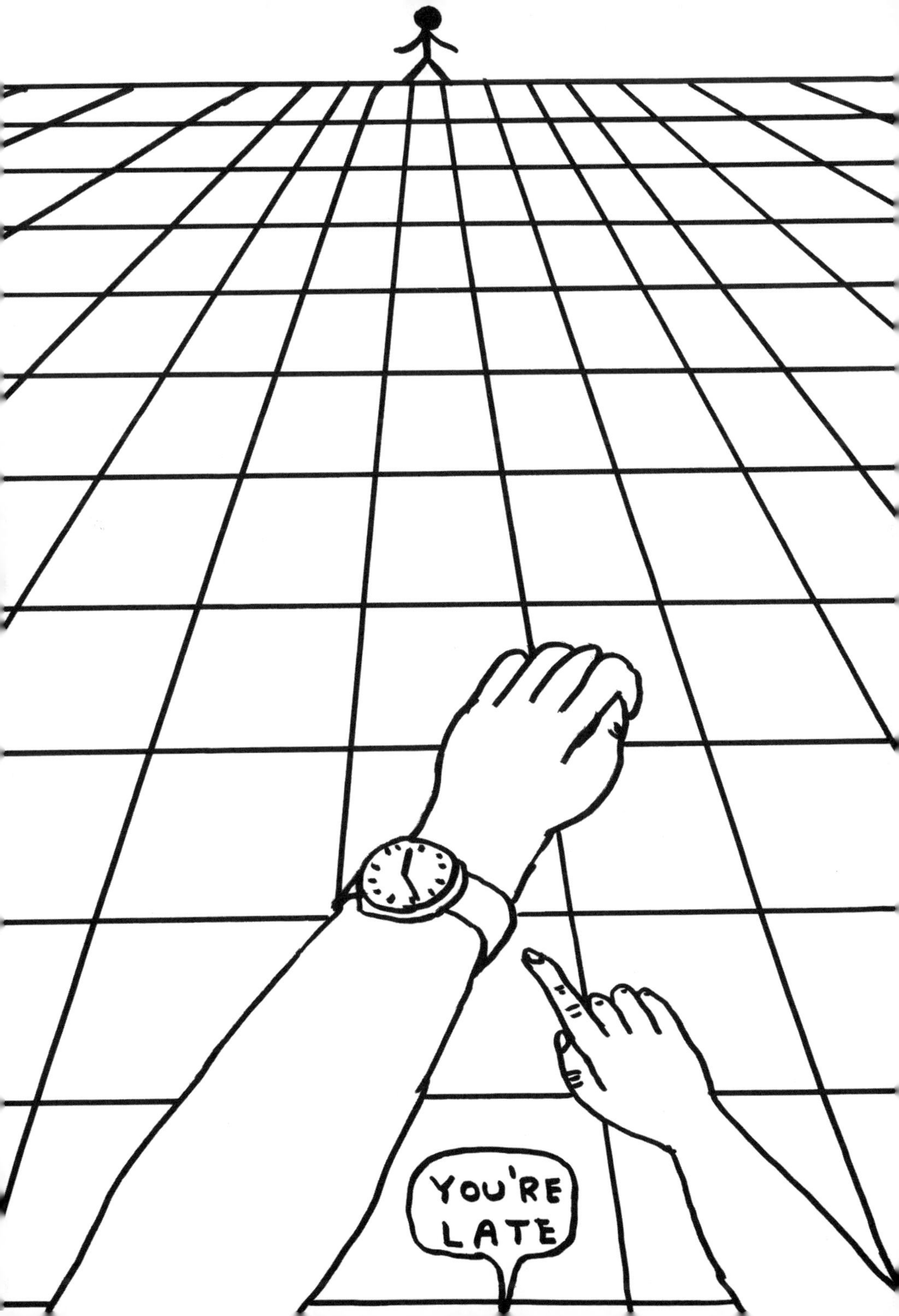

YOU'RE LATE

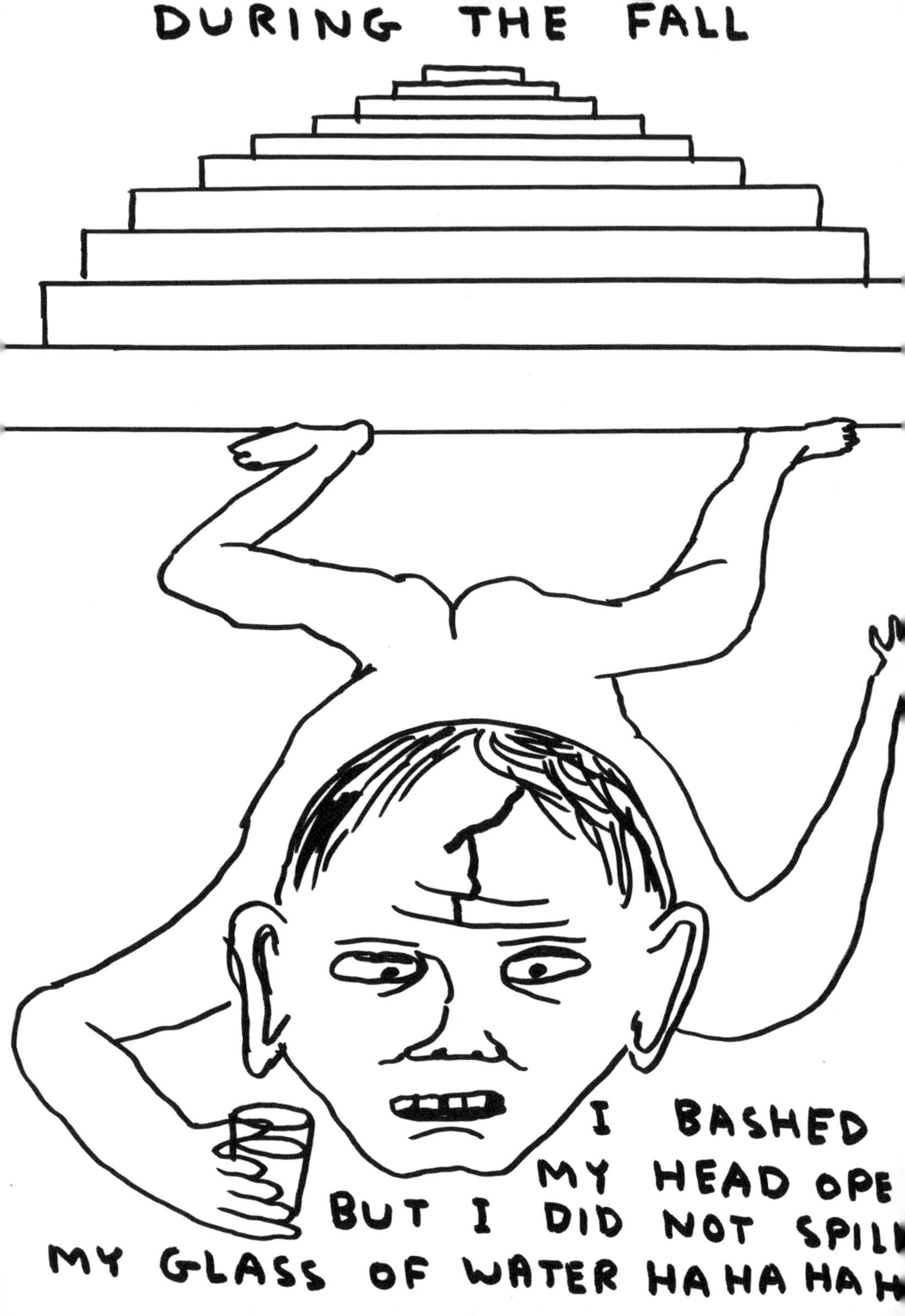

DURING THE FALL
I BASHED
MY HEAD OPE
BUT I DID NOT SPIL
MY GLASS OF WATER HA HA HA H

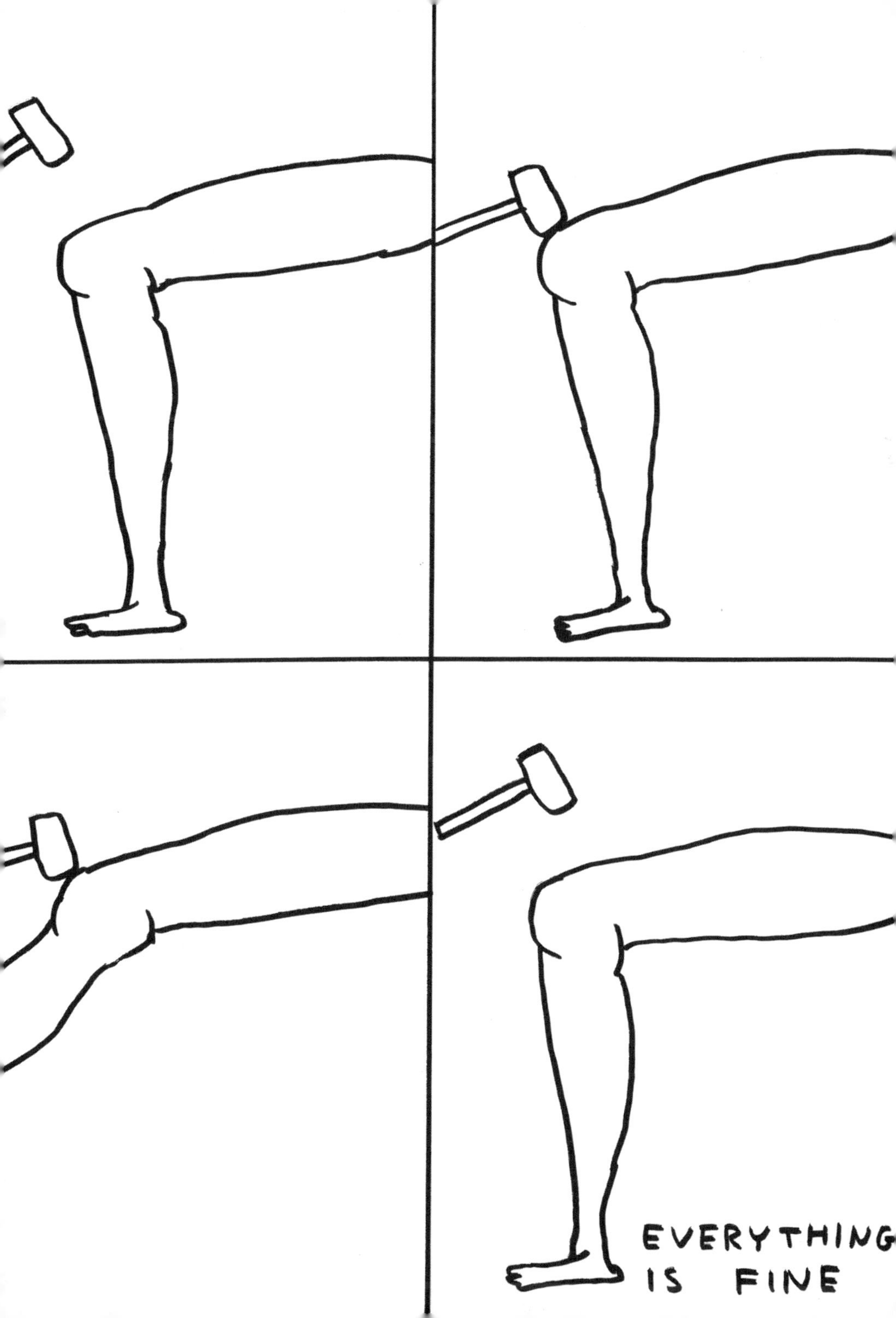

EVERYTHING
IS FINE

NIGHTCLUB

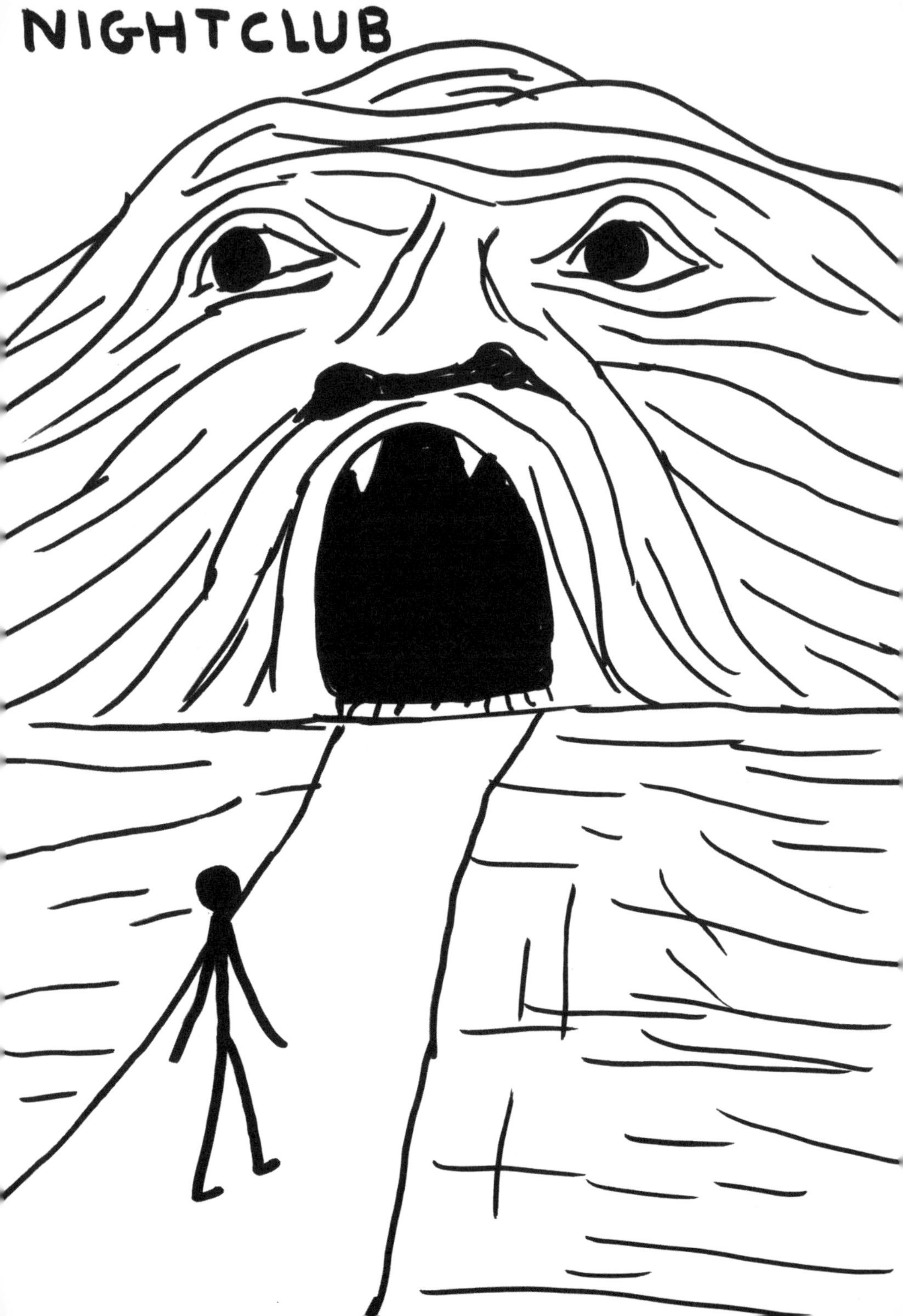

PSSSSSSSSSSSSSSSST

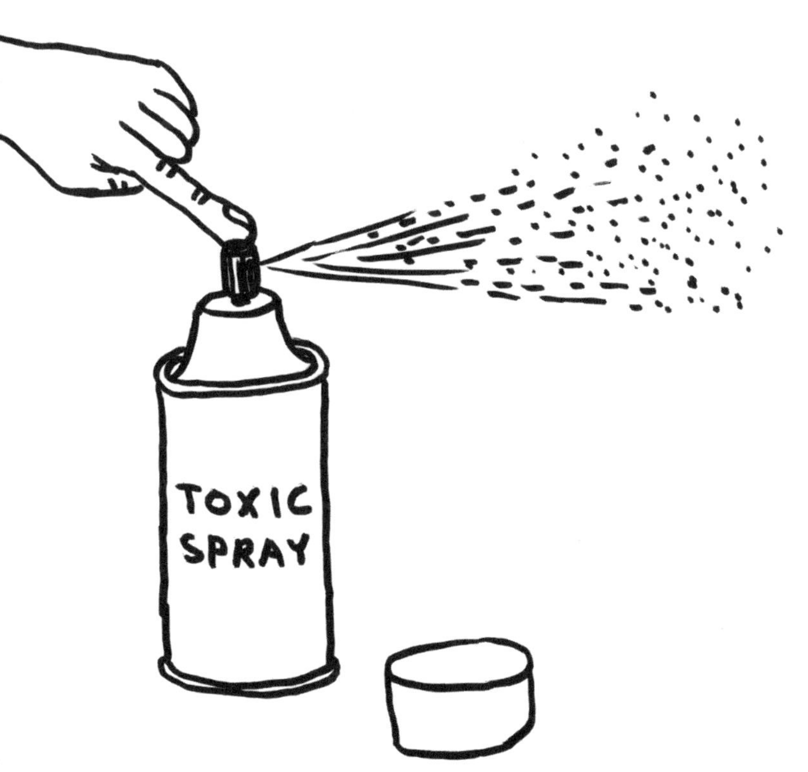

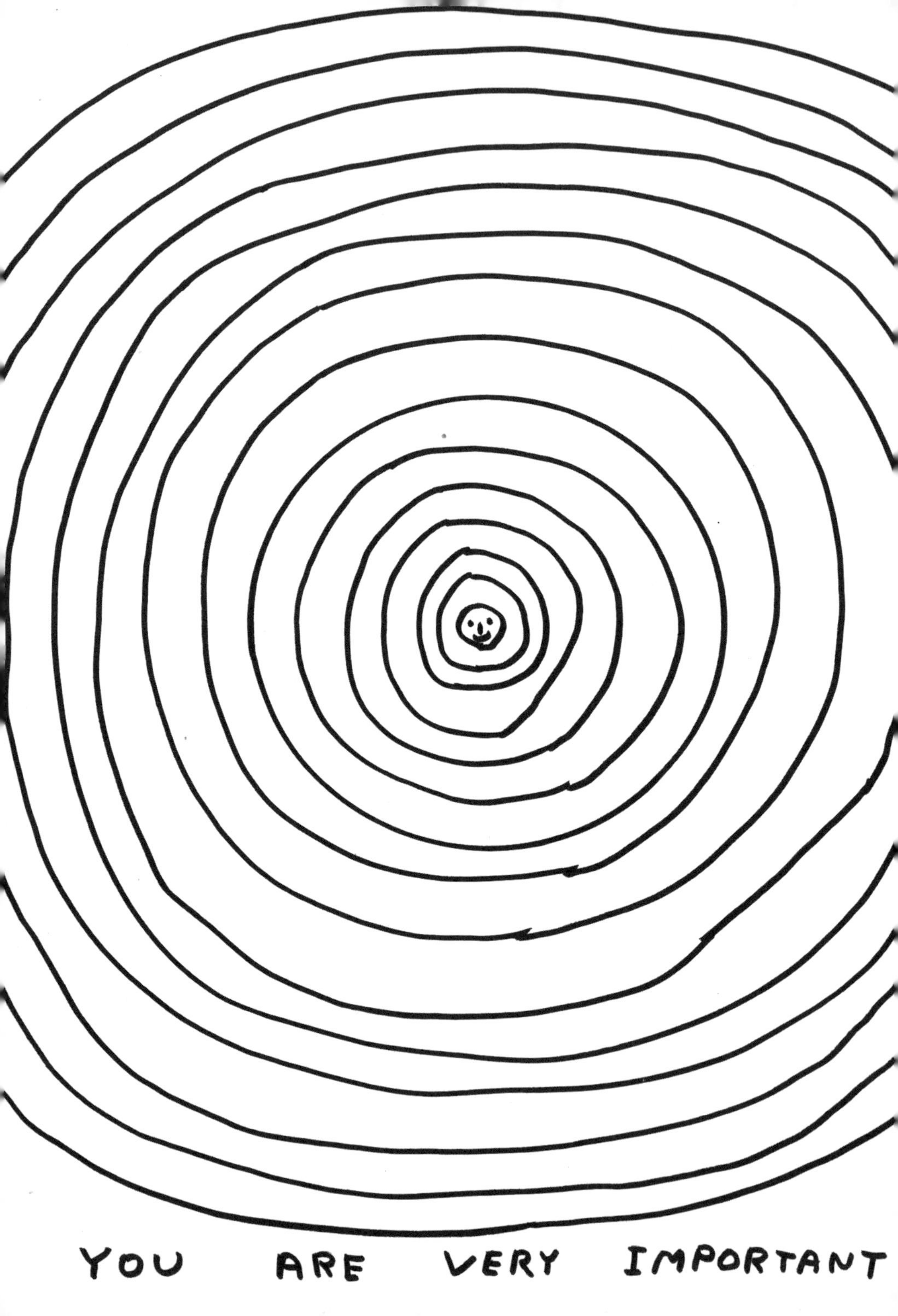

YOU ARE VERY IMPORTANT

FINGER

TONGUE

TONGUE

FINGER

TONGUE

TONGUE

FINGER

FINGER

TONGUE

FINGER

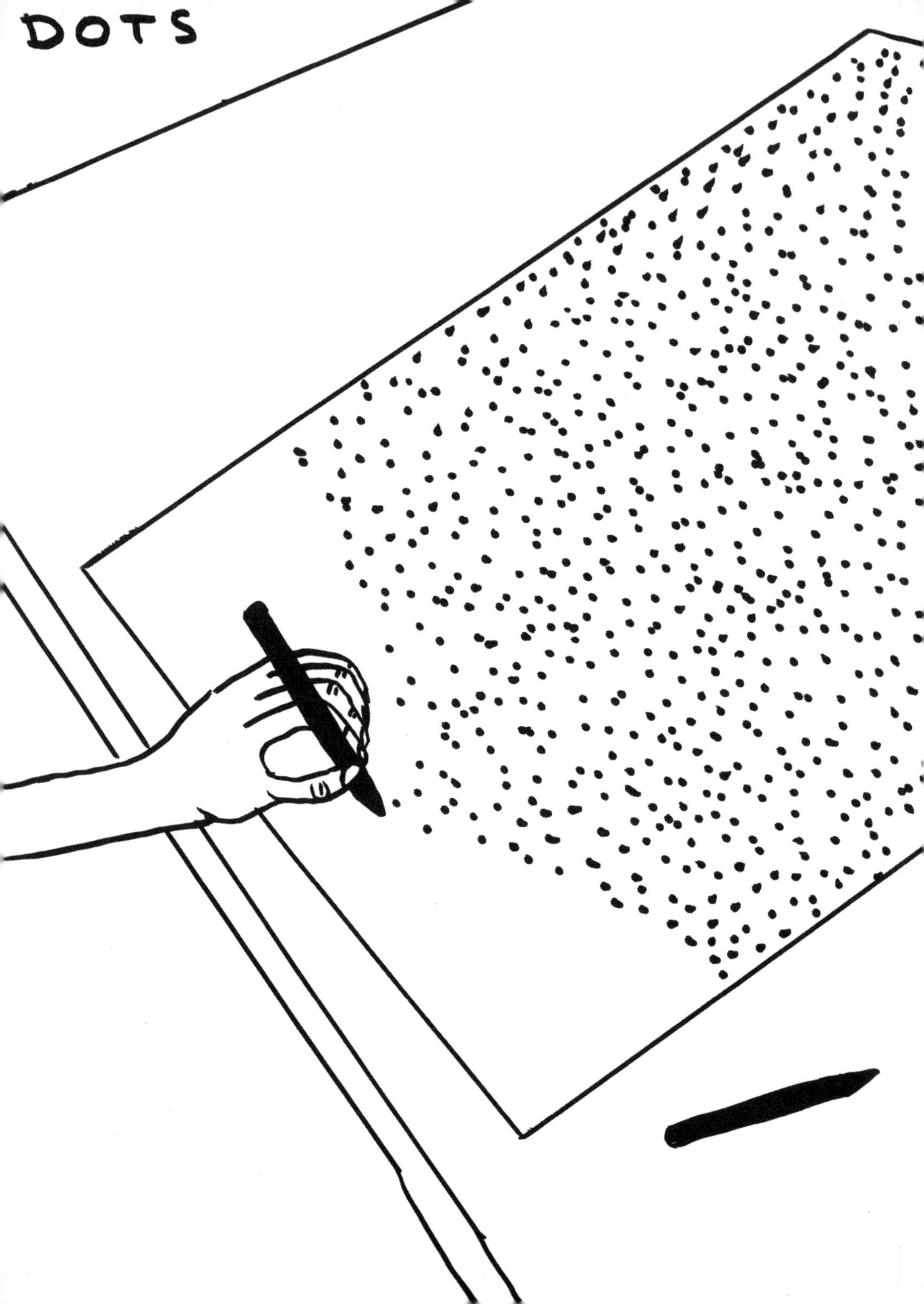
DOTS